AMERICAN IMMIGRANT

AMERICAN IMMIGRANT

My Life in Three Languages

Rosalie Pedalino Porter

Routledge
Taylor & Francis Group

LONDON AND NEW YORK

Originally published by iUniverse

Published 2009 by Transaction Publishers

Published 2017 by Routledge
2 Park Square, Milton Park, Abingdon, Oxon OX14 4RN
711 Third Avenue, New York, NY 10017, USA

Routledge is an imprint of the Taylor & Francis Group, an informa business

Library of Congress Catalog Number: 2010038335

Library of Congress Cataloging-in-Publication Data

Porter, Rosalie Pedalino, 1931-
American immigrant : my life in three languages / Rosalie Pedalino Porter.
   p. cm.
Originally published: New York : iUniverse, 2009.
Includes bibliographical references.
ISBN 978-1-4128-1835-3 (alk. paper)
   1. Porter, Rosalie Pedalino, 1931- 2. Italian American women--Biography. 3. Italian Americans--Biography. 4. Women immigrants--United States--Biography. 5. Immigrants--United States--Biography. I. Title.
E184.I8P727 2011
325.73--dc22

2010038335

ISBN 13: 978-1-4128-1835-3 (pbk)

DEDICATION

To David Thomas Porter, my love, my traveling companion, my greatest source of inspiration—and to the three other important men in my life, Tom, Dave, and Steve

EPIGRAPH

"Without the mastery of the common standard version of the national language, one is inevitably destined to function only at the periphery of national life and, especially, outside the national and political mainstream."

Antonio Gramsci, *Letters from Prison, 1933*

Contents

ACKNOWLEDGMENTS

A passing comment from my son Steve planted the original seed for *American Immigrant*: "Mom, you've seen so much history and been active in important movements—feminism, anti-war protests—and you've lived in various countries and done important professional work, why don't you write about it? I think a lot of people would enjoy reading it."

Writing one's life, then reliving it over and over as the narrative goes through editing and rewriting is a burdensome, sometimes oppressive, task. I found the work much more difficult than my previous, impersonal writings about social issues. And yet I cannot deny there were moments of joy in it as well.

Readers of various drafts who contributed constructive criticism and their support for the overall project include: Alice Allen, Oya Basak, Francesca Della Salla, Blanche Dirito, Gretchen and John Fox, Bob Jelley, Ruth Ann Marucci, Laura Medenbach, Ricardo Munro, Anita and Alex Page, Jane Silva, Gloria Date Smith, Sonya Sofield, and a most wildly encouraging but discriminating reader, Claren Sommer.

Special thanks go to John Fox for expert advice on self-publishing and shaping the story, and to Mary Bagg for her editorial polishing of the narrative and for bucking me up in times of stress. It was Mary in her journalist days who wrote the most comprehensive and coherent piece on bilingual education for the Massachusetts weekly *The Valley Advocate*, whose front-page picture made me a "cover girl" in 2002.

Recognition is due to many friends and colleagues who were willing to refer me to an agent or a publisher and whose help is gratefully appreciated: Rick Balkin, Chris Benfey, Linda Chavez, Alan Lelchuk, John Miller, Diane Ravitch, Mary Jo Salter, Suzanne Strempek Shea.

Two people worked with me most diligently over the years. Son Tom responded in every instance when I needed technical assistance and without whose expert attention *American Immigrant* would be floating somewhere in cyber space. I marvel at this busy father of four for his energy and focus. He managed to read the work-in-progress in several incarnations and do much to get it to the publisher in the appropriate form.

My sweet husband, veteran editor of every line of this work over a six-year period, provided his unbounded enthusiasm. He has endured, along with me, the *Groundhog Day* experience of reliving our lives on every reading. Most importantly, he gave me his complete trust by saying early on—and meaning it, "Dear, I expect you to be honest in your portrayal of our marriage, our family, and our lives together."

Important influences near the end, as I struggled to write the last hundred pages with emotional and intellectual honesty, with dignity and outrage, but above all else with some levity, were Jill Ker Conway's three-volume autobiography, Phyllis Rose's *Parallel Lives* (less because I agreed with Rose's main premise; more because I rose to the challenge of answering her arguments), and Judith Nies' *The Girl I Left Behind: A Narrative History of the Sixties*.

In creating this chronicle, I have relied on interviews, calendars, notes, and scribbles unearthed from my personal archives. Any errors of facts, dates, or places are entirely my own.

Introduction

My voyage from Avella, Italy, in the 1930s, then through tenement-level poverty in Newark and Orange, New Jersey, culminated in a hard-won education, many different occupations, and a family life of full vitality. That audacious story of striving and prevailing, of cultures clashing in often humorous ways, is entertaining. But the most compelling reason to record my life story is the work of my late career—leading a reform campaign to benefit immigrant children in U.S. schools.

Immigration is one of the most contentious issues of twenty-first century America—and discussions involving legal and illegal status, assimilation or separatism, and language unity or multilingualism, continue to spark debate. My part in this is not insignificant. The struggle to give upwards of five million immigrant children our common language, English, and to help these students join their English-speaking classmates in opportunities for self-fulfillment—this is the mission that keeps me working long beyond a reasonable retirement age.

Since arriving in the United States as an immigrant child speaking not a word of English, I have experienced first-hand the struggle to overcome poverty; I've felt the driving ambition to escape working class limitations and climb into educated middle class liberation, all the while fighting parental restraints in a strange new land. Perhaps immigrant stories like mine, of the arrival and the road to full acculturation and comfort, are one of the most American of all themes in our national consciousness. Yet within the universal story, each one of us experiences distinct differences. The elements that have contributed to my rich life encompass family background, conflicts, opportunities, and tremendous luck; a hunger for knowledge; changes in society that opened new worlds for women, and the wisdom or blind chance of choosing a most suitable and supportive husband.

The impulse to document the rise from poverty of my own immigrant family is partly due to my rejection of the current belief that the "American Dream" is no more than a myth and a delusion. We who emigrated a few generations ago believe with our whole hearts that the key to the American identity is, "that this is a land of opportunity in which people can rise from nothing to greatness, depending on their talents and their hard work."[1] How do we reconcile the highest level of immigration in our country's history—more than ten million new entrants in the '90s decade alone, people we may assume are coming to the U. S. to work and better themselves—with author Jim Cullen's assertion that "the gospel of Upward Mobility, in which everybody has a chance to carve his or her own destiny, can be a destructive delusion, serving as a powerful vehicle for blaming those who did not succeed..."[2] Surely Mr. Cullen must have marveled in 2008 at the prospect of Barack Obama ascending to our highest elective office. *New York Times'* columnist Nicholas D. Kristof lauded this possibility long before the Democratic primary put Obama on the ballot: "The step-grandson of an illiterate, barefoot woman in this village (Kogelo, Kenya) of mud huts in Africa may be the next president of the United States. Such mobility—powered by education, immigration and hard work—is cause not for disparagement but for celebration."[3]

Just as my grandparents left their village to flee from poverty and oppression a century ago, certain that their brains and brawn would lead them to a better life, there are millions availing themselves of the same achievable opportunity today. In just forty years, the U. S. population has doubled, from 150 to 300 hundred million, about half of the increase due to immigration. Is this no longer the place for the fulfillment of great hopes?

It was generally understood in my youth that it would take three generations from an immigrant's arrival in the United States for the family to achieve full adaptation and acculturation into American life, upward mobility and economic success. My brothers, my sister and I achieved this success in one generation and I credit a variety of important factors: our growing up at the time of a rapidly expanding economy; two parents with a strong work ethic and traditional values; the accidental good fortune of sturdy health; and, perhaps, the absence of the vices of later generations that decimated so many poor families, specifically the drug culture. All five of us struggled to acquire the higher education our parents could not afford to give us. My values and life experiences, however, have diverged dramatically from those of my four siblings, though we all share a talent for surviving in situations of serious poverty, material and emotional.

From the time I married, I gained special privileges beyond the means of my brothers and sister, though they reached higher levels of material success. Living in academia, I completed an earned doctorate. Having a husband who encouraged and supported my every new professional career move gave me the opportunity to pursue the rewarding work of publishing, lecturing, testifying in court cases, and advocating nationally as a recognized authority on the education of immigrant children. Two high points of my professional work: leading the "English for the Children" campaign, a referendum initiative that gained 68 percent of the votes in the 2002 Massachusetts election, and my part in an Arizona court case that was ruled favorably for our side by the U. S. Supreme Court and in which my work was cited. (*Flores vs. Arizona*, June 25, 2009)

In *American Immigrant* I examine women's roles beginning in the 1940s and continuing to the millennium, from the vantage point of one who grew up in a working- class, male-dominated family, a view radically different from that of the upper-middle-class icons of the "Women's Liberation" movement (in which, incidentally, I enthusiastically participated). Other themes I explore include the emotional price exacted by the dislocation from one's native land and traditions; living and traveling in the Middle East, Europe and Asia;

and, at the end, the rich satisfactions of our immediate family, daily rewards I could not have imagined in my youth.

Historian Forrest McDonald concisely sums up for me the wonder of life: "Whether I am hungry or well fed, whether I am sick or healthy, or cold or comfortable, or honored and respected or despised and kicked and beaten, even that I shall soon be leaving, all is trivial compared to the fact that I got here. I am a miracle, and so, dear reader, are you."[2]

Writing about seven decades of a woman's experiences in twentieth-century American culture, the changes large and small, personal and political, emotional and intellectual that I have undergone and observed—this is, in my first language, "*la storia*," I tell.

PROLOGUE:
ALMOST THE END...

Rome, April 2006. I have invited our sons and their families to take
one more trip to Italy with us, for my latest "big birthday." My husband
and I have lived in and traveled in this land of my birth on countless
occasions. The plan works well as our three sons are seasoned travelers,
sufficiently fluent in Italian to be at ease in most situations. With us are
Tom, his wife Lisa, and their five-year old daughter Emily; Dave and
his new love, Sally Cooney, for whom this is a first time in Europe; and
our youngest son, Steve. Lisa has made special arrangements to visit the
Roman Synagogue and to have a private tour of the Vatican Museums
with a focus on Jewish-related art. We gather each evening at restaurants
we have known for decades, Da Giggetto in the Roman ghetto, Alfredo
alla Scrofa for their world-class noodles, and Da Pancrazio, built on the
ruins of Pompey's Theatre where Julius Caesar was stabbed. The ruins
are preserved, on view beneath the restaurant.

One day, as planned, we take the train from Rome's Termini
Station to Naples, where son Tom picks up a rented van for our drive
to Avella. Our sons first visited the town in 1973 when we made a short
visit to see the house where I was born. In the past dozen years, my
husband and I have revived connections with my Pedalino cousins. My

Zia Vittoria, now in her eighties but still alert and active, is especially happy to meet our sons for the first time, as are my cousins Rosa, Gino, and Rachelle. After lunch, all but *la zia* join us for a stroll around the village. Walking the entire village, including stops at the main piazza to read the names on the war memorial to both world wars (many of the names are Pedalino and Luciano), the church where my parents were married and I was baptized, and the corner where the house in which I was born once stood—even with photo taking, the whole walk takes less than a half hour.

On our way to the van for our return to Naples, Gino, at my suggestion, leads us on a stroll through the beautifully sited cemetery. Avella lies in a flat plain in the foothills of Mt. Vesuvius, the ever-looming, dormant volcanic cone. We walk sedately up and down avenues lined with well-maintained grave markers and marble mausolea, while Gino points out the names of near and distant relatives—our progenitors. Finally Gino tells me we are approaching the tomb of our grandfather, Domenico Pedalino, the only grandparent I knew and dearly loved. As we enter the mausoleum and I spot the engraved name across the dimly lit room, I instinctively dash forward to touch it. Alas, I fail to notice that metal scaffolding is partly in my way, causing me to trip on a metal bar just inches off the floor. I fall with a heavy thud, head cracking against the marble wall. My instant thought is "Am I going to die *here?*"

Perhaps it would have been a fitting end, a closing of the circle, to leave this earth in the very place where my life began and from which I have traveled very far indeed. However, that would be too neat an end to my story. My good fortune prevails. In spite of a broken arm, a badly bruised knee, and blood spattered everywhere from cuts in my scalp, I never lose consciousness. My family, alarmed and shaken by the accident, rallies round, and cousin Gino, a medical technician, urges us not to wait for an ambulance but to go directly to the emergency room of the nearest hospital.

There I am given excellent and prompt medical treatment—stitches in my scalp, an MRI, X-rays, a cast on my arm, cleaning and bandaging the knee—and the welcome news that I have suffered no serious damage to my head, only a clean break in my arm near the wrist. One oddity in Italy's ER procedures: two separate emergency rooms, one for women and one for men. Neither my husband nor my sons can be with me through the tests and treatments. No matter, the women in the family give me solid comfort. At the end, my husband offers our U.S. health insurance cards but we are told, "Non si preoccupa, signore, tutto sta bene, non dovete pagare." Not to worry, sir, all is fine, you don't need to pay.

I have recovered completely from this frightening episode. But the incident focused my mind on bringing to a close what was then a work-in-progress, this attempt to describe and explain my many lives— immigrant, child of poverty, ambitious young woman grasping every opportunity, wife, mother, feminist, constant traveler, scholar, and finally activist and advocate for the education of immigrant children. How I achieved so much, the opportunities availed of, the role models emulated, the providential luck and the staggeringly hard work—it is an intensely American story. And now to the real beginning.

SECTION I

EARLY YEARS, EARLY STRUGGLES

Chapter 1

La Storia (In the Beginning...)

As the oldest of five children born to Francesco (Cheech/Frank) Pedalino and Maria Lucia (Lucy) Luciano, the burden of remembrance is mine. I am the repository of the family chronicles, the secret-sharer, my mother's confidant from earliest childhood once we were removed from Avella, Italy, and settled in the new world. Our family history, though similar to that of many immigrants in superficial ways, followed an unusual trajectory for my own generation. In the early twentieth century, along with millions of other southern Europeans, Pedalinos and Lucianos emigrated to the eastern United States at the height of the heaviest wave of immigration in our country's history, not to be exceeded until the last decade of the twentieth century.

The Pedalino Family

The earliest members of my father's family arrived in New Jersey, worked in clothing factories, and, once established, brought younger relatives from Avella. My father's Uncle Frank (known to the family as *Zi* Frenke) was one of the first in the family to settle in Newark's large and growing Italian immigrant community. (I spell family names and phrases in the Neapolitan dialect phonetically.)

Around 1920, my father's older brothers—Michael and Louis—arrived in Newark to live with *Zi* Frenke's family. In their late teens, these two young men were expressly sent to the United States in order to help support their remaining siblings back home, much as is the custom today among Latin American immigrants. Each week when they received their wages, they handed them to *Zi* Frenke who allowed them each fifty cents, an amount to suffice for clothing, cigarettes, and entertainment. My Uncle Michael loved to tell the story of his once asking *Zi* Frenke if he could have a little extra to buy himself a warm cap. His uncle answered, "No, I have to send all of this to your family in Avella. You'll have to save a little each week to buy yourself that cap."

Michael and Louis worked hard, progressing to foremen positions in the factory. Soon, each started his own men's tailoring shop. They married, started families, and bought homes in Newark. Beyond these similarities, their lives took very different paths. Michael took English-language classes at night school. Sixty years later, on reading the section of my first book in which I relate my experiences in a first-grade classroom where I did not understand a word of English, Uncle Mike wrote me a letter I cherish. He expressed his love and pride in my achievement and described his own youthful adventures learning English; he'd idolized his teacher, Miss Ruth Smith, and would go out of his way to walk her home after class.

From his earliest days in New Jersey, Michael adapted easily to American ways. He apprenticed himself to master tailors from whom he learned skills that he later applied in his own businesses. He studied men's clothing design and joined a professional trade association, gaining such a measure of respect from his co-designers that he was elected president of the association in his later years. Michael alone of the three brothers quickly understood the importance of education and set high standards for his children. Speaking at Harvard University in 1988, Al Shanker, founder of the American Federation of Teachers, described similar aspirations of working-class families of the 1930s in his New York–Jewish-immigrant neighborhood, how they proudly celebrated any child who finished grammar school with an eighth-grade diploma.

Louis, though as hard-working and ambitious as Michael, had an altogether different personality. He, like my own father, was to retain some of the least progressive attitudes from his native village, such as the low regard for women's achievements outside the home. Louis had intelligence and an engaging personality, but these traits were negated by a terrible temper and little tolerance for his wife's or his children's peccadilloes. He did not attain the material success of his brother Michael, though he raised four children and considered his life very satisfactory, in spite of all the shouting, arguing, and carrying on that characterized the often-chaotic household.

It is currently fashionable to characterize the large new immigrant populations that have arrived in the states—people from the Caribbean, Central and South America, Southeast Asia—as very different from southern Europeans. The chief difference, especially for Latinos, is said to be the fact that they can easily return to their land of origin. This back-migration and return, it is said, was not a factor for earlier immigrants who came to the United States to stay. Not entirely true. Although I have no demographic data at hand to support my argument, I suspect my family is not unique in the fact that both sets of grandparents went back and forth a few times, each time to seek economic advantage in the United States and then return to Italy with "the spoils."

Domenico Pedalino, my paternal grandfather, made three separate trips to America in his lifetime. In Avella he was the village baker, the *panettiere* who rose at four every morning to bake large loaves of crusty, chewy bread. No cakes, muffins, or other delicacies were produced in his oven, for poverty was widespread and hardly a family would have bought such luxuries. He first came to America, alone, as a young married man, before World War I, stayed a few years, working as a fruit peddler with a pushcart, and went back. He returned to Newark with his wife Rosa in the early 1920s and opened a fruit and vegetable store that provided well for both of them and allowed them to send dollars to their children in Avella. Again, at Grandma Rosa's insistence, they returned to Avella. In the mid-1930s, they made their last trip to the United States. On that occasion, Grandpa opened a fruit and vegetable store in East Orange, and they lived with Uncle Mike and his family for two years.

Grandma Rosa simply could not adapt to American life. She was a vain woman who cared greatly about her appearance and about dressing in style. She was bold enough to have her hair "shingled," a daring, short-hair style for an Italian matron. Avella tradition dictated that only a well-secured bun pulled back severely from the brow was the proper look. She was a stern and imposing woman who had always harbored a prejudice against American life as "barbaric," a strange notion if one has any knowledge of the primitive nature of Italian village life in those days.

Uncle Michael loved to shock his friends with this anecdotal example of brutish village behavior. A young woman who climbed Monte Vergine daily to gather kindling was being courted, unsuccessfully, by a thoroughly unpleasant young man whom she had sternly rejected more than once. One late afternoon, carrying on her descent a heavy load of sticks on her head, the man grabbed her from behind and slashed her cheeks with a rusty razor. Of course, after her scars healed, she was so disfigured that she had no other option but to marry her attacker. It was no secret in the village, from then on, that he routinely beat her and their children, an egregious fact accepted by the community. At this sorry conclusion to his little story, my uncle would explode in disgust: "And Mussolini wanted to go to Abyssinia to civilize the Africans?"

Grandma Rosa decided early in 1939 to return to Avella to be with her five daughters who were at home, waiting for suitors. It amazed me and embittered my mother that with the continuing poverty on both sides of the Atlantic, five sisters should be encouraged to sit at home like debutantes while their brothers in America, who all had wives and children to support, were expected to send regular contributions to their upkeep. Not one brother dared object.

Grandpa Domenico would sometimes come to Sunday dinner with our family in New Jersey. We enjoyed the infrequent visits with this gentle, quiet man with bright blue eyes who bore a strong resemblance to the late conductor Arturo Toscanini. However it happened, he did not have the foresight to get himself back to Italy before the beginning of World War II in September 1939. When civilian travel was closed, he was forced to stay in America until the war ended in 1945. He suffered terrible anxiety over the well-being of his wife and five daughters. Their home in Avella was destroyed in an Allied bombing raid, but no one in the family was hurt. My father and his two brothers sent food packages through the American Red Cross once each month. I remember helping my mother prepare the packages. They could not weigh more than 4 pounds and had to be a certain size; we had to wrap them in cloth and sew the cloth securely, printing the address in ink. We included coffee, cigarettes, dried legumes, and some of the new, miraculous, powdered soups—Lipton's Chicken Noodle.

Grandpa was on one of the first passenger ships to Italy in 1946, but he did not survive long after his return to Avella. He died of prostate cancer in 1947. The popular notion in the family was that the stress of the war years aged him and caused his death in his middle sixties. *Chi sa?* Grandma Rosa died in 1949.

The Luciano Family

Antonio and Sofia Luciano, with their young son Giacomo, left Italy around 1910 for America, where they settled in New Britain, Connecticut. Grandpa Antonio was a tailor who did alterations in a local men's clothing shop. My mother, Lucia, was born in New Britain in 1912, a happenstance that later turned out to be the salvation of our family. In the summer of 1914, Antonio and Sofia planned a trip to Italy to visit relatives in Avella. They sailed in midsummer, intending to stay only a few weeks, but delayed their return to the states dangerously long. When war began, Antonio, an Italian citizen, was drafted into the army. By the end of World War I, the family could barely find the means to subsist, much less find the wherewithal to return to Connecticut.

After the war, Antonio started a tailor shop in one room of their family home in Avella. Both children were enlisted to help earn the family's livelihood. Son Giacomo was apprenticed to his father and soon became a tailor of men's clothing. Lucia, who had been a star pupil, was forced to leave school at the end of fourth grade. Free public education was limited to four years of elementary school; continuing studies required traveling to Nola or Baiano, the closest towns with *lycees*, and purchasing books and supplies—expenses the Luciano family could not manage, certainly not for a girl child. Instead "Lucietta" (little Lucy) was apprenticed at age nine to a local dressmaker. For what amounted to pennies each week, she was required to work long hours sewing women's clothing by hand, as well as to clean the dressmaker's house, run errands and be a general servant to the whims of her mistress, who had to be addressed always by the respectful title, "La Signora."

Often, when my mother reminisced about her growing-up years in Avella, she would hold back tears over the senseless cruelty of her mentor. Still, she gained valuable experience as the years went by, becoming so skilled as to sew beadwork on silk dresses of her own design, and to complete an entire wedding gown and trousseau on one occasion—not for a village woman but for a summer resident who came from Naples for the *aria fresca* of our country town. When I was a young girl, my mother taught me to sew, embroider, crochet, and knit; skills that she hoped would be useful in my future life.

Lucia was considered a beauty in Avella and, in her late teens, she attracted the attention of Francesco Pedalino, my father, who had a reputation as a handsome, fun-loving, daring young man whose escapades were the subject of local gossip. Francesco, mostly called by his nickname, "Cheech," defied his family by refusing to take up either tailoring or bread-baking. Nor did he show any inclination to be a student, barely managing to finish elementary school. Instead he became a butcher, but not in our understanding of the term as a white-aproned man who stands behind a counter dispensing plastic-wrapped chops and steaks. At that time and place, a butcher was a slaughterer of livestock. Farmers would hire a butcher to slaughter a cow, calf, pig, or goat; skin it; do the requisite cleaning and dressing; and carve it into all the desired cuts.

My father enjoyed the random nature of his trade, the traveling from farm to farm, the unscheduled working hours, the freedom from regimentation—these impulses would remain with him through his adult life, making serious problems for our family's welfare. Nor did my father ever really learn the hard lesson that delaying instant gratification to save for larger benefits in the future makes good sense for people of modest means. On one of my father's butchering jobs, the animal turned out to be diseased, and when my father scratched his face he became infected. The infection was hard to heal and required an incision in his right cheek, leaving scars that marred his face but did not diminish his charm when he smiled—with his bright hazel eyes twinkling and his even, sparkling white teeth.

My Parents Early Years in Avella

Cheech pursued Lucia in classic village fashion, sneaking an occasional unchaperoned walk with her. At age eighteen my father was drafted for his mandatory eighteen months of military service in the Italian army. He was stationed at the barracks in Caserta, a provincial capital not more than 50 miles from Avella. He was homesick, and the proximity to Avella acted as an impetus for taking off without official permission, often to call on Lucia.

According to their marriage certificate, my parents were married on December 3, 1929, in the village church, La Chiesa di San Pietro. They began life together in the home of my mother's parents, who soon after moved to Naples, leaving them the small house where I was born. In 1973, while vacationing in Positano, I brought my husband and sons to Avella for a visit. The tenants who now lived in the house allowed us to walk through the cramped little "front room" and kitchen on the ground floor, the two small bedrooms on the second floor by an outside staircase, and to see the privy in the garden. The house had indoor water faucets but no indoor toilet, its condition little changed or improved since the 1920s. The village of Avella had very little to recommend it in my parents' time, nor has it blossomed into the type of charming Italian town we know from film and song. There are no hotels or restaurants in Avella. The town's population has doubled since my parents' time to 8,000 inhabitants, and there are visible signs of prosperity—large new homes, well-paved streets, municipal buildings. It is not picturesque in the way of Tuscan and Umbrian villages, but it has a spectacular setting, lying in a flat area with steep Monte Vergine and its Norman castle overlooking the town, and well as with its proximity to Mt. Vesuvius.

What little I know of my parents early married years is gleaned from stories related by relatives and friends, since I have no recollections of my own for those years. In fact, for reasons I cannot fathom, I have almost no personal memories of my life until the age of six, when I was taken to America. All I know about my parents' years in Avella is grim. They started out with very little to live on, and the arrival of three children in five years merely multiplied their misfortunes. According to my mother's stories, her mother-in-law was harsh and unyielding, favoring her son and disparaging her daughter-in-law at every turn. Family poverty was so severe that my father would go to his mother's house to beg food for us. His mother would offer him day-old bread but insist that he eat it right there, forbidding him from taking anything to the rest of us. There is an Italian word that describes a person of such stone-hearted callousness: *canaglia*.

On my first visit to Avella in 1953, as a young lady of twenty-two, I became privy to a family secret that, if true, might have explained some of Grandmother Rosa's resentment of my mother. My Uncle Giacomo and I rode the train from Naples to Baiano, where he hired a horse and buggy to take us into the village of Avella. I was concentrating so hard, trying to recognize any sights along the way, that I was not listening carefully to the ramblings of the driver. After he greeted my uncle and learned that I was the daughter of Cheech and Lucia, the driver began to tell ancient yarns about what a rascally character my father was, of how the elders in the family had to chase him to force him to marry my mother when she was so hugely pregnant. As the man chortled and grinned, my uncle lashed out in anger, telling me to ignore this dirty *ignorante, imbecile* who had lost his good sense along with his teeth. The ferocity of my uncle's reaction surprised me, but far more stunning was what I had just heard. If this were true, it might explain the animosity between my mother and her mother-in-law, but it would not justify it.

But wouldn't my parents' marriage certificate, dated approximately thirteen months before my birth in 1931, give the lie to the old man's story? And why would he fabricate such a hurtful lie? Could the date of their marriage have been falsified later to an earlier year? Could my mother have had a miscarriage early in their married life and then a second pregnancy very quickly that gave me birth? I never raised this question with my mother, nor did I ever question other relatives of her generation about it. It remained a mystery for me, one that I chose not to explore further. The strength of my desire to know was not nearly sufficient to risk an instant of suffering for my mother.

Not until October 2004, on a visit with my aunt, *Zia* Vittoria, did I receive confirmation of what I heard from the buggy driver in 1953, which was then denied by my mother's brother. My father did court my mother, led her to think they were engaged, and attempted to abandon her when she became pregnant. According to Vittoria, my mother was on very friendly terms with the five sisters and her future mother-in-law. When the pregnancy and my father's obstinacy became known, Grandma Rosa demanded that he marry Lucia or be banished from her home. I am now certain that my parents married two months before I was born in a forced ceremony that left my father feeling trapped, resentful, and unforgiving. Perhaps my mother and grandmother, having been forced into a relationship with each other, harbored resentments of their own, but I can only speculate.

Wretched as living conditions were in the early 1930s, a new threat was added to the family's woes. Italy, under the dictatorship of Benito Mussolini's Black Shirt Fascists, embarked on its African adventure. The Italian Army invaded Abyssinia (now Ethiopia) and young men were being drafted and sent overseas. Soon, even married men with children were called up. Grandmother Rosa wrote to her sons, Michael and Louis in New Jersey, to ask them to get their brother to the United States. She was informed that the family would be able to emigrate to the United States as non-quota immigrants because of Lucia's American citizenship. Immigration laws were restrictive, and regular quota applicants could be on a waiting list for years. Uncle Michael offered to advance the travel expenses and help the family on arrival.

Now *La Nonna* had a sacred mission—to save her son from being sent to Africa! The only difficulty presented by the American Consulate in Naples was that my mother would have to go to the states alone, as the American citizen, and later send for her husband and children. Then the consular official discovered a recent change in U.S. citizenship law: as of May 24, 1934, children born abroad to American-born women would gain U.S. citizenship at birth. The youngest child in our family, Antonio, fit this new category. Born on June 26, 1934, he traveled to America with my mother on an American passport; we two older children were left with our father, later to travel to the states on Italian passports. The vagaries of U.S. immigration law defy reason.

Convincing my mother to leave her only known home and her entire family took a lot of persuasion. She was a shy, unprepossessing twenty-three-year-old who was being asked to go to a new land when she had never been out of her village; to move to a country where she did not know a word of the language; and to live with Uncle Michael's family when she had not seen the man since she was a young child (and it could hardly be said that she'd *known* him). Most wrenching of all for her was the intolerable thought of leaving two of her children. She resisted mightily. But *La Nonna* used all her powers of intimidation, threatening my mother by saying, "If you don't take my son to America and he's sent to die in Africa, it will be your fault; the curse will be on your head."

Coming to America

On December 4, 1935, Lucia and little baby Antonio sailed from Naples on the *SS Rex*, Italy's premier transatlantic liner on the New

York run. This frightened woman with her still-nursing baby was so deeply traumatized with shyness and insecurity that she hardly ate a full meal the entire time. She lost 20 pounds on the nine-day voyage. On arriving in the port of New York, she was met by Uncle Michael before the passengers even disembarked. Through special connections, he had obtained permission to board the ship and escort her personally through customs and immigration formalities.

Imagine my mother's amazement when she arrived at the home of the Michael Pedalino family in East Orange, New Jersey, a modest three-bedroom house that to her seemed opulent, with indoor bathrooms, a gas stove, and so many other wonders. Aunt Mary gave her a dress to change into, something less severe than the heavy, dark woolen frock from Avella. When my mother failed to come out of the bedroom, Aunt Mary found her in distress because the dress had short sleeves, and in Avella only women of loose morals left their arms uncovered above the elbows. She was coaxed to join the crowd of relatives waiting to meet her and see the baby. This was the first of many adjustments to American life. She dreaded the thought of how her husband would adapt to these new ways, a man who was totally domineering in the village manner.

Lucia lived with her in-laws for approximately one year while she waited for her application to work its way through the Immigration Service and allow the family to be reunited. She cared for baby Antonio (now called "Anthony" but pronounced "Entanee" all his growing-up years), and helped Aunt Mary with household chores and the care of her three children: Rosalie then eight; Domenick, five; and baby Gloria, three. Typical in Italian families, every first daughter was given some form of the paternal grandmother's name (Rosa, Rosetta, Rosalie, in this case), while first sons took a form of the paternal grandfather's (Domenico). That made for confusion on the rare occasions when all the cousins were together and all had the same names.

Uncle Michael employed my mother to do "piece work," a crucial component of cottage industry in the 1930s. He brought home bundles of sewing from his clothing factory—a hundred lapels to be hand-stitched for men's suits, for example, or a hundred collars to be stitched on to jackets. The work was paid for by the individual piece and not by the number of hours worked. This small income allowed my mother to save for the down payment on furnishings for her future apartment, and she could also work in the evenings after her baby was asleep.

There was a great deal of anxiety and uncertainty in the 1930s among families whose members were split between Europe and America; each year brought fresh evidence of the inevitability of war. My mother's nights were silently tearful as she worried over the health and safety of her two young children and the recurring fear that if the visas were not issued soon enough my father might still be sent to war in Africa. She lived for the letters from Avella and trusted implicitly in Uncle Michael's efforts to expedite the immigration process. The lowest point in that year was when she read that I had become dangerously ill with double pneumonia, suffering high fevers and delirium. At that time—before penicillin, antibiotics, or any of the miracle medicines developed during World War II had yet appeared—pneumonia was often fatal. Apparently the crisis passed and I regained my health.

My brother Domenick and I were cared for by our father's sisters, he by *Zia* Vittoria and I by *Zia* Sisinella. It puzzles me that I have almost no memory of the first five years of my life, the time in Avella and the voyage to the United States. Of the few memories I retain, I have a hazy picture of sitting in a room with other children (perhaps a nursery school, *asilo* as they call it), being told to put our heads on our desks and close our eyes and not open them or we would be pounced on by a monster—a *Mammone*. Another is the frightful sensation of hallucinating during the high fevers of pneumonia, screaming that there were giant spiders all over the walls. I cannot bring up any coherent pictures of our daily life, my grandmother, my father, or any lasting impressions of how we behaved among ourselves and with others. My only clear memory of sailing from Naples to New York is of being held up at the railing by my father as we steamed past the Rock of Gibraltar, which I later recognized as the picture on the Prudential Life Insurance policy. Thanks to Uncle Michael we sailed on the *Conte di Savoia*, a highly regarded passenger ship of the Italian Lines, though we were in third class, the bottom.

On arrival in New York Uncle Michael contrived to bring my mother and Anthony on board the ship to meet us. It was an odd encounter that has often been related at family gatherings. Baby Anthony did not recognize his father and cried when he was picked up; Domenick backed away from our mother, of whom he was very wary since he had not seen her for a year. I flew to my mother and wouldn't let her go. She was overcome with joy, but quite stunned at what I was wearing. My mother had spent some of her earnings on a complete set of new clothes for Domenick and several pretty dresses for me. When she met me, I was wearing a drab, black woolen dress and coat. Apparently my aunts had made a vow to the Blessed Virgin Mary when I recovered from my illness that they would dress me in black from then on. It rankled with my mother that she was never told how the aunts disposed of my American clothes.

On arrival at Uncle Michael's house, Aunt Mary immediately dressed me in one of her daughter's bright colored dresses. Uncle Louis' family was invited to dinner, along with the elderly *Zi* Frenke for this festive occasion. After dinner, during the discussion of the rising power of Mussolini and his Black Shirts, my father lifted me on to the table and asked me to sing the popular song of the day, "Facetta Nera," a rousing tribute to Mussolini's soldiers who were bringing *civilizazione* to the Abyssinians. I still remember the dreadful first verse.

Facetta nera, brut' Abyssinia
Aspetta e spera che gia l'ora s'avicina
Quando saremmo vicino a te
Noi ti daremmo un' altro Duce e un' altro Re!

Black face, ugly Abyssinians
Just wait and hope that the hour is approaching,
When we shall be near you
We will give you another leader and another king.

I sang out the verses in a loud clear voice, unabashed, for I had no notion of the meaning. These few years of euphoria for Italian immigrants like my uncles, who derived great pride from the apparent social improvements that Mussolini was making in their native land, did not last very long. From the moment of the attack on Pearl Harbor in 1941 and the alliance between Italy, Germany, and Japan, my uncles and all their friends turned against the Axis powers. I well remember the joy my father and uncles expressed when Italy broke its compact with Germany and declared war on its former ally in September 1943, throwing in their lot with the Allied forces for the rest of the war. The horrors of the German occupation of Italy and the punishments imposed on Italian lives and property as their Army retreated are well documented.

Uncle Giacomo and his family suffered doubly—from the hostile German occupation and the frequent Allied bombings. Far worse were the spiteful acts of destruction inflicted by the retreating German Army, including the blowing up the city's water supply and public utilities. The Lucianos, along with thousands of others, moved into caves on the northern outskirts of the city to escape the air raids, and so survived.

CHAPTER 2
Life in Depression-era New Jersey

Describing our family's hardships in a strange land, the fearsome experience of going to school for the first time in unfamiliar surroundings, knowing not a word of the language of the classroom—the effort to make this account "real" almost defeats me. We lived on Littleton Avenue in Newark, a city housing a large Italian immigrant population. We began our American life in a rented, four-room apartment, furnished by my mother's savings, with a small deposit securing the basics. Every week the furniture store owner came to our house to collect a small payment. Nearby my father had opened his first butcher shop with equipment paid for by Uncle Mike. It was a very unfortunate start. After one year, the business was a total loss. Neighborhood families could barely afford meat once or twice a month, and the existing shops were desperate to hold on to their customers.

First Steps
My mother took me to school soon after we were settled, a walk of three city blocks from our apartment building. She left me with a first

grade teacher and told me to wait for her at noontime, when we would be sent home for lunch. At dismissal time, I was escorted to an exit door, apparently a different door from the one at which my mother was waiting. I began to walk in what I thought was the direction to my house. I walked for what seemed like miles, soon crying when I realized I was lost. As I passed an Italian barbershop where a group of men were lounging outside, they took notice of my plight and stopped to ask my name and where I was going. I was not certain of my exact address but when I said, "Rosa Pedalino di Littleton Avenue," the barber remarked that there was a new immigrant family on that street and I must be one of the children. They called in a passing policeman who took me to the nearest police station where they sat me on the sergeant's desk and gave me an ice cream cone while they asked around for information on my family. I was escorted home by the policeman, there to find my frantic mother and small brothers—all weeping over my disappearance. Perhaps that little escapade impressed me with my lifelong belief that the primary mission of police is to help us.

In less than a year, our family was flat broke. With the small income from my father's store, my parents relied on a supply of hand-me-down clothing from Uncle Mike's family and spent as little as possible on food, utilities, rent, and furniture payments. My mother was an excellent economizer, making the most of what little we had. We had no toys, books, or games. In winter we played indoors, a game we called "jitney bus." As the oldest, I got to be the bus driver, sitting on a little stool and holding in my hand a big metal lid from a soup pot—the steering wheel of the bus. My brothers, playing the passengers, pretended to hand me their nickels as they boarded, and away we would ride, making up fantasy destinations.

It was probably Uncle Michael who investigated what help was available to us from the social service agencies, help that we were legally entitled to since our mother was an American citizen. However it was arranged, we moved to a slightly better apartment on Mt. Prospect Avenue, a wide, tree-lined street with trolley tracks running up the middle. How grand it seemed! Part of the forty-dollar monthly rent was to be covered by the city government, and as well we would receive a very small family stipend in the form of surplus food or clothing. This was called being "on relief" in the 1930s and would now be known as "welfare." Depression-era people were ashamed to let it be known that they were "on relief" or accepting any kind of support—it was considered a *disgrazia*. My parents kept their situation a secret from neighbors, hoping that this "charity" would not be needed once my father found work.

The following description of my early years in an American school appears in my first book, which was published in 1990:

> During those first few months, the hours I spent in the classroom were a haze of incomprehensible sounds. I copied what the other children seemed to be doing, scribbling on paper as though I were writing; otherwise, I silently watched the behavior of teachers and students. Although I cannot recall the process of learning English and beginning to participate in the verbal life of the classroom, I know it was painful. I can remember that within two years I felt completely comfortable with English and with the school community—how it happened I do not know. ... When it finally began to happen, I remember the intense joy of understanding and being understood, even at a simple level, by those around me.

I find *Hunger of Memories*, Richard Rodriguez' account of his experience as an underprivileged Mexican-American child deeply moving and evocative of my earliest school memories. He writes:

> One day in school I raised my hand to volunteer an answer. I spoke out in a loud voice. And I did not think it remarkable when the entire class understood. That day, I moved very far from the disadvantaged child

I had been only days earlier. The belief, the calming assurance that I belonged in public, had at last taken hold. ... Only later when I was able to think of myself as an American, no longer an alien in gringo society, could I seek the rights and opportunities necessary for full public individuality. ... Those middle class ethnics who scorn assimilation romanticize public separateness and they trivialize the dilemma of the socially disadvantaged.

Mt. Prospect Avenue

"Socially disadvantaged"—what a lovely euphemism for being among the poorest of the poor in our new neighborhood. The main reason for moving to Mt. Prospect Avenue was so my father could be near his new job, a half-hour ride on the trolley to the next town of Nutley, where he worked in a butcher shop owned by an earlier Italian immigrant. My father worked from 8:00 AM to 6:00 PM, six days a week, for twelve dollars. His hard-hearted employer would not allow him to take home a scrap of meat for his family. The strict rules of the "relief" agency required that no family subsidy could be granted unless the head of household was completely out of work. Thus every few months an inspector would show up at our house to ask if my father had found work yet, and my mother would always say that my father was out looking for work that very minute. As it is with families of the working poor even now, lying to the authorities becomes a necessity of life.

My mother, thanks to her many years as a seamstress, found a jobber on our street who parceled out "piece work" to ladies in the neighborhood who were skillful enough to do the fine stitching of silk undergarments, intricate embroidery, or lace edgings. I often walked with my mother to the apartment, half a block away, where she would deliver the completed bundle of sewing, always to be greeted by a cold, arrogant "Buon giorno, cosa volete?" (Good day. What do you want?) My mother would answer respectfully, "Signore, ho finito tutto il lavoro. Mi potrebbe pagare cualche cosa, debbo comprare ..."

(Sir, I've finished the work. Could you pay me something, I need to buy…). Before she could finish the sentence he would erupt with a nasty answer: "Pay you, now? I can't pay you until I deliver this to the factory. Then you'll get something. Go, go now." His spinster sister, Emilietta, a meek woman who looked ancient to me but was probably no more than thirty, once said, "Please, why don't you just give her a little something on account …" but she, too, was rudely dismissed. On one occasion, as we were leaving, Emilietta furtively slipped a dollar bill to my mother, who was hiding her tears.

What an evil man. How he reveled in his role of unassailable superiority, lording it over half-a-dozen poor women trying to earn a desperately needed bit. We learned later from local gossip, when my mother no longer was beholden to the scoundrel for work, that the man was promptly paid for all "pieces" delivered but deferred full payment to the women, doling out small sums intermittently, for his own perverted enjoyment. On hot summer mornings, when I woke I would see my mother sitting at the window in her slip, sewing by the early morning sunlight, already perspiring, with a handkerchief knotted loosely around her neck. Yet I don't think I truly grasped the reality of how poor we were.

Our children's world was circumscribed by the walk to school that we made twice daily, since we went home for lunch; the local library, my greatest after-school stopping-off place; and going to Mass and Sunday School at Our Lady of Good Counsel Church on Sundays. We had no car in those early years, of course, and no money to ride the bus or trolley. A grocery store stood on the northeast corner of our block at Coeyman Street, and a small A & P on the southeast corner at Delavan Avenue. Across the wide avenue that we were never allowed to cross unaccompanied, stood Glatzell's German Bakery, source of the once-a-year treat of streusel coffee cake.

Struggling to cover the basic necessities of daily life was a constant for my parents. The official notion that poor people should not receive any help if the father is employed—no matter how little he earns—did not die with our Depression-era generation but was still official policy in recent decades. With a rent subsidy, with my father's meager salary and my mother's even more meager supplementary income from sewing, they could barely keep us fed and clothed and allow my father his cigarettes, which then sold for five cents a pack. My mother, as the American citizen and official recipient of government aid, was required to check in with the relief office in "downtown Newark" every two weeks, a five-cent trip by trolley each way. On one visit they gave her a 50-pound bag of flour to carry home; another time it was a 20-pound bag of apples; occasionally she would be given second hand-clothing that she would alter for us. Lucy wore an old, hand-me-down navy-blue spring coat from Aunt Mary that did not quite fit her; the buttons did not quite come together in the front. It was not large enough or warm enough for winter wear, but it was all she had. On her return home with the giant bag of flour, her dark coat was covered with the white powder, causing her to cringe with shame as she entered our building.

It would be unfair and inaccurate to present a totally bleak picture of our daily lives. We children were blessedly unaware of the struggles to sustain us. Our first year in the Mt. Prospect Avenue apartment, two young men from Avella, my father's cousins—Vincent, a fun-loving, friendly sort, and Livio, a hunchback with little levity in his personality—lived with us and contributed two dollars each a week to cover their room and board, and all meals including a lunch my mother packed for them before they went to their work in a garment factory. A pity they left us to rent their own apartment, since their contribution was so urgently needed.

Coming from Avella where we had never known an indoor bathroom, one of our earliest luxuries was the bathtub, though we did not have hot water on tap. Every Saturday night my mother would heat pots of water on the gas stove in the kitchen to give the three of us baths. Naturally we all were bathed in the same water. Then, dressed in our pajamas, we would sit around the kitchen table for the Saturday night treat—a dab of cream cheese spread on a Ritz cracker, one for each of us. Years later, as an elementary school teacher in the Puerto Rican neighborhood of Springfield, Massachusetts, I was asked to visit the family of little Magalis in my kindergarten class to find out why the child came to school so covered with dirt and smelling of urine. I was assigned this task because I could speak Spanish. I found a family living in a cold-water flat and a mother who seemed totally overwhelmed with eight children from four different fathers, none of whom was in evidence. What a terrible sadness to see such despair on this woman's face and to understand her plight so well.

I count us fortunate, my brothers and me, that our parents were united in their dedication to providing support for us in spite of the almost unrelieved difficulties in their lives, so many of which drove a wedge between them. So much misery, so many arguments between my parents, such bitterness in my father's sense of futility in his "place" in this new country, frustrations that he took out on our mother by berating her every initiative. For example, Elliott Street School offered English-language lessons to the mothers of recent immigrant children. My mother would have taken classes a few mornings a week, while we were also in school, but my father absolutely forbade her to do it, accusing her of wanting to "get ahead of him." This was a pattern that persisted through their entire married life. My father was jealous of any activity that would take his wife away from her domestic responsibilities and, yes, the physical and emotional aspects of childcare were definitely *her* responsibility. My mother was not allowed to wear makeup, not even face powder, and was not allowed to cut her hair, having to keep her heavy tresses in a large bun tethered to the back of her neck. Today we would characterize my father as a "control freak" but that would still be too mild for the grim reality of their marriage.

Somehow they managed, thanks to their careful, frugal ways learned in Avella. All our growing-up years, for instance, my family adhered to a set weekly schedule of meals, nutritious though hardly high on variety. Every Tuesday, Thursday, and Sunday were pasta dinners with a salad or vegetable, and the Sunday dinner included meat when it was affordable. Friday night was meatless for Catholics, Monday nights were "leftovers" nights, Wednesdays always presented a vegetable and bread dinner, and Saturday was the day for making the soup that would serve us for one or two meals. Often on Saturday mornings my mother would send me to the A & P with fifteen cents in my hand to say to the butcher, "Please give me fifteen cents soup meat and a nice piece of bone." She reckoned, rightly, that the butcher would be more generous with a small child and throw in an extra scrap.

I learned economy in the kitchen in those early years, and, as my mother's chief assistant, I also learned the basics of food preparation, house cleaning, sewing, crocheting, and embroidery—all skills considered essential for my future domestic role. Our breakfast was a bowl of *latte e cafe* with a chunk of stale bread dipped in it—little did we know that this beverage would become the trendiest drink at a then-unfathomable place like Starbucks! When in third grade, during a lesson on nutrition, we were each asked to tell the class what we had had for breakfast that morning, I listened to the others before announcing that my mother gave me orange juice, Corn Flakes, an egg with toast, and a glass of milk—a total fiction, but a lie that got me by without hazarding the contempt of classmates who would tease and a teacher who would tell us that coffee stunts your growth, and did my mother want me to be a midget?

Today's poor have access to health care at a level unimaginable in my growing up years, although millions of the working poor and lower middle-class today still do not have enough access to affordable doctors and hospitals. We had no family doctor and never went to a dentist. Each of us had our tonsils removed, however, when we reached age seven or eight, as was then considered the wise course, which required an overnight stay in a charity hospital ward. Our childhood illnesses were cured by our mother's home remedies. Aunt Mary advised my mother to give us a teaspoonful of cod liver oil every morning to ward off colds, and when the cost of this elixir could be squeezed out of the budget, we had to take the foul syrup each morning. Thanks to our good genes, our limited but healthy basic diet that included no candy, our habits of cleanliness, plenty of exercise and sufficient sleep, we grew up quite healthy. My first visit to a dentist occurred when I was eighteen years old. One of my best friends who was working in a dentist's office convinced me to have a check up. My teeth were pronounced healthy and strong and remain so to this day as I round out my seventy-seventh year.

The socialization process for new immigrants—acculturation, if you will—occurs through contact with people in their immediate surroundings. The people it would have seemed natural for our family to be closest to were the Pedalinos who'd come to America before us. But my father's two brothers and their families had little or nothing to do with us. They did not invite us to share holiday meals or family birthdays—we hardly knew our cousins. Why this distance? I believe that Michael and Louis had leaped way ahead of my father in becoming "Americanized." They had married local women and thus had acquired in-laws and a whole set of other relatives. Our visits to Uncle Mike's family were so rare that we were totally in awe of his family and their affluence. On one visit, Aunt Mary peeled a banana and cut it in half, offering one piece to my brother Domenick (whose Italian nickname was "Mimi"). He didn't want the banana but was too shy to refuse it. When no one was looking, he stuffed it in his pocket, the slimy pulp undiscovered for weeks.

Our home at 819 Mt. Prospect Avenue was a two-story, four-family brick building with two flats on each side of a main entrance. We occupied the first floor apartment to the left of the front door; to the right was the married daughter of the owner of the building, Sadie; the owner, Mr. Marchegiano, lived with his family directly above us; and a family named Cortes lived on the second floor to the right. These people contributed more to our understanding of life in America than our blood relatives. To my knowledge, none of these families was "on relief," but in the 1930s keeping such family secrets salvaged one's pride.

Three incidents are still vivid for me and still evoke feelings of humiliation. On warm evenings, residents of the building would sit on the front steps, known as "the stoop," adults chatting, children playing in front of the house until dark, all waiting and hoping for the apartments to cool off. Incidentally, my father never sat on the front steps with us in the summer. This was a social circle inhabited only by mothers and children. I don't know where my father spent his evenings, perhaps with some of his *paisanos* in card games and wine drinking or other inexpensive pastimes. My mother and father rarely spent an evening out together—we were not yet familiar with the concept "baby sitter." Friends came to spend an evening with us or we went to visit, as a family, or to attend the occasional christening, wedding, or wake. This lack of a social life as a couple was partly the pattern from life in Avella, partly the effects of poverty and the stresses it placed on their lives.

Some evenings my mother would bring out a few apples or a peach that she would peel for us. One night, just at dusk, the Good Humor Man ice cream truck came slowly by, bells tinkling, and all of us cried out for him to stop. My brothers and I joined the other children in begging their mothers to buy an ice cream popsicle, the preferred treat. My mother tried to hush us but we were so insistent. Finally, without a word, she turned and walked into the house. Our neighbor, Sadie, took me aside and said, "Don't bother your mother. Don't you know she hasn't got the money for ice cream?" I was crushed by that comment, an eight-year-old girl left to placate her two younger brothers who were in tears.

One winter night after a heavy snowfall, my father took us to the corner to watch the neighborhood children ride their sleds down the Coeyman Street hill. We stood with him, watching longingly as groups of children would jump on a sled for the ride, sometimes falling into the snow banks, sleds sliding away. A couple of times my brothers and I begged other children for a ride, but we were turned down. My father never said a word. But when a lone sled went sliding by he stepped in the way and secured it, turning quickly and leading us away from the street corner. We were so surprised we said nothing and just followed him, walking rapidly past our house and to the next corner, where he took the three of us sliding. Our father was not naturally a thief, and I never saw such an action again. I believe his desperation overcame him, but this impulsive act and the fear of being found with a stolen sled surely made our sledding trips uncomfortable for all of us.

One evening, Mr. Peplin, the owner of the furniture store, arrived at the door. Every week he came to collect the small payment in person. On this occasion I stood near the kitchen stove, unobserved. My father explained, in very broken English, that he didn't have the money this week. Mr. Peplin insisted that he had to be paid, and the argument went around, two or three times. Finally, my father stood up, grabbed the front of Mr. Peplin's shirt, and pulled him to his feet. With Peplin's face close to his he hissed, "Do you want me to go out and rob somebody to pay you? I can't pay now, but I will pay you every penny as soon as things get better." Poor Mr. Peplin, who was Jewish but understood the garbled Italo-English message clearly enough, said, "Fine, fine, Mr. Pedalino, that's fine," and left. Mr. Peplin did not appear at our house for a couple of months. Over time my father paid the entire amount owed and Mr. Peplin was effusive in his praise for the family, urging my parents always to come to his store for new furniture. For the next sixty years, my mother had only kind words for Mr. Peplin and honored him as a prince among Jewish merchants.

Adaptations and Accommodations

Living in an established immigrant neighborhood of mostly second and third generation families—mostly Italian, but with a sprinkling of northern Europeans, Irish, German, English, and a few what we then called "colored" families—was a modest improvement over the original Newark tenement apartment of our first year in the United States. Most of our neighbors were in as dire straits as we were. Our landlord who lived above us, Mr. Marchegiano, was a kind grandfatherly type whom we would occasionally see in the back yard, sitting under the grape arbor he had lovingly tended over three decades. Among his eight progeny was one really bad apple, his son Angelo, reputed to be a small-time criminal who had been discharged dishonorably from the U.S. Army. Angelo hung around his parents' apartment, supposedly looking for a job, but no one believed he was making any effort—he was what in those days was called "a lazy bum."

One day when we were all out of the apartment, Angelo forced his way in through the kitchen window and stole the piggy bank that contained the pennies we three children had saved for over a year. When my parents discovered the theft, my father was immediately certain who the culprit was. He went to talk with Mr. Marchegiano, not to threaten to go to the police—that would not even have been a consideration—but to plead with the man to have his son return what he had taken. The piggy bank was returned, with most of the pennies. Imagine taking something so insignificant. But for an unemployed man, pennies would buy a pack of cigarettes and a beer.

School days were my joy—the way I escaped from the oppression of household duties and the constant reminder that as the oldest in the family I had an obligation to help bring up my brothers. I loved school, once I gained enough confidence in my English to speak easily with friends and make my thoughts known in the classroom. I was a total grind. I believed in the goodness of schoolwork, of getting the answers right in arithmetic, of memorizing the times tables and the names of all the twenty-one South American countries, of writing a sentence without mistakes. It would be a long time before children would grow up wearing T-shirts urging them to "Question Authority." My efforts were rewarded with good grades, and my quarterly report card always elicited genuine approval from my mother and grudging praise from my father, who believed firmly that there was little use in teaching girls much besides the skills necessary to run a household.

Discovering the public library nearby was truly a godsend. From second grade on, I borrowed books from the library every two weeks, reading through the series of fairy stories where I found my first vision of a possible Cinderella future. Walking to school, I often stopped for my best friend, Joan Ferrara, who seemed so much more sophisticated to me since she had older brothers and sisters from whom she learned thrilling things such as popular song lyrics, movie star gossip, and how to apply make up. At home, though my mother always tuned in to one of the Italian radio stations in the afternoons, gradually we began to listen to the American children's programs at the hour before or after dinner, the suspense-packed shows—the adventures of Tom Mix and Jack Armstrong, the All-American Boy; *The Green Hornet, The Shadow, The Lone Ranger,* and *I Love A Mystery*—all interspersed with commercials for Ovaltine and for the only three known cereals: Corn Flakes, Rice Crispies, and Shredded Wheat. And for a Sunday treat, the Marchegianos would pass one part of their newspaper, the *Newark Star Ledger,* on to us—the comics, which we called "the funnies." My sons are mildly skeptical when I tell them that on first hearing voices from the Philco radio in Uncle Michael's house I went to the large upright instrument and tried to peek behind it to see the people I was convinced were hiding behind the set. But it was truly so!

A strange notion took hold of me one day in the spring of my third grade year. Witnessing the severe scolding of Ellery Winters, a classmate who often misbehaved, I somehow began to think that I would be kept after school that day. After lunch, instead of walking back to school, I loitered around the neighborhood until dismissal time, when I walked home. For the next two days I followed the same routine, attending school in the morning and not returning in the afternoon. Of course, my teacher sent home a note and my truancy escapades ended, not without a severe reprimand and a few slaps on my bottom at home. Miss Grundy, the principal, was kind to me and said there was no harm done, that I was such a good student, so well behaved, that my fears had been groundless.

My parent's lives were not strongly centered on our Catholic religion, and we were not sent to a parochial school because it was a few blocks farther from home than Elliott Street School. We were very glad of that, since we'd heard tales of the strictness and abusiveness of Catholic schools and "The Nuns." But we were made to attend Mass every Sunday morning, as well as catechism classes in preparation for the sacrament of Holy Communion. (My mother would have attended Mass with us but was not allowed to go. My father demanded that she stay right in the kitchen to prepare Sunday dinner, which we ate at 1:00 PM.) The common practice is for Catholic children to receive their First Communion in the spring of their seventh year (considered the age of reason). To be economical, my parents made me wait until both of my brothers were old enough, so that we all made our First Communion together in the spring of 1942. It was a terrible embarrassment for me as the only eleven-year-old in the group, but the occasion was celebrated with a bus ride to downtown Newark to have a professional photograph taken of the three of us in our new outfits.

One could not imagine today the level of prudery of my immigrant parents, whose overriding goal was to keep us innocent of depravity by keeping us ignorant of our bodies and their normal development. I had no idea about the onset of menstruation when, shortly after my tenth birthday, I went to the girls' bathroom and found my underpants stained with blood, felt blood dripping down my legs. Naturally I thought I was injured and asked one of my classmates what I should do. She brought me to the teacher, who understood immediately; quietly, in the coatroom, she calmed my fears. She then asked Myra Mackenzie, one of the older girls in our class, to please walk me home and explain to my mother what had happened. My mother thanked Myra, took me aside to bathe, and then gave me one of the folded white cloths, of which she had a ready supply, and a belt with pins to hold the sanitary pad. She explained, "Now you are a young lady and you will have to take care of yourself. You will have this bleeding once a month for a couple of days." That was the sum total of my initiation into adolescence.

Music has always played an important part in my life. From our earliest childhood, we would sit with our parents on evenings when a few friends came to visit, and listen to my father and his friends sing their favorite Neapolitan songs to the accompaniment of a guitar and a mandolin. My father had a beautiful untrained tenor voice and was quite a skilled player of both instruments, which he had brought with him from Italy. We grew up hearing these melodious tunes and the hauntingly beautiful lyrics—"Santa Lucia," "Torn' a Sorrienta," "Senza Mama e Abandonata," "Chitarra Romana"—expressing nostalgia for Italy, for distant family, and for unrequited loves. On long drives in recent years, when I'm in the car alone for several hours, I often pass the time by singing these songs, challenging myself to remember the words, remembering my father and feeling disappointment that his life had such small measures of joy.

In my fifth grade classroom one day, Mr. Rabinowitz announced that musical instruments were on loan, free, to students who would like to take music lessons. I raised my hand with a few other students, and when he called on me to say which instrument I wanted to borrow I asked for a piano. The other children laughed, putting me to shame, when he said, "We can't give you a piano to take home but how about a violin?" I accepted. The first few weeks of my sawing away, practicing scales, were painful for the family, but I persevered and came to enjoy playing the violin for the next two years, even joining the school orchestra. One evening I played in a string quartet of fifth grade music students at a school recital. The occasion called for a new dress my mother sewed for me from remnants, and I had the satisfaction of seeing my mother, father and two brothers in the audience.

Our lives changed suddenly and not entirely in positive ways when my mother decided that with all three children in school all day, she should find full time employment.

Latch-Key Kids

By 1940 manufacturing jobs were increasingly available and unskilled laborers were in demand. My father finally allowed my mother to apply for a job, and her first employment outside the home was at the Table Talk Pie Company. This first step took Lucy away from being a fulltime housekeeper forever. She prepared us for school and gave us each a lunch to carry, leaving home by 7:30 AM to take two buses to the factory. After school I was responsible for taking care of my brothers for the two hours until my mother arrived home. Often I was left chores to do and when I shirked my duties, sitting around with my brothers reading cast-off comic books from our neighbors or just playing in the backyard, I was roundly scolded and given a sound slap across the rear end. Small as her salary must have been, it allowed us to enjoy some new treats, such as the occasional penny for candy, the opportunity to go to the Saturday afternoon movies at the nearby Kent Theater, admission ten cents. At first the little, 3-inch-in-diameter Table Talk pies, which my mother got for free when they were dented, were a wonderful treat, but as a steady diet they became tiresome.

Lucy left Table Talk Pie after six months to start work in a garment factory, for slightly higher pay. Doing work for which she was already skilled led to quick recognition. My mother's hunger for better earnings (and for acknowledgment) impelled her to work harder than the women around her, to sacrifice most of her lunch hour to be more productive, and to completely ignore the chit-chat and gossip that the others indulged in whenever the "forelady" (department manager) was out of the room. She was not popular with her co-workers. Since they were paid by the piece instead of by the hour, her fingers flew, guiding the cloth through the treadle sewing machine. She would never be a poster girl for the union shop.

Lucy's next move, on hearing of better-paying work, was to apply at a factory that made uniforms for the U.S. Army. As fate would have it, the Monday she started her new job was December 8, 1941, the day after the Japanese attack on Pearl Harbor and President Roosevelt's declaration of war against the Axis powers. On that morning I was on my way to school, oblivious of the war news, when, through my own carelessness, I was struck by a car as I skipped across the street near Elliott Street School. The driver was going slowly and stopped immediately to help me. But for a few bruises to my knees and elbows, I was unhurt. He took me into the school where they called my mother to come and take me home. She had only been at her new job one hour, but they allowed her to leave for the rest of the day.

Lucy's professional sewing skills were soon recognized and she was taken off the repetitive, assembly-line work and promoted to the position of department substitute, with a raise in salary. Since she was adept at sewing any part of a garment and doing it swiftly without special training, she would fill in for any absent worker to keep the production lines functioning. Within a few months she was recommended for promotion and a substantial raise—she would become a "forelady," one who oversees a whole department. How naïve my mother was as she announced this great opportunity to my father. He did not praise her but immediately demanded that she turn it down. It was only the beginning of what was to be the destructive pattern of their competition for the rest of my father's life: She would rise to the next challenge and work well at it; he would feel threatened as the *pater familias* and find ways to demean her accomplishments, to impose new restrictions.

Frank, my father, had acquired a very old LaSalle sedan, the kind of car most often seen in 1930s gangster movies, dark grey with a running board on each side and a box-like trunk with rusty hinges. How he ever obtained a driver's license I have no idea, as he read English very poorly. My brother Anthony believes he paid someone to take the written and road tests for him. Frank had left his job in Nutley to work at a slaughter house, butchering cows, lambs, and pigs, and occasionally making deliveries to small butcher shops. We children now had the novelty of a Sunday afternoon "ride" that lasted all of an hour as my father drove us out to the country and we three argued about who would sit at the coveted window seats. The car had no heater and in winter we were bundled in wool blankets to keep us warm.

In the late thirties Elliott Street School began to allow the children of working mothers to stay in school at lunch time, provided they brought their own lunch from home. In the summer of 1942 the school opened a summer session for children of working mothers, with arts and crafts activities, music, cooking, and other non-academic subjects. This was a blessing for our mother, who could be confident that we were under the care of a teacher most of the day. Now we found entertaining new activities to occupy our days: making raffia baskets, for instance, and a carpentry class for girls (highly progressive for that era) in which I learned how to use a coping saw, hammer, and sandpaper. My first lesson in cooking class taught me how to make a lettuce and tomato sandwich on toasted Wonder bread spread with mayonnaise—but no bacon, it was too expensive—and was my initial introduction to the preparation of an "American" food.

Was our school community multicultural or diverse? Not if skin color is the measure of difference. Perhaps two-thirds of the children at the Elliott Street School were of Italian derivation, but many other nationalities were represented: Gerd Haglund, Robert Sommers, and Joe Amstock are some of the names I remember of children who did not share my ethnicity. The shy, quiet girl sitting directly in front of me in third grade, Dorothea Black, was the only "colored" person in our class. (Although the terms for African Americans changed from "colored" to "Negro" and then to "black" throughout the decades, for consistency I will use "African American" in their place). We were friendly in school and in the playground, though we did not live near enough to play together after school. In fact, as I think about it now, I was not allowed to bring anyone to our house to play, nor did my parents allow us to go to the homes of classmates, except for the two girls who lived within our same block. One day I said something to Dorothea about wishing she could come to my house after school, that it was too bad she lived so far away. She glanced at me strangely and turned away, saying, "I couldn't come to your house anyway." When I asked why, she answered, "Don't you know why? 'Cause we're different, ask your mother, she'll tell you." That was the sum total of my experience with race in elementary school. I never asked, as I didn't really think my mother or my father knew much of anything about this country we were living in—they seemed so totally mired in the language, customs, foods, and practices of "the old country" we had recently left.

With America's entry into the war, our lives were filled with patriotic activities at home and in school. War news on the radio and in the newspapers, on the Movietone News segment at the Saturday afternoon movies at the Kent Theatre—even for young children we were aware that a mighty global battle was being waged. And for my mother and father, naturally enough, it was the staple of conversation at the dinner table every night, since their parents, brothers, and sisters were in European war zones. For us, daily life changed when the rationing of food, clothing, gasoline, and heating fuels began, and every family spent its monthly allotment of ration stamps very carefully. We helped our mother save all manner of household goods to be collected and reused in the war effort: flattened tins from canned foods, paper, rendered fat. At school we were encouraged to buy Defense Stamps for ten cents each and paste them into a book which, when filled, would amount to $18.75, the price of a U.S. Savings Bond. We practiced air raid drills, marching downstairs to the basement of the school to sit on the floor together until the "all clear" rang. It was just a fun occasion for us, a chance to tease each other, giggle, and act silly. Mr. Rubinstein, our music teacher, gave us patriotic songs to practice, the first popular songs of World War II: "God Bless America," "White Cliffs of Dover," "Don't Sit Under the Apple Tree" (with anyone else but me).

The first bit of luck to befall our family rested on my father's recent job at the slaughterhouse. Somehow he managed to obtain a special license to slaughter and dress beef and pork to put on sale in his own business. He actually had no business yet, but he had a precious license that was valuable in the war years, when new licenses were not being issued.

Early Entrepreneurship

Frank and Lucy decided they would now go into business together. With a small loan from Uncle Mike they rented a store on Franklin Street in the adjoining city of Belleville, and rented a four-room, second-floor apartment next door. After six years on Mt. Prospect Avenue, and at the very beginning of my seventh grade year, we moved to Belleville. My brothers and I were enrolled in the Franklin Street School, around the corner from our new apartment. My mother left her job in the defense plant and began to learn the butcher's trade. She was always a quick study. This woman who arrived in America a shy village seamstress not only became a skilled meat cutter but learned how to deal effectively with customers, keep accounts, and develop her English-language fluency as well.

At first Lucy and Frank worked together. My father was out of town every Tuesday, to do his butchering at the slaughterhouse and to bring a week's supply of meat back to the store. Lucy soon became adept at running the shop by herself. This was the beginning of better times for our family and more responsibilities for me. On Saturdays I was responsible for dusting, sweeping (we had no vacuum cleaner), polishing furniture, and helping with the laundry, which we washed in the basement and carried up to the second floor to hang on a clothes line outside the back porch. Now that my mother was working right next door to our apartment, there was no time wasted in commuting, and she was readily available for our many small problems and arguments, to minister to the nicks and bruises acquired in after-school play. My mother and I prepared the evening meal together and shared the cleanup detail afterward. My brothers were not expected to do "women's work" since they were not in training to be future housewives. The division of gender roles was concrete—domestic chores were not for boys.

Our sojourn in Belleville lasted only one year, as my parents saved enough to take the next giant step—buying their own property. It was a good year in many ways as I began to mature socially, to respond to the attentions of boys in my class and of eighth graders, especially the darkly handsome Philip Bruno. Miss Murray, an excellent teacher in my unsophisticated view, made me feel immediately welcome and special as "the new girl," seating me near the front of the classroom with the better students.

I basked in the attention and, for the first time, felt popular. Even my one terrifying experience, never to be repeated, of singing in public, did not turn into public disgrace. With some coaching by Miss Murray, I sang Joyce Kilmer's "Trees," a treacly poem set to a treacly tune that turned my face deep pink when I had to sing the phrase, "a tree whose hungry mouth is pressed, against the Earth's sweet-flowing breast" to the leers of all the boys. My only lingering regret in leaving my former school was the discovery that Belleville had no music program in the elementary schools and no violins to lend.

My formal study of instrumental music ended, but not my love of the popular music of the day—the big bands of Harry James, Benny Goodman, Glenn Miller, Artie Shaw; the male and female vocalists who sang the songs of romantic love and sad separations in this first year of the world war—Helen Forrest, Ella Fitzgerald, Vera Lynn, the Andrews Sisters, Bob Eberle, Bing Crosby, and "The Crooner," Frank Sinatra. One of my favorite pastimes was the occasional after-school visit with a neighbor's high-school-age daughters who, in 1942 slang, were "hep to the jive" and who began to teach me to jitterbug. On Sunday afternoons my brothers and I would join other children on our block to take the short bus ride to the movies in nearby Bloomfield Center, a long afternoon's entertainment with a feature film, cartoons, Movietone News, and a serial that ended each week with some "Perils of Pauline"–type heroine dangling by a fingernail. Two memorable movies of that year, with songs that my generation has never forgotten: *Casablanca* ("As Time Goes By") and *Holiday Inn* ("White Christmas").

Starting Anew in Orange

In July 1943 we made the move to 71 South Day Street in the city of Orange, the building housing our store and apartment that my parents would not leave until 1966 when the State of New Jersey bought the property from them to build part of Route 280, a major east-west highway. I was to spend many unhappy years there, bitterly resenting the fact that our living quarters were not separate from the store, that we didn't live in a real house with a porch, front lawn, and other American amenities that my school friends enjoyed. But in the first few years on South Day Street I was not yet so class conscious.

The house lot measured 25 feet x 100 feet, and the red brick, two-story structure filled the entire space except for a backyard that was about 20 feet square. The first floor front was our grocery store and meat market with an 8-foot x 8-foot walk-in ice box where the quarters of beef, veal, and pork were hung. Behind this area there was a small utility room, a half bathroom, a kitchen, and sun porch/homework/ game room. Second floor contained three bedrooms, a large kitchen, and a full bathroom. True to stereotypical Italo-American form, my father had the backyard cemented over except for a one-and-a-half-foot stretch of garden around the edges—where he grew tomatoes, basil and parsley—close to the chain link fence.

For that neighborhood we were somewhat privileged as home owners. The half-dozen streets south of Main Street in close proximity to South Day Street formed the hub in which two or three generations of Italian immigrant families lived, many in rented apartments above their own small shops, bakeries, grocery stores, florists, dry goods stores. A small but growing number of African American families, recently arrived from southern states to work in defense plants and local businesses, were beginning to share our neighborhood. We did not know the word segregation at the time. All eighth grade students in the northern half of the city went to Central School together. We all came from the same working-class families and our classroom demographic was influenced not by color but on achieving a roughly equal number of boys and girls. Today we would describe the make up of Central School as "diverse," since it included racial and ethnic minorities, concepts of which we were blissfully unaware. On rare occasions I would be allowed to bring a girlfriend home with me after school, but this was mostly discouraged as my domestic duties came first.

My brothers were enrolled in Mt. Carmel School, which happened to be just around the corner, and they were now old enough, as prospective altar boys, to begin studying the responses in Latin for the Mass. Domenick and Anthony, now ten and eight years old, began to be assigned chores at home such as carrying buckets of ashes from our coal-burning furnace in the basement out to the bins on the curb, hauling out trash, clearing our sidewalk of snow, and helping my father with his now annual wine-making in our basement. My father was always a difficult man—never patient with us, always demanding and imposing new duties and certainly very seldom giving praise or showing appreciation. We were his vassals, indentured servants expected to obey his whims and commands. We soon realized that having both parents in the home business meant a level of scrutiny and imposition we had not experienced before. My brother Domenick suffered the most, being required to help in the store after school every day when he was aching to join his friends in baseball, basketball, and other sports. His only break came on days when my father was out on meat delivery runs or playing bocce at the Avellino Social Club nearby.

I found one of the most inspiring educators in all my elementary school years in our science and math teacher, Miss MacDowell. Her love of astronomy lit a life-long passion for the cosmos in me, this little Italian kid whose parents did not even know of the existence of our solar system. She did not assume, as some of our teachers did, that children from Italian homes were barely educable and all destined for factory jobs and early marriage. We enjoyed the dignity of her respect, hard task-mistress though she was. Our English teacher, Mrs. Rumsey, a soft-spoken, chubby woman with thick glasses, managed to maintain order and civility in the classroom as well as generate interest in the literature we read—the well-selected poems and short stories. But Mrs. Rumsey was a source of embarrassment as we all knew she had been married a year and was *expecting a baby*! There was no sign of pregnancy yet but just the thought of it made the girls squirm and the boys tell crude jokes. Such prudery, on present reflection, seems fit for the twelfth century, not the twentieth.

In the spring of my eighth-grade year I began to feel pain in my joints, especially the wrists and ankles, pains that were inexplicable. After inquiring in the neighborhood, my mother took me to the Orange Orthopedic Hospital clinic for a preliminary check up. I was seen by a young resident who recommended blood tests and the results, reported to us on our next visit, were shocking. The doctor diagnosed an early onset of rheumatic fever, a heart ailment we had never heard of, and prescribed a drastic treatment: complete bed rest for one month, as much time as possible in the sun, and at least one or two years excused from physical education classes at school. The doctor warned that I, a thirteen-year-old, was not to leave my bed to walk to the bathroom, I was to be carried or to use a bedpan.

My reaction to this devastating news was more a terrible disappointment at missing the last month of school and eighth grade graduation activities than any true understanding of what was a serious ailment. For my parents it was a terrible blow. Other than when we had our tonsillectomies, none of us had ever been to a doctor. The burden on my mother was more onerous than I could know at that time. Not only was she now obliged to carry my meals upstairs to me three times a day and see to my toilet situation, but she was working in the store every day in addition to her housekeeping chores. What we had not yet been told was that my mother was pregnant for the first time in ten years, already in her fourth month.

The Central School principal accepted the medical situation and excused me from the end-of-year exams, assuring my parents that I would be graduating from eighth grade with my classmates and would proceed to Orange High School in the fall. Every day, my mother would carry me into my parents' bedroom at the front of the house, as it was airy and sunlit. I would be left with books, magazines, and a radio. The solitude was broken occasionally by a visit from a girlfriend, and by my brothers who sometimes kept me company after school. The radio provided me with popular songs, soap operas, and a large ration of war news, culminated by the riveting reports on June 6, 1944, D-Day, and the days that followed. Miss MacDowell came to visit me on the last day of school, bringing me an autograph book signed by all my classmates and a gift—my first bottle of scent, *Friendship's Garden.* My mother and I were so touched by Miss McDowell's visit, and when my teacher was brought up the stairs from the store, I sensed that my mother was embarrassed to be found covered in her long, stained, butcher's apron.

My illness hardly made any impact on my physical condition as I no longer had any pains in my joints and felt no other discomfort. But it made a huge change in our summer routine. Previously we had made a few day trips to the Jersey shore, bringing a large picnic lunch with us in our old LaSalle sedan, but for my health's sake we were now to have our first vacation by the sea. We arranged for a whole week in Long Branch, a shabby resort full of boarding houses that catered to a large Italo-American working-class clientele. My further good fortune was to be invited to spend an additional week with a family friend, Anna

Evangelista, to give me the benefit of the sunshine cure recommended by our doctor.

My week alone with Mrs. Evangelista passed by too swiftly as we spent part of every day on the beach and in the surf. She was a genial person, far more Americanized than my parents, but she did warn away a young soldier who flirted with me on the beach, telling him politely but firmly that he should not be paying attention to a thirteen-year-old. The week with my parents in Villa Rosina was a novelty for my brothers and me. A "villa" it was not, more like a cheap English seaside resort, but to us it was heaven. Each family had a bedroom that accommodated as many people as the number of cots that could be fitted in. Each family had its own set of pots, pans, crockery and kitchen implements. Our typical day began with my mother going to the local market for fresh produce, doing laundry by hand, and keeping us from underfoot until we all walked across the street to the beach after lunch with our paraphernalia—umbrella, toys, towels. There we were forbidden to go into the water for one half-hour after lunch (none of us yet knew how to swim) to avoid getting cramps and drowning, the conventional wisdom of the time. On our return from the beach, we would shower and while my brothers played and my mother and I jostled the other women for space at the stoves. Every evening my father would arrive, after an hour's drive, to take a brief dip in the ocean and to sit down to a full-course dinner, followed by a family stroll on the boardwalk. My later vacations in Cap d'Antibes, Torremolinos, Rio, or Capri never quite met that first thrill of Long Branch, New Jersey.

We were finally told that our mother was expecting a baby. That summer was fraught with two anxieties for me: How hard would it be to become a full-fledged high school freshman among 1,200 other high school kids—could I even find my way around the building much less keep up with the classroom work? And what would it be like to have a baby in the house, a new brother or sister—what new responsibilities would *that* place on me?

Chapter 3

High School

Was there ever a New Jersey girl who had higher expectations for fun, socializing, and freedom from parental restrictions than I when I first entered the halls of Orange High School? Not likely. Intellectual stimulation was not the first thing on my mind. Confusion over my place in the hierarchy of the 350-student freshman class was predictable since I had only lived in the City of Orange one year. Since I missed the last month of school, there had barely been time to make any friends. Though I did not belong to a "clique" (which we pronounced "click"), I would be automatically lumped in with "the Italian kids" at the start.

Our student body would now be characterized as "diverse," though this distinction was unknown in 1940s America. The socioeconomic/ethnic/racial/religious profile of our students' families would fit this general description:

—65 percent working class (factory-workers, white collar workers, small shopkeepers), 30 percent educated professionals, 5 percent or less on public welfare;

—35 percent families of recent Italian immigrants or of Italian ancestry, 20 percent of Irish extraction, 30 percent of northern European stock, 13 percent African American, some living in Orange several generations, some newly arrived from the south); 2 percent Asian, mostly Chinese;

—85 percent white, 15 percent non-white;

—95 percent Christian, evenly divided between Catholics and Protestants, 2 percent Jewish, 3 percent "unclassified."

Walking wide-eyed through the corridors, trying to find my first scheduled classes, my initial anxieties soon passed as I found many of my classmates similarly lost. My parents had no education beyond the fourth grade in a village school, and were blissfully unaware of the mingling of boys and girls, before, during and after class in a modern city high school. It was up to me to teach them about the exciting range of after-school activities, clubs, athletic events, and just "hanging out" that is considered a normal part of high school life. They took a dim view of any school obligations beyond the 2:30 PM dismissal time that would keep me from my responsibilities at home. Freshman year was notable for these reasons: I began to make friends outside the Italo-American neighborhood; I learned of more challenging academic courses than the secretarial track I had been steered into; and my sister was born, an event which would have the most immediate effect on my thirteen-year-old self.

On October 31, it was announced that an after-school dance for freshman students would be held that day from 3:30 PM to 5:30 PM, an informal "mixer" in the school gym with music by record player. I ran home to tell my mother about the dance and to change into a newer sweater and skirt. My mother was sitting in the rocker in our kitchen behind the store, her long white butcher apron covering her pronounced bulge in front. Breathlessly I pleaded for permission to go back to school for the dance, promising that I would be home by 5:45 at the latest to make dinner for the family. My mother quietly gave her approval and urged me to go and enjoy myself but not to be late returning. I was unaware at that time that my mother had been feeling contractions and was waiting for my father to take her to the hospital. She wanted me to be gone before my father's arrival, knowing that he would insist I stay at home.

What a thrill for me—my first dance. Mostly we girls danced together, as we had been practicing at home, but I was asked for one dance by a tall, blond, blue-eyed, cutie, Guy Decker. My head was filled with fantasies of more dances with more boys as I walked home.

A Baby Sister

When I walked into the store I found my brothers waiting for me. I learned that Mama had gone to the hospital to have the baby and Papa would be back later. How closely my parents had guarded us from most of the basic facts about sex and procreation. We had no idea our mother was so close to term—it was simply not a topic of discussion. My mother was in labor until the next morning when our nine-pound baby sister Francesca was delivered after a long but uncomplicated labor. Since hospitals then did not allow young children to visit patients, our first peek at "Francie" was not until five days later when she was brought home.

Not having the baby delivered at home by a midwife, as had been her experience with the first three children born in Avella, was an unsettling experience for my mother, who had never before been examined and treated by a male doctor. On each prenatal visit my father asked to be in the examining room and the doctor, who was of Italian descent, accommodated his request. This deprived Lucy of any private discussion with her doctor about access to birth control. In 1945, after my brother Frank Jr. was delivered by Caesarean section in the sixth month of my mother's pregnancy, the doctor recommended surgery to prevent further pregnancies, but my father adamantly refused to give his permission. My father saw any suggestion of birth control—condom use or surgical intervention —as a threat to his manhood. He totally rejected the doctor's persuasive arguments.

The care of our baby sister in the early years was my mother's constant preoccupation. She was completely responsible for the family butcher shop/grocery store, doing everything from serving customers with groceries, cutting meat to order, stocking shelves, checking deliveries, while my father was running a butcher shop in Belleville, about a half-hour's drive away. In between serving customers, Lucy would tend to her baby, who was kept in a baby carriage in the kitchen behind the store during the day. Making baby formula, sterilizing bottles, and laundering diapers were added chores, since commercially packaged formula and disposable diapers were not to appear for another decade. The concept "daycare center" was not known. Extended families were the norm in neighborhoods like ours in those days, and grandparents, maiden aunts, unmarried uncles, or whoever was nearby and not employed helped with the care of preschool-age children. My mother had no such relatives and my father's brothers and their wives were politely unavailable.

Living directly behind us, our backyards touching, was an immigrant family with eight children, from Udine on the Italian-Yugoslav border. Our two families became friendly and my mother got the idea that Teresa, the mother of the family, might be willing to do a little baby tending, perhaps a few mornings a week, in exchange for a regular supply of meat from our store. Teresa, who was and had always been what we now call a "stay-at-home Mom," often complained of the difficulties of raising a family on her husband's earnings as a ditch digger for the local public utility company. Teresa agreed to help, and her presence in our kitchen to take care of Francie relieved my mother of the anguish of hearing her baby cry and being unable to leave the customers for more than a few minutes. Sad to say the arrangement was ended after a few weeks when Teresa's husband announced that he did not want his wife to be out "working"; she should stay in her own house. My mother was deeply embarrassed and hurt at such a senseless and self-defeating action. With meat rationing in effect, Teresa's family was receiving a benefit more valuable than just a few dollars.

After school hours, of course, my brothers and I all had our assigned chores. After a snack of milk and cookies or some small treats from the store (there was never time for baking a homemade cake—that was a middle-class luxury for the nonworking housewife) my brothers were allowed some outdoor play time with neighborhood boys at the local YMCA. My after-school time was essentially spent taking care of Francie and helping with cooking and laundry. Feeling the crush of constant home responsibilities certainly gave me the impetus to join school clubs that met after 2:30 PM in order to enjoy a few more precious hours of freedom, though I am by nature a gregarious sort anyway, a "joiner." Selfish? Yes. I well knew how much my mother needed me. But as I became friends with girls whose lives seemed completely carefree—they sat in soda shops flirting with boys after school, went on dates, wore lipstick—I wanted so much more than my role as chief assistant to my parents.

In sophomore year I elected to take Spanish I, shunning the Italian I class as too stultifying and predictable. And so I happened on the field of language study that would later become my professional area of expertise. After Spanish, I loved my English courses and cannot praise Orange High School enough for a curriculum that exposed us to an excellent variety of American and English literature. Imagine us kids from low income families reading *Ivanhoe*, Sir Walter Scott's *Idylls of the King*, Shakespeare's *Julius Caesar* and *Macbeth*, George Eliot's *Silas Marner*, as well as the great Americans Stephen Crane, O. Henry, Thoreau, and Dickinson—what a richly inspiring experience! Our teachers had yet to be informed that we should be reading stories about ourselves and our neighborhood, selections we would find "relevant" and would "identify with." Mrs. Goldberg, Miss Calloway, Miss Feind,

Miss Mannion—teachers with exacting standards who knew their subject and made it exciting for us—certainly expanded my horizons far beyond South Day Street and further stimulated my love of literature.

By the end of sophomore year, with solid grades and budding friendships with students who were beginning to be recognized for their talents in drama, athletics, and school politics—in short, kids who were active participants in many areas besides academics and not just marking time before leaving school at age sixteen—I understood my personal need for more challenging course selections. But I was advised to take the practical classes in shorthand, typing, and accounting—business skills that would prepare me for white-collar work after high school graduation. No counselor informed me of the possibility of winning a scholarship if I took more academic courses and got good grades.

Socially my opportunities for making friends and pursuing the "crushes" we fastened on different classmates were quite limited. Aside from school club meetings, I had a difficult time carving out afternoon time to be with friends, much less getting permission to go out in the evenings. Saturday mornings were taken up with housecleaning, with afternoons free for shopping or visiting with girlfriends, although even this time was often limited by my babysitting duties. Sunday was the only day I could count on an entire afternoon and early evening of freedom. After morning Mass at Mt. Carmel Church, Sunday dinner preparation and washing up, I was allowed to go to a movie or visit with friends. Finally, at age fifteen, I was freed of the obligation to take my brothers with me everywhere, a burden I had despised.

On rare occasions I would be allowed to go to a party at the home of one of my girlfriends. My father would drive me to the address of the gathering, believing that there would only be a group of girls involved, and he would return to drive me home at 10:30 or 11:00 PM at the latest. He never knew that these parties were the typical social occasions of high school boys and girls, with soft drinks, brownies or other treats, and silly games like "Pass the Orange" and "Spin the Bottle," a most thrilling, end-of-the-evening game that gave us the chance to learn how to kiss. Had my father known of even these innocent pastimes he would have kept me at home.

In recognition of my expanded duties at home after the birth of my sister, my mother offered me a weekly allowance of four dollars, which I could save or spend on myself. In mid-1940s terms, when Cokes were five cents, hamburgers at White Castle ten cents, full school lunches thirty-five cents, and admission to the movies fifty cents, this was a generous sum. After the first few months of spending at the Woolworth 5 & 10 (*Tangee* orange lipstick, *Evening in Paris* cologne, Frank Sinatra records), I read an ad for a bank savings account called a "Christmas Club," which was designed to teach the joys of saving small amounts weekly that would accumulate by the end of the year, just in time for Christmas shopping. My mother urged me to open an account. Starting with a dollar a week deposit in the Orange Savings Bank, I soon increased my weekly savings to two dollars a week and transferred the sum to an interest-bearing account. From that early start, over the next eight years I saved a total of $1,300, more than enough to pay for the European trip in 1953 that radically altered the course of my life.

I credit my mother with teaching us the important lesson of deferring immediate pleasures for future advantages, a practice we children had never observed in our father. The differences between my parents in their whole approach to life were immense. My father loved each one of us, in his overly protective, domineering ways, and certainly there were times when we saw his caring side. But he was a hard man to understand. For his time and his background and for the dislocation of being forced to leave the village life of Avella, he was not unusual in his autocratic ways, but even conceding all of this, my father was not a good husband, not a sensitive or gentle father, and a very poor businessman who failed in one attempt after another, falling back time and time again on Lucy's work to support our family. What is especially galling is that he had an unusual opportunity to expand his butcher shop and grocery store, given his slaughterhouse license and the booming business during the war and in the immediate postwar period. He wasted every opportunity through a combination of short-sightedness, lack of ambition, contempt for the customers who patronized his shops, and the corrosive effects of my mother's success at his chosen trade, a competition that seemed to drive him to be mean-spirited and dismissive of her contribution to the family.

Yet my father was well-liked by a small group of friends, generally recent immigrants, and members of the Avellino Social Club where he spent every evening drinking wine and playing cards or bocce. He ridiculed anyone who tried to carry on an intelligent conversation, praising some illiterate friend whose son was earning a living as a gas station attendant and disparaging my brothers and me for wanting to continue our studies. He seemed to cultivate men of lesser accomplishments and of small means, provided they liked to spend evenings at our kitchen table, eating, drinking wine, and joining in joking and singing.

How to explain or defend my father's manner with us as children and as young adults? He did gradually change his brutal, heavy-handed ways over time and mellowed considerably in his later years, after we had all started our own families and we all, in different ways, developed affectionate relations with him. But the restrictions he had imposed on us, the heavy responsibilities, the tongue-lashings, and the occasional slaps we had all been subject to—most especially my brother Domenick and I—these experiences were not to be easily forgotten. In my mother's case, the years of being so ill-treated turned her into an unforgiving partner in their later years, when they were alone together in retirement.

I have often reflected on the seemingly illogical pattern of child-rearing in Italian families of our acquaintance, parental behavior matched in my own family. Babies and young children were indulged, cosseted, and overprotected –spoiled rotten, was the term we used—"don't let the baby cry, pick him up, quick"; "little Mary wants a candy, let her have it, so what if it's dinner time"; "how cute, Joey is throwing everything on the floor, *ma che mascalzone.*" Soon enough, though, there was a dramatic change: growing children were expected to shoulder family responsibilities, obey parents unquestioningly, contribute earnings to the family finances as soon as possible, and resist any impulses to be independent or rebellious—the latter being the very signs of growing up that are understood as normal in American families. And the sense of obligation to one's parents was instilled deeply and early. Perhaps these were the ways of uneducated Italians of meager means, a combination of narrow-minded village ways and the hardships of Depression-era America. It was a set of attitudes totally at odds with what I would observe when I married into the upper middle class Porter family.

Here's how my Porter in-laws appeared to me on first acquaintance: parents owe everything to their children and children are not expected to consider their parents' needs for one instant. Parents are expected to provide a nurturing home, indulge all reasonable (and some unreasonable) demands, always be supportive, and always take care of themselves without relying on their grown or even aging offspring—it's a one-way street, not a reciprocal arrangement. I felt I had gone from one extreme of imposition to another. That my husband and I came to accommodate these wide disparities in upbringing and find a more balanced way when we raised our own children is a marvel.

Enter Frank Jr.

At the end of my sophomore year, on June 29, my mother was rushed to the hospital, six months pregnant. She gave birth by Cesarean section to a healthy, six-pound baby boy, Frank Jr. After eight days she was discharged and her doctor advised her to be at complete rest for the next few weeks, not climbing stairs more than once a day, not lifting anything heavy. These admonitions might as well have been said to the hospital walls. Even with my being home for the summer and entirely at her side to help with the children and the household, my mother had to go right back to work in the store. I saw her terrible weakness and how she barely managed to drag herself through the days. It was at times like these that I saw the extent of my father's lack of compassion or consideration for his wife.

With a new baby, an eighteen-month-old, and three older children to care for, he expected her to resume the heavy physical work of the store, and to subsist on few hours of sleep as the baby required night feedings. Never did my father get up at night to let her have a little more sleep. Every evening, when my father returned from the other store, often bringing heavy loads of meat in the trunk of his car, he would walk into the house and my mother would go out and unload everything—it was expected of her. I can still see my mother's face as she struggled to carry each heavy load into the walk-in refrigerator and hoist it up on to the hooks. One night I awoke as my mother was returning to her bedroom from the upstairs kitchen with a warmed bottle to feed baby Frank, Jr. I saw her walking in small steps as she clutched the wall for support, wincing with pain at each step. I felt such resentment toward my father, mentally calling him "*canaglia,*" the ultimate word for hard-heartedness.

About a year after Frank Jr.'s birth, I was at home when my mother asked me to call her doctor to come immediately because she could not stem a profuse bleeding. Her doctor arrived in a half hour, and I overheard his telephone call for an ambulance to treat "an incomplete abortion." I learned years later that my mother had enlisted the help of an elderly neighbor who was known to have ways of ending unwanted pregnancies. My mother survived and, though what she had done was clearly illegal as well as dangerous to her life, the doctor managed to record it as a miscarriage. Luckily for Lucy and for our whole family, that was her last experience with pregnancy, at age thirty-four. Whatever precautions were taken from then on, my mother never opened this subject for discussion, not with me or with my sister. Certainly our father was sufficiently alarmed over the incident to have taken heed.

Continuing Struggles

In the fall of 1946, as I returned to school for my junior year, relations between my father and me were very strained, sometimes erupting into open warfare at meal times, the hour when we were all together. I bitterly resented his imposition of unreasonable rules on my social life—no wearing makeup, no going out in the evenings to school dances or athletic events, no dating, and very little free time. I was fifteen, and, of course, I over-dramatized my plight, convincing myself that my life was blighted. I learned to be a liar and a sneak, highly inventive in finding ways to evade my father's harsh rules.

At the same time, I despised his treatment of my mother, who had mostly regained her strength by the end of the summer but urgently needed help for the two youngest children during the school day. My father should have hired a shopkeeper to take charge of the store and allow her to focus on her home and family. Instead he hired a sixteen-year-old slightly retarded boy, the son of some acquaintance of his, to be a "mother's helper." Joe, a simple fellow whose family was grateful that he had any employment at all, would take two buses from his home in Newark, arriving at our house by 8:00 AM. He would spend the day doing any chores my mother directed him to do—hanging up laundry, rocking the baby, running errands. Joe was a cheerful boy whose limitations were obvious to us, and I'm afraid my brothers and I were not always kind to him. Certainly his help was better than no help at all.

Both my strong resentments caused me to commit some desperate acts that November. Missing so much of the social life my friends enjoyed had become a daily source of anger. As much as I lied and made excuses to my friends about why I was not going to dances, basketball games, and other evening events, I dreaded being labeled a girl who was "kept strict," the demeaning view of Italo-American girls with unassimilated fathers. I had been invited to the Thanksgiving Dance by Hans Henrickson from my Spanish class, who flirted with me at lunchtime every day, and I decided that I would go—somehow. To Hans I explained that my family would be visiting friends out of town for dinner that night and my father would drive me to the school dance—that was how I covered up for the fact that I could not have a date pick me up at home. On the night of the dance I told my parents I was going up to bed early because I was very tired. I fashioned a pile of clothing under the blankets and made a round shape covered with a scarf on the pillow for my head. Since my tiny bedroom was at the rear of the second floor with a door to the back staircase, I left by that door and ran to the school.

I met Hans and our friends and was having a wonderful time when, about an hour later, I saw my brother Domenick looking for me on the dance floor. I left my friends and rushed over, only to be told that my father was waiting outside in the car and I was to leave immediately. It was a windy, rainy night and, apparently, I had not closed the back door firmly enough when I left. The door blew open and when my mother came to close it and saw what looked like her daughter lying still while rain was driving in through the open door, she was horrified—until she discovered that her "daughter" was but a pile of clothes. She could not cover up for me and guessed that I might have gone to the high school.

Quickly recovering from my alarming situation, I told my friends that my mother had become ill and had to be taken to the hospital and that I was needed at home right away. I was in fear of my father's wrath when we drove home. He did scold me, of course, but was otherwise unusually quiet, which was not his usual manner. My father now understood that we had come to a serious impasse on the house rules for me. A few days later Uncle Michael came to visit and talked with my father about how he should begin adapting to American ways. The topic of "dating" was discussed; Uncle Michael related his experiences with his daughter Rosalie's high school years and explained how young boys and girls conducted themselves when they went out in the evenings. I remember my father's words (in Italian at that time) exactly: "Date, what date? What do you mean? Some boy I never saw before, and I don't know his family or where they come from, is going to drag my daughter out of the house, have his fun with her, and then throw her in front of the door? Is that what they do in America?"

At that time I could only cringe with embarrassment, sitting by mutely while my uncle, a level-headed man with a sense of humor, disarmed my father with anecdotes about how harmless these dates were. By the end of the evening, my father had agreed to some relaxing of the rules, and allowed that I go to the Junior Prom in December, a huge concession.

However, in the next week there was an equally explosive family crisis between Lucy and Frank that alarmed all of us and, again, called for the presence of mediators. It had long been our family practice that my father would invite whole families of friends to come for dinner and visit for an evening, often on very short notice. We were accustomed to seeing my mother standing at the kitchen stove and sink for hours, cooking and serving and washing up while everyone else sat and enjoyed themselves. Rarely did we have the experience of going to the homes of friends for similar hospitality. With five children to care for as well as working in the store six-and-a-half days a week, my mother was utterly exhausted by the end of each week.

When an invitation came to my parents from the Evangelistas, friends in a nearby town, to spend Thanksgiving Day with them, my mother was so pleased. For once, she would not have to be the one to do all the work, since my father just barely tolerated the traditional turkey dinner and demanded that other special dishes be prepared for him—rabbit stew, lasagna, wild mushrooms. My father stunned us all by calling the Evangelistas to say that no, no, we wouldn't go to their home but they must all come to our house because he preferred to be the host. What an uproar ensued! We had never seen our mother so outraged or so brave about opposing our father. She absolutely refused to do it, reminding Frank that she was the one who did all the work and now that they had a chance to be the guests instead of the hosts, he was wrong to make such an inconsiderate and downright thoughtless move. They almost came to blows. I was livid at my father's selfishness and believed my mother should take us away and get us all out from under his tyrannical ways.

A neighborhood couple who were close friends came into the discussion, placating my mother and admonishing my father to be more considerate. I chimed in with my opinion that they should separate. My father dismissed my comment as the stupidity of a fifteen-year-old, but his friend turned to me and said, "Don't ever say that to your mother. Where could she go? She has no family in this country and no money. Keep your ideas to yourself and your mouth shut."

After so much aggravation, my mother did prevail—we went to the Evangelistas for Thanksgiving Day dinner and enjoyed it. I considered it a tiny victory for my mother.

December 1946 was a month of excitement in the anticipation of going to my first formal dance. My cousin Rosalie gave me a pale pink gown and white rabbit-fur jacket, hand-me-downs she had once worn as a bridesmaid. I learned that my date Hans Henrickson, who was not yet old enough to drive, had made plans for us to go with another couple and we would be traveling in a Jeep. In these first postwar years, not many new cars had yet come on the market and Jeeps had real cachet. When Hans came to call for me, I was waiting in our second-floor living room. My mother, who was waiting on customers in the store, left them and came upstairs, still wearing her long white butcher's apron with blood spots on it. I introduced her to my date, who had brought me a gardenia corsage that he pinned on my shoulder. For a sixteen-year-old, he had enormous presence of mind, as I'm certain he had never found himself in such a surreal situation before. He gallantly said to my mother, "Mrs. Pedalino, you're so young, you look like Rosalie's sister." My mother smiled her beautiful smile and answered graciously. She gave a gentle word or two about our not staying out too late, that midnight was the curfew, and we left.

The whole evening—dancing in the school gym, going to the Rock Springs Corral Inn for more dancing to the new Nat "King" Cole hit *The Christmas Song,* and kissing all the way home in the back seat of the Jeep—was a thrill I savored for the rest of my time in high school. For those few hours, I put the embarrassing differences between Hans and me completely out of my mind, as did he, I'm certain, a willing suspension of reality. And, in fact, it is a trait I developed that served me well in all the years I lived at home—seeking and finding enjoyment and making the most of all sorts of situations, in spite of the hard realities of family life.

Sadly, Hans lost interest in my company rather hastily after seeing my home setting. By the end of Christmas vacation he had found a new girlfriend from his own neighborhood. Disappointing, but not surprising. High school social groups were fairly homogeneous, based on class, religion, or ethnicity for the most part. Protestant kids from the middle-class neighborhoods centered their socializing at youth clubs such as Young Peoples Federation (YPF) at their churches; Catholics went to Catholic Youth Organization (CYO) dances; a sorority for Jewish girls provided the nucleus for their dating opportunities. School-wide events, of course, drew the attendance of all groups, and extracurricular activities attracted a mix of students from different communities with shared interests such as the arts and athletics.

One of the scandals in the high school class before mine was the romance between Pat, the beautiful blond daughter of City Commissioner Walter Savage (Irish Catholic) and Jimmy Mariani (Italian Catholic). They were only allowed to date because Jimmy introduced himself to her family as James Martin. Shortly after high school graduation, Pat found herself pregnant and, facing her family with the sudden need to marry, she and Jimmy were now forced to reveal his real name and background. Her family was furious over the deception but quickly arranged a private ceremony to cover the shame of what would surely be the birth of a "premature" baby.

In junior year I switched to the academic track and took more history and language courses than were required in the "secretarial" block. I joined the drama, chess, debating, and Spanish clubs, wrote for the school newspaper and the yearbook, activities that gained me friendships with a wide variety of students. I was ranked in the top 10 percent of my class. After all the fun of senior-year activities, the graduation parties and the formal, cap-and-gown ceremony that thrilled my parents, I dreaded the thought of life after high school, of losing contact with friends who would be leaving for college.

How lucky for me that I had not captured the attention of some "nice Italian boy" in the neighborhood who might have tempted me to an early marriage and what would surely have been a far less adventurous life. Odd as it may sound, I was also lucky that my family was in straightened circumstances and needed my help financially, or my father might have prevailed and kept me at home to help with the housekeeping. Now it was time for my entrance into the world of work, and for my free spirit to continue demanding a larger measure of independence while I still lived at home. At seventeen I did not imagine that I would complete a college degree twenty-six years later, or that I would become the first Pedalino to earn a doctorate, honors my father never lived to see but which gave Lucy some of her greatest satisfactions.

SECTION II

EARNING A LIVING, GETTING A LIFE

CHAPTER 4

Women's World of Work

June, 1948: Rosalie Pedalino, seventeen-year-old high school graduate, has just completed her first full week in her first job at the Prudential Insurance Company in Newark, New Jersey. Friday at 5:00 PM, the clerks pick up their paychecks and dash for the elevators. In the crush, Rosalie is pushed firmly into one, and the door closes. Seconds after someone pushes the button for "Lobby," there is a sudden jolt, a red emergency light appears; the elevator stops, and then suddenly begins to move again, slowly. Someone shouts, "Stop the elevator!" But no amount of pressing buttons stops its steady descent. Someone else shouts, "We're all going to die!" Rosalie's instinctive, immediate, and banal thought is, "I'm not going to get to spend my first paycheck." The elevator glides down seventeen floors, finally coming to rest in the basement. Relief is followed by restlessness and mild panic. "Call for help

on the emergency phone!" "Don't talk—you'll use up
all the oxygen!" In a few minutes a building engineer
succeeds in prying open the doors and everyone is free!
Welcome, Rosalie, to the world of women workers,
circa 1950.

June, 1998: At a dinner party in Massachusetts, three
academic couples and a visiting professor from the
University of California/Berkeley, enjoy an extended,
postprandial discussion. The local professors of
literature or art history teach at Mount Holyoke College
and the University of Massachusetts. As is inevitable at
local dinner tables, the talk turns to women's lives and
careers—obstacles overcome. The hostess recounts her
dismay that she was pressured to attend Smith College
when she really did not want to go to a single sex
school. A second woman deplores the fact that she had
to go to Berkeley where her father is on the faculty. The
third woman acknowledges that she had a great time at
UMass but would have been happier at a small private
college. Rosalie, feeling stifled by these expressions of
victimization, finally erupts with, "Dammit! I would
have given anything to go to college right after high
school, instead of going to work in a factory to help
support my family. I can't listen to any more of this."

These two vignettes form parentheses around my work life—
opening at age seventeen when I was excited at the thought of
working in a large office (with the naïve hope of romance and adventure),
and closing fifty years later as I settle now into the position I hold
among professional colleagues. Admittedly I am less sympathetic with
my female friends of middle-class upbringing, but I honestly try not
to be dismissive of their feelings. From my early part in the women's
liberation movement of the 1970s, I have understood the almost

unbridgeable gap between the perceptions and experiences of working-class women and our more privileged sisters, differences we explored in our hundreds of "consciousness-raising" sessions. Let me recapture now the reality of a very different era of women's empowerment.

How very little my parents expected of me! When I was sixteen my father declared that I had had enough schooling and should now stay at home to help my mother with their two youngest children, three-year-old Frances and one-year-old Frank Jr., while she worked in our grocery store. I objected vehemently—school was my only escape from the humdrum life at home and the only place for fun and socializing with peers. My mother pleaded my case and convinced my father to allow me to remain in high school until graduation. Her greatest, most-often expressed ambition was "that you get a job as a secretary in a nice office, so you can wear clean clothes every day, and not have to do that hard, dirty factory work I used to do."

Ethnic Stereotyping

Although my high school grades had been excellent, as the first child of immigrant parents I knew nothing of scholarships or tuition grants that might have given me the opportunity to go to college. No counselor at Orange High School advised me to seek such assistance. Like most girls in my neighborhood, I was advised to take the secretarial course of study, the "practical" skills courses for post–high school employment, not the college-prep concentration. Italo-Americans were not expected to have college ambitions—that was for the Jewish and Protestant kids. We resented the stereotyping and subconsciously determined to "show them" some day.

At the time, however, even a tuition scholarship would not have been enough, for two reasons: first, my father opposed the very notion that I would go on to a higher education, much less that I might go away from home—that was unthinkable; and second, it was very clear to me that I needed to earn a paycheck to contribute to the subsistence needs of our family of seven souls. My father's little meat market and grocery store in Newark had failed due to his poor management, and he had returned to the little store on South Day Street where my mother barely eked out a living for all of us. Whenever my father joined her in running the store in our home, customers began to drift off to other shops in the neighborhood. Soon enough, my father would grow restless and start another venture, leaving Lucy to mend fences. How much I envied my cousin Rosalie, who was then starting her junior year at the College of New Rochelle.

When I try to understand the roots of the tremendous drive that energized me and my brothers and sister, the psychological underpinnings of the ambitious paths we all pursued, it seems there were several elements that strongly affected us. Our parents' very low-level goals for each of us were absorbed daily, in the stated and implied messages we imbibed with our daily nourishment. Our natural response was to rebel against our parents' narrow visions. But at the same time these two people, Lucy and Frank, had passed on to us their courageous genes, the bravery they and other young immigrants possessed that impelled them to leave the comfort of family and familiar communities to risk resettlement in foreign places. In the next generation, my husband and I would be the only two in our respective families to strike out for far off adventurous places, the only ones to permanently leave the towns in which we had grown up.

Perhaps another impetus for rebellion on my part was the seemingly insuperable distance between my parents' prescription for my future (early marriage and a duplication of their ways), and what I perceived of Uncle Mike's aspirations for his daughters (college days and careers to precede marriage). Lucy and Frank were still operating on the values of Avella while I was developing a consciousness of life beyond Orange, New Jersey.

In my senior year of high school, my Spanish teacher, Betty Giordano Shaw, invited four of us who were her prize students to a picnic on the grounds of Montclair State Teachers College to show us around her alma mater and encourage us to think of a career in teaching. I was the only one in the group who was seriously interested—oh, the idea of being a Spanish teacher!—but I had to admit that it was impossible for me. In 1990 when my first book was published, I received a call from Mrs. Shaw, who had heard about my book through the coincidence of being the private tutor of my nephew, Frank Pedalino II. What a delicious satisfaction to talk with the one high school teacher who had shown me such encouragement.

The dream of being a teacher was unattainable, but a friend urged me to apply to the Berkeley Secretarial School in East Orange as a day student. A year's course would prepare me for executive secretarial positions, I was told by the admissions officer who interviewed me. Although I was admitted in late May, just weeks before high school graduation, I visited the school to withdraw my application and to beg for the return of my fifty-five dollar deposit. That was the amount of money I needed to pay for the rental of a cap and gown for the graduation night ceremony and to buy a gown for the senior prom. I recall the kindness of the admissions officer who got a special dispensation to have my deposit returned.

My First Job—As a "Purger"

The year 1948 was a great one for high school graduates looking for entry-level jobs. The post–World War II economy was growing at a fast pace. Unlike the high school dropouts who were already working on production lines or doing manual labor on construction sites, we high school graduates had more genteel options. And, of course, we "girls" did not expect to be in the work force for very long, as we hoped to find husbands who would rescue us from the drudgery. I learned that the Prudential Insurance Company in nearby Newark (a thirty-minute bus or trolley car ride away) hired high school graduates. I was hired and began work at the end of June. My gross starting salary for a thirty-seven-and-a-half-hour work week was twenty-nine dollars; less taxes and Social Security deductions, I netted a little over twenty-five. Of this, I gave my mother twenty dollars and kept the rest for commuting expenses (five cents each way on the trolley), clothes (a modest dress could be purchased for under ten dollars), cigarettes at twenty cents a pack, and a weekly movie for fifty cents.

It was a ridiculous job. Along with a dozen other recent high school graduates, we were assigned to update the files on life insurance policy holders who had died. We, the file clerks, were called "purgers." Each morning the section head would bring out a large number of five-inch-square cards, each of which held all the information about an individual policy holder. The section head would then make a pile of cards, push them down firmly with her hand, and measure a seven-inch stack with a ruler. This was the quota to be completed by each clerk by the end of the day. Each of us would then take our stack to the file cabinets where we would pull the policy holder's folder, make a notation on it, clip it to the card, and put it in the appropriate bin. In my entire three months at the Prudential, I worked solely on names beginning with the letter "H." Need I say the work was stultifying?

Nevertheless, I learned lessons of office etiquette: the rules that had to be strictly adhered to (punctuality) and those that could be ignored (extended conversations at the work station); how many bathroom breaks it was safe to take; what constituted an acceptable lunch to bring from home; how to befriend girls of little ambition and dubious taste in clothes (many of the girls wore dresses more suitable for evening, cocktail dresses now out of fashion, for instance, giving our office a raffish appearance).

Within the first few days I found an easy companionship with the youngest women, the new hires like me. We soon confided in one another that we had no intention of staying at "The Pru" for the rest of our lives. In fact, the six girls with whom I became friendly all said that they had lied on their job applications, as they were only working for the summer before starting college in the fall. We reveled in our future freedom from "purging." I lied, too, to my new friends about going off to college. I could not bear the thought of being lumped in with the women who had been in that office for years, marking time while they saved money to marry their boyfriends.

How did we get through those seven-hour work days? Well, there was a lot of gossiping, we all smoked, some told dirty jokes, some hummed or sang snatches of popular love songs. One day, while searching for paper clips, I found a deck of playing cards in the drawer of the table where we all worked, and as I fanned them out I gasped in amazement at the various positions of sexual intercourse they depicted. One of the girls grabbed them out of my hands and snapped, "Don't look at these, you're too young, you don't know anything."

Some truly unbelievable discussions took place around the worktables of the purgers, revealing the uniform lack of even basic facts of life. One such discussion remains with me still. On hearing of a former employee in our department who had left to have a baby, my favorite "old" girl in the office, twenty-five-year-old Sylvia, said to us with perfect conviction, "I never knew how a baby could come out of the mother's front end where the pee-pee comes out. But somebody told me it's like this. The baby is real small when it's in the mother's stomach, but when it hits the air, it blows up like a balloon." We all gaped at each other, but some of the women nodded their heads in agreement.

In late August, one by one, my good friends began to desert the purging life as they prepared to go off to Goucher College, St. Lawrence University, Douglas College for Women, and other schools. Immediately after the Labor Day weekend, I heard of a job not more than a five-minute walk from my house, a secretarial job in a lawyer's office. I had taken two half-year elective courses in high school—typing and shorthand—and though I was not a great success at either, I believed I could fake it. As we say in the present day, "Fake it 'til you make it."

A Legal Secretary

I interviewed with Commissioner Ovid C. Bianchi in his law office at 327 Main Street, Orange. Lawyer Bianchi needed a fulltime secretary for his private office. Bianchi also kept an office in Orange City Hall where he was the Commissioner of Revenue and Finance. Though he knew my salary at the Prudential, he offered me a starting salary of twenty-five dollars, explaining in a kindly-old-granddad manner that I could afford to take a smaller salary to work near home. I was more than willing to accept it for what appeared to be a far more interesting job and oh, the thrill of being around *lawyers.*

Ovid C. Bianchi was a handsome man in his late sixties with wavy silver hair, a trim moustache, a deep basso profundo voice. He had been a city commissioner for twenty years and had a high level of political expertise, making it his business to attend every christening, wedding and wake in the large Italian community, as well as to pay his respects at all suitable events in the Irish and African American communities. Bianchi was the only son of an upper-middle-class Italian family from Milano who had given him the classical names Ovidio Cesare. He had very little in common with the Italian families from Naples and Sicily who made up the bulk of our immigrant community and, in private, held these people in low regard—except quadrennially when he appealed for their votes.

On my first day, I was totally clueless about how to manage an office. I sat at a desk behind a low wooden barrier, where clients sat to wait for their appointments, on the second floor of a building that housed an electrical appliance store and a Jewish deli on the first floor. My office machines consisted of a manual typewriter and a telephone. Beyond my desk area was the door to Bianchi's office, a pleasant room with large windows facing on Main Street and North Essex Avenue. I dutifully sat next to his desk, when called, to take letters in shorthand and to take instructions for various tasks. Gradually I became acquainted with the files of all the clients, the status of each active case, and the best manner in dealing with clients in person and on the telephone. Since Bianchi's lawyerly work was conducted at a stately, not to say dilatory, pace, clients often called to find out why their affairs seemed to be in perpetual limbo. "When is my case coming up for a hearing?" "Has my will been typed up yet?" "Why is he going for another trial postponement—I thought we were all ready for next week?" "Does Bianchi have the title search done for the closing on my house?" I spent a good part of my time on these phone calls, offering logical-sounding excuses and putting a positive, hopeful face on each client's case. In time, I took on more responsibilities in the drawing-up of wills, documents related to property purchases, and to civil suits. Today I would be called a paralegal.

Bianchi's time was divided evenly between his City Hall office and the private law firm, though politics and city government engaged his interest more than his civil law practice. The cases that came to Bianchi were quite ordinary affairs and the only real excitement I found in my two years in that office was during the city elections in the spring of 1950. I was allowed to spend some of my time working on campaign activities with the City Hall crowd. Bianchi had the script down pat—speaking at social gatherings, at school and church and community centers, at weddings, funerals, christenings and Bar Mitzvahs, wherever he could get an invitation. Of course, there were no radio or TV appearances—it was all done in person and with a personal touch. One evening at a rally for the Commissioner, just a few months after the beginning of the Korean War, Bianchi proclaimed in a passionate voice, "We want to bring our boys home from this terrible Corinthian War!" I concealed a smirk, but most of the audience was blissfully unaware of his gaffe.

I found a friend, another legal secretary who lived nearby, and beginning with our walks to and from the office in 1949, Ruth Ann Marucci and I enjoyed an on-going friendship, and still do.

At the end of my first year with Bianchi, I was given an evaluation and told that I had shown good ability in mastering office routines and skill in handling daily communications with clients. My salary would now be raised to thirty dollars a week. At eighteen, with my first raise in hand, I felt like a seasoned worker! After another year went by, I became restless with the job and my earnings. I scheduled an appointment with Bianchi to ask him if my work was satisfactory and, if so, was I not entitled to another salary increase. He answered "yes" to the first question and "no" to the second, actually saying, "Why do you need more money? You live with your family, you walk to work, and you don't have to spend a lot of money on clothes to work in this office." What an insult. Little did I know at that time that Bianchi, a cheapskate, had made a practice of hiring young high school graduates and paying low wages until they left to get married or take better jobs.

In September 1950, I read that the RCA Company in nearby Harrison, New Jersey, was advertising for office workers. I applied, was interviewed, and offered a secretarial job in the Personnel Services Department at a starting salary of forty dollars per week, a bold 30 percent increase. When I resigned and gave two weeks notice, Bianchi professed surprise. He wished me well but did not offer to meet the higher salary.

Spreading My Wings at RCA

The Radio Corporation of America was not only a radio network with broadcasting stations across the country, but a manufacturing giant producing record players (RCA Victrola—remember the trademark dog sitting attentively, listening to *His Master's Voice?*), phonograph records, and vacuum tubes of all sizes for communications equipment used by the military. RCA, under the leadership of the fabled entrepreneur David Sarnoff, was a pioneer in the production of the earliest television sets, the new glamour industry that would entirely change public entertainment. The main production facility for radio and television tubes in Harrison employed 9,000 people working in a cluster of seven enormous factory buildings.

The twenty-minute commute by train appeared adventurous, as I had only been on two school field trips by train to New York City. My house was a short walk from the Delaware, Lackawanna, and Western railroad station. From the Harrison station, it was a ten-minute walk to the factory. All employees except top management were required to punch a time clock on arriving for work and on leaving at the end of the day. Office workers were expected to arrive by 8:00 AM and leave at 4:40 PM, with a forty-minute lunch break. The factory operated in staggered shifts around the clock: 7 AM to 3 PM; 3 PM to 11 PM; and 11 PM to 7 AM. The RCA Radio Tube Factory had large defense contracts with the U.S. government for the Korean War effort, the U.S. "incursion" that started in June 1950.

During my interview I was given a description of the Personnel Services Office where a secretary was needed. Personnel Services published a factory newspaper, ran a radio station, organized intramural athletic events (bowling, swimming, softball) and entertainment (musicals, factory celebrations) and more. Essentially, it was in the business of morale building for the factory workers, and I realized immediately that I was created for this job! As offbeat as it sounded in advance, my first day on the job was beyond unusual.

George D. Watson, director of Personnel Services, photographer Joe Dooley, and clerk Mary Obrzut made up the staff. I chanced to start work on the first Monday of October when the company was launching a month-long competition between the seven factory areas to see which could increase productivity the most. It was called the "WBTM Contest," for World's Best Tube Makers. The opening event was a parade through all the factory areas by the very popular swing band of Woody Herman (some twelve jazz musicians), while Joe took photographs and I was to record the names of all who appeared in the photos with the band for the company newspaper. I was given a map of the factory areas and told to direct the band members as they tooted their songs from one work area to another. The girls on the production lines loved it and shouted cheers; the foremen, all men, of course, applauded. I was scared witless that I would lead the band to the wrong place or commit some other blunder.

By the end of the morning we were back in the office, where Joe developed the photographs. George prepared the text for the story and captions for the pictures; the layout had been partially prepared in advance. By mid-afternoon, George presented me with a large package and said, "Sis, you will have to take the whole newspaper layout to our printer in Asbury Park. No one else is free to go. Take a taxi to Penn Station and catch the 4 PM train. You'll be in Asbury Park by six and the printer will meet you at the train. Then you can catch a train back home. I'll see that you get paid for the overtime."

I gulped and prepared to go on this errand. When I called my mother to say that I would not be home until eight or nine that night and explained the nature of my errand, she said in a worried tone, "Your father will never believe you—do you have to go?" Of course, my father's suspicious nature would misconstrue my lateness; he'd be convinced that I was sneaking out for illicit fun. Nevertheless, when I arrived home at 9 PM, tired and hungry yet eager to tell the story of my adventurous day, the whole family appreciated the account.

What I loved about working at RCA was the variety of activities, the ability to move around the various manufacturing and office areas, and the opportunity to meet young people who had interesting careers as engineers, psychologists, and lab technicians. Although most young women of my age and limited education might have preferred a straight secretarial position with stable and clearly defined duties, I gloried in the flexibility and occasional wackiness of the Personnel Services assignment. Essentially I was an errand girl: filling in at the radio station occasionally to broadcast factory announcements and spin records of popular songs requested by the workers; gathering results of athletic competitions among factory teams to write up feature stories; giving occasional guided tours for new recruits, such as the groups of engineers starting their training programs at RCA; and even doing the mundane—typing and filing—on occasion.

I must admit that the distance from home gave me more freedom to slip the restraints my father tried to impose on my social life. There were legitimate occasions when I was required to work overtime and my parents knew this meant a bigger paycheck. But it also gave me the chance, under the guise of having to stay past the official office closing time, to go out for drinks with friends and take a later train home. Challenging my father on the time I was to be home from evenings out with friends made a constant war of wills between us. As the oldest daughter of an old-fashioned Italian father who was determined not to adapt to American ways, I provoked many scenes, causing anguish for my mother and nervousness for my younger brothers and sister who were spectators.

To my embarrassment now, I did not handle my freedom to roam during the work day very well. I was called on the carpet by old Mr. Watson for taking far too long on errands out of the office and, of course, he was right. When a small eruption occurred over an unintended slight to Watson's loyal henchwoman, Mary Obrzut, I was recommended for transfer to another department. The transfer was intended as a punishment; I would now be tied to a desk as secretary to Dr. John May, director of one of the engineering departments. Yet this unwelcome transfer soon had a bright side.

Dr. May turned out to be a jolly round elf of a man with a great sense of humor. I met several handsome young engineers, some of whom I dated. I learned a great deal about Time and Motion Study, the quasi-scientific, careful observation and recording of repetitive motions on the assembly lines in the factory to determine more efficient ways of increasing productivity and cutting down on fatigue. I suppose we would now call it ergonomics, the area monitored by OSHA today. But the single most important event in the year I worked for John May was my being called on as an interpreter for a group of young engineers from Rome who were to spend three months in training at RCA.

Dr. May, who was assigned the responsibility of mentoring these six young men from the Italian Marconi Company, enlisted my help informally. All had studied English and had a fair command of the written language, but they lacked fluency in speaking and understanding the spoken language. One of the engineers, who was always referred to as "the short one," apparently fell in love with one of the factory girls within the first two weeks and ran off with her, to the great chagrin of his colleagues. It was generally believed that to secure himself a permanent place in the United States "the short one" married the first available woman who was willing.

I became especially friendly with two men from the group, Franco Miccinelli and Fabrizio Paolelli. Both were full of fun, teasing me with stories of their patrician families in Rome who, they said, always dressed up in togas on Sundays. Fabrizio and Franco were housed for the three months in an East Orange residential hotel where they were the only guests less than eighty years old, and where the meals were designed accordingly. In the spring of 1952, when Fabrizio and Franco set sail for Europe on the *Queen Mary*, I was given leave to see them off on the ship. On the way to the New York docks they begged the driver to stop at the Rutgers University student store so they could each buy college sweatshirts with which to impress their Roman friends. Franco and I struck up a friendship that we still enjoy today with our spouses, children and grandchildren. Our families have made many visits back and forth between Milano and Massachusetts, with an unforgettable and magical Christmas when the Miccinellis gave my family the use of their cottage in the Alps for a skiing holiday. In 1987 Paola Miccinelli, Franco's twenty-four-year-old daughter, spent a semester with my family in Amherst while she did graduate research in biology at the University of Massachusetts.

One other benefit of the RCA years was my discovery that the company would pay half the tuition for college courses taken by employees if they could be shown to be professionally useful. Thus I embarked on my first adventures in higher education. Rutgers University had a city campus in Newark, a ten-minute train ride from the Harrison factory site. I applied to take three courses—English Composition, Introduction to Psychology, and French. You may well wonder how I ever justified that taking these courses would improve my secretarial skills. At the time I was intrigued with the work of the psychologists in our department and had a vague notion of majoring in that field, so I took a chance and my stipend was approved.

I began at Rutgers in September 1951. My classes met every Monday, Wednesday, and Friday evening from 6 to 10 PM. I would finish work at 4:40 PM, eat a quick supper in the RCA employee cafeteria, and zip over to Newark. After classes I took a half-hour bus ride home and walked the rest of the way, a little bit risky in my neighborhood. Neither of my parents really believed that all this extra studying was necessary, but I prevailed over my father's objections. I began to think of myself as a "college girl" of sorts.

It was in French class that I met Blanche Gutowski, a lively young woman close to my age whose day job was in a New York City travel agency. Over cigarettes during breaks between classes, we discovered we were both keenly interested in foreign travel. (I explore in the next chapter how our plans to travel abroad together a few years later dramatically changed both our lives.) Blanche and I remain friends and still see each other with the fresh young eyes of twenty-year-olds who relished playing Emily Kimbrough and Cornelia Otis Skinner, the two American women who wrote *Our Hearts Were Young and Gay* about their hilarious travels.

Perhaps the most fateful incident involving the RCA Company and my family—one not to be appreciated for many years, to be sure—was the hiring of my younger brother, Anthony, on his graduation from Orange High School in June of 1952. When my brother applied for work, I spoke to the office manager in the Personnel Office on his behalf. My brother began in the mail room, then was promoted to teletype operator and, since neither job paid very well, he asked to be transferred to factory work. He worked six months as a materials handler—he carried large loads of empty cardboard boxes to the assembly lines where the women workers would fill them with vacuum tubes; it was not an intellectually challenging job, but it paid a higher salary. After the Korean War ended in 1953 and RCA's contracts with the Department of Defense ran out, RCA began reducing its work force and Anthony was laid off. Subject to the draft, he volunteered for the U.S. Army and served two years at Fort Bliss in El Paso, Texas. On his discharge, RCA gave him his job back and thus began my brother's rapid, steady advancement (aided by his taking college courses at night to earn an undergraduate degree) that culminated in his position as a senior vice-president of the NBC Television network, an RCA affiliate. No one in our family could have anticipated such a star turn.

So it was not surprising that when our youngest brother, Frank Jr., was seeking employment after U.S. Army service in Germany from 1966 to 1968, Anthony was in a high enough position to help him land a place in the RCA Global Communications Division. Frank went on to a stellar career in telecommunications, working at various times for ATT, Sprint, and others. However, the greatest excitement for the family was Frank's assignment to the traveling team maintaining White

House communications for President Carter's trip to Africa and Brazil. What a thrill for all of us to bask in the glory of our brother's sudden local fame. Frank Jr., too, started in a modest job and advanced rapidly, taking college courses after work to complete both an undergraduate degree and an MBA.

But after my two years at RCA I set my sights on New York City for adventure and fun in the glamorous world of advertising. Why advertising? On a one-week vacation in New England in August 1952 I'd met a handsome young man who was an account executive at Foote, Cone & Belding in New York. His tales of the daily excitement of working in that field encouraged me to strike out in a new direction.

Geyer Advertising, then Kenyon & Eckhardt

Ad agencies hired bright young men and women, just out of college, who were determined to become leaders in creating advertising campaigns that would make them rich and famous. The standard practice was to put these ambitious young people in the lowest of the lowly jobs— mailroom letter sorter, delivery boy, file clerk, secretary—and expect them to work their way up: unless, of course, they were connected by blood ties to a high executive. In October 1952, I was hired by the Geyer Advertising Agency at 735 Fifth Avenue as a secretary, with a salary of fifty-five dollars a week, to one of the writers in the Public Relations Department. After withholding taxes and Social Security deductions, my take-home pay amounted to about forty-eight dollars, out of which I contributed fifteen to my parents, paid for train transportation (about eight dollars per week), covered my expenses for clothing and entertainment, and managed to put a small sum into savings.

The dress code of the times was strictly in force: a different outfit every day that included a hat, gloves, purse, high-heeled shoes, girdle, and stockings (those were the days before panty hose). On the 17th floor of the Squibb Building, located at the corner of 57th Street and Fifth Avenue, we were a short block from Central Park, across the street from Bergdorf Goodman, Tiffany, and the Plaza Hotel—oh, what a chic place to be! But our actual workplace hardly resembled the New

York office setting I had seen in Hollywood movies. Offices of account executives and officers of the company were situated in the outer tier with windows looking out on the city, while a large inside room filled with a dozen desks was where we secretaries sat. Every one in that room (except me) was a college graduate doing the entry-level work like taking dictation from her boss, typing, filing, and answering the telephone. Every one of us smoked at our desks. We gossiped, went out for long lunches, and sometimes for long coffee breaks—these were the perks that made up for the meager salaries. Some did persevere and end up in the big offices with the big salaries; most elected marriage and retreated to the suburbs after a few years of advertising "adventures."

Some days there really was excitement: the morning that account executive Ernie Byfield came directly to the office in his tuxedo from a grand night on the town, to announce that he had had a marvelous date with Sharon Douglas, daughter of the U.S. Ambassador to the Court of St. James; the unveiling of the new "Take Tea and See" campaign for Tetley tea (which we immediately renamed "Take Tea and Pee"); Bett Feisler's announcement that she would be attending the coronation of Queen Elizabeth II, courtesy of her fiancé at the U.S. Embassy in London. Quirky events like these lifted the day-to-day work well above the dreariness of the ordinary business office. My little Public Relations group consisted of the department head, Edward Thomas, and two executive writers, Joseph Meehan and Virginia Livingston Grimes, with one secretary for each—Betty Schreiber, Claire Carroll, and me.

There was a department ritual I came to cherish. On our birthdays we would each be told not to leave early and then called to a meeting in Mr. Thomas' office after 5 PM. The first time I was asked to report to the meeting I was quite nervous, wondering if I had failed at some task. On entering Ed Thomas' office I found all five co-workers assembled and they all shouted "Happy Birthday." On his conference table was an elegant little cake with candles and a bottle of sherry. We were all treated to the cake and to the Pedro Domecq Amontillado. I amused my husband with this story one day when we were having a glass of sherry before Sunday lunch. Since he has never worked in a business office, he considers this exotic.

I enjoyed working for Virginia, an intelligent, kind, worldly woman in her late forties who treated me in a friendly, respectful manner at all times. She had never married and only on one occasion let down her guard in an after-hours conversation to say that she deeply regretted not having stood up to her stodgy family when they judged her fiancé to be "unsuitable" and made her break the engagement. She gave me this avuncular admonition when I was deeply troubled over my engagement to a man my family disapproved of. Still, she had her eccentricities. More than once when I would be seated across from her, taking dictation, she would answer the telephone to hear her mother say that Stalky missed her. Virginia would then launch into a dialogue with her dog Stalky and then tell me what Stalky was saying back to her!

The Geyer Agency was not in the top tier but was considered a respectable middle-sized organization. Our secretarial salaries were average for a thirty-five-hour week with a two-week annual vacation. The Geyer Agency even permitted me a six-week leave after one year (two weeks paid vacation, four weeks without pay) to go on a European tour. In a later incarnation, in the 1970s when I became an elementary school teacher, I was dazzled by the thirty-hour work week and the liberal sprinkling of holidays throughout a school year that lasted only thirty-seven weeks. I immediately discovered, however, that there were no perks like long, Martini-enhanced lunch hours, no gossiping around the water cooler, no arriving late some days and leaving early on others. Public school teachers are actually expected to be in their classrooms at least a half hour before the students arrive and to stay after classes at the end of the day, to supervise their student's lunchtime or even eat lunch with their students—and they can barely escape for a bathroom break. More about this routine in a later chapter of my life.

After approximately eighteen months at Geyer, the company experienced a downturn in earnings, and each department was ordered to reduce staff. As the newest hire in my department, I was given two weeks' notice. Virginia took me out to lunch at the East of Suez restaurant and gave me a little "going away" gift that I still have, a long *faux* gold chain with unevenly molded chunks of green *faux* jade. She offered to call a few of her contacts in other agencies and got me an interview at Kenyon & Eckhardt that resulted in a new job two weeks later.

K & E was a much larger agency with such accounts as Lincoln Mercury, Frigidaire, and the prestige clients Piper Heidsick Champagne and Romanov Caviar. The offices on Park Avenue and 47th Street provided lovely little luxuries such as the coffee wagon that circulated through our offices each day, mid-morning and mid-afternoon, with beverages and pastries; and the "telephone wiper," a woman dressed in a white lab coat who very efficiently wiped each telephone instrument with a disinfectant each week. As secretary to the assistant head of the Public Relations Department I soon found opportunities to do more than just secretarial work, like writing an occasional press release.

The agency's clients sponsored some of the great early television programs of the 1950s: *Your Show of Shows, The Ed Sullivan Show, The Dean Martin and Jerry Lewis Comedy Hour.* It was a heady atmosphere for a girl who still lived at home with her Italian immigrant family in Orange, New Jersey, but who yearned to be a modern, sophisticated woman. One day the great jazz band leader, Benny Goodman, dropped in at the office; another day it was Robert Cummings, the movie star and lead player in the weekly series, *Father Knows Best*; the Piper Heidsick Company once sent a case of champagne to the office to celebrate an especially successful ad campaign, and we all sat around drinking the bubbly out of paper cups and eating caviar on *ficelles* from the local deli—it was such a lark.

I'd been at K & E a mere six months when, for personal reasons, I resigned to take a second jaunt to Europe. On my return home at Thanksgiving time, I decided to chart a new course, forsaking advertising in favor of finding a job that would allow me to use my fluency in three-and-a-half languages: Italian, Spanish, English and *un petit peu de Français.*

The Maidenform Brassiere Company

While living in Rome for a few months in the fall of 1954, I had applied for a job with the *Rome Daily American* newspaper. Although I was not hired, the notion came to me that it would be interesting to look for a New York job with a company that did business in the international community, perhaps earning myself a higher salary as a bilingual secretary. The first employment ad that caught my attention mentioned an opening for a Spanish/English bilingual secretary at the Maidenform Brassiere Company. I scheduled an interview with the head of the export division, more as a joke than anything else.

The Maidenform Company occupied three floors of an office building on Madison Avenue at 35th Street, with a similar floor plan as the ad agencies I had worked for—executives with windowed offices, drudges in a large room without views. I was welcomed in a perfunctory manner, no warmth whatsoever, by Mr. Sol Rubinstein, a stocky, expensively suited junior executive with an unlit pipe in his mouth. The interview conversation followed a predictable pattern. Mr. Rubinstein was rather humorless, certainly not the quick-witted type of "personality boy" I was accustomed to in the ad agencies. When we got to the questions about my fluency in Spanish, Mr. Rubinstein handed me a copy of *Time* magazine *en Espanol* and asked me to read from it and give him a translation. As I opened the magazine, the telephone rang and he asked me to wait. With a moment to scan the magazine, I found a page with very little text, a Coca Cola ad. Promptly I read aloud the entire text, then looked up and gave him a literal translation. He said, "That sounds fine. Are you interested in the job? The pay is sixty dollars a week and the hours are nine to five, two weeks vacation after a year. Any questions?" To my own surprise, I said, "When do I start?" I had it! With just three years of high school Spanish, I had taken a huge chance promoting myself as a "bilingual" anything. I now realized that Sol, my soon-to-be boss, had no knowledge of Spanish at all.

Maidenform was founded by Ida and William Rosenthal, women's underwear designers who'd invented the sized cup-style bra in the 1920s. But the company owed its success and preeminence in the world of brassieres to the business acumen and driving ambition of Mrs. R., as she was colloquially characterized in the *Fortune* magazine cover story about her. A family-owned company (Sol was one of the nephews) with factories in Hoboken, New Jersey, and Santurce, Puerto Rico, Maidenform sold bras around the world and dominated the market in the United States. In the 1950s the company's "I Dreamed ..." advertising campaign was a prize winner. The series debut in 1949 pictured a well-accessorized young woman (with gloves, hat, and handbag) wearing the most attractive of outfits—but a topless one, except for her bra. The ad was accompanied by the slogan, "I dreamed I went shopping in my Maidenform bra." The campaign—with fanciful departures from the original slogan such as "I dreamed I had tea at the Plaza ..." or "I dreamed I went to the Met ..."—continued for several years. I heard an anecdote about this ad in my first week on the job. It seems that the agency that prepared the ad for the Mexican market wrote, "Sone que iba por las calles en mi brassiere Maidenform," which does not translate as "I dreamed I went walking" but as "I dreamed I was a streetwalker." Many laughs in the office but not a joke for the New York ad exec that lost the account.

My two years at Maidenform were a revelation on several levels. It was my first experience as the only Christian in an entirely Jewish organization. I felt completely at ease here and I found my work more varied and challenging than anything I had done before. I translated all correspondence that came to us in Spanish, Italian, or French; composed letters in those languages; acted as interpreter at Sol's meetings with foreign representatives; and attended the twice-yearly presentations of the new lines when buyers from around the world came to New York. But I found the office intrigues, gossip, jokes, and such a little less interesting than at the other agencies I'd worked for, since most of the secretaries and clerks at Maidenform were not college graduates trying to break into a glamorous field but high school graduates with less ambitious goals.

But what a boon to my social life, to be able to say, offhandedly, on a first date or at a cocktail party, "I'm with Maidenform Bra," a line that was inevitably followed by the comment, "Oh, do you model?" and a surreptitious glance at my bosom. Actually, although all of my two years at Maidenform were entirely occupied with normal secretarial duties, I did have one modeling assignment that I kept to myself—it would have been too scandalous to reveal to family or friends in 1955. One day, in the middle of the morning, Sol called me into his office to say, "Mr. R. is in the middle of making adjustments to a new design and Grace, you know, the model who's here every afternoon, has called in with the flu. He needs a 34B to just model for a half hour, just for a fitting. Would you be willing—I think you're the model size? You'll be paid a small bonus for the favor." Yikes, I couldn't believe my ears. Of course I said yes. I had seen Mr. R. around the office, a gentle, grandfatherly man who always seemed distracted but was perfectly polite to all the employees. So, I did the job and was paid fifty dollars for my half hour. I didn't say a word about it to anyone for years.

Just before leaving Maidenform's employ, I missed a great opportunity. I called the Broadway agency we used to get theater tickets for popular shows when foreign buyers came to town. As we discussed what Broadway show was hot for the following week, the agent said, "Miss Pedalino, there's a new play opening in two weeks that is going to be the hit of the century! It's a musical by Lerner and Lowe, based on the Pygmalion story, with Julie Andrews and Rex Harrison in the leads. I can hold two tickets for you, if you're interested. It's going to be a blockbuster." Without much thought I turned the offer down, missing my chance to see *My Fair Lady*, something I still regret. But at that moment I was greatly preoccupied with my imminent departure from Maidenform to become a stewardess on international flights for Pan American Airways—up, up, and away.

Before "Coffee, Tea, or Me?"

Odd as it may sound, the idea of seeking work with an airline that flew to all seven continents came to me from a cloistered nun. In late winter of 1956, I went on a spiritual retreat weekend with my best friend, Ruth Ann Marucci, at the Convent of the Cenacle, home of the cloistered Ursuline nuns in the Bronx. From Friday evening to Sunday noon, observing a vow of silence, we were to spend our time in reading, prayer, and meditation, with one lecture each afternoon, a nun reading to us at meals, and the opportunity to have a private conversation with one of the religious. I had been intrigued by the writings of Catholic theologian Thomas Merton, SJ, whose *Seven Storey Mountain* and *The Waters of Siloe*, accounts of a life of silence in his Trappist monastery, were best sellers. But being a life-time compulsive talker, I did not appreciate until that weekend how wonderfully the absence of talking concentrates the mind.

In my allotted thirty minutes with young, charming Mother Bishop, I told her briefly about my work, my interests, and the recent severance of a romantic attachment, principally on religious grounds. I confessed to be searching for new worlds to explore and new ways to escape the limitations of my educational, familial, and financial resources. After only a short reflection, she said, "Rosalie, you have a rich talent for languages, some business experience, some college credits, and a strong streak of adventurousness, a love of travel to the "faraway places with strange sounding names," the popular song describes. Yes, we do have some small contact with life outside the convent, even though we never set foot outside the Cenacle. Have you considered applying for work as a stewardess on one of the two U.S. airlines that fly exclusively to other countries? I don't think you would want to do that kind of work just to fly from Pittsburgh to Omaha. But with Pan Am or TWA you would be using your language skills, indulging your love of travel, and being paid a salary. What do you think?"

That idea was so instantly appealing that within a week I found myself calling the Pan American Airways personnel office in Long Island City, New York, to find out about their requirements for stewardesses and to have an application form mailed to me. Pan Am was the elite airline; it had started the first American flights across the Pacific and Atlantic and to all seven continents in the 1930s as "American Overseas Airlines" and then changed its name to Pan Am after 1949. Basic requirements for stewardess candidates were non-negotiable: at least two years of college or a Registered Nurse degree, fluency in a foreign language, height between five feet two and five feet seven, weight to be proportionate to height (but slender), an attractive appearance, and a friendly personality (being what we now call a "people person"). On arriving for my interview, I felt confident of all the above except the height, since I believed myself to be barely five-one. But I stretched my shoulders and neck as much as I could when I stood to be measured— and I made it!

After a rigorous six-week training course in a class of twenty-five other young women, more than half from European countries, we earned our wings and were ready to be scheduled for flights. We had learned the basic skills, such as heating and serving meals in the confined spaces of an airplane; personally demonstrating safety procedures and narrating the instructions in English and one other language, depending on the destination (flights to Paris, for example, included all announcements in French); securing the cabin for take-off and landing; and leading an emergency evacuation in case of a crash landing. There was also an extraordinary training session led by a Red Cross officer on how to cope with medical emergencies on long flights—heart attacks, asthma, epileptic fits—and how to deliver a baby in the aisle of the plane, with privacy, if all the seats are occupied.

My mother knew I had taken the job with Pan Am and would soon be flying away, but I had not yet told my father. Better to wait, I thought, until I graduated from the training program and actually had the assignment. My first trip was to Frankfurt, Germany, an eighteen-hour flight that included stops for refueling in Newfoundland and Ireland. I now told my father that I had a new job working on big planes flying to many countries, and that my first flight would be to Germany where I would be able to visit my brother Domenick, who was stationed in Mannheim with the U.S. Army. I said I would be back home in four days and would then have a week to rest before starting out on another trip. My father, who still expected me to be home before midnight when I went out with friends, surprisingly made no objection to my spending days or even weeks away. I believe he had finally concluded two things about his perennially rebellious daughter: that I had gotten beyond the age when I might have disgraced the family by "getting into trouble" (being a teen-age unwed mother), and that at twenty-five I would probably never marry and be an old maid who would have to support herself. All during my flying days, my father actually took pride in my travels and bragged to his friends, for example, when I brought him a special round of French cheese or a bottle of Irish whiskey.

My father, of course, had never heard the stories of the round-heeled ways of stewardesses and pilots or he would have forbidden me from taking any such job. But the rumors of the promiscuous life of the flight crews were largely exaggerated. Most of the pilots were married with children, and in those days that meant "hands off." Most of the stewardesses were looking for husbands, not adulterous affairs. We traveled together, worked together, but didn't sleep with each other. In the whole year of my flying career, I saw very little unseemly behavior. In the ethos of the fifties, we dated lots of different men but felt under no compulsion to have intercourse with any of them.

Flights were long on those propeller-powered planes—the DC 4, DC 6, Boeing Stratocruiser, Lockheed Constellation. A flight to London that today takes six hours then required at least one refueling stop at Gander, Newfoundland; Goose Bay, Labrador; or Shannon, Ireland, making it a ten- or twelve-hour trip. Our cabin crew of three served cocktails and dinner, then dimmed the lights and hoped that most of the passengers would sleep so we could take an hour's rest before starting preparations for the breakfast service. We were on our feet for all but an hour, serving approximately a hundred passengers and six members of the flight crew.

On the elite Stratocruiser flights there were only thirty-five passengers; they occupied large plushy seats and enjoyed the comfort of actual beds in the large overhead compartments, a separate cocktail lounge down a small spiral staircase, and meals prepared by Maxim's Restaurant in Paris. On these flights we had more leisure time and we were instructed to be cordial and hospitable to the passengers, to memorize their names and make polite conversation. Among the most memorable people I met were the conductor of the New York Symphony, Erich Leinsdorf; the madly handsome Mexican-American tennis star, Pancho Gonzalez, who invited me to be his guest at the Forest Hills matches; violinist Isaac Stern and his family, who invited me to attend rehearsals at the Pablo Casals Music Festival in Puerto Rico; a genuine "great White hunter" from Africa named Lee Merriam Talbot; and Sergio Hamann, the nephew of the president of Brazil, who took me dancing and to sports events in Rio. But the one who impressed me the most was Andres Segovia, world-renowned classical guitarist from Spain. On that particular flight from New York to Buenos Aires there were not many passengers and I had the great good fortune to spend over an hour in conversation with Mr. Segovia, mostly in Spanish, discussing our favorite authors, current world problems, and our families. What a delightful, courtly gentleman! At the end of the flight, he took me aside for a moment to say, "Senorita Pedalino, you've told me how very much your father appreciates the classical guitar. Please get in touch with me on my next concert appearance in New York and I will have a pair of tickets saved for you."

This was truly my dream job, perfect for that period in my young life: two or three flights a month, each lasting from four to twelve days, with a week or more of free time in between. A typical schedule would be this one, from my July 1956 Flight Log: a trip to London, departing New York's Idlewild Airport (now called JFK) late afternoon Thursday, stopping in Shannon, and arriving in London early on Friday morning, with two days at a hotel, expenses paid. Most of the crew members went directly to their rooms to sleep away most of the day, but not I. After two hours' sleep I was ready to explore the city. On my first trip to London, I fulfilled a long-held desire to see the Rosetta Stone at the British Museum. What an overwhelming experience; I wept at the sight of this incredible rock with the three different writings—Cuneiform, Egyptian hieroglyphics, and Ancient Greek—that Cambridge archaeologist Michael Ventris had translated for the first time. Seeing this physical representation thrilled me. We all went to the theatre, a bargain with tickets costing less than two U.S. dollars, did a bit of shopping, and walked in the parks.

My second trip for that month lasted fourteen days, starting with a flight to Paris; one day's "rest;" then a flight to Beirut, Lebanon, where the cabin crew remained for a ten-day layover, going on three round-trip flights between Beirut and Teheran; then back to Paris and home to New York, after which I was entitled to a ten-day leave. My salary of fifty-five dollars a week covered eighty hours of actual flying time per month, not including the requirement to be on duty at the airport for briefings four hours before flight time and to remain to file paper work after the flight. When we worked longer on the actual flights, we received overtime pay according to union rules.

The cabin crew engaged in petty thievery—at least what I saw was petty indeed. On one of my first flights the purser handed me $6.50 as we landed in Paris and said, "This is your share of the free liquor from first class that we sold to tourist-class passengers." When I declined, as I had done nothing to earn it, she shushed me with, "Don't sweat it." I had not seen the sleight-of-hand that she employed in this little scam. On my third flight to Teheran, I was so exhausted by the long hours on my feet and the intense heat that I elected to stay on the plane and sleep during our four hours on the ground rather than go into the city again for sightseeing or shopping. The purser, Opal Hess, the only fifty-year-old stewardess I had ever met, said she would be buying caviar to resell in Paris on our way home, and would I like to invest in a pound for myself. I agreed. Opal returned to the plane with 2 pounds of fresh, Caspian Sea caviar, for which she had paid two dollars per pound. We stored it in the little refrigerated compartment on the plane and then in our hotel refrigerator, transporting it to Paris where we were paid four dollars a pound for each package—a net profit of 100 percent. I could weep to have that caviar now!

Every stewardess has stories of dangerous mishaps, close calls on landing or take-off, but I'd rather relate two farcical occurrences. On my first flight to Frankfurt, Germany, we were not an hour out of New York when a woman with a heavy German accent asked for a glass of milk to settle her stomach. I brought the glass on a little tray and, as I was leaning over to hand it to her, the plane took a sudden, steep drop. A long column of milk rose out of the glass, straight in the air, then splashed all over the woman's chest. I was embarrassed and apologetic; she was terribly upset that her suit jacket was soaked in milk, but she announced that it was not my carelessness but an "act of God."

The second mishap occurred in the middle of the night. We routinely prepared a breakfast of freshly scrambled eggs, Canadian bacon, sweet buns, juice and coffee for all one hundred passengers and the crew. Preparing the eggs took the longest. We set a narrow stainless steel shelf across the entrance to the galley, and secured it at both ends. Then we broke twenty eggs into each of five large plastic containers. After adding a little cream and seasonings we would seal each container tightly and shake it vigorously. Now the eggs were ready to be cooked, twenty at a time, in an electric skillet.

I had barely finished breaking eighty eggs into the containers when the steel shelf collapsed, spilling all the eggs in a river that ran down the center aisle. After a moment of paralyzing panic I woke up the purser, who stared in horror at the egg river. Fortunately, almost all the passengers were sleeping and the cabin lights dim when we began sopping up the raw eggs with hundreds of paper towels. We did manage to salvage the bit that didn't spill from the bottom of each container. Now I had to report "the accident" to the captain. He swore aloud and fixed me with a piercing stare. "Just tell the passengers that we're serving a Continental breakfast this morning. Don't mention eggs unless somebody asks. And that means we won't have eggs for the crew either, damn it. I'll radio ahead and get permission for the crew to have breakfast at the Shannon Airport and that'll be charged to this flight." I feared my Pan Am career had just ended. I never did receive an official reprimand, though the story became part of airline legend, especially the finale: passengers walking up and down the aisle wondering why their shoes seemed to stick to the soggy carpeting in the aisle!

I resigned from Pan Am, without giving the required two-weeks notice, in September 1956—a romantic but impulsive act that ultimately backfired, and which I fully describe in the next chapter. I had, needlessly as it turned out, given up my carefree, fun-loving, gallivanting-around-the-world occupation. Having to find other work, I was soon back to the nine-to-five grind in a job hardly worth noting. I was hired as the bilingual secretary to the president of a New York firm that exported plumbing fixtures to Latin America. Z. E. Meyer (he did not use his first name, "Zadoch," but preferred to be called Ed) was the most foul-mouthed individual I'd ever encountered, a shocking difference from the speech decorum that prevailed in the other offices I had worked in. It was a depressing time for me, with nothing to lift my spirits in the Meyer office. Those few months of handling correspondence and telephone conversations about bidets, toilet bowls, and sinks were truly the nadir of my early working years. When I saw an ad in the *New York Times* announcing that Pan Am was seeking Spanish-speaking stewardess candidates for their Latin-American division, I applied and was hired again.

My return to the flying life, not to the European and Middle Eastern routes but to the Caribbean and South American countries, exhilarated me, and I was determined not to give it up easily again. Returning to the traveling life I loved, there were new worlds to explore—Brazil, Venezuela, Argentina and many visits to Puerto Rico. But this carefree, bachelorette period, as I'll soon explain, lasted only six months.

CHAPTER 5
Love Stories

August 21, 1953: A powder-blue Cadillac convertible parks in front of Frank and Lucy's grocery store on South Day Street. Carmine Salvatore, a family friend, helps load Rosalie's five suitcases in the trunk, while she bids her father, sister, and brothers goodbye. Mr. Salvatore drives Rosalie and her best friend Ruth (along with Rosalie's mother, who will wave goodbye from the dock), to Pier 44 in New York to board the USS *Constitution*, a ship of the American Export Lines en route to Napoli. He then presents Rosalie with a bon voyage gift, a white beaded evening bag. This European voyage of six weeks, intended as a light-hearted tour before she settles down to marry her fiancé, will have unanticipated consequences.

August 15, 1957: Dave and Lee (Rosalie) Porter, married ten days earlier, drive a Porter farm truck, full of luggage and steamer trunks, from South Day Street to Pier 44 in New York City. They are boarding the USS *Independence*, sister ship of the *Constitution*, for a honeymoon trip to Italy, and will then head to Istanbul, where they will live for the next two years. This is the final move prefigured in Rosalie's life over the years—the breaking away from family and friends. It is a wrenching sorrow for Lucy who will never have her oldest daughter nearby again.

During my years between high school graduation and marriage I made constant efforts to distance myself from the narrow life of my immediate family and to attain ever-greater independence. Precisely at the mid-point of this period, in 1953, my parents gave me permission to travel to Italy to visit their relatives, and this single event changed my life forever. But there were many missteps, false starts, and plain bad behavior I am not proud of—both before and after the liberating trip—in my relentless quest to make friendships with a wider range of people, to meet more interesting beaus, and to achieve upward social mobility. Most of those opportunities arose through the variety of jobs I held (and which I describe in Chapter 4).

In this chapter I shift my focus from work and move on to discuss what kind of social life a young woman of my class and family limitations—one who was striving to leap "above her station," as the English would say—could expect. I reflect on the cultural gap between my immigrant family's ways and what I perceived to be the ways of "average Americans," especially as they were portrayed in the popular songs and movies of the day. Sometimes, while writing this part of my story, it felt as if I were recording a way of life totally foreign to present ways—like the study of a primitive society à la Margaret Mead's *Coming of Age in Samoa*.

It is a well-established fact that young women in the immediate post–World War II years, the early 1950s, felt pressured to marry and start families. This is not to say that there were no college-educated women who made a career their first priority, but they were a minority. Yet we had some outstanding role models: Clare Boothe Luce, Amelia Earhart, Eleanor Roosevelt, and Margaret Bourke-White were the "serious" ones I marveled at, and I had no less admiration for pop icons such as Billie Holliday, Ella Fitzgerald, and Sarah Vaughan. But the marriage imperative was especially strong for working-class women whose career choices were limited to white-collar office work or production-line factory work as they marked time before finding a husband.

Truth to tell, I had few dates in the first year or two beyond high school. I met hardly any young men in my law office job, and (luckily!) I did not attract the attention of any of the "boys" in the neighborhood where my father was known to be very strict; none of them were brave enough to approach me. It was a time of palling around with girlfriends, going to the movies, gossiping, talking about our ambitions and our hopes of finding the "right type"—ideally a handsome Catholic college graduate, potentially a good provider, and an accomplished kisser. No one possessing all those attributes appeared on our horizons, not at the YWCA weekly dances or at any other gatherings.

Thanks to my friend Ruth, with whom I walked to and from work every day, I found ways to extend my sphere of social activities. In addition to her fulltime job, Ruth had kept house for her father and four brothers since the death of their mother four years earlier. Ruth's family was quite outstanding in our neighborhood. Her seven brothers all went to college, in the 1930s and 1940s, entirely supported by their father's earnings as a gardener and through scholarships, summer work, and the G.I. Bill tuition grants for World War II veterans. My parents liked and respected Ruth, and they considered her to be a steadying influence on me, their rebellious daughter.

Ruth's aspiration to find a college-educated husband led her to plan, in 1949, the first year of our friendship, one of our first "scouting" trips. On a cold, gray Saturday in mid-November, we went by train to New Brunswick, New Jersey, to attend a Rutgers' University football game. The following year I was invited by a former high school classmate to be his guest at the Princeton-Navy football game, and he asked me to bring a blind date for his roommate. Ruth and I boarded the train in our best suits, new cashmere sweaters, gloves, and high-heeled shoes; our dates met us at the station and whisked us away to the Cottage Club for lunch, then the game, a cocktail party, and so on. We had a wonderful time and I made a hit doing the Charleston, a dance from the 1920s flapper era that was the craze. The young men invited us back for a second weekend and, again, we enjoyed ourselves tremendously. But that was the last invitation we got. Since we were not able to stay overnight but had to take the train home on Saturday night, our dates lost interest in us "Cinderella" girls. No more "Going back to Nassau Hall."

Next Ruth proposed that we go to the New Jersey seashore for a weekend in the summer, and my parents approved, thinking we would be staying with Ruth's cousins when we were actually staying at a boarding house. Always, at every single opening to independence, I had to deceive my parents about what I was actually doing. This posed risks for me that I gladly took rather than suffer in the tight clasp of their control. My first taste of total freedom from parental restraints lasted from early Saturday morning, when we took the train from Penn Station Newark for the two hour ride to one of the shore towns, until Sunday evening when we returned home. We stayed at one of several respectable, family-run guesthouses that catered to young women. They all offered well-appointed bedrooms, shared bathrooms, and rules about visitors (no men allowed above the first-floor parlor). Those few weekends each summer that we could afford to go to the shore were heaven to me—days on the beach, and evenings in bars where we met so many neat young men, most of whom were college students or recent graduates. We soon discovered that there was a well-understood self-selection in the demographics of the shore towns' youthful weekend populations. Belmar attracted Jewish vacationers, while Avon-by-the-Sea and Spring Lake were heavily Catholic, and so we chose the latter two towns.

Looking back on those weekends of fifty years ago from the vantage point of today's sex-obsessed society, it does look awfully tame—and it was. We were conditioned to view premarital sex as taboo and believed that flirting, dancing, some kissing. and perhaps a bit more intense action with a serious boyfriend or a fiancé were the limits. We accepted and strove to stay within those limits. We expected our dates to try to go a bit further (but not on a first date) and that was part of the ritual, understood and observed by most. Smoking and moderate drinking were acceptable for young women; vulgar language, drunkenness, or a reputation for promiscuity (what we called "putting out" or being "round-heeled") doomed any young woman as an unsuitable marriage prospect. My friends and I knew almost nothing about contraception. It was the conventional wisdom of the time that the less we knew, the less likely we would be to indulge in risky sexual experiments. The pervasive fear of pregnancy or venereal disease effectively inhibited our behavior.

The Men In My Life—My Days as an Artful Dodger

Though it was never admitted, my father and I had a tacit understanding regarding my contacts with young men: as long as he did not actually see anyone coming to our house to take me out, and as long as I was home by a reasonable hour (11:00 PM preferably, midnight the absolute limit), he seemed to evade the reality that I actually went out on dates. The onus for monitoring my activities was on my mother. Had I fallen into evil ways, she would have been entirely to blame. It was such a dishonest arrangement on everyone's part, but it was the best I could manage at the time. I'm afraid I did not set a good example for my brothers and sister.

Making excuses for why I had to meet a date at Ruth's house, or in front of the cinema, constantly taxed my imagination. The excuse of meeting at my office was a credible one, especially when I worked in New York. During periods when my father was working in a store some distance from our home-based grocery store, I could count on his not arriving home before evening and could have a date call for me at home, though it was risky. But when my father's ventures failed and he was reduced to working in the store at home, I had to adapt my strategies considerably. My life was not grim, but it was a tricky balancing act.

Popular music was always important to me as an easy means of self-definition and for indulging my fantasies of romance. From the late 1930s on, I memorized the lyrics of popular songs I heard on the radio, part of my English-language learning. As young women, Ruth and I considered the ultimate thrill to be on a date in New York at Birdland or Bop City jazz nightclubs, listening to the coolest cats— Dizzy Gillespie, Errol Garner, George Shearing, Oscar Peterson, and Tito Puente. Secretly I nurtured a yearning to sing like Ella Fitzgerald or Anita O'Day. In the 1980s, when our youngest son Steve, a serious piano student by high school age, began playing jazz classics, I would sing along to his accompaniment, right in our own living room, at cocktail hour. Steve was amazed that I could recall the lyrics to even some of the more obscure songs of my youth. My husband joked that if I had not filled my memory bank with such trivia I might have become another Einstein. Why ever do all those song lyrics still reside in my thoughts, accessible on demand, not only the Cole Porter or Harold Arlen or Irving Berlin masterpieces but even mediocrities like *Walking in a Winter Wonderland, A Shanty in Old Shantytown, One Meatball*?

Bopping along, on the lookout for romance and adventure at every turn, I met my first serious love, Frank Fordham Ward, at the East Orange Tennis Club on a sunny Saturday afternoon, October 6, 1951. I was introduced to Frank by a girlfriend who had eyes for Frank herself. We made light conversation while watching a doubles match and, a few days later, Frank called to invite me to a play at the Paper Mill Playhouse in Millburn. Frank was tall (six feet four) handsome, bright, athletic, amusing, a Duke graduate with a master's degree from NYU, and at age twenty-eight, a financial analyst with a New York bank. He was definitely in the "dreamboat" class.

From our first few dates, we discovered mutual interests in music, dancing, theater, and books; our conversations never lagged. Without my saying why, Frank understood that I would not invite him into our home yet. When he called for me, I would be ready to answer the bell and walk right out, or he would pick me up at my brother's apartment. This was an uneasy arrangement for both of us, but once we were out together we took such delight in each other's company that it ceased to matter. A year of such evenings went by, and, though we were so very much in love, we were careful not to talk about future plans or of formalizing our relationship. Differences of social class, religion, and ethnicity posed serious obstacles: Frank's father was an architect, my father a butcher; Frank belonged to the First Presbyterian Church in East Orange and I to Mt. Carmel Roman Catholic Church; Frank's ancestors came from England and Germany a hundred years earlier, my family and I were recent immigrants from Italy. The Wards represented solid Anglo-Saxon Protestant respectability; my family was hopelessly outclassed. Bad enough being Italian and Catholic, which might have been overlooked if my parents had been professionals with a suburban home and a sizable bank account, but my parents, of course, were not.

By Christmas 1952, when Frank had received notice that he might be recalled into the Navy for active duty in Korea, he asked to meet my parents. On a Sunday afternoon he came for espresso, bringing my mother a small box of chocolates. The visit, in our kitchen behind the store, lasted an uncomfortable half hour, with all of us joining in a stilted conversation before it was time for the two of us to leave for a cocktail party. I was paralyzed with embarrassment for my parents' heavily accented English, just wishing they could have made a better impression. Frank's manners were impeccable. He complimented my mother on her resemblance to me and talked with my father about his car.

Stalemate—and Solution

We continued to date. We would meet on the New York train most mornings and enjoy the forty-five-minute commute together. I had yet to meet Frank's parents and there was still no declaration of serious intentions on his part. He had now turned thirty and I was just twenty-two. In March 1953, after a year and a half of dating, I had come to the conclusion that Frank would never ask me to marry him, that he lacked the courage to overcome the problems we would face with his family, and that I had to take a drastic step to separate myself from this romance that was going nowhere. I asked my father for permission to take a trip to Europe with my girlfriend Blanche (though I couched it in terms of "going to Avella to visit my grandparents and cousins") and, to my immense surprise, he said "Yes." I had decided that six weeks away would give me enough time to get over Frank Ward. My mother raised a small concern: "Do you think you're making a mistake, spending everything you've saved to go on a trip when you should be saving it for when you get married? People in our class don't go on trips to Europe." I was momentarily saddened at her small ambitions but assured her that I would save up again.

The five months leading up to our departure was a time of high anticipation. We were only a few years beyond the end of the World War II, and European travel was just beginning to be the *ne plus ultra* of chic for young Americans. Blanche, the friend who would accompany me, worked for a travel agency in New York. She used her connections in planning our trip, making hotel reservations and often getting us professional discounts. It was a time of transatlantic crossings by ship—few would fly because it was too expensive. Who would want to get to Paris in twelve hours when you could sail on the *Ile de France* for five days of merrymaking? We settled on sailing from New York to Naples on August 21, traveling north through Italy, Switzerland, France, England, and then home on the *Queen Mary* by early October. I was far from the first person in my office to go on such an extended voyage—it was very much the "in" thing to do. My office mates gave me a bon voyage luncheon and the popular *Fielding's Guide to Europe*.

Though Frank and I continued to see each other regularly for weekend dates, I affected a nonchalant, lighthearted manner as I began to distance myself emotionally. Blanche was only allowed four weeks leave from her office, so she decided to fly to Italy and meet me there a few days after I arrived by ship. I never told my father that I would be sailing on the USS *Constitution* alone, a prospect that intrigued me.

Not until one week before my sailing did Frank finally stun me with a proposal of marriage. He said he loved me and believed we were absolutely right for each other. Would I be willing to meet his parents and announce our engagement on my return from Europe? It took me only a few moments to shift from my set idea of bidding Frank a final goodbye to responding to his proposal: "But why should I go to Europe, then? I love you and want to marry you. I'll just cancel my trip." He replied, "No, no, you mustn't do that. You've been looking forward to this great adventure and you don't want to disappoint Blanche at the last minute. You must go and enjoy it all, and I'll be waiting for you."

How odd. I was so overwhelmed by this show of backbone that I accepted the delay in announcing our engagement. We had been dating for almost two years, lived in neighboring towns, yet we had wrapped ourselves in a social cocoon of friends and acquaintances that did not include either family. It was not normal, but I had accepted it. Now, when we should be making concrete plans for bringing our families together, ironing out religious differences, deciding on where to live and when to start a family of our own, I was being urged to take a long, expensive trip. I truly never entertained a moment's skepticism about Frank's proposal, letting myself enjoy the euphoria of his loving attention and the thrill of the voyage ahead.

It was the custom for travelers to host bon voyage parties on shipboard during the hours before the noon sailing. On any given day a dozen or more ships would be mooring or departing along the docks of mid-town Manhattan. Friends were allowed to board the ship and celebrate until the big toot signaled time for visitors to disembark. We vied for invitations to see someone off. One of our favorite office stories was about our co-worker Margo, who drank so much champagne in a stateroom party that she passed out as the SS *France* began to pull out of its berth in New York harbor. She awoke and ran to the captain's office screaming to be let off the ship. The captain radioed for a tugboat to come alongside, and then she was abruptly lowered over the side in a rope bosun's chair and fined a few hundred dollars. With an armful of American Beauty roses from Frank, two other beaus waving champagne bottles, my three closest friends and my mother around me, I was a princess at last. I kissed them all goodbye and dived ecstatically into my new incarnation.

The Voyage and Its Outcomes

The story of my meeting David Porter in the lounge of the USS *Constitution* during the first few hours after the ship sailed is a family classic, recounted on too many public occasions. David Thomas Porter of Elba, New York, population 500, graduate of Hamilton College, recently released from Navy jet pilot training, and a sometime journalist, had been hired on a three-year contract to teach English at Robert College in Istanbul. On the first page of my trip diary I wrote: "After I unpacked my suitcases in the cabin, met my three roommates, and signed up for a table in the Cabin class dining room (second sitting), I came to the lounge for tea at 4 PM. I'm now sitting near a really cute guy, writing my first diary entry." Tea and biscuits were brought and, as I noticed that my fellow tea drinker was reading the *New York Herald Tribune* (NOT the *New York Times*, as family legend has it) I demurely asked, "If you're not going to do the crossword puzzle, may I have it?" He turned with a smile and said, "Sure. My name's David Porter." Thus began a conversation that is still going on, fifty-five years later. Over tea we became acquainted, and I was invited to have cocktails with Dave at 5:30 PM. On arriving in the lounge, I was introduced to Claren Sommer and Bob Jolly, two new acquaintances of Dave's who were also going to Istanbul to teach. I could almost hear my inner voice exalting, "Let the parties begin."

Nine days from New York to Naples, with stops at Gibraltar, Cannes, and Genoa on the way, turned into a nonstop house party. Within a day or two of getting acquainted, a nucleus of hardcore revelers was formed: half a dozen young men heading to Robert College, Istanbul; a dozen Smith College students going to Spain and Italy for their junior year abroad; a dozen or more young graduate students, lecturers, and U.S. Embassy people going on foreign assignments. Since the late-night partying kept most of us from getting to the breakfast tables, the typical day began after lunch with sunning and swimming, soon followed by cocktails. One unforgettable sight was the chubby Smithie Iris Love (later to be famous as a world-class archaeologist and socialite) in a too-tight bathing suit, with a fake ivy crown on her head, standing on a table singing "Roll Me Over, In The Clover." We all observed the ship's rules about dressing for dinner and joined in the organized evening activities. My shining moment at the impromptu talent show came when I was pushed out on the dance floor to dance a wild Charleston. We danced, drank, smoked, flirted, sang bawdy college songs, and just generally enjoyed the freedom from responsibility that is implicit in an ocean voyage, the suspended days between continents. For sheer *joie de vivre,* we ended one night by jumping into the pool in our party clothes.

As I reminisce about this now I am struck by how much we still enjoy the friendships initiated on that ocean crossing. In September 2003 my husband and I hosted a fiftieth-anniversary house party for the people who met on the ship or in Istanbul in 1953. Five couples gathered with us on Nantucket Island—the Sommers, Jollys, Grants, Dodds, and Gillards. While we no longer have the stamina or the inclination for all-night partying, we had wonderful discussions about the varied travels and careers we've pursued. Early on the last morning, as we stood with Bob and Connie Jolly at the pier waiting for the ferry to take them back to the mainland, Bob turned to us with a bemused expression and said, "You know, it's quite amazing. All of us are still married to the same mate. None of us got divorced—not that we didn't think about it—but we didn't do it." That fact alone would stamp us as "different" today, most likely to be thought lacking in courage or imagination.

I developed a measure of fondness for David Porter on those nine days of shipboard shenanigans, charmed by his intelligence, sense of humor, and affability—he was not just a fun-loving companion but a man in whom I glimpsed an underlying basic decency and solid character. This was my "fling" before settling down to suburban bliss in East Orange, New Jersey. We ended many an evening or early morning with pensive moments on deck, enchanted by the sight of the French coast and the thought of approaching the fabled Europe of

Hemingway and Fitzgerald, the prewar writers who had given us such romantic notions.

The American Cousin Comes to Napoli

Arriving in Naples on a sunny Sunday morning, I recognized Grandfather Antonio Luciano and Uncle Giacomo on the pier. David and his friends would go to the Santa Lucia Hotel for a week's sojourn before boarding the Lloyd Triestino Lines' *San Giorgio* to take them to Istanbul. We all talked about getting together for sightseeing in the Naples area, but I knew my first few days would be heavily committed to the family visit. Once cleared of customs and passport formalities, ushering a porter with my suitcases and a trunk full of clothing and gifts for my uncle's family out to the taxi, I was greeted with hugs and kisses and the comment that I looked just like my mother, Lucietta. They had not seen me since I left for America as a six-year-old child. My grandfather's comment was, "She doesn't look like a village girl any more."

We arrived at my uncle's apartment where he and his wife and four children occupied the ground floor apartment of the building caretaker, consisting of a small living room, one bedroom, and a tiny kitchen. All available space was taken by the "matrimonial" bed and by the folded cots used by the children: Antonio (thirteen), Maria (eleven), Lucia (eight), and baby Angelo (three). My uncle proudly announced that he had arranged lodgings for me and my American friend who would be arriving in a few days. An elderly professor and his spinster sister, on the third floor, had graciously offered to have us sleep in their guest room. We boarded the ancient, iron-cage elevator and moved my suitcases to the professor's apartment. *La cuggina d'America* had arrived.

By noon, when I had only been with the Luciano family a few hours, I was overcome with extreme exhaustion and asked for the chance to take a short nap. I had not anticipated the intensity of their attention or the strain of conducting all these conversations in Italian, since my relatives knew not a word of English. I was stared at by six smiling faces whose eyes betrayed such a hunger for great things from my visit. While I tried to answer their questions about life in America, the strain made me almost tongue-tied. I had the strongest impulse to run away, but I retired for a few quiet hours to gather strength to play the dutiful "American cousin" for the next few days.

By the end of a long afternoon of catching up on years of family history on both sides of the Atlantic, while I drank the strong espresso and ate a pastry, with all eyes trained on me, I had an inspiration. I asked Uncle Giacomino if he would please call the Santa Lucia Hotel for me so I could talk with a friend from the ship. When I heard David's voice and his first few words in English, I broke into uncontrollable weeping. I explained that I needed to see him, that I couldn't stand the strain of this intense family gathering. Could he save my life and see me for a few hours? Without a moment's hesitation he said that I'd caught him minutes before leaving for an opera performance at the *Teatro San Carlo*, but that he would take a taxi to my uncle's place right away. Joy! Uncle Giacomino was disappointed that I would be going out for the evening and quite disapproving when the friend turned out to be a man. He said I was now in his care and he was responsible to my parents for my safety. But I declared that my parents had enough confidence in my good sense to have allowed me to go on this trip and that in America young women were allowed independent outings without chaperones. With that, we jumped into the waiting taxi and sped down to the harbor where we strolled, talked, and spent the evening dancing under the stars at a popular nightclub. What a tremendous relief to be with a person of my language and culture! This and other adventures of our early friendship would eventually form the foundation for a lasting love.

On returning to 183 Corso Vittorio Emanuele we found Uncle Giacomo pacing on the pavement in front of the apartment, waiting for my return. I informed my uncle that we had had a pleasant evening with American friends near the beautiful bay of Naples and that our friends had organized a trip to Pompeii and the Amalfi Drive by chauffeured car for the next day. He would understand that I must go. Clearly this did not sit well with him, but he made no objection.

Iris Love, the Smith student and Classics major, hired a car with driver and guide to take David, Claren Sommer, and me with her on this grand tour, all expenses covered by her parents. It was a glorious day, from the obligatory stop at the cameo factory where we resisted buying anything, to the ruins of Pompeii which were then a novelty for American tourists, to an al fresco lunch on a balcony restaurant in Amalfi where the strolling musicians who sang arias from "La Boheme" were rewarded with a tip that probably set them up in their own establishment (we had not yet figured out the exchange rate of lire to dollars).

At Pompeii, Iris bribed the guard to sneak us into the excavated site of the old whore house where the guide nonchalantly described the sexual positions depicted in faint colors over each stall-like cubicle. She also had him unlock the wooden covering over the carving at the doorway of the Villa of the Vetii Brothers, which portrays a man with a disproportionately large penis on a scale under the Latin slogan, "Worth Its Weight In Gold" (the guide translated for us). Unlike the sophisticated Iris who declared that "Mummy has been to Pompeii three times and has never gotten to see the obscene rooms. She'll be green with envy when I tell her," we three were embarrassed, avoiding each other's eyes. Secretly though we knew we now had a titillating story to tell.

Fortified with such an exotic tour, I now found myself able to cope with a day in Avella, my birthplace. My mother had instructed me to dress well, with hat, gloves, purse, and high-heeled shoes; my appearance would signal the standing of our family in America. This was no hardship for me, as American women travelers in 1953, not yet having discovered blue jeans, dressed that way most of the time. There in Avella I made an important visit to my mother's godmother, Nennela, and sat with her and her son, a stocky, thirty-ish bachelor with a prematurely balding pate; he hardly said a word while his mother described his work as a draftsman and his sterling character. The following day, at 7:30 AM, Nennela and her son arrived unannounced in Naples at my uncle's apartment. Uncle Giacomo called up to the professor's apartment, asking me to come down immediately. In my pajamas and bathrobe I arrived to find everyone seated for the requisite espresso. Nennela announced the reason for her visit: "Rosa, you are the image of your mother whom I love very much. Now, I have a gift for you, this gold medal of the Madonna di Pompeii on a gold chain. I have come to ask you to marry my son. I know you have only just met, but I'm sure your mother and father will approve. You know he is an only child and will inherit my house in Avella. I am willing to allow him to be married in America. Then you will live with me."

This was a stunner. I looked around at the equally surprised faces of my uncle and aunt. Without further hesitation, I said, "I am grateful that you bring me such an honorable proposal, but I regret to say I am already *fidanzata*, engaged to be married in America on my return." With this, I pulled a small snapshot of Frank out of my purse. Nennela was visibly chagrined. Her son said not a word. Soon they left to return to the village. My aunt and uncle were pleased that I turned down the offer as they had some ancient grudge against Nennela.

Late that evening, my friends and I waited at the Stazione Centrale in Naples for Blanche to arrive. When the last train from Rome pulled into the station and there still was no sign of Blanche, we taxied to my uncle's house, where we found Blanche waiting; she had arrived earlier than expected. To my uncle's great consternation we all talked at once, making plans for leaving for the Isle of Capri the next day. We were careful to leave out the name of the island, since Uncle Giacomo would recognize it and be furious that I was heading off to Capri with my men friends. We agreed to meet at the boat station the next morning. After David and Claren left, I informed my uncle that Blanche and I alone would take a tour of Capri the next day, and then leave directly for Rome to continue our tour of Italy. He was quite disappointed at the shortness of my stay, having envisioned at least a few weeks of my sitting with him over espresso. But I showed him my itinerary with the dates of hotel reservations in Rome, Florence, and Venice. Blanche and I retired to the professor's guest room, talking and giggling most of the night, keen to move on.

Goodbye Uncle and Clan—for Now

My uncle rode to the port with us in the morning and we bade him goodbye. David and Claren took the next ferry. Once all joined on the island, we hailed a taxi to take us up to the central piazza. On the way, the driver pointed out to us the grandiose yacht in the harbor belonging to the deposed king of Egypt, Farouk. He warned us not to go to any parties on that boat, as the fat "king" was a terrible seducer of young girls.

We found rooms at La Pineta, a modest bed-and-breakfast near the main piazza, swam and lunched at Gracie Fields' glamorous Piccola Marina resort, where Claren, a world-class diver, showed off his stuff; we danced under the stars at the Quisisana, and took the obligatory rowboat tour of the Blue Grotto with the oarsman singing "O Sole Mio." Blanche and I bought our first bikinis and Capri pants, but I would not have the courage to appear in public in my teeny-weeny bikini until four years later, when David and I returned to Capri for our honeymoon. Though staid and proper by today's standards, for the mores of the 1950s Blanche and I were having a racy adventure. Here we were staying next door to two young men friends, getting together on the balcony outside our rooms each morning, in our pajamas and bathrobes, for breakfast! Everyone in New Jersey would have been scandalized, and that's what made it so much fun.

The episode with my friends from the ship ended when we all returned to Naples to head in different directions. David gave us his address at Robert College and urged us to change our plans and take a trip to Istanbul to help him celebrate his twenty-fifth birthday a few weeks later. We said we'd give it some thought. And so, they sailed off to the Near East and we headed north on our prescribed itinerary.

After touring the major central and northern Italian cities, we decided that we could skip "cuckoo clock and chocolate" Switzerland and go to Istanbul instead, with an overnight in Athens on the way back, resuming our planned itinerary in Paris. We sent telegrams to David in Istanbul and to Blanche's office in New York where our travel and hotel bookings would be revised. The lads in Turkey wired back their delight at our plans. Were we crazy or what? No one we knew had ever extended a European tour that far to the east. I had never been on a plane and the thought of flying was another attraction. We were booked at the Park Oteli, site of many a spy thriller. David, Claren, and their friends were wonderful hosts, taking us to the incomparable Hagia Sofia, Blue Mosque, Taksim Square, Galata Bridge, the Golden Horn and up the Bosphorus to the European Towers of Rumeli Hisar where the Turks conquered the city in 1453 and where the Robert College campus had been established in 1863. The experience of exploring exotic places in the company of familiar companions is hard to beat. I learned later that David and Claren's stock rose sky high when word got around that they already had two American women come all the way to Istanbul to see them!

I fell in love with the city and especially the college area, situated as it is in the choicest hills overlooking the Bosphorus and Asia, this being the only city in the world that sits astride two continents. On our last afternoon, as we stood in front of Claren's tiny "music house," gazing at the wooden fishing boats skimming by and listening to a recording of Debussy's "Sirenes," I thought I would die of such pure bliss. Perhaps this is the kind of "high" that is induced by drugs, though I am not knowledgeable about such states.

Nevertheless, we left our friends that evening and pledged to write to each other. David promised he would see me on his return to the United States in three years, no matter what my marital status. Then we flew to Athens, via *El Al Israel*, to spend a day walking around the Acropolis, and a clear moonlit evening sitting on the marble seats of the amphitheatre watching a performance of *Oedipus the King*.

A Serious Distraction

On to Rome to change planes for a Pan American Airways flight to Paris. Immediately after takeoff on this Boeing Stratocruiser, the funny airplane shaped like a pregnant cow because of the cocktail-lounge bulge underneath the passenger compartment, Blanche and I descended the spiral staircase to join the crowd, and a merry group it was. We were soon chatted up by an Australian engineer on a business trip for International Harvester, and who was based in the company's Karachi, Pakistan, branch. A swashbuckling sort who had piloted a fighter plane in the Pacific in the war against Japan, he had never been to Europe, and he soon enlisted us to explore Paris with him. Colin Edward Cagnacci, self-taught, up-by-the-bootstraps, enormously charming, widely read, a good dancer and a quick study, had the salesman's knack of making friends easily. As we became acquainted, I understood the great affection he bore his modest, working-class parents in Queensland, third-generation immigrants originally from Italy, and of how very proud they were of his success. Colin, an area representative for the farm machinery company in Pakistan and Afghanistan, lived in Lahore and traveled widely in both countries. This trip included a stop in Chicago, International Harvester headquarters, a signal that he was being vetted for promotion.

I was dazzled at my sudden splash in the international high life: the Folies Bergère, dancing in Paris night clubs, dinners in famous restaurants, the glamour of walking along the Champs Elysees at noon or watching the sun come up over this fabled city from the height of Sacre Coeur—for a New Jersey kid hungry for a bigger life, this was a taste of haute cuisine. The effect of my travels and my acquaintance with new people and places had spawned in me a growing discontent at the thought of returning to my former life. These particular experiences had a powerful impact on my thinking at the time: the simple excitement of foreign travel, the confidence of finding myself appealing to a number of interesting men, knowing now that I could sparkle in almost any conversation and hold people's interest; the awakened desire to see and know more of this world's beauties once having seen the treasures of the Louvre, the Vatican, and the mosques.

But the most transformative experience was the discovery of the importance of my native land. The tour of Italy gave me a new appreciation of its value to Western civilization, the richness of its history, art, food, and style—*sprezzatura.* This aspect of my travels led me to reexamine the attitudes I had grown up with—that we Italians in America were second-class citizens, an inferior lot that was barely tolerated. To declare myself free of this embedded inferiority was a cleansing, liberating thought. The question that soon followed was whether I truly wanted to marry a man whose family would always treat me with subtle (or overt) condescension, having signaled already that I was such an inferior choice that they could avoid even the slightest social contact.

Not ready to make any hasty changes, I did spend considerable time in many discussions with Blanche reflecting on my choices. Our journey ended with a stormy, wind-lashed crossing of the north Atlantic on the *Queen Mary*, days of such violent tossing that we two were often the only ones at our dinner table, most others taking refuge in their cabins to be sick in privacy. Halfway across the ocean the ship's captain announced that we could not dock in New York, due to a longshoremen's strike (no one would be there to unload the ship), and would be docking instead in Nova Scotia, where all the passengers and their luggage would be loaded onto trains for a three-day trip to New York City. The announcement was greeted by shrieks and groans— everyone had friends and family meeting them at the New York pier, and we all had to send telegrams with the change of plans. But it was one more unusual twist to an exciting six weeks, and the train trip turned into another round of Bridge playing, smoking, drinking, and storytelling. Each of us assumed his own escapades in Europe were uniquely fascinating.

"How ya gonna keep 'em down on the farm, after they've seen Paree?" That popular post–World War I song best characterizes how Blanche and I behaved on our arrival home. We were obnoxious, European-travel snobs, too willing to relate the minutia of each and every day we'd been away. We had not anticipated that, as happy as our families and friends were to see us again, they were really uninterested in the details of our travels. They didn't seem to appreciate that we had been profoundly transformed by our experiences, as we privately believed. My mother and father only wanted to hear about whom I'd seen in Avella and what they had to say. They had absolutely no interest in my descriptions of Roma, Firenze, Venezia, or even Napoli, much less Paris or London.

But my reunion with the "love of my life" had the most surprising outcome. On our first evening together, as I marshaled my thoughts for a preliminary discussion of our plans, I detected a subtle coolness in Frank, an aura of discomfort. For two who had been so deeply caring, it was proving difficult to recapture our old closeness. He seemed intensely keen to hear about my adventures, but when I playfully quizzed him about his activities, he hesitated before saying, "Well, I have to tell you that I met someone while you were away. I've been dating a girl I met at my parents' country club, Dorothy Dyer. It's nothing serious. We've just had some good times together." I readily admitted that I had dated different men I had met in my travels, casual encounters. We were at an impasse, each one waiting for the other to declare a new *modus vivendi*. Without actually spelling out a new set of rules of engagement, we both understood that we would continue to see each other but each would retain a measure of independence. Coward that I was, I had not the heart or the courage at that point to tell Frank my honest feelings about the serious impediments to our sustaining a happy marriage. Our two families could never be friends, and the resulting strains would have a destructive impact on us both. The handmade lace veil I had bought in Venice for our wedding would be stored away, not to be worn for four decades.

Enter Colin Edward Cagnacci

I resumed my work at Geyer Advertising, took up the usual round of social life, and enjoyed a brief whirl with the Australian engineer, Colin, who had arrived in New York. He insisted on a visit with my parents and arrived for the Sunday afternoon espresso ritual, full of bonhomie and elegant tales of tiger hunts in Hyderabad, or of crashing his plane "into the drink" in the Pacific. My father, who loved to hunt and brought home many a buckshot-riddled rabbit and pheasant for the family, was struck mute with incomprehension. After Colin left, my father admitted that he had not understood much of what was said by this man who "talked funny," and did he really kill tigers? Lucy and Frank had never met an Australian and were not happy that I had brought this stranger around. I, on the other hand, was beginning to be attracted to Colin, who at thirty-two cut a dashing figure. He was at ease with my humble home above the store, assuring me that his family's cottage on a small sheep ranch in Queensland was even more modest.

Thus began a new and mostly long-distance courtship. Colin had been divorced from a young woman he had married in Australia during the war. He courted me with letters, telegrams, and telephone calls from Chicago, San Francisco, Hawaii, Hong Kong, and Karachi. My friends, especially Blanche who was fond of Colin, were intrigued by the notion of my possibly marrying such an international sophisticate and taking up residence in Pakistan, with side trips by camel over the Khyber Pass and into the wilds of Afghanistan. It was all too exotic! Frank Ward still hovered around and we sometimes dated, as friends, and shared some lovely, no-pressure evenings; an occasional letter arrived from my friend David Porter in Istanbul, filled with hilarious tales of teaching English to Turkish teenagers and of his vacation travels in the Middle East. I felt free, unencumbered, and in demand!

Gradually, Colin became more serious about marriage. In the spring of 1954 he sent me a beautifully worded, formal proposal, to which I answered "yes." As we would be married in Orange, New Jersey, with Colin arriving from Pakistan just in time for the ceremony, I now inquired about the procedure for a marriage ceremony between a Catholic and a divorced Protestant. My discussion with a Jesuit priest was a terrible disappointment. Looking back now from the post–Pope John XXIII / Vatican II reformation of church rules, I can hardly credit what the priest dictated to me at that time. If Colin was a suitably baptized member of the Presbyterian Church in which he was first married, then his first marriage would be recognized by the Catholic Church and I could not marry him. The suitability of the baptism rested on whether he had been baptized by total immersion, that is, completely dunked in water, or whether the water had been poured over his head. If the former, the baptism was not recognized and the first marriage would not have legitimacy; if the latter, then too bad for us, I was told.

On learning that Colin had been legitimately baptized, I also discovered that we could petition my church for a dispensation, but that it could take years for it to work through the bureaucracy. Of course, one often read of famous celebrities or heads of state being granted dispensations, but for the ordinary Catholic it was mostly an exercise in futility. My Jesuit advisor did offer one other hopeful suggestion. We could shorten the application process if we went directly to Rome instead of starting the paperwork in New Jersey. In spite of my strong dismay with my Church over the ridiculously hair-splitting rules, I was not yet ready to abandon my religion over this. The plan we made was to meet in Rome in September, I making the trip from New York, and Colin joining me from Pakistan. Giving up my job and going back to Europe a scant year since my "grand tour," seemed so grossly irresponsible to my parents that they argued with me for weeks. In fact, my father was so incensed that he stopped talking to me completely before my departure and for several months after my return.

I sailed from New York on the French Lines' SS *Flandre* with Joanne Neville, an office acquaintance, and high school friend Gloria Date, who was stopping in England to visit relatives before moving to Rome for an extended stay with her mother's cousin, Ed Hill, editor of the *Rome Daily American* newspaper. My guiltiest memory from that five-day ocean crossing is that Gloria was almost continuously sea sick and lying in her bunk, and that I spent almost no time keeping her company, one of the worst examples in my life of neglecting a simple humane obligation.

After a week in Spain, I arrived in Rome for the romantic interlude with Colin and our appeal to the Church bureaucracy, which sorely tried us both. We were happy to be together and renewed our plans to be married the following year in New Jersey, with the unrealistic expectation that a Church wedding would be approved by that time. Colin returned to Pakistan. I stayed on in Rome for another month, applying for jobs in several offices, thinking that by staying in Rome, at the very "headquarters" of the Church, I could make things move along more rapidly—a totally nonsensical idea. But are not many of us full of impulsive, unrealistic ideas at age twenty-three?

Finally, with my money running out in early November, I sailed home. My family's reaction to my return was quite subdued, and they conveyed their strong impression that I had been derelict in my duties to them, having made no financial or other contribution for two months. I snapped back smartly into my role of Italian-American daughter, taking up my usual home chores. Finding a job with the Maidenform Brassiere Company in New York as a bilingual secretary set me on a solid earning and savings path again. Colin made a gesture to reassure my parents of his serious intentions with a handsome diamond engagement ring, and our letters, telegrams and phone calls continued apace. Lucy and Frank were not comfortable with their prospective son-in-law, and they were justified in their unease as they had only met him once for a half hour. They were aghast at the idea of my leaving Orange to live in a country they had never heard of, possibly for the rest of my life.

Exit Colin

Though the next few months were not difficult in any large ways—I was comfortably occupied working in New York, enjoying the satisfaction of using my language skills in my job, filling my free time with activities involving my brothers, sister, and friends—I gradually began to doubt my own serious intentions. After six more months of our long-distance courtship and the growing belief that no dispensation from the Church was imminent, I faced the reality that a Church ceremony would not happen. It was not my religious convictions alone that troubled me. I reluctantly admitted to myself that what I loved most was the excitement of the life Colin represented, more than Colin himself. I kept my private reappraisal entirely private for another month by which time, in March 1955, I was ready to announce my change of course. I am not proud of the fact that I gave Colin the excuse of religion as the reason I wished to break our engagement. It was a very sad conversation for both of us.

I sent back Colin's ring. My family and close friends were certain I had made a difficult but wise decision.

Once again I was a free agent, and in no hurry for emotional attachments. Working at Maidenform was interesting and paid well for the times, sixty dollars a week. It also provided one of the perks of the needle trades, entree to some of the showrooms where clothes were bought at discount prices. This was decades before "discount" stores or designer "outlets" for clothing were even thought of.

Strange as it may seem in the multiculturalist ambience of the last decades of the twentieth century, my two years in the Maidenform offices never resulted in anything resembling an office romance. I was the only non-Jewish employee and, while I felt completely at ease with the executives and with the other secretaries, no one ever offered to introduce me to an eligible bachelor they knew. It was a time of ethno-religious separatism—the lines were clearly defined and mostly observed. In the 1950s, one in ten Jews "married out;" by the 1990s it was one out of two, and this evidence of assimilation is a cause for serious concern for American Jews. The women in the office regaled each other with tales of their weekends at resort such as Grossingers, a hotel in what they laughingly referred to as "The Jewish Alps," the prime mating territory of the Catskills. There was hardly any interest in my exotic travels because, after all, vacation time was principally intended for finding a husband, preferably a "doctor-doctor" or a "dentist-doctor." One close friend, Phyllis Friedman, confided that after four years of going to the Catskills for her two weeks' vacation, with her parents' blessing, she decided she wanted to do something different. She said, "I told my father, Dad, you know I majored in Spanish at Syracuse, and this year I want to take a trip to Mexico for my vacation, and try speaking a little Spanish." Her father's reply was a classic. "You want to go to Mexico? What, you want to marry a Mexican?"

Actually one office mate, Howie Hirschorn, made attempt at matchmaking. We liked each other and enjoyed casual banter over coffee breaks. One day Howie shyly announced that he knew the perfect guy for me and asked if I would agree to his arranging a blind date. Howie was doing an accounting job for a lingerie manufacturer whose son, Gabriel, was the candidate—good looking, right age, right religion (Lebanese Christian) and considerably wealthy to boot. I went on the blind date with "Gabe," cocktails and dinner at the New York Athletic Club, about as sedately upper class as any place I had ever been in. But for all the correctness of the markers, it was a painfully dull evening for both of us—we found absolutely no common ground, there was no spark. A gentleman to the end, Gabe drove me all the way home to New Jersey. *Finito.*

While I was marking time, the world around me was not standing still. My two brothers, Domenick and Anthony, were both drafted into the U.S. Army. Domenick was sent to Mannheim, Germany where he served as a Military Policeman during the high alert of the Hungarian uprising in 1956; Anthony spent his Army career at Fort Bliss, El Paso, Texas. Although we were not at war, the national draft continued to take young men away from their jobs and schooling for two years' duty. Frank and Lucy worried that their sons were at risk should the Russians attack us, a constant Cold War anxiety.

The 1950s were exciting years for rebels, all later propaganda by baby-boomers to the contrary. We were aggressively anti-Communist but opposed to the actions of Senator Joe McCarthy and his witch hunt, joyous when he was finally brought down. We were intoxicated by the new progressive jazz of Dizzy Gillespie, Illinois Jacquet, and Stan Kenton. Latin dances were the rave and I became a wild devotee of the Cha-Cha-Cha, Mambo Samba, and Merengue, foregoing the jitterbug and lindy hop of the 1940s. And there was great excitement over the progressive social movements, "tolerance" for racial differences, railing against anti-Semitism—these were the focus of songs, books, movies. We all read *Gentleman's Agreement, To Kill a Mockingbird,* and we were moved by Frank Sinatra's *The House I Live In* and Billie Holliday's *Strange Fruit;* we went to see *Pinky, Love Is A Many-Splendored Thing,* and *South Pacific,* just a few examples of how popular culture and entertainment reflected on (and stirred thoughts about) ideals of racial equality and equal opportunity.

The Return of David Porter

In the fall of 1955 Blanche left New York to enroll at Catholic University in Washington, D.C. There she met John Browne; the couple soon wed and settled into married life. David Porter returned from Istanbul to be drafted into the Army. The old friend of my early European adventures, someone who shared my interests in literature, travel, history, and art, was a welcome occasional companion. Typically, he would call my office to say he was en route to New York City and might I be free to have drinks and dinner with him? I would drop whatever plans I had and agree to meet him. On one such occasion we met "under the clock at the Biltmore" for martinis, then went on to the Versailles Restaurant for dinner and to hear Edith Piaf in person for her poignant rendition of *La Vie en Rose*. Her performance was superb, though the charge of five dollars for a pot of espresso coffee was so outrageous that we talked about it for years. A cup of coffee from Chock Full o' Nuts, that era's Starbucks, then was ten cents.

David's return to the states was occasioned by a draft notice he had never anticipated when he signed the three-year contract to teach at Robert College in Istanbul. He had enlisted in the U.S. Navy after graduating from Hamilton College in 1950 and, after six months of jet pilot training at Pensacola, Florida, he resigned his officer's commission and was granted an honorable discharge. Four years later, he was sent a notice that he was still subject to the draft to complete the two years' mandatory service. He appealed the draft notice on the grounds that he was doing a more important service for America by teaching English in a country that is a valuable ally of the United States, but his appeal was rejected. He was ordered to return to America and serve eighteen months in the Army.

At age twenty-six David was surely one of the oldest recruits at Fort Dix for basic training, and the experience was not one he cherishes. Soon he was assigned to Fort Jackson in Columbia, South Carolina. At least he was on the East Coast now, and we could meet in New York or Washington for a date whenever he could wangle a weekend pass. These dates were always enjoyable, but neither of us looked at the other as a lover or potential mate—we just had companionable times together, neither feeling an urgency to make any serious commitments.

Soon after arriving at Fort Jackson, David had a stroke of good luck. Through letters from friends in Istanbul, he learned that his former colleague Sam Grant was also stationed at Fort Jackson with the responsibility of teaching English to young men from Eastern Europe who had escaped to West Germany during the Hungarian Revolution. These refugees were offered U.S. citizenship if they enlisted in the U.S. Army for five years. They came from a dozen language backgrounds, including Polish, Czech, Hungarian, and Albanian, and most knew no English. Sam spoke to his commanding officer, requesting an assignment for David as an English-language teacher. What luck! Instead of being sent to artillery or clerk-typist or cooking school, David would be doing work for which he had practical experience. He was pleased to be working with Sam, and to have a good friend with whom to go out on the town, though the town of Columbia was a cultural backwater in those days. Still, the two like to say even today, "Well, we protected that area—the Commies never took South Carolina."

When did David and I begin to look at each other with new eyes? By the summer of 1956, the realization slowly dawned on both of us, after a three-year acquaintance, that we were highly compatible, and always delighted in each other's company. Could this be love? Should we begin to consider a future together? David invited me to drive up to Elba, New York, to visit the Porter family in early summer when I was on a week's leave from flying. The visit was a great success. David's mother, brother, and sister were genuinely warm and welcoming. The Porter home, built by David's late father in 1928, was (and still is) the largest and most impressive house in the small town of Elba. I met several family friends and took a tour of the family farm on "the muck," the local term for the rich black soil that produces onion and potato crops. My long train ride alone back to New Jersey was a good time for sober reflection. I finally admitted to myself that this wonderful man with whom I had spent so many carefree hours in so many different situations was more than a friend—he was the perfect loving partner I had hoped to find, perfect in that he shared my aspirations. Evidently my dear David was having the same thoughts.

At the end of August, after a short flight from New York to Bermuda, I found David waiting for me at Pan American Airways arrival areas at the Idlewild (now JFK) Airport. Still in my stewardess uniform, he whisked me into Manhattan and down to Greenwich Village for drinks and dinner at Minetta's Tavern. We were sitting at the bar having cocktails, surrounded by a happy, boisterous crowd of visiting firemen in town for a convention, when David told me how much he loved me and asked me to marry him. How sweet the memory of that moment! I accepted, expressed my love in return, and we embraced for a kiss to the cheers of the firemen who overheard it all!

It was the Thursday night before the long Labor Day weekend. David wanted us to marry during the weekend and go back to Fort Jackson together for the remaining year of his Army duty. He called his commanding officer and was given an extension of his weekend leave. I called Pan American and resigned my stewardess job, entirely contrary to company rules requiring a month's notice. We both went to work on the wedding which we hoped to have take place in three days' time. I did my part, bringing David to meet the family and announcing our hasty plans, making an appointment with Father Andrew at Mt. Carmel Church, buying a dress for the ceremony. David called an Elba friend now living in New York to come to Mt. Carmel Church and sign an affidavit to the effect that David Porter was single, had never been married, had never been in jail, and was not a criminal.

Our interview with Father Andrew, who was to perform our marriage ceremony started out smoothly enough. Soon he turned to David and said, "I am satisfied that you are an honorable person and that you will be a good husband. But since you are not Catholic, I must ask you to agree to three conditions if you wish to marry Rosalie, and they are these: you will not interfere with your wife's practice of her religion, you will not use birth control, and you will promise to allow any children to be baptized and raised in the Catholic faith." We sat in silence while David absorbed these very explicit rules that, I must confess, I had never questioned. Finally, David replied, "I need some time to think about all of this. It is just too much to agree to so suddenly. We need to talk this over together between the two of us and come back with our response."

That evening and all the next day, Saturday, we talked. We reviewed all the wonderful things we loved about each other, what a solid base of understandings we shared, the reasonable expectation that we would create a strong marriage and raise a family together, and on and on. David was adamant that he could not in good conscience agree to conditions that, while allowing me to continue my religious observances, were anathema to him as a confirmed agnostic. He had been raised in a liberal Protestant tradition, free of religious obligations, had never been baptized, and held generally negative views of organized religions. We both wanted desperately to be married and take up a life together, now. At home, I revealed the problem to my mother, who was shocked and puzzled by this turn of events. She asked, "Does David love you? Then why doesn't he just tell the priest what the priest wants to hear, sign the papers, and after you're married, you do whatever you want?" I was appalled. How could she, a lifelong communicant in the Catholic Church, even think such a thing? I said to her, "Mom, David is a very good person. He has great integrity and I admire him for it. He will not lie to Father Andrew. I just wish I could figure out what to do. I really feel terrible." My mother simply did not understand.

By Sunday night we were exhausted. We acknowledged that our discussions were now hopelessly repetitious. We could not see a way to make it work. We decided to put everything on hold for the time being. David would go back to his Army camp and I would explain to my family that there would be no wedding the next day. Suddenly I realized that I had given up a job I loved in my eagerness to wed. But the most heartbreaking thing was the separation from each other so suddenly after the high exhilaration of believing we were starting a new life together! David and I equally felt the crushing disappointment, he on his return to camp without a wife, and I in my search for a new job and resumption of life at home.

We wrote long letters, talked on the phone often, and I even took a weekend trip to Columbia, South Carolina, to visit David. It was a bittersweet reunion. We still could not get around the religion mismatch. Both families, though they knew almost nothing about each other, were firmly in favor of our marriage. David's Army buddy, Sam Grant, urged him not to lose this lovely prospect—marry her, he advised. By Christmas, after three months of fruitless debates, we agreed to call it off. What sad news to convey to family and friends who all admired David and felt he was my destined mate. I reached the depths of despondency, hated my job, and lost so much weight that at 103 pounds I had to alter most of my clothes. It was becoming painfully clear to me that getting married in 1950s America might just be beyond my reach, since I had now mismanaged three attempts.

January 1957 brought an unexpected reprieve from my unhappy job among plumbing supplies. Pan American advertised for stewardesses with fluency in Spanish to staff flights to the Caribbean and South American. In some trepidation, I submitted an application to the New York office and was granted an interview. Incredibly, I was rehired, and I promised to never, ever again resign without giving ample notice. Suddenly, in spite of the heartache of missing David, I was given an opportunity to travel to new countries and to explore the different cultures of Latin America. After six weeks retraining in Miami, I resumed flights out of New York.

David and I were in touch now and then and even met in New York once, soon after his release from the Army, when he was passing through the city on his way back to Washington. We made no mention of our cancelled marriage plans. For my part, I deliberately kept my emotions in check, not daring to hope that we could ever be a couple again. He and Sam settled in Washington for the summer, sharing a house with a group of bachelor bon vivants. David was taking a graduate course at Georgetown University and enjoying his freedom from military life. My longtime friend, Blanche, was living with her husband and child in a Washington suburb where she occasionally invited me to visit for a weekend, since my Pan American Airways flight schedule allowed me about two weeks at liberty each month.

Thus the stage was set for the concluding act in the drama "When David Met Rosalie." On the first weekend in August, my two closest friends, Ruth Marucci, and my cousin Rosalie Pedalino, joined me for a weekend in Washington. I called David to let him know I would be in town. He invited me to take a swim at the Sheraton pool and to have dinner. As we chatted, he suddenly became very serious. With a half smile, he said, "I've been in touch with Robert College in Istanbul and they've offered me a job as head of the English Department in the middle school. I'll be leaving in about two weeks. Would you come with me?" After a brief pause while I recovered from my surprise, I asked, "Is this a proposal of marriage?" He said, "Yes, of course."

The next part of this exchange is not entirely clear in either of our minds, and it was the source of a major problem later. I believed David to say, "Let's not let the Church business come between us now. Let's be married here in Washington in a civil ceremony and then we'll make it up with the Church later. It would be best not to go to New Jersey, since they have a three-day waiting period for a marriage license. We can be married in Washington on the same day we get our license and have our blood tests." I was in a total daze. Here was our last chance to make the commitment to each other. I knew that if David left for Istanbul without me we would never come together again. David said, "I think it would be helpful if we just went away for a day to talk things over and make plans, without your girlfriends, my house mates, and everybody else around. Let's drive down to Williamsburg tomorrow and stay overnight. We'll come back on Saturday and make our announcement to everybody."

Off to Colonial Williamsburg, leaving all our friends in suspense. It was a lovely little interlude and just the right place to make our peace with each other. In mid-summer Williamsburg is almost empty of tourists. Now we got down to the myriad details of getting married, visiting families, gathering whatever was to be shipped with us for two years in Turkey, rearranging travel, passports, all to be completed in

time for the two of us to sail on the SS *Independence* on August 15—
and it was now August 3. On our drive back to Washington we stopped
at a jeweler in Richmond to buy gold wedding bands.

We were euphoric on our return as we announced our intentions
to my friends. Blanche, Ruth, Rosalie, and Blanche's husband John
were elated by the announcement, but when we said it would be a civil
ceremony there was deep consternation. Sam Grant had no such scruples
and agreed immediately to be our best man. I called my mother in New
Jersey to tell her the news and she said, "That's good. And who are you
marrying?" My brother Anthony's wife Dee agreed to be my matron
of honor. They would all, except my father, drive to Washington early
Monday morning to join us for the ceremony. Blanche and John would
host a small reception at their apartment, but my Catholic friends felt
conscience-bound not to be present at the marriage ceremony, which
hurt me deeply at the time but did not alter my love for them. I called
the Pan American Airways office to inform them that I was resigning
immediately and, once again, they were furious at my disregarding
company rules and imposing on other peoples work schedules. I braved
the nastiness, certain that I would never need that job again. In those
quaint, pre-feminist days, stewardesses were not allowed to keep their
job if they married, and certainly not if they had children.

Bright and early on a hot, humid Washington Monday morning,
August 5, David and I began the round of blood tests, license application,
and securing a judge in Alexandria who would perform the ceremony
at 4 PM. Blanche's husband had been an usher in a wedding party the
day before and still had the lease of an air-conditioned limousine (a rare
luxury in those days), which he put at our disposal for the day. Blanche
and John made one last attempt to help us "do the right thing." They
urged us to talk with a priest friend of theirs to see if we couldn't find
quick access to the Church's blessing. What a folly. The crusty, cranky
cleric, a double for the Irish actor Barry Fitzgerald, was not in the least
friendly or conciliatory. He merely warned us that if we went ahead
with this civil business I would be risking my immortal soul. That was
not the kind of good counsel I wanted that day.

By now, family had arrived from New Jersey (my husband would later jokingly say that my two brothers might have been "packing," to make sure he would go through with the wedding this time). We left for the Court House in Alexandria where an elderly, soft-spoken, Traffic Court Judge/Justice of the Peace joined us in legal union. (Thirty years later, our son Tom would marry Paige Thompson, in the garden of the same Court House. And that same year, when we hosted a lavish thirtieth anniversary party, my friends and my cousin sincerely apologized to us for not having stood with us at our marriage ceremony.)

Porters and Pedalinos Joined

We were finally and definitely married!

I've not mentioned the Porter family's reaction to our impending marriage, but David, of course, called his mother in Elba, New York, to tell her of our rather sudden plans to marry. She could not reach Washington in time for the ceremony and was pleased that we would visit her and the rest of the family in Elba before leaving the country. David's sister in New Jersey was away with her family but would be back the following week to see us off. What a whirlwind nine days.

One day in New York City took care of having my name changed on my passport, getting a double cabin on the ship, informing the Near East Colleges Association (administrative office for a dozen Middle Eastern American colleges) that David *and wife* would be traveling together to Istanbul with the necessary changes in salary and stipends. David's sister, Marge Philipp, accompanied us into the city and took me on a round of shopping to fill out the wardrobe of a new bride. We spent two days in Elba, where we were celebrated by family and friends. I was immensely happy to be among the Porters—brother Roy and his wife Bobbie and children, sister Dorothy (Dud) Pixley and husband Frank and their son—they gave me a genuinely warm welcome. Back to New Jersey for a family dinner with my father's two brothers, Michael and Louis, on the last night before we sailed. After much wine drinking, and some Neapolitan songs, my Uncle Michael turned to David and, pinching his cheek, said, "Look at him. What a handsome boy. He almost looks like a Pedalino!" That, Michael intended, was the ultimate compliment.

We had brought a few steamer trunks from Elba, in the back of a borrowed pickup truck. I packed clothing, some table linens, silverware and wedding gifts, anything that fitted in and might be useful. We'd been warned that the Turkish economy was in bad shape and that supplies of consumer goods in the shops were very meager, but that didn't really sink in with either one of us. At the last minute, before locking the trunks, my mother took four cans of American coffee from the store shelves and put them in. I thought it a silly gesture but let it go as I did not want to hurt her feelings. How valuable that little gift would be, I could not have guessed.

Time to kiss the family goodbye, a painful leave-taking. There was sadness for me at the thought of going so very far away from them, and even more for my parents who had themselves left their parents in Italy, never to see them again. But, at the same time, for us, *i sposi,* all was ecstasy. We were still afloat on the intense wave of activities in preparation for our departure. Now we could focus on the immediate prospect of nine days at sea and a week in Rome and Capri before sailing from Naples to Turkey. No doubts, no trepidations. The relaxed time between Orange, New Jersey, and Istanbul would be a lovely honeymoon, affording us a carefree interlude before taking up our long-desired life together.

PHOTOGRAPHS

All photos taken by family, unless otherwise noted.

Pedalino family in Avella.
Seated, Grandma Rosa Ferrara Pedalino and Grandpa Domenico
Pedalino. Standing from left, Giuseppina (on chair), Rosa,
Vittoria, Francesco (author's father), Emilia, and Gigetta. 1919

Lucia Maria Luciano Pedalino,
author's mother, 1935

Passport photo, author at age 6, father, brother Domenico, 1936

First Holy Communion,
Our Lady of Good Counsel
Church, Domenick,
Rosalie, Anthony,
Columbus Studio,
Newark, NJ, 1942

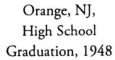

Orange, NJ,
High School
Graduation, 1948

David Porter, Rosalie Pedalino, Claren Sommer,
Blanche Gutowski, Isle of Capri, 1953

Author, Pan American
Airways Stewardess in
Ankara, Turkey, 1956

Author, husband, and mother of bride, on
wedding day, August 5, 1957

Rosalie, David, arriving in Istanbul from
Naples on SS. San Giorgio, 1957

David, seated,
Davey (age 2)
and Tom (age 3),
University of Rochester
Alumni Review,
April/May 1962

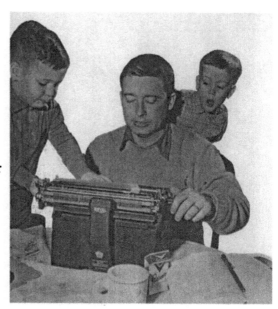

Author, fifth grade teacher, Armory Street
School, Springfield, Massachusetts, 1976

70th birthday party for author's mother, seated, Lucy, Anthony;
standing Rosalie, Frank, Jr., Frances, December 1982

Banquet in Kyoto, Japan, author, husband,
and Professor Hiroko Uno, 1983

THE UNITED STATES
DEPARTMENT OF EDUCATION

*Reposing special trust and confidence
in the integrity and ability of*

Rosalie P. Porter

I have appointed her as a Member of

National Advisory and Coordinating Council
on Bilingual Education

By the Secretary of Education:

Date: *June 17, 1985*

Certificate of appointment to National Advisory and Coordinating
Counsel on Bilingual Education to U. S. Congress, June 17, 1985

Plovdiv, Bulgaria, author (standing at right)
on lecture tour for USIS, May 1988

Jeffrey Amherst
Bookshop poster
by Howard
Gersten,
proprieter

Book signing, author and husband on right, May 17, 1990

Author (back to camera), shaking hands with
Pope John Paul II, Rome, 1992

Catholic marriage ceremony, Newman Chapel, University
of Massachusetts, Father Norman Bolton, Irene Leonardi,
author, husband, Steve, Tom, and Dave, August 1996

Alan Alda, Aliette Goldmark, Arlene Alda, author,
Villa Serbelloni, Rockefeller Study and Conference
Center, Bellagio, Italy, September 1997

Author's three books, published 1990, 1996, 2004

Three sons, Tom, Dave, Steve, in 1969 and in 2006

Four grandchildren, from oldest to youngest: David Gamliel, Carley George Porter, Addison Rose Gamliel, and Emily Avery Porter, 2007

Three couples, Steve and partner Ed Lee, Dave and partner Sally Cooney, Tom and wife Lisa Perlbinder, Amherst 2007

50 Years of Love and Adventure, Anniversary celebration
for David and Rosalie, Amherst, August 2007

SECTION III

PARALLEL LIVES,
POWER SHIFTS

CHAPTER 6
An Enduring Partnership Begins

May 13, 2004—Lee and Dave Porter, son Tom with his 13-year-old stepson, David Gamliel, are seated in Albert Long Hall on the Bogazici University campus in Istanbul, Turkey. Professor Oya Basak regales the audience with a long, witty introduction of the concert pianist, Stephen Porter. Oya has been a close friend of the Porter family for four decades. Among the audience of Turkish university students are a dozen American friends of the Porters who, by coincidence or by design, are on hand for the concert. It is a moment of supreme joy for this family whose origins are here, at the place once known as Robert College.

The Turkish Years
August 15, 1957: The honeymoon voyage begins. The ocean crossing on the SS *Independence* was a restorative interlude. On arriving in Italy,

we spent a full week in Rome and Capri, and had a short visit with *lo zio* Giacomo in Naples. My uncle and his family were surprised but happy that I had married the young American who had been my companion on my madcap adventures four years earlier. We sailed for Turkey on the Lloyd-Triestino Lines' *San Giorgio,* a small ship that followed a romantic course from Naples through the Corinth Canal to Athens; then on to Izmir, the Dardanelles, and to dock in the Sublime Port—Istanbul, once Constantinople.

In these special circumstances, when we were leaving our former lives, families, and friends to take up new roles in a relatively unfamiliar part of the world, the leisurely pace of intercontinental travel permitted time for us to make a comfortable transition. Once the days of transoceanic travel by ship passed into obscurity in the 1970s, the jet-propulsion of hordes of travelers around the planet eliminated the comfort, romance and exoticism of earlier voyages.

Docking in Piraeus, for example, for the obligatory half-day visit to Athens and the Acropolis, gave us a second chance to admire this marvel of human ingenuity at close range, to walk among the gigantic caryatid columns, a physical proximity no longer allowed to tourists. On our return to the *San Giorgio,* we left our camera in the taxicab. Dave ran back to try to catch the driver, who was speeding away from the docks, while I boarded the ship. Within minutes, the "all ashore" sounded, and the crew prepared to raise the gangplank. For one horrifying moment I thought we would set sail without my husband, and he'd be stranded without his passport! One second before the gangplank was uncoupled, Dave ran across the pier and leapt on board.

It was thrilling to arrive in Istanbul again, to be met officially this time as members of the Robert College community, once the truly Byzantine customs and immigration formalities were completed. David had been hired to head the English Department for Robert Academy, and to be housemaster of Theodorus Hall. Our home for the next two years would be the housemaster's apartment in that venerable building (colloquially referred to as "The Odorous Hall), together with eighty-nine Turkish teenage boys, two American resident teachers, and two

Turkish tutors. When we arrived at the door of our quarters, David carried me over the threshold, a gesture I treasure. There was not time to take more than a swift glance around and freshen up for dinner at Will and Doris Whitman's house, a short walk away from the campus quadrangle. On our return, we postponed a close examination of the apartment for the next morning; we were utterly enervated by the day's tensions. Our bedroom was equipped with two old Army cots and a small chest of drawers. Our bathroom included a claw-foot tub and a makeshift shower attached to a copper hot water heater fueled by a wood fire that we were too exhausted to attempt at that hour. As I curled up alone on my little cot, I was suddenly swept by a tremendous homesickness, *anomie*. What was I doing in this strange place, and who was this man I had promised my life to? I wept in muted anguish until my husband comforted me with this gentle reassurance: "We're going to be all right, Zelda."

A bright, sunny morning restored our spirits. Our living quarters, three large rooms with magnificent views of the Bosphorus from every window, were almost entirely bare of furnishings. The kitchen had a two-burner electric hotplate set on a marble-topped chest of drawers. No utensils, silverware or crockery, no stove, and no refrigerator. David had been expected to arrive as a bachelor who would take all his meals in the college dining room. Though we were warmly welcomed in the faculty dining room, we soon decided that we wanted our privacy at meals. The challenge would be to set up a workable situation in the housemaster's apartment at a time when supplies of consumer goods were severely depleted, a situation for which we were not well prepared. Since our hasty marriage and rapid departure from America had taken the Robert College administrators unawares, there had not been time to warn us about what useful supplies to pack in our trunks.

The Turkish government, in the mid-1950s, launched an ambitious program to improve the country's economy by building highways, commercial sites and housing, and by laying pipelines for oil and gas delivery. In order to promote these national priorities, practically all imports of consumer goods were severely restricted in order to favor the import of steel, concrete, and other essentials. Local industries were not yet advanced enough to produce the things we take for granted in Western countries. We could not, therefore, go to downtown Istanbul and buy a refrigerator or a stove or sturdy cooking utensils or any but the most poorly made dishes and glasses. Turkey had not yet begun to produce frozen foods and very few canned fruits and vegetables were on the market. No foreign alcoholic products were imported. But the one unavailable item that was most distressing for natives and foreigners alike was the lack of coffee. For the entire two years of our residence in Turkey, there was no coffee on the market. The Turks, who had treated the world to Turkish coffee for five hundred years, were now reduced to drinking only tea, a situation deeply resented but tolerated. It was pure luck that my mother, the good Lucia, had slipped four cans of American coffee among our clothes in one of the trunks! The only household goods we were bringing with us were eight place settings of silverware and a chrome-plated electric coffee percolator.

Our first few days on campus, before the arrival of students and faculty, were devoted to organizing our household. No friend in Orange, New Jersey, could have imagined the scenes we faced—the deep disappointments that were more than balanced by the generous spirit of the Robert College community. First priority was to make our needs clear to the woman in charge of allocating college furnishings, the admirable Mrs. Armen Turgil. She managed to provide us with a real bed and a tiny kitchen stove within days, but we were without a refrigerator for three months. In the warm early fall, I kept butter, milk, and other perishables in the refrigerator of Ann Milnor, wife of the Robert Academy principal, and made the short walk to their home, up and down hill, several times a day.

Our first visit to the on-campus *bakkal*, or what I expected to be a grocery/convenience store, totally shocked me. We entered a dusty, dim room with a wooden counter and shelves that were entirely empty. In front of the counter was a huge sack full of rice and another full of dry beans. On the counter stood a scale, a cash box, a stack of newspapers for wrapping purchases, and a few loaves of bread. As we walked out,

I fought to restrain tears of incredulity. We would have to obtain our groceries, meats, and produce from the nearby village of Bebek, a long trek up and down the steep Robert College hill.

Another surprise was the status of the local meat supply and the quality of butchering. If the butcher in Bebek had any meat at all, it was hung on a hook outside his small shop, unrefrigerated. It might be a side of beef, but most often it was lamb or mutton. There was no differentiation between cuts of meat—when the butcher understood how many kilos of meat we wanted, he would hack off a chunk and slap it into a newspaper. It would be up to me to make something out of it. Without a car, we walked down the steep hill to the village and carried our purchases home with us in string bags. On occasion we would be offered a ride on our friend Claren Sommer's scooter or in his tiny car, a British Lloyd two-cylinder that barely made it up the hill with two people in it. For the most part, we made the trek on foot.

Many new acquaintances loaned us basic china and glasses, and some sturdy pots and pans. But most importantly they gave us a wealth of information on how to manage the daily routines. I learned to be ready with a saucepan when the *sutcu* (milkman) arrived every evening on his donkey. He came to the door to measure out a liter or two of milk and pour it into my saucepan, for which I paid him some few *kurus*. With the aid of a borrowed cooking thermometer, I heated the milk to 120 degrees for 20 minutes—*voila*, it is pasteurized! I telephoned each evening to the green grocer in Bebek for fresh fruits and vegetables that would be delivered the next morning, saving me some of the walking trips. I was put in touch with the *tavukcu* (chicken man), an enterprising youth who called on us every few weeks. Into my kitchen he carried his little suitcase, opened it to unpack several small packages wrapped in newspapers—a scrawny chicken weighing no more than a pound and a half at best, a piece of highly seasoned salami. We haggled a bit over the price, in a good-natured fashion, and the purchase was made.

As we began attending faculty dinner parties I realized that, without canned or frozen foods, we were all limited to the same three or four vegetables in season. Wonderful as the fresh, naturally ripened produce was, we found ourselves keenly eyeing the market for the next season's bounty, for the first strawberries or spring peas. My first attempt at making a fruit pie had me following instructions in my new Betty Crocker cook book, the best basic "how to" for wives of the 1950s. I discovered a new product in Bebek, canned sour cherries. After tossing the cherries with sugar, cinnamon, and a little lemon juice, I decided to taste one and, to my surprise, I bit down hard on a cherry stone. The processing of cherries did not yet include removing the pits! I did not mind the extra half hour spent on removing every cherry stone since it would have been terrible if we had put our guests at risk of breaking a tooth.

We were a very traditional, friendly community, with every one of the established families entertaining the newcomers and extending all manner of assistance and advice—from references to doctors, ways of getting around without cars, and how best to *pazarluk* (that is, to bargain the price of goods in the Grand Bazaar) to organizing sightseeing tours on weekends. Social events on campus included afternoon teas, bridge parties, dinner parties, cocktail parties, musical or dramatic performances by the faculty, or special performances by visiting dance companies, musicians, and theater groups. We had an introduction to a Turkish businessman who had dealings with our brother-in-law in New York. Albert Ben Muvar and his wife Laurette turned out to be a delightful young couple with lively interests in the social life of the city. They were our guests at a number of Robert College events, and we met them in the city on occasion. One evening at the Karavansarai Night Club, when the band struck up a Charleston, my husband announced that I was a noted Charleston dancer. Albert swept me out to the dance floor. He was an incredible dancer and the floor was immediately cleared for the two of us. We had such fun kicking up our heels at the fast rhythm and received loud applause at the end.

Learning to be a housewife in such a daunting situation forced me to rely on the advice of cooperative friends, not on the gadgets we would have considered essential back in the states. We made do with so little of the conveniences in American homes and were proud of it. For example, I made my own peanut butter, and rolled up balls of *tel kadayif* and baked them in the oven to make a faux shredded wheat cereal, but the oddest thing I learned to make was vodka. Turkish vodka was the only "hard liquor" available on the market, besides Raki, but it was very expensive. Tobacco shops sold pure alcohol, legally. I was instructed in the simple art of making vodka at home. "One liter of distilled water boiled with a small amount of sugar; let cool and add one liter of alcohol and the thin peel of one lemon. Strain through a clean cloth, put in bottles and store in a cool, dark place." The vodka might be aged for only a few hours if we were having a party that night, or it could be stored for a longer time to achieve a smoother quality. And so it was that I became the vodka maker in our family for the next two years, mixing it with fruit juice and *Portakal* liquor to produce the "Hill Cocktail" of Robert College lore.

Being so far from both Pedalino and Porter families allowed us to work out the foundations of our married life in ways that would not have been possible if we had had the interference of our two totally different clans. Some of those strains emerged later when we moved back to the United States, but by then we had bonded in a relationship that promised to be sturdy enough to withstand the stressful times.

One of the festering, unresolved issues hanging over us during those first two years was the matter of our uncompleted marriage, that is, our civil ceremony before a U.S. Justice of the Peace, which did not meet my expectations as a Roman Catholic for a true sacramental blessing by my church. The few days between David's marriage proposal and the beginning of our lengthy voyage to Istanbul gave me an excuse to leave the matter in limbo. Shortly after arriving at Robert College, I raised the question of when we would have a religious ceremony. David drew back from the vague promise he had made earlier. I felt sadly disappointed that my understanding had perhaps been more wishful thinking than a real commitment from my husband. We faced the same dilemma that had stopped us from marrying a year earlier: the Catholic Church made very firm demands on non-Catholics: the couple would not employ artificial birth control; the non-Catholic partner would not interfere with the Catholic partner's practice of faith; the couple's children must be baptized and raised in the Catholic faith. For David, the third requirement was the most repellant, although he found the first two unappealing as well.

In our first year at Robert College I tried to attend Mass at the tiny Armenian Church in the village nearby but on each of these occasions David would express his disapproval by his silent sulks. Even a polite discussion of the problem became increasingly emotional. My husband's firm agnostic principles would not allow him to impose any religious beliefs and practices on our future children—that was it, plain and simple. I felt aggrieved at being deprived, essentially, of my faith. We could not live together very long without a compromise on someone's part. I reasoned, privately, that I had but two choices: either I should divorce my beloved husband in order to remain a Catholic, or I should put aside my religious practices and keep my commitment to the intelligent, moral husband I had come to love and appreciate. Was this a foolish rationalization? Perhaps. Was my capitulation wise? Yes, in light of the subsequent years of a strong, loving partnership of immensely greater satisfactions than I could have imagined at that time. We changed each other's attitudes significantly over those years.

The women, the faculty wives with whom I formed strong attachments and for whom I had the greatest admiration as exemplary wives and mothers—my role models—appeared to be of uniform composition. All shared middle-class, Protestant backgrounds, all were graduates of prestigious colleges—strong representation from Smith and Mount Holyoke—all expressed liberal political views. I was not the brunt of any overt social-class snubs, but still I felt out of my element. I wanted to be one of them but knew that I could not change myself, retroactively, to fit their mold. We openly discussed housekeeping minutiae, shared books and magazines that were in short supply, traded ideas on world events and U.S. policies and politics, but they deemed some topics—birth control or abortion, for instance—unsuitable to be brought up in my presence. They all were engaged in part-time teaching, which I was unqualified to do. One day I overheard a silly conversation between two of my women friends with small children. One of them said she had asked her four-year-old daughter what she wanted to be when she grew up and her daughter answered, "An airline stewardess and fly all around the world." At that they both laughed and the other woman said, "She'll grow out of it, not to worry." Since that was my last job before marrying, I felt demeaned.

David and I began an unlikely friendship with a young couple teaching at the nearby *Kiz Kolej* (American College for Girls), the sister school for Robert College located a few miles away. We had first met David and Mary Alice Sipfle on the ocean crossing and soon after we began to have an occasional dinner together. They were both recent graduate students from Yale, David had completed his doctorate in philosophy and Mary Alice all but her dissertation for the doctorate in French. We were an unlikely foursome. The Sipfles were intellectually stimulating, polished conversationalists with a sharp sense of humor, good Bridge players, but they were teetotalers. We were more sophisticated in the ways of travel, social life, partying, drinking, smoking. We found common ground in a love of good food and our evenings centered on a well-cooked dinner and hours of Bridge, with good conversation. The Sipfles had brought a Virginia ham with them, a real treasure in a Moslem country, and it hung from the ceiling in their kitchen as a prized possession. After Mary Alice delivered their first child, Ann, and recovered her energy, we were invited to be their guests for a Christmas dinner that featured that precious ham.

The Sipfles were destined to have the most profound influence on both of us. Dave Stipfle's example as a talented teacher and intellectual became one of the prime factors in my husband's decision to pursue a doctorate in literature and a career in university teaching when we returned to the United States in 1959. Mary Alice presented me with a competitive challenge, planting a seed that would lie dormant for a dozen years or more before sprouting. I did not at that time ask myself if I could one day complete my studies for an undergraduate degree, much less a doctorate like Mary Alice, but I felt a subconscious stirring in that direction. Also, the two proudly stated that their marriage was firmly based on the notion of a 50–50 sharing of domestic duties. What an amazing idea in 1958, even for a liberated academic community, that a husband would take turns diapering the baby, washing dishes, giving the baby an early morning feeding and occasionally allowing his wife to sleep late. It was certainly a way of life that my husband would not dream of embracing. A rigid, gender-based division of duties would prevail well into the future for us.

Domestic issues aside, it was an exhilarating time to be living in the Near East, next door to the USSR, which celebrated the fortieth anniversary of the Russian Revolution in November 1957 by launching the first projectile into space, the Sputnik. Turkey represented our strongest ally, allowing the United States to maintain naval and air bases on its soil, bases for the constant aerial surveillance of the Soviet Union. The Bosphorus, the deep-water linkage between the Black Sea and the Sea of Marmora and the Mediterranean, flowed beneath the Robert College hill, affording us daily views of Russian oil tankers, probably ships carrying KGB spies, part of our Cold War mentality.

The U.S. military presence was barely visible, but access to the goods sold on the American bases was a wildly sought-after benefit. One of the most intense topics of gossip in our college community was the question of who among us had "PX privileges." Who among the college administrators had the privilege of going to the stores maintained on the U.S. military bases, the Post Exchanges, for service men and their families? Since so few consumer goods were available in local markets, the appearance of coffee or Scotch or a canned ham raised suspicions among the rest of us. There was almost no social mingling of the college community and the American military families. It was understood that the military considered Istanbul a hardship post and could not imagine why any Americans would actually choose to live here. Someone once overheard the Robert College people referred to by an Air Force officer as "civilian slop-over."

We also wondered who among our colleagues might be an agent of the CIA. Then as now there were nasty stories of the obtuseness of CIA activities. One of the English teachers at Robert College did, in fact, admit to us years later that he was recruited by the CIA before leaving for Turkey. His assignment was to read the daily Istanbul newspapers and report on anything suspicious. For this he was paid thirty dollars a month and given those golden PX privileges. The absurdity of this was in his total lack of knowledge of the Turkish language, meaning that he had to rely on the family's housekeeper to do the task for him.

Money changing was another exotic experience. The official exchange rate at the time was 2.6 Turkish lira to one U.S. dollar. My husband's contract paid him $1,800 per year, most of which we earmarked for special treats like vacation travels in Europe and the Middle East. He was also paid a Turkish lira salary, which covered our living expenses, and we were provided a rent-free college apartment. To subsidize our vacation travels, it was necessary to trade some dollars on the black market, a commonly accepted practice. However, the many ways of making these exchanges involved intrigues straight out of the Eric Ambler spy novels. All the old hands at the college had contacts downtown where an exchange for as much as eleven lira to one dollar could be made directly, say at a certain café in the flower market, or during tea time in the lobby of the Pera Palas Hotel, or at a street-corner yoghurt stand. More elaborate exchanges involved sending dollars to a Swiss account for a Turkish businessman who would trade them for lira at an inflated rate. We felt very daring, but I suspect the Turkish authorities were not unaware of this penny-ante activity and just let it go on as a mild sort of pastime for foreigners to get their jollies. Just the illicit trading of a few hundred dollars paid for our two-week winter trip to Beirut, Jerusalem, Cairo, and Luxor.

Summer in Germany and Spain
We were modestly helped with occasional infusions of dollars from the Porter family farm in Elba, New York, in which my husband owned a share. It was an informal arrangement—no annual accounting or profit reports, no regular income to rely on—but brother-in-law Roy, who managed the farm, would send a small check whenever it was needed.

At the end of our first year in Istanbul, we took our savings and with Roy's help we ordered a small car in Germany, which we would pick up in Dusseldorf and use for our summer travels before driving it back to Turkey. In those days American tourists routinely bought their cars in Germany, England, France, or Italy and had them shipped back to the United States at a considerable saving over buying foreign cars at home. With careful budgeting, and the advantage of a strong dollar, we managed to travel for three months in the summer of 1958, mostly in France and Spain. Our last month of the summer found us on the Island of Majorca in a rented villa with Robert College friends. It was here that we marked our first anniversary, and where a doctor confirmed that I was pregnant with our first child, due seven months hence.

My fluency in Spanish and Italian, and a limited knowledge of French, made our daily contacts with hotel clerks, waiters, shopkeepers, ticket sellers, and other members of the service sector easy to handle. Since my husband also had a modest command of Spanish and French, we enjoyed many wonderful conversations with local residents and with travelers from other countries, exchanging views of contemporary literature, world events, local arts, music, foods, and festivals. At a time when a liter of good table wine in a Spanish bodega cost the equivalent of twenty-five cents (you brought your own bottle to be filled from the barrel), our daily maid who arrived at 7:30 AM, in time to light a fire in our wood-burning stove to cook our breakfast, was paid a dollar a day. She asked me if I would also give her two eggs a day for her little boy and I readily agreed. For this we were scolded by our next-door neighbors who complained that we Americans were paying too much and ruining the economy for local residents!

As the summer odyssey drew near an end, we left Majorca and boarded a Mediterranean ship in Marseilles, with our little Taunus car, and sailed for Athens; from there we would set out to drive to Istanbul. There was absolutely no guarantee that an American resident bringing in a car—whether by driving it in, bringing it aboard ship, or having the car delivered later—would actually succeed in having the car released from customs. Some cars were released without a problem while other cars were impounded for months. An American station wagon, ordered for the president of Robert College, was kept for almost a year while one technicality after another impeded its release. Driving north from Athens through desolate mountainous country, over rutted, perilous roads, it was a relief to arrive in Alexandropolus and then Thessaloniki for overnight stays. One meeting in the middle of nowhere relieved the tension. On a deserted mountain road, a Greek shepherd with a staff suddenly appeared and motioned us to stop. When we pulled up near him and rolled down the windows, he said, "Change American dollars?" Away we roared, thankful for the comic relief.

Our anxiety level rose as we approached the Greek-Turkish border station at Edirne. We drew up to the guard post and were motioned to step out of the car and asked for passports. The customs officer examined our documents and then made a cursory examination of our suitcases. When he opened the boxes packed with an infant's layette, items we knew we could not buy in Istanbul, he asked, "Where is the baby for these clothes? Are you going to sell these?" I made my best effort with gestures and my few words of Turkish, pointing to my stomach, to indicate that the "*bebek*" was coming and the clothes were for that anticipated baby. The officer finally understood and smiled. With greetings of "Allaha ismarladak" (may Allaha go with you), he handed us back our passports and waved us through. What a relief. We had overcome the enormous border hurdle and now had the convenience of a car for the coming year.

Year 2: A Radical Change in the Robert College Culture

Returning to our Theodorus Hall apartment, to the familiar campus sights and friends, we both felt fairly confident in our roles, David in his teaching and heading the English Department, I in my wifely responsibilities and in making preparations for our first child. Nothing could have prepared us for the change in *dramatis personae,* the arrival of a new group of teachers who would alter the social life of the college community and start what would later be called, "The Golden Age" of expatriate life on the Bosporus. For an account of that period from

a child's eye view, read Maureen Freely's *The Life of the Party*[5]. For
the American teachers who arrived, whether single or married, with
or without children, all embodied a view of life abroad that differed
significantly from the current style. The new arrivals were well ahead
of their times, prefiguring the fabled 1960s era of sexual liberation.
Here was their opportunity to turn over the mundane—the housekeeping and child-rearing—to easily available and low-wage servants,
and to make the most of the freedom to pursue local pleasures. The
newcomers were not about to adapt to the traditions, somewhat stuffy,
of the present community but were determined to remake it in their
own hedonistic ways. It was truly a sea change that enveloped all of us,
affecting friendships, marriages, sexual orientations, and careers.

David and I found ourselves in both camps, taken up with the racy,
fun-loving new crowd for parties, sightseeing expeditions, and sports
events, but still quite happy to enjoy the company of the established
families. Academic communities can be insular, gossip-ridden nests
of back-biting personalities striving to outdo one another, perhaps
even more so when situated in a foreign country. Cut off from the
moderating influences of our families in America, we created our own
rules of acceptable behavior. Young couples, fresh out of graduate school
or low-wage teaching jobs, who had struggled back home to afford an
occasional babysitter for an evening out, now found themselves with
free time for new friendships, travel, love affairs—in an environment
that while celebrating the "life of the mind" and the dazzle of
stimulating conversation also tolerated the indulgences of the body to
a high degree. Coupled with the exoticism of living in a cosmopolitan
city at the crossroads of Europe and Asia, it was an intoxicating life,
both exciting and frightening for me.

The stepped-up pace of our social life began to raise my anxieties.
David became fast friends with several of the new teachers, a talented
crowd who began the custom of dashing off to a local bar, on the spur of
the moment, for long bouts of drinking and conversation, well into the
evening hours. These impulsive off-campus flings became a common
practice. The "boys" needed to get away from wives and children now

and then. What disturbed me was the assumption that wives should not expect to be informed, just "be cool" and carry on, go ahead with dinner or wait it out. I found the idea personally insulting and said so, another subject of disagreement between us.

Experiencing the novel physical changes of pregnancy, finding an American-trained doctor for the prenatal visits, seeking information on the latest birthing practices from the campus wives who had recently delivered babies in Istanbul (the popular Lamaze, natural childbirth method, for example), took up a good deal of my time and thoughts. My parents had assumed that I would return to the states to have the baby and worried over my news that I would stay in Turkey. We, like most of the other Americans we knew, felt duty bound to stay the course. As long as there were no obvious problems, and I was fortunate to be in good health, we could safely expect to deliver our baby at the *Amiral Bristol Hastahanesi*, the American hospital in Istanbul, as others had done. And, indeed, that was the case.

Thomas Avery Arrives
On the evening of February 26, I cooked a special birthday dinner for our bachelor friend David Leeming, who was just out of Princeton and sometimes a mite homesick. He was delighted with the American-style fried chicken and with the heart-shaped cake covered with pink frosting. During the night I began to feel the first labor pains, but having been cautioned by my women friends *not* to rush to the hospital at once, since first babies were notoriously slow in arriving and that the pains might be false alarms, I said nothing until morning when I woke up my husband to tell him the pains were now quite close together. Nevertheless, we made a quick breakfast and, when our maid arrived, informed her that we would be leaving for the hospital. She screamed and made a huge fuss, incredulous that we could be so calm about it all. Driving from the college to the hospital took a miserable forty-five minutes as we bounced over the cobble stone streets. Dr. Vedat Yeginsu, our doctor who had trained at Massachusetts General Hospital in Boston, met us at the hospital; after a brief examination he

whisked me off to the delivery room, motioning to David to sit in the waiting room. Before I could inform the doctor that I wanted no drugs but a natural birth, I was given a spinal injection and prepared for the delivery. The baby came so quickly, not fifteen minutes after arriving at the hospital, that suddenly our beautiful little boy and I were being wheeled out of the delivery room to be met by my husband who was astonished to see us and quickly asked, "Are you all right? Is it a boy or a girl?"

I wrote all the details to my family, so that they, too, could marvel at this momentous event. We were too naïve to know what an ordinary occurrence it was. But the ways of the Turkish hospital were not at all what common practice was in those days in American hospitals. The baby arrived just before noon. At 5 PM my husband arrived with flowers, stuffed toys for the baby, and three of our bachelor friends bearing champagne and cigars. Imagine the party scene in my hospital room! When the nurse brought baby Tom in for a feeding, she was not at all censorious about the noise, the imbibing or the cigar smoking. After my husband and our friends left for an evening of celebration in the city, the mother of one of our students walked in with a baby gift as I was eating my *sis kebap* and *pilaf* dinner—apparently visitors were not screened or limited at any time. Hospitals in the United States in those days did not allow anyone to visit but the husband of the mother and the grandparents of the baby, and only during restricted hours.

The following day David brought me two treats from our kitchen: a small jar of American peanut butter that we had won in a Bridge tournament (that was for my morning toast), and the remaining half of the Leeming birthday cake. In the evening, when I lifted the cover on the cake platter I was horrified to discover that there were dozens of roaches feeding on it. Sanitation was not up to American standards, yet the hospital had an excellent record for its maternity ward.

Thomas Avery Porter weighed five pounds three ounces at birth and lost two ounces in the first few days, but he was perfectly healthy and pronounced ready to go home at the end of five days. With what trepidation we bundled our precious child into the car for the drive home. We were now totally responsible for this new person, immediately concerned to keep him sufficiently warm and clean and fed. For the next few weeks my entire life centered on the baby who cried for a feeding every three hours, day and night, restricting me pretty much to the apartment. Breast feeding was the healthy and popular practice recommended by our doctors, but Tom was not gaining enough weight and the more I worried, the less plentiful was my milk supply. After six weeks of problems, I was advised to wean the baby to bottle feedings with a powdered formula, Similac, an American product now available at the U.S. military store. Thanks to a professor with the coveted "PX privileges," we were able to buy a generous supply of Similac, which I mixed with boiled water to produce Tom's bottle feedings. It proved to be what he needed and he soon showed better weight gains and slept for longer periods.

We had no crib but traded our chrome-plated electric percolator for a modest baby carriage, which became Tom's home until we returned to the United States. We thought the carriage with its detachable body and folding legs for car travel was an absolutely grand piece of equipment. But when we arrived in New Jersey for my family's viewing of their first grandchild they were horrified. In New Jersey Italo-American culture, the first child must have an elegant and expensive pram, something to make the neighbors envious, something suitable for a royal prince. David and I had no such pretensions.

Our last four months at Robert College were a time of adjustment to the role of parents, to serious deliberations about what career David would pursue on our return to the United States—advertising? law school? graduate school in literary studies? My own daily life was far more restricted than my husband's and sometimes it reduced me to tears. One day, as I started down the hill for a morning walk with Tom in his carriage, I spotted our car approaching, and David waved as he and three friends left for downtown to play tennis at the Hilton Hotel courts. I felt hopelessly neglected. One day, when Tom was a few weeks old, our friend Mary Alice Sipfle called to say that she would take me downtown to the matinee of a French film and that my husband would be the baby sitter for those few hours. It was my first child-free outing in a month and I relished every moment of it.

We wanted very much to visit the sites of some of the antiquities on the coast of Antalya before leaving Turkey and planned a trip for the college's spring vacation, when Tom was six weeks old. We would take along a supply of formula and of the new marvelous invention—disposable diapers. One of the American teachers in our building, Peter Morley, made the trip with us, sitting in the back of our little car with Tom in his carriage bed. It was a memorable visit to Bursa and its Blue Mosque, but the wonders of Ephesus and Pergamum, Greek and Roman ruins, delighted us much more. Both sites stood in lonely splendor, amphitheater and temple ruins well preserved over thousands of years, and we were the only tourists strolling among these treasures. One early morning we set up our Coleman stove and cooked our breakfast at the top of the mountain overlooking the magnificent Greek amphitheater, imagining the timeless lines of Aeschylus or Sophocles being declaimed. For a thoroughly modern note, a handsome young boy came up to sell us a bouquet of poppies for a few liras.

All went smoothly until the third day. As we were remarking on the facility of traveling with an infant, we stopped for a picnic lunch by the side of an orchard full of the pink-blossomed Judas trees. Then, the car would not start. David, who had grown up around farm machinery and had been driving a car and flying a plane by age fifteen, checked the motor, the fuel and oil levels, all to no purpose. We were stranded in open country, far from any town, a worrisome situation. As we sat by the side of the dirt road, a camel caravan came into view and slowly made its way past us. It didn't even occur to us to try to ask for help. Then David tried one more time to start the motor, and this time it started. With no further mishaps we arrived safely back in Istanbul, full of stories. The post-vacation parties at the college were veritable competitions for who had been to the most interesting, exotic, weird, inaccessible, or yet-to-be-discovered-by-the-public places. A typical conversation I overheard revealed one-upmanship at its best: "I've just come back from Egypt, did the Valley of the Kings, Cairo, the pyramids—fabulous," and the response was, "Ah, but did you go to El Faiyûm? Now that's not to be missed.".

After due deliberation, my husband decided he wanted to enter graduate school for a doctorate in literature. He applied to the University of Rochester, which offered him a full tuition scholarship and a stipend of a thousand dollars, a generous offer he accepted. We would live in Rochester, New York, for the next three years, just thirty miles from the Porter family farm in Elba. David's mother, Bertha Thomas Porter, assured us that she would cover our monthly rent on an apartment near the university, and we could count on occasional support from the family. My husband chose the University of Rochester both for its excellent faculty in English and because it would situate us close to Elba for a few years. He was concerned for the health of his brother, Roy, who had recently had major surgery for cancer of the colon.

Our two years at Robert College had given us the opportunity to be ourselves, to begin to know each other, unfettered with the impositions of in-laws and friends of our youth, to build friendships that, unknown at that time, would last for decades. It was not a topic I ever discussed with my husband, but I secretly harbored fears that the heated social climate at Robert College would have a harmful effect on our marriage. I felt we had had enough of the high life and high jinks on the Bosphorus and were leaving at just the right moment. Time to take up new challenges elsewhere. Our return to the states would be by ship, the usual mode of travel between continents in those days and the most economical way for us to bring our household goods and car with us. We sailed from the Yolcu Salonu on a sunny morning in June 1959, leaving behind the waves and shouts of many friends on the pier as the SS *Ege* drew away from the docks.

Leaving Istanbul, Discovering Positano

Our good friends Mary Alice and David Sipfle and their baby Ann were with us, and we planned to travel in Italy together once we landed in Naples. On arrival we made the obligatory visit to *lo zio* Giacomo and his family, who were keen to meet baby Tom. We soon left the city to drive south along the coast to a village that had been recommended to us—Positano. Beyond the bay of Naples and the city of Sorrento, situated on a steep mountainside, the resort city next door to its even more famous neighbors on the Amalfi Drive, Positano was still largely unfamiliar to American tourists but a popular vacation spot for the European cognoscenti. We had written ahead for lodgings at the Villa Franca, a very modest, small, family-run hotel at the very top of the mountain overlooking the beach and seaside. The Russo family provided spotlessly clean rooms, each with a small balcony; they served breakfast and either lunch or dinner al fresco, all at an affordable daily rate. We planned to stay one week.

Once unpacked, the four of us started down the winding hill, our babies in prams, to explore the town center below. We were starved for European food and for variety. In fact, at the very first bakery café, we stopped for espresso and pastries. The temptations were too great for some of us. Dave Sipfle and I consumed too many Neapolitan *pasticciotti—sfogliatelle, cannoli, baba*—to the considerable annoyance of our spouses.

We asked Signor Russo if he could recommend a local woman to babysit for Tom and Ann, perhaps a few hours each day, so that we adults could go to the beach. We feared the heat and sun were too severe for our babies. He introduced us to his niece, Mena, a gorgeous seventeen-year-old who seemed to have stepped out of an Italian movie. She turned out to be not only beautiful but entirely reliable, caring for the two children our first week in Positano. When the Sipfles left to tour northern Italy, we were so happy with our situation that we decided to stay on at the Villa Franca. Mena took such good care of Tom, walking him up and down the hill in his carriage, sterilizing the bottles and preparing boiled water for the formula—she did it all for the princely sum of one American dollar per day! Those three weeks on our own before sailing from Naples on the SS *Independence* proved to be a blessed rest and recuperation period before diving into the rigors of graduate school, setting up a household on a very limited budget, and confronting what we had been blissfully able to avoid for two years: adapting to and negotiating the differences of our two family cultures.

The Rochester, New York, Years

These initial "re-entry" scenarios prefigure the different ways in which we would react to our two families after our independence of two years:

On arriving in Orange, New Jersey, we spent a week with my family. My parents gave us their bedroom in which they had installed a new crib for baby Tom. There was much boisterous celebration of our return and of the first new grandchild, visits from neighborhood friends, wine drinking and singing to the accompaniment of guitars and mandolins in the evenings. During the day, my mother was busy in the family grocery store, and we spent most of the time in the kitchen and on the porch visiting with my brothers, my sister, and with my mother when she was free.

It was stifling for David to be constantly surrounded by so many people in such close quarters, and hardly ever able to enjoy an adult conversation. All the exchanges seemed to be focused on the baby's little gestures and the anticipated baby due soon to my brother Anthony's wife, Dee. This was not a household that ever had the time or inclination to develop the fine art of conversation. There had never been a college graduate in our family, much less a graduate student preparing to pursue a doctorate. This was entirely new territory for Lucy and Frank, and yet they expressed their approval and their willingness to help us in any way they could, even though they had no idea why my husband was going back to school.

Driving from Orange to Elba a few days later, we were welcomed to the lovely Porter home, where David's old room had been prepared for us with a new crib for the baby. The house that David's father had built for his family in 1928 is the most imposing home in Elba, even today. At the time we came back to America, brother Roy and his wife and six children, plus David's mother, lived in the three-story, five-bedroom residence with a "ballroom" on the third floor. Roy ran the family farm in his home office at the rear of the kitchen wing with a secretary who helped manage the day-to-day business. Pearl was the full time African American maid whose time was well occupied with the household and the six children, who ranged in age from Posey at four months to Portie (Roy Avery Porter III) at fourteen.

To me the household appeared to embody everything I aspired to: middle-class respectability; gentle manners; intelligent, well-educated, even-tempered adults (or so they all seemed). For example, it appeared to me that members of this family did not make loud complaints or fuss about things. It was midsummer and the days and nights were mostly hot and humid. At my mother's house, electric fans circulated the air for some relief, and yet everyone loudly complained about the heat, the humidity, and the mosquitoes. At the Porters, however, there were no fans, and certainly no air conditioners, in any of the very stuffy bedrooms, but no one ever remarked about it. Nothing was said, and I understood that one was expected to ignore physical discomfort and just "bear up." How very civilized.

We made quick work of finding an apartment in Rochester near the university and gathering mostly hand-me-down furnishings from the Porters and Pedalinos. The month in Elba gave me an insight into the dynamics of David's family, which, of course, was no more idyllic than any similarly situated group of people in the 1950s. I began to make the acquaintance of his oldest sister, Dorothy Miles Pixley (Dud), my husband's closest sibling. Dud had majored in Spanish literature at Wellesley but had never pursued a career or work outside the home. She dabbled in local theater and literary projects, read extensively, and was an active member of the Episcopal Church. She doted on my husband and seemed delighted with his chosen career path. She was married to Frank Pixley, a businessman/farmer who very much doted on her and on their adopted son, Penn.

We spent a few evenings out with Roy and his wife Bobbie, who impressed me as an amazingly serene woman for a mother of six. They made a handsome pair, both slim and attractive, dedicated golfers, with a lively social life. I noticed that no drinks were served before dinner, no drinks or wine at meals, and was told that Mother Porter had never tolerated drinking in her second husband, David's father. She was convinced that it contributed to the break up of her first marriage years before. Therefore, social drinking had to take place at bars and restaurants, never at home. Oddly to me, Bobbie, who was a teetotaler, never passed judgment on the drinking habits of her husband or his friends. In spite of the elegance and spaciousness of the Elba house, Roy and Bobbie confided that they were eager to build their own home nearby and had even had an architect's plan drawn up, since they found daily life with Mother stifling.

I had high expectations for the graduate school experience ahead. Though it was David who would be the real student in the English Department, I looked forward to reading the literature on the course syllabi, to giving my support by typing all his scholarly papers, and to making new friends among the graduate students' wives. Even before classes started, David devoted summer hours to boning up on his French for the required exam in a modern language. I discovered a course in Spanish literature of the seventeenth century that met two afternoons a week and registered as an auditor at no cost, with David's promise to be at home with the baby for those two hours.

That first semester established the pattern of our lives for the next three years, with few interruptions. Our roles were defined by the mores of the 1950s. David was entirely dedicated to his intellectual studies, and a more serious worker I had never seen. He studied late almost every night with few exceptions for weekends. My job was to keep up the household, shopping, cooking, cleaning, taking care of our son, and, indeed, I was recruited to do my husband's typing. I had been a very good typist in my secretarial days, and, since I read most of the books my husband was reading, I enjoyed the stimulation of typing his critical essays. But the primitiveness of the technology! We had an elderly manual typewriter and essays had to be typed with eight or nine copies, which was done by rolling that number of sheets of paper, interleaved with carbon paper, into the typewriter. To correct a mistake required very careful erasing of each copy. It was a laborious task, but no better method existed.

My Spanish course was exhilarating and I looked forward to each class, not only for the stimulation of the literary discussions in Spanish, but for the pleasure of being among adults and out of the house. Alas, after that first semester, David decided he could not baby-sit and we could not afford to pay for the service. Much as I regretted it, I accepted the fact that my own studies would be delayed for a few years.

At the first university social affair, where all the graduate students and their wives or girlfriends gathered, I met several congenial women with small children who were just as eager as I to fraternize while our husbands were occupied. We met for our children's "play sessions" in each other's homes and provided each other with information on child-rearing practices—the latest word from Spock, Gesell, and others on nutrition, weaning from the bottle, hours of sleep—and the latest academic gossip, scandals, or achievements. In that first semester at the University of Rochester, I learned that I was pregnant and that our second baby would be arriving in May, when Tom would be just fifteen months old. We had certainly not planned to have a second child so soon, but we reasoned that the two would grow up companionably close. Financially, the expenses of two small children were not appreciably greater than for one and the delivery at the University of Rochester's Strong Memorial Hospital would be almost free of charge. The University provided its graduate students with an excellent medical plan that included prenatal care, delivery of the baby, and postnatal care for the token sum of twenty-five dollars.

None of us in the graduate school could afford to be extravagant. Social life was pretty much limited to an occasional dinner party at each other's homes, an evening out at a concert or movie, or, for us, a Sunday dinner in Elba with the Porter family. We established connections with neighborhood high school girls who would mind our children for a few hours in the evening for twenty-five cents an hour. The main sustenance for all of us, the compensation for living within limited means, was the exhilaration of reading, discussing, and analyzing the novels of Austen, Trollope, Thackeray, Tolstoy, Dostoevsky, Flaubert, Cervantes; the plays of Shakespeare, Marlowe, Webster, Molière, Goethe; and the

English poets. What a rich feast to occupy our hours when we were not otherwise engaged in household chores. We wives shared our husband's preoccupations with literary criticism, aesthetics, and high culture. My education was continuing informally in ways that would not earn me college credits but was no less rewarding.

Visits to my Pedalino relatives in New Jersey were limited by distance (an eight-hour drive each way), my husband's intense work schedule, and a subtle discomfort I sensed in him when we spent a few days with my family. At Christmastime 1959 we made the trip, our first holiday with my family since our marriage. Three days of noisy feasting and wine drinking in the kitchen behind the grocery store ensued with much fuss made over the two babies (Tom and my brother Anthony's son Frank); much joshing of Frank Jr. and Francie, my teenage siblings; and the endless recounting of family fables. My brother Domenick introduced us to his fiancée, Marie, and announced their plans to marry the following summer. And my parents loaded our car with groceries and some prime cuts of meat when we prepared to leave. Frank and Lucy were proud of their son-in-law, although he was inscrutable to them. They were delighted with my obvious good health at this point in my pregnancy. David suffered through the days in Orange with fairly good grace, but I knew that secretly he was hiding his disenchantment with the family scene.

1960 Brings David Lawrence and JFK

Our first year in Rochester coincided with the most exciting political campaign that we had yet experienced. We and our graduate student friends were riveted by the events leading up to the primaries, and the jousting over John F. Kennedy's run for the Democratic Party nomination. For the first time since 1928, a Roman Catholic aspired to the presidency. In spite of his religion, which at that time was considered an almost insuperable liability, JFK personified everything we admired: intelligence, youth, high-level speaking and writing skills, a keen sense of humor, Ivy-League credentials, war-hero stature, an attractive aristocratic wife, and something they called "vigah" up in Boston. The academic community adored JFK and was willing to accept his sincere assurances that the Pope would not inhabit a Kennedy White House. Even my darling agnostic husband, who had very little tolerance for organized religions, became an enthusiastic Kennedy supporter.

The two events of 1960 that dominated our family were the birth of our son David Lawrence in May and the election of JFK in November. My second pregnancy proceeded as smoothly as the first. I felt more confident, partly because I could talk more easily with my American doctor than I'd been able to with my doctor in Istanbul. Again, I watched my diet and kept my weight gain to a total of eighteen pounds throughout the whole nine months, which was considered healthy at that time. In those days every woman I knew smoked cigarettes, though we all knew they were the cause of lung cancer, and that smoking should be reduced during pregnancy, and we all had a few drinks on special occasions. As the due date approached, my husband joked with me that I must try not to go to the hospital until I had finished typing his last term papers, though I could barely get around my bulky belly to reach the typewriter keys. In fact, a minor complication led my doctor to bring me into the hospital on May 25 to induce labor, and David Lawrence arrived at the end of the afternoon, weighing in at a hefty 8 pounds and 4 ounces, a second beautiful boy. Five days in the hospital was the accepted stay, but it seemed much too long a time to be away from my fifteen-month-old Tom, who was not allowed to come into the hospital to visit me.

We adapted to the new baby and to our more crowded living space. Baby Davey and Tom shared a tiny bedroom, and when one awoke for a night feeding or to start the day at 6 AM, his cries awoke the other. Sleep deprivation causes the debilitating exhaustion that leads to mild depression in the first few months of caring for a new baby; I suffered my share of it, but eventually it passed. For most of us the situation improves as our baby gets on a more reasonable feeding schedule and begins to sleep for uninterrupted stretches through the night. The practice of co-parenting, however, which would have given me some relief, was decades away from becoming the expected norm.

My husband never got up to give any of our children a bottle feeding in the middle of the night, never got up early to change their diapers or to give the boys their breakfast so that I could have a little extra sleep. It was simply not to be. No matter how resentful I felt, or how much I appealed to his sense of fairness, I had to accept what was fairly common for the times: separate spheres of responsibility. Our lives were not made grim by this disagreement. Throughout the five decades that we have lived together, we have negotiated responsibilities constantly and come out the better for it, one bending to accommodate the other or vice versa in different situations.

The dynamic political campaign of JFK focused our idealism and taught me something about the ways of upper-middle-class attitudes. David's father, Roy Avery Porter Sr., a prosperous businessman who had been considered for a position as Secretary of Agriculture, was a Republican Party stalwart in New York State. No one in the family, not David's sisters or his brother, would have contemplated voting for a Democrat, and certainly not for a Roman Catholic, especially not Dud and Marge who were devoutly committed to the Episcopal and Presbyterian churches, respectively. My husband's political apostasy was attributed to his being temporarily in the clutches of "those left-wing college professor radical Commies." A revealing incident occurred at the time of the first televised Kennedy-Nixon debate. Shortly after that evening, on a visit to Dave's sister Dud and her husband, the debate came up. My husband said, "Wasn't that terrific, to see the two candidates live, on the stage before the whole country, having to answer questions from the reporters. Kennedy was the absolute winner—better speaker, had more facts at his command, and was more at ease." Dud and Frank looked at him in total confusion. Dud said, "But David, that's not what happened at all. We watched the whole thing. Nixon was absolutely the winner, no question about it." For sister Marge, when the topic came up years later, she flatly stated that she would never vote for a Catholic, period.

On an August day, when we knew that Kennedy would be coming to Rochester on a campaign swing through upstate New York, we stood at the edge of the sidewalk on the road from the airport to cheer this charismatic, handsome devil who sat nonchalantly waving and smiling, high on the backseat of a convertible that drove slowly by. We were so enthralled at the sight of him that each of us actually believed JFK had looked into our eyes. Election night, and the overnight vote count that lasted until mid-morning the next day, bore out our optimistic hope that he would be elected, and he was. Pure joy. A victory for liberalism, good looks, and the elegance of articulate speech—no wonder the Kennedys and their "Camelot" were mythologized around the world. In our naiveté, we thought the loser, Tricky Dick Nixon, had been permanently banished from the political scene, little imagining the circumstances of his triumphal return in eight short years.

The three years in Rochester passed in comparative serenity, each of us working hard at our self-assigned roles. Caring for two small boys involved long hours for me and only brief reprieves. There is no question of David being a loving and committed father, but his involvement with the boys was not as great when they were infants as it became once they began to speak, to walk, to run, to exhibit individual personalities. He established an early camaraderie with the boys in physical activities which would lead them into sports later, as well as in developing their language skills—reading aloud, reciting nursery rhymes, word games of all sorts, and drawing sketches of all manner of mythical figures for the boys' delight. I, too, became involved in play activities with the children that I had never experienced as a child myself. For instance, I took enormous pleasure in reading children's fairy tales with repetitious narratives, the Mother Goose rhymes, the marvelous stories of Beatrix Potter—ideas for these readings and other activities that came from my hours spent with other graduate student wives. We were so proud, my husband and I, that our Tom could recognize all the letters of the alphabet, and name all the forty-eight states on a U.S. map puzzle by the age of two! And his brother Davey achieved the same. The two brothers sparred a little, competed for our attention, and soon became each other's best friend and boon companion.

My husband and I were brought up quite differently, so we had mild disagreements about child discipline, but we were in total agreement about the boys' daily schedule. They were early risers, up by 5:30 or 6:00 AM, so that's when I started my day. David would usually have studied late into the night and would sleep until 7 AM or so. From their earliest days, I encouraged the boys to follow a reasonable schedule: play until noon, nap in the early afternoon, play activities until dinner at 5 PM, and then baths and bedtime story reading, with lights out by 6:30 PM. David and I had our dinner after the boys were tucked in, a time for grown-up conversation at the dinner table, until they reached the age of six and seven, when we gathered for family meals together every night of the week. Those earlier separate meals involved extra work on my part, but the daily schedule was healthy for the boys and it was definitely a pleasure for David and me to have had some moments of quiet alone. I felt justified by no less an authority than Dr. Spock, who advised us that whatever routine we established for our growing children, whether strict or easy going, it was important to be consistent. I was the only one among my siblings who routinely enforced an early bed time for the children, and had to take a lot of family joking about it on our visits to New Jersey, where our nieces and nephews stayed up hours later than Tom and Davey.

The Saga of Ruth's Visit to Rochester

Both Porter and Pedalino families helped us with our expenses in those graduate school years, and we felt not a moment of false pride. From the Porter family we received financial assistance. From my family, whose circumstances were much more humble, we received occasional gifts of clothing or toys for the boys, and packages of groceries and meats from the store on South Day Street. My parents would cut and wrap ten pounds or so of meat, freeze it, and then make up a box, well insulated with layers of newspapers, which would be mailed to us by overnight express, arriving in a still partially frozen state. These packages were the best my family could offer and we celebrated the arrival of each one. This practice resulted in an event that has passed into the realm of family epic.

Ruth, best friend of my youth, made plans to visit us in Rochester for a weekend, stopping in Syracuse on her way home to see her brother, Dr. Amerigo Marucci, at Syracuse University. My mother asked Ruth to carry a package for us and gave her a 20-pound box of frozen meat. Ruth boarded the train at Newark Penn Station in the early morning and placed the package of meat in the overhead rack for the eight-hour journey. A few hours later, a snowstorm began which turned into one of the biggest blizzards of the winter of 1961. The train slowed, stopped for several hours, and then restarted. By the time the train arrived in Rochester, several hours late, the meat had thawed and blood began to drip from above. It was a terrible embarrassment for Ruth, who had to get the conductor's help to wash the blood off the train seat and to find a new wrapping for the package. On arrival in the Rochester train station, it took several attempts to find a taxi, but the snow was so deep that the driver only brought her to the end of our little street, which had not yet been plowed. By now, with Ruth hours overdue, David and I were truly alarmed. Standing anxiously at our front window, looking at the heavy falling snow, we suddenly saw a distraught-looking woman slogging down the middle of the street, dragging her suitcase and carrying a big box, looking at house numbers. It was Ruth! We ran out to bring her into the warmth and shelter of our home. We were hilarious over the story of her trip, which is still a sure-fire laugh getter at family gatherings.

After the birth of our second son so soon after the first, David and I agreed that we needed a better method of birth control than the Catholic-approved "rhythm system." My doctor prescribed a diaphragm and spermicidal jelly, the most effective method in use at the time. We were both content to be raising two boys, marveling at every stage of their development. At the university, David's academic performance was outstanding. He was assigned to teach a class in American literature each semester, which carried an increased stipend, and he derived immense satisfaction from both teaching and participating in graduate seminars. The concentrated study program he had designed allowed him to complete all course work for the doctorate in three years, working right through every summer. The university's public relations office selected David for a cover story in the alumni magazine, an article about a typical graduate student with a family, published with the title "Men of Distinction." Looking back at that magazine story now, we are especially amused at the photo of David at his typewriter, cigarette dangling from his lips. I stand nearby handing him a cup. The caption reads: "Wife Lee gives support and coffee."

One Vacation in Three Years

Our only real vacation in those graduate school years was a summer trip to Cape Cod when Tom was two-and-a-half and Davey just over a year old. With our Robert College friends, David and Mary Alice Sipfle, who would be coming from Minnesota, we each rented a very modest cottage for a week together in Harwichport. We brought along our high-school-age baby sitter, Suzanne Heckman, to help with the children, allowing us adults an evening or two out, and giving her a chance to see the Cape. It was an enjoyable week at the seashore, and an incident occurred that belongs at the very top of the "it's a small world" category of anecdotes.

On our first day in Harwichport we drove to one of the beaches, unpacked children, toys, blankets, and umbrellas, then climbed over a dune to spread our equipment on the sand. We settled in our beach chairs to watch the children at play and to scan the Atlantic horizon. Soon, we all took note of a man who was walking along the water's edge because he was dressed in a suit, shirt and tie, polished shoes, and a straw hat—unusual for the beach. As he came closer, my husband said, "It can't be possible, but that guy looks like Herbie Lane, the bursar at Robert College." We continued to stare and decided that it *was* Herbie. My husband called out to him, and he walked over to chat with us. What a coincidence that three former residents of Istanbul, Turkey, would chance to meet on a Cape Cod beach. We learned that Herbie's family owned this section of the beach and he liked to stroll along to see how it was being enjoyed by the public. It was a wholly unexpected event that gave our vacation an extra little thrill. A few years later, Herbie and his Russian wife, Sophie, died on an airliner that was blown up by terrorists over Yugoslavia.

David Chooses the University of Massachusetts
Our last year in Rochester brought David the anxieties of deciding on a doctoral dissertation topic, finding a teaching position for the fall of 1962, and organizing our move to a new place. Professor William Gilman of Princeton University hired David as a research assistant during the summer to help with a book on Ralph Waldo Emerson. Gilman later guided my husband to decide on the poetry of Emily Dickinson as the subject of his doctoral dissertation. Universities across the country were expanding, enrolling more students and creating more teaching positions, a boom time for job seekers in the humanities. My husband and a half dozen of his friends sent off letters of inquiry to various universities and traveled to the late December meeting of the Modern Language Association in Chicago for three days of interviews with prospective employers. This annual meeting of the professional association for the literary fields is sometimes snidely referred to as "The Meat Market," the marathon interview sessions for recruiters and applicants. Typically, graduate students received several job offers for tenure-track teaching positions, and would have the luxury of choosing a school offering the highest salary, the greatest prestige, the best location, or some combination of the three.

After a round of letters and negotiations during the early months of 1962, David accepted the position of Assistant Professor in the English Department at the University of Massachusetts in Amherst. We began to shift gears, mentally, from the informal, shabby gentility of graduate student life, to assuming the identity of real grownups, with a fully employed head of household earning a reasonable income at an annual salary of $6,400. A weekend trip to Amherst to meet the English Department head and look at a house to rent gave us an opportunity to view the college town where we would make our home.

I was particularly pleased at the thought of living in a New England town near Boston and New York City, and closer to my Pedalino relatives in New Jersey.

Leaving Rochester would be no great hardship; the city had never really enchanted either one of us, although we regretted moving farther away from the Porter side of the family. I felt loved and respected by my husband's family and had grown genuinely fond of all of them, especially my mother-in-law. As I became better acquaintance with Bertha Porter, I came to appreciate her intelligence and good humor and to admire her fortitude in surviving two failed marriages yet devoting herself to the four children she raised largely on her own. She once said to me, apropos of the two husbands who disappointed her, "They should put on my tombstone, 'She Tried.'" Many years later, in recounting this anecdote to my husband, I added, "And on my tombstone it should say, 'She Tried Too Hard.'"

CHAPTER 7
David Thomas Porter, Ascendant

The decade of David, of his rapid rise in the world of academia, and of our family's overseas adventures, began on an auspicious note, once we secured the lease of a fully furnished house with an acre and a half of lawn and woods just one mile from the center of town and barely two miles from the university. We stored what meager furniture we owned at the Porter home in Elba, and managed to buy a Ford station wagon with help from Dave's interest in the family farm. On the first Saturday in July, my husband drove off in the little old German car and I started out in the carefully packed station wagon with three-year-old Tom and two-year-old Davey. Our babysitter, Suzanne Heckman, came along to help me along the way and spend a few days with us seeing a bit of Massachusetts. It was a grueling trip, with stops every few hours to use the bathroom and to give me a break from having to concentrate so hard on the New York State Thruway. David had arrived at the house in six hours; my trip took four hours longer. What a relief for all of us when I finally pulled up the long driveway to be greeted by my husband, who had been sitting on the front steps anxiously watching the road for hours!

Our first experience with the niceties of small-town life occurred immediately. We were dismayed to discover that neither one of us had taken out extra cash from the bank to see us through the three-day July 4th holiday weekend. In the days before ATMs, cash withdrawals had to be inside banks during the short "bankers' hours." Girding ourselves for probable disappointment, we drove into town where Dave walked into Russell's Liquor Store and explained our plight to the owner, asking if he would cash a small check for us. Old Bill Russell, seasoned in the ways of faculty types by his decades of doing business in Amherst, genially offered to cash a fifty-dollar check for us, all the help we needed. His trust was not misplaced as we are still loyal customers, forty-five years later.

An invitation to a party honoring the retiring chairman of the English Department, Max Goldberg, introduced us to Dave's new colleagues and their wives. Cocktails and dinner at the home of Professor Joseph Langland brought together most of the department members who were currently in town and us few new arrivals. We discovered a lively group, including Dick and Jo Haven, just back from a sabbatical year in India, and Anita and Alex Page, returning from a year in Pakistan. There were good-humored speeches and a modern dance executed on the lawn, by a member of the Drama Department, to Bach's "Goldberg Variations." We seemed to have landed in a bower of high culture.

English Department morale was high with the growth in student enrollments; that meant many new faculty positions as the university rapidly expanded from 8,000 to 25,000 students in a dozen years. Four semesters of English courses were required for all students. Staffing these courses created openings for half a dozen or more new hires every year. As with our earlier experience at Robert College, we arrived at a more or less placid era in American campus life. We had emerged from the dreadful Communist witch hunts of the McCarthy era, the Korean War, and the disastrous Bay of Pigs invasion of Cuba by the

Kennedy administration, but we were not prescient—no one imagined the societal upheavals, assassinations, war, and urban violence ahead. College-town social life in our first few years in Amherst centered on genteel dinner parties, the interests of traditional couples with young children, and the imperative for our husbands to produce published works as well as teach their classes. With his typical wit, my husband fantasized a cartoon he would draw for *The New Yorker*: two tweedy young, pipe-smoking professors in front of a campus building, one saying to the other, "In academia, 'cosa nostra' is Publish or Perish." David was fully occupied with fulltime teaching and writing his doctoral dissertation, a critical study of the poems of Emily Dickinson. But his time was not nearly as burdened as it had been when he was in graduate school. Often he came home early enough to play with the boys in the backyard or the nearby park, and part of the weekend was free for family activities.

I inquired at the university admissions office about the possibility of taking a few courses for college credit, as an undergraduate degree candidate, resuming the college work I had begun a decade earlier. I was quickly accepted, probably given consideration as a faculty wife. In September we enrolled Tom in Mr. and Mrs. Grose's private nursery school for three- and four-year-olds, five mornings a week. "Baba Grose" was a retired math teacher and his wife had taught music and art—they were ideal grandparent types. For our Davey, we found Mrs. Lovell, a kindly local matron, to come and care for him three mornings a week while I went to my classes at the university: "Masterpieces of Western Literature" and "Spanish Literature of the Golden Age." These arrangements freed me to be on campus three mornings a week for classes and library research. After giving the two boys lunch, they napped for a couple of hours, allowing me time to study. Perhaps the most enjoyable event of our first fall in Amherst was the English Department Picnic, an annual outing at the Quabbin Reservoir on the second weekend in October when the leaf colors were at their peak. (*New York Times* Columnist Russell Baker once remarked about New England leaf colors, "Hey, you see a million leaves, you've seen 'em all.") The picnic with English Department families was such a happy occasion for our sons that, many years later while Dave and I were out of the country and Tom and Dave were college students home for the weekend, they went to the English Department Picnic on their own.

But the most frightening event in that fall of 1962 was the Cuban missile crisis and the threat of nuclear disaster, which had a personal aspect for us. On first moving to Amherst, we had felt relatively safe from Cold War terrors in this area of the Connecticut River valley. Soon we learned that under the rolling hills not five miles south of our house, was a military facility buried three stories under the "notch" in the Holyoke Range, one of the control centers for the Strategic Air Command bombers that were in the air around the globe at all times, loaded with "nukes." Those October days, while Russian freighters seemingly loaded with long-range missiles steamed towards Havana, were times of terrible anxiety. Waking one night to the sound of a low-flying plane, we both sat up in bed fearing an attack. We felt vulnerable, as a primary target, should a nuclear war begin. Blessedly, that did not come to pass and we soon calmed back down to normality.

Getting back to school again, especially the two-semester survey course of readings from the Greeks to the mid-twentieth century, satisfied my craving for works unfamiliar to me, especially the plays of Sophocles and Euripides, the English and Italian writers of the Renaissance period, and the incomparable Dante Alighieri. Discovering the timeless beauty of *La Divina Comedia* elevated my spirits, not only for the genius of the structure and language of the work but because it was of my own heritage. But I derived the greatest pleasure from Professor Irving Rothberg's Spanish literature class where he lectured in Spanish (of course!), and all classroom discussions were in Spanish as well as term papers, rigorous standards I met. The academic year ended on a high note for both of us, I with high grades, and David with high approval for his teaching and for successfully completing his doctoral dissertation. David traveled to the University of Rochester as Mr. Porter to sit for the oral defense of his dissertation, and returned as Dr. David T. Porter, earned Ph.D.

Discovering Nantucket Island

To celebrate the new "doctor," we inquired among friends about some interesting Massachusetts place for a week's vacation. Wally and Ann Silva, a young student couple from Nantucket Island, gave us a lead to a rental cottage at a very low rate in the off season. With our two sons, we sailed to the island that would open a new world for the entire Porter extended family. The weather on the little island thirty miles off the coast of Cape Cod was uniformly cold and rainy most of that week. We bought yellow slickers for all of us and huddled on the beach in the fog and drizzle; we bought firewood and built warming fires in the little cottage where we sat reading while the boys played board games; and we explored the island from end to end. On the one evening that we secured a babysitter and went to the famous Opera House Restaurant for drinks and dinner, we fell totally under the spell of island glamour. Peter Benchley sat in one corner, and a few other arty types were scattered among the diners. On the last day, as we walked up the gangplank of the ferry boat to sail back to the mainland, the sun finally appeared, illuminating a dazzling view of town and harbor. We succumbed to the island's magic.

Working and Studying

Our second year in Amherst we rented a different house for the year, from another family going on sabbatical leave. It was too soon to buy property since David's position at the university was on a renewable one-year contract. Both Tom and Davey were now in nursery school every morning of the week. That fall semester of 1963, I enrolled in a graduate course in twentieth- century Spanish literature at Smith College through the Four-College Association, which allowed students at Amherst, Mount Holyoke, and Smith colleges, as well as the University of Massachusetts to take courses at any of the institutions. We were only eight students in this graduate seminar that covered a wide variety of readings in the early twentieth-century literature of Spain and Spanish America, and carried a heavy load of critical writing for classroom discussions.

David's career at the university looked brighter, with the prospect for a promotion and tenure measurably enhanced by the doctorate and his first few published articles. At the time, tenure decisions were generally made after six years of teaching, a long enough period to fairly evaluate a faculty member's teaching and the quality of his research and publications. But for veterans who had served in the military, a tenure decision could be made after only three years. Tenure is the ultimate academic perk: Institutions of higher education confer tenure on selected faculty, which guarantees that the person can remain on the faculty until retirement. This lifetime job protection can only be withdrawn for serious cause, and assures that no one can be fired for political reasons or one's speech content. Hence, it is the guarantor of academic freedom. Since highly qualified professors earn far less than their peers in business or other professions, tenure, along with the short academic year (twenty-eight weeks) and a sabbatical leave every seven years, are among the important factors that attract young people. I must add, however, that the seemingly short teaching schedule, long vacation, and sabbatical leaves are not leisure time but the essential periods an academic must devote to scholarly research and writing, and my husband made maximum use of that time, working long hours all year round.

David's heavy investment in concentrated scholarship produced its first reward when his dissertation was accepted for publication by Harvard University Press in the spring of 1964. David's star shone brighter now among his colleagues on the English Department faculty. With a greater sense of optimism that we might indeed become permanent residents of the town, we began to consider purchasing a house just as we learned that our first Amherst rental house was now on the market. It was an easy decision to make an offer on a house we knew so well, and to return to 106 West Street. We had found the neighbors congenial, especially the Campbells next door whose children were our boys' playmates.

Buying our first house required a down payment, and we had not yet accumulated any savings. Dave's brother Roy agreed to buy out my husband's share in the family farm for a very reasonable $30,000. This was a tremendous windfall for us and the first use we made of it was to put a $6,000 down-payment on the Amherst house, which was listed at $20,500, and put the rest into savings. It was the first time in our seven years of marriage that we felt financially secure. Still, now that we had committed to a monthly mortgage payment of $150, we agreed that I would put my studies aside and find part-time work to help with our expenses for a year or two. With my background in secretarial work, experience in advertising and public relations, and fluency in three languages, I hoped to find something at the university.

The ideal position was offered to me at the end of the year—advertising and public relations manager at *The Massachusetts Review*, a scholarly magazine of art, literature, and social issues published on the university campus. This grandiose-sounding job paid only twenty-five-dollars a week but offered great benefits. I worked three mornings a week while my sons were in school; I would be paid for six weeks' vacation in the summer, and there would be liberal time off for family illnesses or emergencies. Certainly the opportunity to work with editors and be in contact with writers and artists was very appealing. *The Mass Review* (MR) was in its fifth year of publication and already enjoyed a high reputation for the quality of its art reproductions, poetry, fiction, and critical essays. *The Mass Review* job would stretch into an eight-year association for me. When I left to resume my undergraduate studies in 1972, my salary was sixty dollars a week.

Sister Fran Marries

In April of 1964 my sister Frances married her high school sweetheart, Jerry Della Salla, a construction worker who had grown up in our neighborhood in Orange. We had met Jerry only once when he and my sister came to Amherst for an overnight visit with us, a liberty I was amazed my father would allow. We liked our prospective brother-in-law on first acquaintance, noting his intelligence and earthy humor. They were both young, Fran nineteen and Jerry twenty, both hewing to the traditional Italo-American pattern of working and saving money to buy the furnishings for their first apartment. (How quaint this must seem to young people in our postfeminist era—that young "dating" couples would not cohabit, would probably not begin engaging in sexual intercourse until just before or immediately after their wedding vows, that they would *first* pool their savings to set up a home and *then* begin to live together and bear children! Well, we feminists certainly changed all that.)

Their wedding was a formal affair, paid for by my parents, with all the gifts of money going to the young couple. The typical wedding gift in Italo-American circles, then as now, is not silverware or china but an envelope containing cash, *la busta*. Each guest tucked the envelope into a white satin drawstring bag kept beside the bride's chair as they came to congratulate the couple. My Anglo-Saxon relatives and friends considered this vulgar, but I privately thought it was a great way to help working-class couples starting married life.

David and I attended the ceremony and the reception at the Crystal Lake Casino in West Orange, though we were not included in the bridal party. I did not dwell on it with my husband at that time, but I was very disappointed that I could not be matron-of-honor for my sister because I was not a practicing Catholic at that time. It was only one of such disappointments: I could not be a godmother at the Christening of any of my nieces or nephews, or serve as sponsor at their Confirmation ceremonies. To their credit, my parents never asked about my religious observances, never expressed dismay that we had not had our sons baptized and were raising them outside of any established religion. They understood David to be an ethical, moral person and chose not to dwell on why we did not follow the family religion. I believe my parents treated us differently from my brothers and sister, to whom they gave frequent and vocal advice, because they were somewhat in awe of my husband, the professor.

Decade of Upheavals
The 1960s (oh that decade!) with its social, political, and international upheavals, wrought enormous changes that filled our lives with equal

parts of excitement and anxiety. My brothers and sister and I experienced the sixties as a time for creating and shaping our next immigrant generation—having had the benefit of recently living through an economically viable ambience, an atmosphere of optimism, one that reinforced our belief that our hard work would inevitably result in upward social mobility. But my path diverged from theirs, given my place in academia. David and I participated in the *social* movements around us: civil rights demonstrations, anti-Vietnam War protests, the sexual revolution brought on by Dr. Rock's birth control pill, and the women's liberation movement. Coming in the wake of the assassination of JFK, the moment of ultimate tragedy for my generation—and yes, for the generation who witnessed it just short of their own coming of age—on the murders of Martin Luther King Jr. and Bobby Kennedy, and on urban riots and unprecedented campus violence, I can well understand why this period has been over analyzed and romanticized beyond all other decades of the twentieth century.

We who inhabit academia pride ourselves on being the most progressive thinkers in the nation, dragging the rest of the country after us to accept what we know to be beneficial for everyone. I'm not attempting to write a social history of the period here, but an account of how it played out in Amherst paints a fairly representative picture of a progressive college community. Faculty and students, as well as town representatives, gave unanimous support for the civil rights movement. But opposition to the Vietnam War was so intense and consistent that Amherst held the longest weekly vigil in the nation, eight years of silent Sunday demonstrations on the town common.

We also saw how corrupt the well-intentioned movements could become when they radicalized, when the sincerity of equal rights for African Americans and peaceful public outcries against war converted into intolerant, violent, and destructive actions—the idiocy of the "Free Speech" movement of Mario Savio at Berkeley promoting obscenities; the negation of free speech on campus if it was not antiwar. When Vice President Hubert Humphrey, while running for the presidency in 1968, came to speak at our university, he was booed out of the hall. There was no tolerance for unpopular viewpoints, and we witnessed total abdication of responsibility by college administrators when students who destroyed property, including professors' teaching materials, disrupted or shut down classes. Can any reasonable person justify the destruction of research notes and papers belonging to a professor of literature as an action to "stop the war?"

Retired Amherst College professor Leo Marx, speaking about the period years later, lauded the actions of students in the 1960s and judged them to be "the greatest generation the world has ever seen." Superlatives for that decade have never been in short supply, always linked to the demeaning of the 1950s. I became fed up with the posturing and self-importance of nineteen-year-old males who were exempted from the military draft as students and then, hiding behind the safety of their deferments, presumed to judge draftees— believing that they themselves were "making the revolution" when they protested or demonstrated. As one of my husband's colleagues in the English Department responded when I asked him if he was going to a scheduled "sit-in" on the war, "Not me, I stopped masturbating a long time ago."

In spite of my disillusionment with some of the campus scenes, I was engaged in antiwar activities during the entire period of the American presence in Vietnam. Nothing I've learned since that time has changed my belief that it was wrong from the time JFK sent 16,000 "advisors" and allowed the overthrow of the South Vietnamese government, to the trumped-up Tonkin Gulf Resolution of the U.S. Congress and LBJ's escalation of the war, to Nixon and Kissinger's feints at diplomacy, all this ending in the final horror of the last Americans leaving by helicopter from the roof of the U.S. Embassy in Saigon.

A few of us Amherst women began our protest by writing letters to our congressmen and to President Johnson; then we went on to collect signatures on petitions, to hold signs on street corners, to read the counterculture press (*I. F. Stone's Weekly*, for example), and attend lectures. I joined a local demonstration, sitting in the road blocking the entrance to Westover Air Force Base in Chicopee Falls to protest the renewed bombing of North Vietnam. When we were ordered to move, I sat with the others until we were taken to jail. After a few hours we were released. The officials charged us with disturbing the peace, admonished us not to repeat the offense, and told us that if we complied our arrests for the civil disobedience would not be officially recorded. The peaceful demonstrations went on for so many weeks that the court in Chicopee Falls could not bring us all to trial. I went to Washington on an overnight bus ride in 1972 to march with the thousands of protesters at the Lincoln Memorial. And I was able to do this in large part because of my husband's willingness to take care of the children in my absence. As the boys and our marriage grew, David became more and more supportive of my need to branch out on my own, both personally and professionally.

One serious concern in our family was for my brother Frank Jr., who on graduating from high school in 1964 was accepted as a scholarship student at Rider College. Frank was the first and only one of us five siblings fortunate enough to go directly from high school to college. Somehow my parents were scraping together enough to pay his expenses. But Frank was not a serious student, and he flunked out by the end of his freshman year. He was now subject to the draft. Frank tried, with the help of his brothers, to enroll in another college, but by the fall of 1966 he was serving in the U.S. Army. In a piece of good fortune, Frank was shipped to West Germany after completing his training as a Military Policeman. My parents' fears were laid to rest as the posting to Europe was considered a relatively safe place to serve one's military duty.

The social upheavals that preoccupied us at that time did not keep us, personally, from making our family life and the experiences of our growing children our focus, one ultimately more fulfilling than imbibing the rarified Amherst air. In the fall of 1965, after several more short vacations on Nantucket Island, we searched for an affordable house that would become our summer residence, some sort of "handyman special." There were several good reasons for this investment: David's teaching schedule ran from September to the end of May, so he could do his scholarly writing there in the summer; we had begun to find interesting friends on the island; and property was very modestly priced. After looking at several houses that were listed at $7,000 to $12,000, we made an offer of $10,500 on a house in the center of town. This antique, built by a seaman on a whaling ship in 1833 for $600, is a classic Nantucket "half-house" with five fireplaces (no central heating), on a very small lot, gray-shingled in the manner of all homes on the island, and needing a tremendous amount of work to make it habitable. We took title in October 1965 with plans to move in the following June.

An Unplanned Event

"The best laid plans of mice and men, aft gangly aglee," said the Scottish poet Robert Burns. My husband applied for a one-year lectureship abroad under the Fulbright program, a government-sponsored exchange of scholars and students initiated by Senator J. William Fulbright of Arkansas. David had expressed a preference for Italy. Tom and Davey were now old enough to travel easily with us and to benefit from the experience of not just visiting but living in another country. Harvard University Press announced it would publish David's *The Art of Emily Dickinson's Early Poetry* in the spring of 1966. Should he be selected for the overseas lecturing opportunity, the 1966–67 academic year would be a convenient time to go, since our sons would be in the early primary grades.

Tom was so advanced in reading and arithmetic in his first grade classroom that in mid-year his teacher recommended that he be moved up to the second grade; she considered him capable of completing the two grades in one year. After serious consideration, we approved. Tom's teacher advised us, "Don't make a big fuss over it with Tom. I'll tell him we're moving him to a different class to see how he likes it. Just treat it casually at home." Indeed, we worked so hard at being casual about this proud moment that Tom said to us years later, "I came home to tell you and Dad that I had moved to the second grade and you both said, 'Oh, that's nice.' And you changed the subject. You never wanted to talk about it and I thought that was really weird."

On the afternoon of December 31, 1965, I went to my doctor's office to learn the results of a pregnancy test I had taken a week earlier. The result was positive. Clearly, we had been careless with our birth control practices and my doctor estimated that my baby would arrive in August. That was an unplanned-for announcement with which to greet the new year. We'd thought we had the perfect, two-child family, but we immediately adjusted our thinking and decided we could well adapt to the new addition. But deep down I knew that my desire to return to my college studies would have to be set back another five years. And then, in mid-January, my husband received notice that he'd been awarded a Fulbright Lectureship for the following academic year at the University of Catania, on the east coast of Sicily.

On an evening that neither of us will ever forget, as we stood together in our kitchen with a drink in hand, to celebrate the good news, David said to me, "We're going to have to decide what to do. Too many things are coming together at the same time. We've just bought a summer house to fix up, we're going to have a baby next summer, and we have a chance to live in Italy next fall. How many of these things can we really do?" I thought very carefully, and then answered, "We can do it all." And so we did, undaunted by the logistics of it all, heady with optimism that all would work out well.

Steve Arrives on Nantucket Island

Since we'd planned to be on the island for the whole summer, we decided to find a doctor on Nantucket Island and have the baby delivered there, rather than returning to Amherst near my August due-date. We took up residence on the island in early June and began the heavy physical labor of making this sturdy but neglected house into a livable place. David and I did all the work—cleaning, repairing, buying used furniture from the thrift shops, and bringing in hand-me-downs contributed by my family. We found a high school student, a "mother's helper," to live with us for the entire summer; she would care of the boys mornings and evenings, leaving her afternoons free to go to the beach with her friends. My health did not suffer from the work, which included doing laundry in an ancient washing machine and carrying heavy loads up to the second floor to hang the pieces on a clothesline that extended from the window to a tree with an old-fashioned pulley arrangement. Our budget was so tight that we did not even install a telephone that summer but took periodic walks downtown to use the public pay phone. We were momentarily panicked when my doctor announced that based on X-ray pictures we might have twins, but on later scrutiny he decided that would not be the case.

Although we had talked with Tom and Davey often about the coming of a new baby brother or sister, they were both in tears when I had to leave for the hospital on Monday afternoon, August 8. This time I felt much better informed, having taken a series of classes in the Lamaze method and had learned to do deep breathing to relax and control the labor pains. David was allowed to sit with me for a few hours, reading to me from *The New Yorker*. But the medical establishment had not yet progressed to the point of allowing the husband to be in the delivery room or to take photos or film the birth, practices that would become commonplace in later years. The birth was uncomplicated and shortly after midnight loud cries were heard as the doctor held up our healthy 8 pound, 4 ounce baby boy. The tiny Nantucket Cottage Hospital hosted only one mother and baby the whole five days I was there. If I heard a baby's cry in the night I knew it was our Steve.

Each day I was allowed to order lunch for myself and for my husband, and he was encouraged by the nurses to bring a carafe of wine for us to share, a novel and civilized practice. Our resident babysitter cared for the two boys when David came to the hospital, since they were not permitted to come to my room. I absolutely luxuriated in the five days of rest and had sufficient time and good professional advice to help initiate breastfeeding successfully. It seemed to both of us that with all the travel ahead, and setting up a home in another country, it would be beneficial to the baby and more efficient for all of us if he were breast fed and not reliant on my sterilizing bottles and finding safe drinking water for mixing with powdered formula.

A Year in Catania

The year in Sicily would be one of the most rewarding times for our young family, but it took enormous energy, organization, and mutual cooperation, as well as adjustments in family dynamics, to bring it about. Tom and Dave started school in September on Nantucket, to fill their time until we would leave for Sicily in early October. Dave was so unhappy in this temporary school that he complained of a stomachache every morning, pleading to stay at home. I sensed that the boys felt too much of my attention was being given to their baby brother. My husband had all the burdens of traveling back and forth to Amherst to get that house ready for renters and to gather his academic materials for the coming year. He also felt somewhat ignored. I was coping with the extreme exhaustion brought on by lack of sleep, making preparations to close the Nantucket house for a year, pack for the ocean voyage and for the year in Sicily, make travel arrangements, and get new passports. By the time we sailed for Europe, David and I were barely on speaking terms from the stresses of the recent months.

In the midst of all the angst of September, my mother called to say that she was so eager to see our new baby that she would come to Nantucket for a few days. She would be flying from Newark to Boston and then to the island. We were very happy to hear of her visit, but worried about her traveling alone. On her one other trip to visit us in Rochester she failed to hear the announcement of her connecting flight and ended up in Buffalo, where she was eventually put on a flight to her correct destination. Lucy's presence was such a lovely interlude, though, distracting us all with the pleasure of her company. The visit with us, and the exploration of the island, lifted her spirits also. She and my father had just seen my brother Frank Jr. off to Germany and had spent long hours at the hospital on two occasions in recent weeks, for the birth of grandchildren.

Lucy brought us a piece of family news that, late for me by twenty years, was an instant delight. The family store and apartment on South Day Street had been taken by eminent domain as it stood in the path of a new state highway to be constructed. Hallelujah!! This superhighway had been talked of for years. How I'd eagerly longed for our family to move to an acceptable house. How I suffered the shame of living "in back of the store" through my high school years and beyond, knowing what a poor impression it made on all but the hardiest and most determined young men. Now, at last, my parents had received a fair market price for the property and Lucy, on her own, had found and contracted to buy a house in the nearby suburb of Livingston, New Jersey. On our return from Sicily, we would visit my parents in a real home and not the hated South Day Street neighborhood.

Finally, our departure day arrived. On October 7, having shipped our heavy baggage in steamer trunks earlier, we locked the door on 59 Fair Street, bade our neighbors goodbye, and boarded a small plane for the flight to Boston. The next day we went aboard the SS *Cristoforo Colombo* of the Italian Lines for the eight-day voyage to Messina, Sicily. On being shown to our connecting cabins we discovered that the description had been somewhat misleading. The two third-class cabins, each with steel bunk beds, were so tiny that the baby carriage would not fit and our baby would have to sleep in the corridor. This, of course, would not do. David immediately went to the Purser's Office and arranged for us to move up to Cabin Class (second class), to a large cabin with two sets of bunk beds, a private bathroom, and ample space for baby Steve's carriage—his home. The upgrade was money well spent. It gave us additional services that made our voyage with a seven-year-old, a six-year-old and an eight-week-old not only comfortable but enjoyable. Some of our friends and relatives thought we were reckless to be embarking on such a trip with small children at all.

The Italian Lines was noted for good service and fine cuisine. We brought our boys to the dining room for breakfast and lunch. Tom and Davey spent part of each day in the children's playroom where two attendants supervised their activities. The boys were also included in the special children's dinner each evening, allowing their parents to dress up for cocktail hour and dine with other adults. Our baby was tucked in for the night and the cabin steward looked in on him every half hour. During the day, the mild weather allowed us all to spend time on deck, in the swimming pool, or engaged in some of the deck games. The week turned out to be carefree and restful. On docking in Malaga and then in Naples, we took Tom and Davey ashore for short sightseeing trips while a nursemaid cared for baby Steve on the ship. The boys were especially excited about seeing Mt. Vesuvius, their first volcano, and visiting the ruins of Pompeii.

Our arrival in Sicily, after such a pleasant interval at sea, was a serious disappointment. David and I are natural optimists. We had assumed that, having traveled widely and having mastered the rigors of life in the Middle East, we could confidently handle the details of moving to a European country, especially since I am fluent in the language of that country. Our naiveté was in not understanding that every new situation presents new sets of problems and not the same ones that had already been met—and resolved—elsewhere. From the docks in Messina, once through customs, we took a taxi to the railroad station, following a horse and wagon with our trunks and suitcases piled on it, moving slowly through city traffic. At the station, the taxi driver strongly urged us not to board the train but to hire him to drive us the 150 miles to Catania. When I said no, he became abusive. Our baggage was piled on the station platform, waiting to be loaded on the train. The taxi driver screamed at us, "They don't know how to handle these trunks. Look, they'll break open," he said as he viciously kicked at the locks. We were horrified. My husband threatened him in English while I shouted in Italian to leave us alone or we would call the police. Our two boys were alarmed and baby Steve began to cry. What a poor start. This was not much of a "*Benvenuti in Sicilia!*"

The train ride along the coast under a heavy rain, past high mountains covered with cactus plants, with an occasional ruined country house, made me think of all the Italian film comedies, like *Divorce, Italian Style,* set in just such scenery. For the sake of our boys we were cheerful, and they were such good sports, implicitly trusting their parents, a trust that was sorely tried in the next few weeks. On arriving in Catania, the hotel where we expected to stay appeared to have no record of our reservation. The desk clerk found us rooms elsewhere. We were settled by mid-afternoon, anticipating an early dinner and early bedtime for all of us. How could we have forgotten that no such thing as an American-style, early dinner can be had in Europe? At seven-thirty the hotel restaurant would open. I left the family and walked to the nearest grocery store to look for crackers, peanut butter, and jelly for snacks. The closest thing I found to peanut butter was a jar of Nutella, ground hazel nuts and chocolate, which sounded great to me but was turned down flat by our boys. For the next two weeks at the Gran Hotel Costa on Via Etnea, named for Mt. Etna, which stood immediately in our view at the top of the avenue, we adapted to Sicilian hours for meals, as we went about the business of looking for a house, a car, and a school for our two sons.

In the short space of two weeks we were directed to the Labor Exchange, where we met and hired Maria Stanganella, a country woman seeking her first job as a nanny/housekeeper; we bought a used VW; we found a spacious apartment in the nearby seaside village of Acicastello; and we found a school for Tom and Davey. Maria was the lynchpin, the essential support person who cared for baby Steve each day in the hotel while we took the older boys with us on all the errands. As soon as we met Maria and interviewed her, we were both impressed by her quiet, unassuming manner and obvious intelligence.

After looking at a number of apartments in and out of the city, we chose the place in Acicastello, a three-apartment complex set in the middle of lemon groves on a hillside overlooking the Mediterranean, with an outdoor play area for the children and a village at the foot of the hill within an easy walk. The owner, Signora Calabretta, a shrewd business woman, had previously rented the apartment unfurnished, and was reluctant to assume the responsibility of furnishing it for us. However, she was open to negotiations and, though this may sound stereotypical of Italians, I believe the sight of baby Steve and his brothers cinched the deal for us. *La famiglia* matters.

School for the boys presented the most urgent challenge. I had given them short lessons in Italian during the summer, with Italian picture books, and David and I had planned to put them in the nearest Italian school for our eight-month stay, expecting that they would learn Italian quickly in this "total immersion" situation. While we were house hunting, we hired a tutor to give the boys lessons in the basic vocabulary they would need to start school. It was a disappointment; the tutor had the boys spend the hour copying one word at a time, "mela" for example, in a lined notebook. Rather than teaching basic phrases and vocabulary, she spent all her time correcting their handwriting which, of course, was different from the cursive taught in Italy. No, no, this was not at all what we wanted. We cancelled the tutorials.

Next we visited the Acicastello village school, talked with the principal and observed a class. We learned that classes were held from 8:30 AM to 1:00 PM six days a week, with a short break for snacks in mid-morning. It appeared that much of the instruction was in rote learning exercises, copying sentences or math problems from the board, with choral recitations by the whole class. It hardly seemed to engage the students. Knowing that the boys would miss much of the content, we the parents would have to obtain books from America and tutor the boys every afternoon so they would not be behind in their subjects when we returned home.

We made a hard decision to go against our original plans. We found an American school at the U.S. Naval Base at Sigonella, about a forty-five-minute drive from our village. On entering the base to visit the school, we found ourselves in a replica of an American suburban town, with an elementary school that looked exactly like the one in Amherst. Tom and Dave met the first- and third-grade teachers who gave them a warm welcome, and we discussed their enrollment with the principal. Bus service was provided, since most of the students were the children of American families living off the base. The yearly tuition of six hundred dollars per child would have been prohibitive for us, but when David appealed to the Fulbright Commission in Rome they approved a grant to cover it. Twenty years later, the Sigonella base was in the international news as the place where they imprisoned the Arab terrorists who murdered Leon Klinghoffer when the Italian cruise ship *Achille Lauro* was hijacked.

On the day we settled our boys in school, the last big hurdle, we stopped for lunch at a seaside restaurant and somehow, in some indefinable way, we began to really talk to each other, the stresses of the past several months melting away. David would be teaching American literature at the University of Catania a few days a week, Maria proved supremely competent at caring for Steve and maintaining our household, and we two would have many opportunities to go sightseeing together. Unexpected holidays from teaching occurred frequently—*sciopero* was the operative word—a strike of the train, bus, or taxi drivers, post office workers, university cleaning staff—any of these brief interruptions caused classes to be cancelled. Then there were the many scheduled holidays for saints' feast days, commemorations of famous battles or wars, and the local, provincial, or national elections. Truth to tell, David's teaching duties were very light.

I had the luxury of reading and spending blissful hours with baby Steve. I was free to go shopping in the city, once I mastered shifting the gears of the standard transmission on our VW, and to join the American Friendship Club, which brought together American women and women of Catania in meetings, social events and charitable activities. Since Maria worked six days a week, every Saturday we left Stevie with her and took the older boys on day trips to explore the wonders of Taormina, Siracusa, Piazza Armerina—lovely jaunts that always included a mid-day meal in restaurants where the boys practiced their Italian by deciphering the menu and ordering for themselves.

They adapted very easily to their new school and made friends. Tom even joined a Cub Scout group in his class, though it was very rare that they could play with school friends since they all lived so far apart and had long commutes by bus. At 7:15 every morning, David took the boys to the Agip Motel coffee bar where the school bus would pick them up for the forty-five-minute ride to school. David and I would go to the Agip together at 4 PM for a cappuccino and to pick up the boys on their return. Their daily routine left only a few hours for outdoor play before dinner and an early bedtime. David, with our landlord's consent, commissioned the local ironmonger to build a set of swings and install them in our backyard, with a long sliding pole for shimmying down. We began an evening activity that proved quite satisfactory to all: teaching the boys how to play a challenging card game. First they had to be bathed and in pajamas to take part in "The Clean Hands Bridge Club." These two lads of six and seven proved themselves capable and soon picked up a pastime that is still a part of every family gathering.

Not all our family entertainments caught their fancies. We bought a subscription to the nine-performance opera season; each boy was given the chance to attend an opera with us. We thought the splendor of the Opera House, the guards standing stiffly in Napoleonic uniforms, the opulent staging of such dramatic works as *Aida* and *Madama Butterfly* would pique their interest. Alas, we were mistaken. The only thing that kept each boy passively in his seat was the promise of pizza after the show. Much as they were unhappy being left at home with Maria on those opera evenings, nothing induced them to return for another performance.

We had very little social life. It was simply not a part of the academic culture of the University of Catania, whose professors did not form a social community in the manner of American university faculty. We made a few good friends, however, in John Lindsay Opie, an American lecturer, and in Philip and Irene Leonardi from Connecticut. Philip was the other Fulbright lecturer assigned to Catania to teach at the local lycée. The Leonardis arrived with three small children, taking an apartment in downtown Catania. It turned out to be a fourth-floor walk-up, a daunting situation, but they coped very well. Irene and I became fast friends, and our two families often gathered together for a midday dinner along the sea, inexpensive excursions due to the strong dollar/lire exchange rate. Irene and I collaborated on the production of a cookbook for the American Friendship Club, a collection of international recipes contributed by the club members: *Collezione Culinaria Sotto L'Ombra del Etna.* Editing, proof-reading, and nursing the little book through to completion gave me my first taste of the joys of publishing, and the cookbook sold well to raise money for the Club's charities in the city.

All in all, it was a good year for each one of us. Had we been in Amherst, we could never have afforded a nanny/housekeeper to give my husband and me so many lovely times together, or to have given our older boys the thrill of seeing the marvels of Sicily's rich heritage, the Roman amphitheatres, Greek ruins, the natural beauties of the island that included the biggest live volcano in Europe in our backyard. As for Stevie, I had the pleasure of guiding and observing his every development in that first year of his life. Maria was fond of our three boys but *Stefanuccio* was her special love. In late spring we left him with Maria, taking Tom and Davey on a three-day trip to Palermo, Agrigento, and Segesta, making a complete circle of the island.

Only in Sicilia
Our relations with our neighbors, our landlord, and the merchants and service people in the village of Acicastello were uniformly pleasant but for one mysterious situation that could only happen in Sicily. Beginning suddenly in late February, our water supply stopped every afternoon at 4 PM, with not a trickle from any faucet. Maria had no idea why this was happening, and the family living in the next-door apartment was not affected. After more than a week of this unexplained annoyance, we decided that there must be a problem between the municipal offices in Acicastello and their control of the water to our apartment. We went to the town hall and asked to talk with the mayor. I explained our situation and asked what could be the cause, was there a break in service because of a physical problem or was there an unpaid water charge? The mayor, *lo sindaco,* fixed us with a baleful stare and quietly promised that he would investigate. Within a few days, the water supply was fully restored but we were given no official explanation. Maria learned

from our neighbor's maid, some time later, that the mayor passed on the word that the American family was not to be "inconvenienced." Apparently the owner of our building, Signora Calabretta, refused to pay "protection" to the local Mafiosi and they used this little annoyance to send her a message. We were actually amused by the incident at the time, but horrified a few years later when we learned that Signora Calabretta had had an unfortunate but fatal "accident." On leaving the apartment to drive down the very steep road, her brakes failed and she crashed into a wall at the foot of the hill. It was ascertained that the brakes had been tampered with. These details were revealed to us in 1980 when we visited Maria while on a lecture tour in Sicily. However, even though thirteen years had passed, she warned us never to reveal the source of the Calabretta story or to tell it to anyone while we were in Sicily.

One of the perks of academic life is the opportunity to travel to interesting places to deliver scholarly papers at conferences. During our year in Sicily David had two such invitations, each unusual in its own way. In November 1966 he traveled north to give guest lectures in Firenze and Pisa, just weeks after the most damaging floods in modern Florentine history. He saw first-hand the tragic effects of the overflowing Arno River and the massive efforts by an international gathering of art restorers to rescue the masterpieces. In the spring of 1967, David was invited to participate in an American literature seminar in Rome. Through an ad in the *Rome Daily American*, we found an American military family in Rome that would trade their apartment in Rome for ours in Sicily for two weeks. David went ahead of us and I flew to Rome with our three children and Maria. Once settled, I obtained tickets for seats at St. Peter's Basilica to attend the Pope's weekly audience. Tom, Davey, and I, and Maria holding baby Steve, were led to seats in the first tier on the main alter. What a thrill for Maria, a devout Catholic, to see the Supreme Pontiff at such close quarters. She confided that it was the greatest experience of her life.

Before leaving Sicily to return to the United States in June 1967, we resolved to provide for Maria. She had never worked outside her home until she came to help us. Her husband, who had gone to Germany to work in the Ruhr Valley coal mines, was seriously injured and returned to Italy an invalid, suddenly putting her in the position of family wage earner. First, we found an English family with a new baby who hired her immediately. Then we paid extra installments into Maria's state retirement fund. She was grateful for our help, kept her job for another dozen years, and retired with a comfortable pension.

Back to the Real World

Once back in the states we returned easily to the pattern of Amherst life. The three years that followed, before our next overseas residency, reflect the middle-class American norms of the period. Tom and Davey now walked the half-mile to their elementary school, a wonderful improvement over spending three hours a day on a school bus. They thrived in the classroom, resumed friendships with neighborhood children, and participated in team sports—Pee Wee League baseball, ice hockey, and basketball, each in its own season. Tom began cello lessons but only persevered for a year. Davey took up the cello a few years later in a more serious way and continued right through high school, playing in the school orchestra. They were both good readers and, consequently, became good writers. Our practice of reading to the children at bedtime now changed into their own habit of reading to themselves before lights out. Tom reminds me that we had a Summer Reading Club which featured a ten-cent reward for each book read and reported on (to Mom); we kept a list of titles, and the dates they were completed by, on the refrigerator door. Birthday parties were such simple, homey affairs, compared to what we see today of children being celebrated in "function rooms" with professional clowns, magicians, and other entertainment. Typically, we invited six or eight boys for an organized activity such as a baseball game or other sport at the nearby park, followed by a picnic lunch and a homemade cake.

Summers on Nantucket Island in the "handyman special" antique house meant equal parts home repair and scholarly research for David, and home repair and child rearing for me, with enjoyable afternoons on the beach for all of us. My husband organized a pick-up baseball team with all the children we could corral into action; Tom and Davey did a variety of things—from tennis lessons to guided nature walks to children's theatre to just plain riding bikes in the neighborhood. We made new friends on the Island and became part of the social life that included dinner parties, cocktail parties, and beach picnics with our children. In the midst of all this socializing, two encounters stand out—two magical evenings when we sat around a dinner table, once with novelist Saul Bellow and once with poet John Ciardi.

An especially strong friendship grew between David and me and the Silvas, a couple with children the same ages as ours. Jane and Alby were both from Nantucket families (Alby was the twin brother of Wally Silva, who had first suggested Nantucket as a summer destination). Wally and Alby's father ran the largest car dealership on the island, and Jane's parents operated the Cliffside Beach Club. We spent many an evening together at each others' homes or at an occasional splurge dinner at the Opera House. What our family loved most were the odd Sundays when Alby would pile all of us into his huge Jeep Cherokee for a picnic at Great Point, with clam digging and fishing. One Sunday we spotted a beached whale from a distance as we drove along the water's edge, and the children were excited by the thought of climbing on the great carcass. Alas, as we got near the whale that had washed up in a February storm, the stench was so foul and the flesh looked like melting wax. We drove past it at great speed. But the picnic on Sunday, July 28, which almost ended tragically, is one of our family's most vivid Nantucket memories.

Alby had dug up and opened two dozen cherrystone clams, and we were devouring them with our drinks, when there was a cry for help. A nine-year-old girl had been caught in the riptide, her fifteen-year-old babysitter swimming out to rescue her was also being swept away, and the girl's mother was about to start out to save them. Jane and Alby, seasoned islanders, saw the danger immediately. Alby started the Jeep and tore down the beach for help, scattering all our picnic food from the tailgate on the sand. At Jane's insistence, the mother stopped at the water's edge as Jane and Howard Jelleme jumped into a small dinghy and rowed out toward the swimmers, who by now were hundreds of yards out at sea. They caught up with the two, and Jane held their arms, since the boat was not large enough to hold everyone; in that way they towed them back to shore. Alby had reached a phone and called the Coast Guard station. A rescue boat was launched, and a helicopter dispatched, but by then the rescue had been effected[6].

A small postscript to the dramatic rescue illustrates both the frugal ways of New Englanders and the potential repercussions of hasty actions. Once the survivors had been bundled in blankets and taken to their home, we turned to the task of gathering up our scattered belongings. Clothes, fishing gear and picnic items were packed haphazardly among children and adults. Jane even scooped up the baked beans, half in the pot and half in the sand. After settling our own children, David and I drove over to the Silvas for drinks and the salvaged picnic—we needed to unwind and replay the event a few more times. Jane had meticulously rinsed the sand out of the baked beans and baked them again, adding more bacon and brown sugar. In our hurried efforts to leave Great Point, our clothes were mingled together, and when the Jeep arrived at our house I gathered an armload of what looked like our own things, brought them into the house, and distributed them among the bedrooms. On a chair near my husband's side of the bed I deposited his clothes to be sorted later for the laundry. The following day, David left the island to do some errands in Amherst, returning two days later. When he finally got to the sorting of his clothing he held up a pair of khaki trousers and asked me, "Whose pants are these?" Clearly he never could have worn the trousers, they were much too large. Aghast, I said, "I don't know." "Then how did they get on the chair next to my side of the bed?" "Oh, Lord, I have no idea. But, wait, wait. They must be Alby's. When we left Great Point we were in such a hurry, our clothes were all jumbled together and I must have brought them here by mistake. Yes, yes, of course that's what happened." And, indeed, that was the truth of it. I am grateful for the unshakable trust between us, that my husband would not (and should not!) doubt my word.

A Family Separates, Permanently

From that summer of 1968 on, our niece Patty Porter began spending her summers with us as a "mother's helper," allowing us evenings out and giving her an opportunity to have a welcome vacation away from her family; her parent's troubled marriage was in the final stages of dissolution. After years of Roy's increasingly erratic behavior, partly due to excessive drinking, Bobbie finally decided to leave the Porter home in Elba, New York, with her children and sue for divorce. She waited until after the big family gathering for Mother Porter's eightieth birthday in June 1968, a celebration which included granddaughter Pamela's graduation from Elba Central High School and Dr. David T. Porter's delivery of the high school commencement address. David was the first graduate of Elba High School to earn a Ph.D. He gave a wonderful speech, touching briefly on the two significant issues facing the United States: civil rights for African Americans and opposition to the Vietnam War. For Mother's birthday, we gave a contribution in her name to the NAACP, which seemed to puzzle her. But she was a good sport and thanked us sincerely.

It was soon after this event that Bobbie left Elba and her husband of twenty-two years, a step that opened a deep rift in the family. On one side were my husband and his sister Marjorie who, while they loved their brother dearly, were well aware of the long years that Bobbie had tolerated a bad situation; they felt sympathy for her plight. On the other side, sister Dud and Mother Porter became fiercely protective of Roy and expressed outrage that his wife and the mother of his six children would dare to leave. This division of attitudes persisted for several years, beyond the death of Mother Porter. The effects of the divorce wrought havoc on the children.

Bobbie left Elba with fifty dollars in her bank account and was forced to find work immediately. She had been at home raising children since her marriage and had not completed her undergraduate degree. Roy's resistance to the divorce meant that he refused to pay child support and tried vigorously to convince the children to leave their mother and live with him. It was a family split that the children, in their adult lives, never fully recovered from, some blaming their mother for their problems. Bobbie, in fact, after starting as an aide in a home for mentally retarded young women, gradually worked herself up to an administrative position in healthcare and completed a master's degree in her field. Though the family was reduced to a much lower standard of living than the one they had enjoyed in their early years when Roy's farm income was high, Bobbie managed to support their needs. Patty Porter spent three summers with us on Nantucket, establishing a bond with our three sons that has lasted to this day. Her presence and her help made our vacation times far more enjoyable than they would have been without her.

A Year in Staffordshire, England

In summer 1969 David received an invitation to be a guest lecturer at the University of Keele in England for the spring semester 1970. We invited Patty to go with us. She would have the opportunity to attend an English high school and to travel with us in Europe during school vacations. She was thrilled to leave Lyons, New York, to spend her year as a student at the Orme School for Girls in Newcastle-under-Lyme, Staffordshire. On the evening of December 31, 1969, with our niece and three sons, we winged out of Boston's Logan Airport en route to London. David and I felt immense relief to be on our way after the very hectic days of preparation for moving abroad, and, sipping a good Martini before dinner we toasted the voyage. "If we left the water running in the bathtub or the coffee pot on the stove—we can't do anything about it. So, let's just relax and look forward to London."

Soon the captain sent his greetings over the loudspeaker and announced a contest. Leaving Boston at 9 PM East Coast time, traveling at a certain rate of speed across the Atlantic Ocean, and considering the time zones involved, the captain asked if anyone could estimate at what time we would actually reach midnight and the new year. About ten minutes later, Tom, sitting in the row in front of us turned and said, "Dad, I've figured it out. Tell the captain that at 10:37 Eastern Standard Time we will be at the point of midnight over the ocean."

We called the stewardess, who took Tom's scrap paper with the figures on it and his name to the captain. Soon we heard this announcement, "Our contest is won by young Tom Porter, age ten, from Amherst, Massachusetts. Congratulations, Tom, and a bottle of champagne is the prize but I guess it'll go to your parents."

Our arrival in England on New Year's Day of the new decade was so completely different from our first day in Sicily. We had both been to England on more than one occasion and chose the Basil Street Hotel for our three-day family holiday before proceeding to Keele. Patty and the boys were dazzled by the London sights at holiday time—the shops (especially Hamley's toy store, the British equivalent of our FAO Schwartz), crowds, Christmas lights and decorations, and the quietly formal service at the hotel. There was a moment of humor when the white-gloved waiter serving us an elegantly sauced fish course was asked by our niece for a bottle of ketchup. The startled waiter quickly covered up his embarrassment and brought out the plebian sauce on a silver platter. The great treat for Patty, Tom, and Davey was going to the theatre to see *You're A Good Man, Charlie Brown*, their first live performance by Broadway actors.

Our travel to Stoke-on-Trent, the nearest city to the village of Keele, taught us two things about the British Railway: it would take us from Keele to London in just under two hours and we could enjoy a complete three-course dinner in the dining car for about five dollars. David Adams, director of the Bruce Center for American Studies at the university, met us and delivered us to our new digs, a three-bedroom apartment for visiting professors right on the campus. Keele was one of the first "red-brick universities" opened after World War II to expand the British university system and open up study opportunities for many more young people. The extensive land and lovely manor house had been donated to the government by the Sneyd family, and classroom and dormitory buildings were added. Faculty apartments and individual homes were sited around the main college buildings, making for a well-designed and cohesive community. We were immediately satisfied with our apartment in the Horwood Flats, snug fit though it was.

Tom and Dave walked to the Keele St. John's School in the village with a large group of neighborhood children; Patty was enrolled in the Orme School for Girls in Newcastle-under-Lyme, a short bus ride from Keele; and three-year-old Steve attended the Infants' School on the university campus three afternoons a week, while Professor Dad walked to his classes and tutorials, leaving me our car. One of our first shopping trips involved buying Tom and Dave suitable clothing for school. They were expected to wear grey wool, knee-length pants (what we call Bermuda shorts) and dark knee socks. We were instructed to buy them plimsoles (sneakers), anoraks (windbreakers) and Wellingtons (high boots). The boys were not happy to leave behind their warm corduroy trousers for this weird outfit, but after the first day of school we never heard another complaint. They were happy to look like all the other boys. Niece Patty had to be outfitted in a navy blue skirt and sweater, white shirt, and school tie. Later on in the warm weather, Patty wore a striped cotton dress and straw hat, a uniform she thought was so droll that we had to take several snapshots for her friends back in the states.

David's teaching load was heavier than had been his assignment back home, but he found the students very keen and his colleagues to be an interesting and friendly lot. Here we found a familiar academic social life akin to the ones at the University of Massachusetts and Robert College in Istanbul—the close community of residential colleges—but quite different from our experience in Catania, Sicily. Invitations to dinner parties and teas introduced us to the friendly group of colleagues and their spouses, and we responded by hosting our own evening get-togethers.

Tom and Dave were taken up immediately by schoolmates and, since they were both good athletes, their teacher, David Price, introduced them to soccer, the sport the British call football. He assigned the Yankee brothers places on the first squad and they did us proud. Academically they were amazed at the rigor of their English school, with more subjects and higher expectations than their school back home, but they rose to the challenge. What they loved almost more than anything at St. John's were the lunches, which really were dinners. With what gusto they described sitting down at tables set with real crockery and silverware, where each week one student did the "dishing up." The meals included some variety of meat, a vegetable, two kinds of potato, and a "pudding" or dessert, such as the infamous treacle pudding. They fell in with their classmates, eating such oddities as "bubble and squeak" (cabbage!), sausages that seemed to be made mostly of oatmeal, and other concoctions they would never have consumed at our family table. Soon they adapted to the English idioms and pronunciation, much as Tom had easily mimicked the Texas accents of his classmates at the American school in Sicily. The "code-switching" was most dramatic in our three-and-a-half-year-old Steve who would be talking with me in his normal Massachusetts voice as we walked to his "school," but on meeting the first few children in the schoolyard he would immediately switch to a higher pitch and affect the English speech of the Midlands, seemingly without conscious effort.

The eight months in England were a more successful overseas experience for the entire family than the one in Sicily had been. Perhaps this was largely due to the friendly community, but knowledge of the language helped a great deal, as did the ages of our children—they were old enough to be intrigued with new places but not yet rebellious teens—and of course the presence of our Patty was invaluable. She, too, though occasionally homesick, was fascinated with being in England. We used every weekend to tour local sights of historical interest (castles and manor houses such as Little Moreton Hall were popular draws) or to travel to London, Oxford, the Lake District, Stratford-on-Avon, and the ruins of Coventry Cathedral. Davey sent a postcard picturing Shakespeare's house to a classmate in Amherst who wrote back to ask, "Hey, Dave, what's a Shakespeare house?" A weekend trip to Fishguard Landing in Wales, to acquaint the children with the Welsh roots of their grandmother Bertha Thomas Porter, revealed three pages of Thomases in the local telephone directory, as well as sixteen listings for the name "David Thomas." We discovered an unusual tourist attraction in the potteries (the five towns renowned internationally for their production of bone china)—the Wedgewood factory. Odd as this may seem, Tom, Dave, and Patty were quite taken with the skilled craftsmen making and decorating the delicate pieces and with the displays of antique sets of porcelain made for kings, czars, and pashas. Tom stated that he would like to work at Wedgewood's some day, an indication of how thoroughly he felt a part of Midlands life.

And what were my special pleasures in Keele? The secure knowledge that all were functioning happily in their various places; the satisfaction of mastering such mundane things as driving on the left side of the road, managing to shop and cook with the narrow range of English foods (no pasta, no good hamburger, and no pizza to take out); the ability to go out with my husband on the spur of the moment for a pub lunch or a special museum excursion, thanks to our niece's presence; and the three afternoons a week when I was totally free to indulge in *reading for pleasure*. A lending library van would stop by the Horwood Flats weekly. For the first time I felt ready to tackle Henry James—he had failed to sustain my attention twenty years earlier—and I read his entire works, along with those of Doris Lessing, Matthew Arnold, E. M. Forster, and a number of the more contemporary English authors. Our niece developed a love of literature, following our viewings of *The Forsyte Saga* and *Howard's End* on the BBC.

Springtime in Rome, II

Thanks to David's growing reputation as an accomplished speaker and scholar, he was invited to give two weeks of lectures at Rome's Centro per Studi Americani during the April spring break. Of course, we were all excited about the trip to our favorite European city. Through an ad in the *Rome Daily American* I contacted Douglas Macalindon, an attaché at the Irish Embassy in Rome who offered to rent us his villa on the Via Appia, a place large enough to accommodate our family, since his own family would be away at the time. Done! We embarked by train to London for an overnight before proceeding to the Channel crossing and a train that would take us to Rome. Shopping at Harrods's, the most famous department store in the world at the time, we fixed up

Tom and Dave with navy blue blazers, and gave the children a tour of the amazing assortment of goods from all over the world.

Steve, who'd had a minor cold for a few days, became ill that evening with such a high fever that he went into convulsions. We called an ambulance from the hotel and rode with him in it to a nearby hospital. The attending doctor brought down Steve's temperature and told us that there was no sign of any serious problem, just a more severe cold than we'd realized. Now we were faced with the dilemma of whether the whole family should proceed with the trip, or whether David should go alone. We decided to go ahead together.

We had not yet learned to regard the assurances of travel agents and house renters with less trust and more skepticism. Although the train ride and Channel crossing were uneventful, the rest of the trip was fraught with annoying inconvenience. In the late afternoon we boarded the super train on the French side and crammed ourselves into a compartment with three narrow steel cots on each side, bolstered by the anticipation of enjoying a good French meal in the dining car that evening. Contrary to our expectations, we learned late that night that there was no dining car and that the train would not stop at any place where we might buy snacks and drinks on the station platform— *merde!* If our travel agent had told us, we would have brought our own picnic supplies with us. Not until we changed trains in Milano the following noon did we find a dining car that provided a much appreciated lunch. Alas, Steve's fever continued, and as he dozed on my lap he became ill and vomited on the front of my dress. Immediately the nearest passengers offered their handkerchiefs and held him so I could clean up.

On our arrival in Rome's Stazione Termini we separated—Patty and I to take Steve to the American hospital, David and the two boys to go out to the "villa." The doctor prescribed antibiotics and assured us that Steve would be well in a few days. We took a taxi out to the house we'd rented. It was dark as we pulled into the courtyard of the Macalindon place, and what we saw was a stucco building situated directly on the road, the famous Via Appia Antica leading out of Rome to the south.

We entered a poorly lit foyer and, upon hearing familiar voices, walked in on a scene we never would have expected in Rome. Tom, Dave, and their father were seated around an ancient trestle table being served hot tea and baked beans on toast by Moira, the Irish maid! The ground floor kitchen, lit only by a bare bulb of less than 25 watts hanging overhead, resounded with the roaring traffic that sped by outside. I asked Moira to show us to the bedrooms so I could settle Steve in for the night. They were minimally furnished—more bare-bulb overhead lights. Dust-encrusted windows and heavy black spider webs signaled that no one could have occupied these rooms in months, if not years. It was a subdued family that made the best of that first night in our "villa," but David and I shared a late-night resolution to move out as soon as possible.

Morning brought a bright sunny day and our landlord, Dennis Maclindon, who showed us around the garden, brought a doctor friend to look in on Steve, whose fever was slightly lower. He also offered to take me to the nearest market to buy basic groceries. Charming fellow that he was, we were not reassured about staying. We left Patty with the boys, and David and I went into the city center to find new lodgings, securing two large rooms at the Hotel Sorrento e Patrizzia on Via Nazionale. Since the city was now beginning to fill up with pilgrims for Palm Sunday, we would not be able to move into the hotel until Monday. Resigned to spending the weekend on the Via Appia, I did what would become a family tradition on taking up residence in a strange place: prepared a dinner of pasta and salad, our favorite comfort food. We informed Macalindon of our coming move, a change of plans he accepted with equanimity. We learned later that his family had left for Ireland a year earlier, but he had preserved the fiction of their being on a short vacation in order to keep collecting the family housing allowance from the embassy.

We fell into a fairly comfortable pattern for the next two weeks with David going to his "palace" every morning to teach (the Centro per gli Studi Americani is located in the Palazzo Antici Mattei). He loved to walk up to the Campidoglio with its equestrian statue of

Marcus Aurelius, and there collect his thoughts on that day's lecture while enjoying the magnificent views of the Roman Forum. Mornings the children and I did chores; afternoons we all gathered for lunch and sightseeing. Public transportation in Rome serves the citizens well and we got around by bus, tram, and walked miles every day to some new and some familiar places—Villa Borghese, the Etruscan museum in Villa Ada, the Coliseum, St. Peter's Basilica, the scene on Via Veneto. Out of town trips included a day at the ancient Roman port of Ostia, with its marvelous mosaic tiles. One disappointment was a long, fruitless bus ride to Villa d'Este on a Monday, only to discover that many of Italy's museums and antiquities are closed that day.

Continuing to look for a less-expensive living situation, I found an ad for an apartment offered by a young American couple, and we ended our last week in Rome with five days in this beautiful top floor apartment with a balcony overlooking the Vatican. All in all, with Steve entirely recovered and the many delights of the city, we agreed that going with Professor Dad to Rome was a great idea.

David rented a van to drive us north before boarding the train to England. En route to Firenze, we looked for a place to stop for our picnic lunch, since Italy's autostrade did not yet have the excellent cafeterias and convenience stores that are in place today. Turning on to a dirt road, we arrived in a farmer's courtyard. The farmer who greeted us was hospitable. He said we were welcome to spread our picnic nearby and that we would enjoy the view across the valley to the town of Assisi, an unexpected pleasure. So many, many times in Italy during our visits over fifty years we have found such cordiality—people who will lead someone to an unfamiliar address, or take time to help foreigners who may not speak the language of the country.

On our drive north, heading toward the train and our ultimate destination, Keele, we made a brief visit to the thirteenth-century Giotto frescoes in Assisi, spent a few days in Firenze to view as many of the riches of this museum city as we could, and then boarded the train for Milano. Having a few hours there before our train to England would be ready, David took the older boys and Patty to see the Duomo while I shopped in the nearest grocery store for Italian delicacies to take back to Keele. We all met in the station for coffee with our dear friend Franco Miccinelli and his daughter Paola. We bought sandwiches, fruit, and bottled water for our overnight train trip; we dared not rely on the promises of the French railways.

Anti–Vietnam War Activities

At Keele in that spring of 1970, as on U.S. college campuses, university students were becoming active protesters against the Vietnam War. Shortly after the horrendous event at Kent State University in Ohio, where four students were fatally shot by National Guard troops attempting to quell a demonstration, a student group at Keele set off a bomb that destroyed the small building housing the Registrar's Office. Though no one was hurt, this act of violence so close to our apartment frightened us. The community was deeply divided over the ethics of using violence to promote peace in Vietnam. My sentiments were entirely against the American invasion of Vietnam, and I remain convinced that it was one of the worst acts in our history, but I never approved of the increasingly violent actions of the antiwar groups.

One day there was a light-hearted demonstration at Keele: a nude sit-in in the very middle of the campus on the first really warm, sunny day in June. A dozen or so students disrobed, lay on the grass, and sunned themselves—that was their war protest!—all of it photographed by the *News of the World* tabloid, to the embarrassment of the university administrators. It caused such a stir that questions were raised in Parliament about the outrageous behavior and whether grants for student rebels shouldn't be cut. Certainly our sons ogled the nudies when we walked by on an innocent errand, but none of us quite understood the connection between their nude sunbathing and Vietnam, except the eternal impulse of youth to *epater les bourgeois*.

On Dave's tenth birthday we took our two older sons to London for the day. We strolled through Westminster Abbey, pointing out the graves of famous writers and prime ministers. Next we visited the British Parliament, walking into the House of Lords and then the House of

Commons where we, as the only visitors at the time, were allowed to sit on the green leather seats on which all the elected members sit for their famous and often raucous deliberations. Lunch at the prestigious Cadogan Hotel was the treat, since we had long ago discovered that a good restaurant meal never failed to please anyone in our family.

As we approached the end of August and our time in England was drawing to a close, David and I began seriously to consider the attractions of English life, while the terrible disruptions over the major issues of civil rights, war, and poverty in America daily riveted our attention on the BBC news. Daily life in Keele, Newcastle-under-Lyme, and Stoke-on-Trent, our immediate area, seemed far more gentle, courteous, and well mannered than what we knew of U.S. ways. David Adams, my husband's friend and colleague who headed American Studies at Keele, began probing the possibility of offering my husband a permanent appointment to the faculty. It was not an opening to be summarily dismissed. The urgency influencing our possible move to England was the desire to shield our three sons from involvement in a war which seemed to have no end. Other attractions in England included good friendships, the ease with which our sons adapted to their schools and peers, and the access to other European countries. David was obliged to return to the University of Massachusetts for at least one year after being away on leave, and that year would give us time to explore the idea of transplanting our family.

As typical academic travelers (the "cheap international set"), we made arrangements to go home via a fly-by-night (pun intended) charter airline, since it would cost us only about eighty-five dollars per person, London to New York. It was always an adventure, traveling by charter, but the savings were considerable. We took ourselves to a bed-and-breakfast in London the night before the flight in order to arrive at the airport by 5 AM. After a three-hour wait, we were informed that the plane that was to take us to New York was late in leaving Madagascar—the company, Court Airlines, had only one plane—and the delay would likely last the day. Most of the passengers were left on their own, but the families with children were gathered, placed on a bus, and taken to an English country inn where we could spend the day at the airline's expense; we had rooms to nap in and lovely grounds where the children could play. We all marveled at this unexpected act of charity. That day in Little Bardfield Hall, built in 1583, was the most pleasant sendoff from our English hosts, a day that Tom and Dave often recount.

Now we would rejoin family and friends and take up the threads of ordinary life while giving serious thought to becoming permanent expatriates. My mother, who spoke no English and was lacking in worldly knowledge, had been courageous enough to leave Italy in 1935 to take her family away from Fascism and economic deprivation. How much more easily could David and I make a transoceanic move, we who had traveled and lived in different countries, spoke several languages, and were part of an academic network. We truly did not anticipate the tremendous upheaval in American society now underway—the beginning of the women's liberation movement, especially—that would have consequences for both of us, ushering in a gradual shift of emphasis in our family from the strong focus on David's career and the striving for upward mobility to a new emphasis on my own interrupted education, career development, and the changing relationships with our growing sons.

CHAPTER 8

The Decade of Emerging Women

Late September 1970—Word spreads about a meeting
to organize Amherst Women's Liberation consciousness-
raising groups: all interested women are welcome.
That evening meeting radically changed the outlooks,
marriages, and families of many women, mine included.
While our family was in England feminist leaders
in Amherst had begun the local movement. At this
organizing event the entire roomful of several dozen
middle-aged, academic wives thrilled to the talk of
liberation and gasped at the new look of the younger
speakers—bra-less, boob-bouncing women in Army
boots who wore no make-up, showed off unshaved legs
and underarms—and registered shock at their obscenities
and aggressively anti-male rhetoric. We were asked to
commit to forming random groups of ten that would
meet weekly for the coming year, discussion groups to
heighten our awareness of how we had been victimized

214

in our male-dominated society and to learn how to change all that—locally, nationally, globally! Yes!

The experience of meeting with a group of strangers—never mind that we were self-styled "sisters"—to talk about our early years, our sexuality, our children, husbands, parents (before the advent of the catch-all word "relationships"), and, of course, our victimization, created a dichotomy in my emotions and attitudes. At one and the same time, I yearned to bond with my new friends, be like them in opposing the male sex and throwing off the shackles, but I clearly sensed the wide gulf separating us—my working-class origins and early experiences did not remotely fit with the privileged backgrounds of almost every woman in my group. All my adult life I had striven mightily to become middle class. I perceived my position as a faculty wife in a New England town as the *desideratum*—I'd arrived. Now I was told that what I aspired to was not worth achieving—us women of the educated middle-class, it appeared, had also been trampled underfoot.

My support group included a fifty-year-old artist, the wife of an art historian; two sixteen-year-old high school girls (one the daughter of the artist); a Hampshire College faculty-wife social activist; a 6-foot 2-inch Amazonian poet/graduate student; a thirty-ish University secretary; and the young bride of my nephew David Philipp, a young man who had just started doctoral studies in biochemistry at the University. Nineteen-year-old Wendy Farrington Philipp, daughter of Sir Reginald and Maude Farrington of Nassau, Bahamas, was the first to drop out of our group after attending two evening sessions and finding the rhetoric totally baffling and in some ways frightening.

The first meeting was at my house and I served coffee and homemade cookies. One of the women immediately said, "The first rule of this group will be that no one should serve anything." As heads began to nod in approval, Amazon spoke forcefully, "Don't tell us how to behave in our own homes. In my culture it would be considered an insult not to offer something to guests, even if it's only a glass of water. You do what you want when we meet at your house." After this startling announcement at our first meeting, Amazon soon left us; she declared that she "didn't need this shit."

Someday when my granddaughters ask me, "Grandma, what did you do in the feminist revolution back in the olden days?" I'll say, "I did a lot of things and I learned a lot." I learned much about class, political posturing, excuse making, rewriting history, moral relativism, and utopian thinking. I also quickly understood the legitimate yearnings for equal opportunity, for reproductive rights, and for questioning traditional ways that bound women unfairly. My husband was mostly tolerant of the support group and willingly did the child-minding on the evenings of the weekly meetings, though he sometimes tired of the interminable discussions between the two of us about feminist issues. Unknown to me, our son Tom, eleven years old at the time, would often sit at the top of the stairs listening to the discussions when I thought he was safely asleep. He confesses he found it mostly mystifying and sometimes silly. Example: on the subject of the availability of birth control and abortion, one of the two high school girls suggested, "Maybe we should just *not* give birth control to black women until the black population grows to make up 50 percent of this country, then we'll have equality and less racism." That idea was treated respectfully but not endorsed by anyone in the room.

This was the beginning of the era of nonjudgmentalism. In fact, one of the strongly promoted attitudes among us was that any lifestyle women choose is to be respected and supported, meaning out-of-wedlock births, lesbian couplings, choosing to live on welfare, or abandoning one's children to "find oneself." The only lifestyle that was not much to be admired, noted a friend in the movement, was the traditional marriage and family arrangement. She and I perceived that we who were choosing to remain married and raise our children in traditional households—though we might be "getting liberated" in many ways—were not going to be the role models for younger women.

In the two or three years of my participation in different aspects of the movement, it became increasingly clear that we feminists were not connecting with working-class women or the truly disadvantaged.

Eventually we would, but that would happen in some undesirable ways. My personal contribution locally was to be trained to counsel women on "problem pregnancies," newspeak for abortion. Even as a nonpracticing Catholic, I would never have chosen an abortion for myself, but I sympathized with women who found themselves in dire circumstances for raising a child. Before *Roe v. Wade* abortion was not legal in Massachusetts, but we had researched the possibilities available in nearby states. After an interview, and after offering information on resources such as adoption agencies, we would give leads to the nearest clinic in New York City that performed the procedure for a token cost. If necessary we helped with expenses. I have since modified my early enthusiasm for "free abortion on demand" and believe a few modest curbs on *Roe v. Wade,* such as the ban on partial-birth abortion and keeping the parental notification for underage girls, are both reasonable and necessary.

Another bit of counseling I volunteered to do, since my movement sisters felt inadequate to the task of talking to "minority" high school girls, was to hold open conversations on sexuality and safe practices for young teens. I met with small groups of young African American and Puerto Rican girls from nearby Springfield and Holyoke who were seeking basic information about how to behave with boys, how to keep from getting "knocked up," how to keep a boyfriend without having to "put out." Having grown up with little guidance about the workings of women's bodies or the specifics of sexual intimacy, albeit in a much more "chaste" world, I realized how desperate these young women were for information, some even for a confidante. I had no qualms about talking with the girls. The discussions were frank, earthy, indelicate—no tip-toeing around physical activities, no euphemisms for body parts. My aim was to instill pride in these young girls, fire them up to believe in their personal worth, encourage them not to succumb to the loutish neighborhood boys or predatory older men but to value themselves and to seek the opportunities for a better life, to rise above the dismal situations they saw in their own families. The key to their personal futures lay first and foremost in absolutely avoiding two dangers: pregnancy and/or dropping out of school.

Approaching my fortieth birthday, I counted my life fulfilled in many ways, although capable of improvement. I was slightly overweight and discovered the new Weight Watchers organization whose weekly inspirational meetings and "weigh-ins" provided another avenue for conviviality with local women. I enrolled with the goal of losing twenty or so pounds and achieved my goal weight in five months, just in time for a new summer bikini. The lessons on good nutrition were useful.

I continued working at *The Massachusetts Review*, the small salary helped our family finances and, even more valuable, the experience itself provided a stimulating connection to the editors and contributors. And yet I planned to leave the magazine job when our three sons would be in school all day. I expected to enroll as a full time student at the University in fall 1972 to complete my undergraduate degree and take up a professional career. I had no quarrel with the notion that I should carry on in my role as the mother and wife—assuming the physical care for my sons and husband, with David's minimal help—while he earned the salary that supported all of us and kept rigorous focus on his writing for publication. But it was also my time to focus on my long-postponed goals.

Celebrity Status

During the 1971 Christmas vacation (yes, we still called it by its official, national holiday name, not yet having dreamed up the euphemisms of multiculturalism that would come a decade later), our boys were fascinated by a noontime television quiz show on NBC called *The Who, What or Where Game*. On a few occasions we sat together and called out answers to the questions. In my irrepressible manner I often called out the right answer, to my sons' delight. Tom said, "Mom, you should go on that show. You'd win every time." In fact, when it was announced on screen that NBC would welcome contestants, Tom wrote and asked that they invite his mother to be on the show. A few weeks later, a letter came from NBC with an invitation to call for an interview in New York City.

I made a date for mid-February during the children's school vacation, giving us an excuse to spend a few days in New Jersey with the Pedalino cousins. I took Tom, Dave, and their cousin Frank into the city for a tour of the New York Stock Exchange and the NBC-TV studios. I was led to a classroom with a few dozen other applicants. We were given a written test of general knowledge with questions on world history, geography, current events, sports greats, and movie stars. We were questioned aloud and urged to be as fast as possible in raising hands to give answers. That was the end of the test. To the great surprise of my entire family, I was called to appear a few weeks later.

I took myself to New York City with one change of clothing (on the chance that I would be on the show more than one day), fully expecting to make one appearance and return home. Arriving at the studio with half a dozen other hopefuls, we were given the ground rules: be very alert to press the buzzer and answer questions instantly—speed was better than accuracy; be lively in our facial expressions, show emotion; and, in the words of the producer, "Be adorable!" The shows would be taped, two or three a day, and broadcast a few weeks later. I was in high competitive mode as I won the first game and was rushed off stage for a change of clothing and fresh make-up. As we were coached by the show's host, I was asked what I would like to say about my work, hobbies, or family. I said I would like to mention my involvement with Amherst Women's Liberation. No, they would not allow that—don't say anything that might sound controversial to the audience. That prohibition fired me up to go in and fight once more, and I won the second game, but we were now out of time at the end of the afternoon. This small-budget show did not pay for anyone's hotel room or meals. I was turned out into a snowstorm with bus fare to New Jersey to spend the night with my brother Anthony's family. And I was admonished to be on time for the next day's taping at 10 AM. This particular game show posed serious questions to the contestants, no cream pies in the face, but the winnings were modest. Still, having now won seven hundred dollars, I was eager to continue.

There was great excitement both in Amherst, where my sons could hardly contain their amazement, and in New Jersey, where my parents and siblings lived. The next morning, I boarded an early bus for the forty-five-minute trip into Manhattan. The massive snowfall slowed traffic and in the Lincoln Tunnel we were suddenly stopped. After a quarter hour or so, I asked the driver if he knew what caused the hold up and learned that an accident in the tunnel had to be cleared away. Horrors! I saw the minutes ticking away. When we finally emerged on the New York side of the tunnel, I barely had time to catch a taxi to the studios where the producer was ready to put a substitute in my place. That morning I was vanquished, but honorably; I returned to Amherst the winner of $835, a small vacuum cleaner, and a large case of Mary Kay cosmetics. True small-town stardom followed when the game show was broadcast on national television and shown in the Amherst Regional Junior High School cafeteria, with a front-page story in the *Amherst Record* featuring celebrity Mom and son Tom on March 24. Of all the anecdotes about the event, my brother Anthony's was the funniest: "My high school classmate from the old neighborhood, Ferdinand Raimondi, is a fireman in Orange. Ferdinand was eating lunch in the station house with his pals and watching *The Who, What or Where* show when he did a double take. 'Hey,' he said to his teammates, 'that looks like Rosie Pedalino. Nah, it can't be her. They wouldn't put anybody from South Day Street on television.'"

Changing Tastes

The school year ended on a high note. Dave was a star student, winner of the fifth grade math prize, a cello player, and an all-round athlete; Tom, also good at sports, had survived his first year in the big world of junior high school without succumbing to drugs or running away from home; and Steve had finished a year of nursery school and was ready for kindergarten. With niece Patty Porter, our trusty mother's helper, we left for our eighth summer on Nantucket. Tom and Dave, however much they loved the beach, had had enough of being away and they made quite a fuss about missing Little League Baseball and other activities in Amherst; they were nearing teenage-hood, the time when peers are so important. Steve, however, was happy as a lark, learning to ride a two-wheeler bike and following his brothers around. David and I were disenchanted with the latest trend to make the island an ever more precious and high-priced resort. The wealthy Bienecke family, entrepreneurs and arts supporters, bought up quite a lot of the run-down wharf-area artists' shacks and began upgrading everything for a tonier clientele, which started a new escalation of property values. We complained bitterly about the rapid rise in costs—imagine, a thirty-five-cent ice-cream cone!

Our Nantucket friend Jane Silva, canny businesswoman but homebound mother of four, devised a plan for a new enterprise that sounded quite daring at the time. Her parents owned the Cliffside Beach Club, where they ran a small snack shop on the beach that sold the typical summer fare—hot dogs, hamburgers, soft drinks, and ice-cream popsicles—with just counter service, no seating. Jane's idea was to build a small restaurant on that site, a place where she would serve lunch, not only to beach club members but to the general public. She would start with a limited but elegant menu—an omelet and salad, Portuguese bread, and a glass of wine, the omelet ingredients changing each day—and charge a flat price, $3.50. We applauded her idea, the novelty appeal of the only beach-front restaurant on the island, but scoffed at the notion of charging such a high price! Still, we encouraged Jane to do it and were among her first customers. Not only did her modest little place succeed in that form, but The Galley Restaurant rapidly improved in size and quality, expanding to serve dinners and cater social events. Jane's astute management and the later involvement of her sons, David and Geoffrey, have made it one of the most impressive resort restaurants on the east coast. She is fortunate to have sons who willingly made the family business their professional career.

For all the enjoyment we'd found on Nantucket, especially the friendships, at the end of the 1971 summer we decided that we'd had enough. We put the house on the market. Our summers would take new forms, allowing more scope for our son's activities in and out of

Amherst. Given the upswing in real estate prices on the island, our house sold quickly for an amazing $38,000, almost four times what we'd bought it for six years earlier. Just before title passed to the new owners in early January 1972, David and I made a last trip to remove a few personal possessions, since none of the furniture was worth taking. Certain as we were that we had made the right decision, it was still emotionally wrenching to walk out for the last time, leaving a home that held so many happy family memories, especially as the birthplace of Steve. It's the return year after year to the same rooms, finding the same familiar things, that builds such a physical sense of place. Each time we leave a place we've lived in, I am compelled to take away with me some quotidian object whose sole value is to evoke the past.

Coincidentally, in January 1972, we were surprised by an unexpected visit from Jane Silva and her four children. Jane announced that she had left her husband. She had decided to move her family to Amherst, enroll the children in the town's excellent school system, and return for summer seasons to Nantucket, where she'd continue to run her restaurant.

Without much registering our amazement at her pluck, we made them all comfortable. Within a few days I found Jane a furnished house, available for sublet from January through June, while the owners were on sabbatical. With the children in school Jane set about finding work and learning the ways of Amherst life. Within a few weeks, a much-chastened Alby arrived, convinced Jane to take him back, and promptly found work in the area. It was a reconciliation that lasted several years and cemented our friendship even more strongly, though in the end our friends couldn't reconcile their differences, and the marriage ended in divorce.

In early 1972 the profit from the Nantucket house sale gave us a sense of financial solidity, which we translated into two splurges for the family. The first was adding on to our Amherst house. Local architect Bill Gillen drew up a plan for a large "family room," and a laundry room with a new entrance to the rear of the house. With an acre and a half of land, we had room to add on without preempting the backyard space for sports. In early April, we had a formal, ribbon-cutting ceremony as we filed into the new TV/game/study room, with each of us contributing a song, poem, or comic remarks.

The second was my taking the boys to Puerto Rico, the island I loved in my Pan Am stewardess days. For the April school vacation week, we accepted a standing invitation to visit the Cavallaro family, South Amherst neighbors who had moved to Puerto Rico to start an English-language radio station. The Cavallaro children had been schoolmates of our boys. The first view of San Juan and its exotic tropical scenery intrigued my sons, and being with their good friends Francesca and Gina and their five siblings was a constant source of glee. But unbeknownst to the boys, we had landed in the midst of a highly charged situation. Somehow, during the entire week of daily sightseeing—to El Yunque, Puerto Rico's tropical rain forest, to Luquillo Beach, to the famous El Morro fort in the Old City, and to El Comandante to see their first horse races—the boys were insulated from the troubles in the house.

My first hint that things were not going well was in the shabbiness of their house and its furnishings. In Amherst, where Augie owned the town's prime radio station and my good friend, Ann, kept a lovely home, the family clearly had middle-class status. The radio station in San Juan had turned out to be a bad investment, and supporting a family of nine, with all the children attending a private Catholic school had reduced Ann and Augie's standard of living. Our first evening at their home, Ann whispered to me that she would be serving the children Kool Aid drinks because Coca Cola was just too expensive. At the end of the week, I treated the children and Augie to pizzas while Ann and I went out for an evening on our own. Not only were their finances stretched to the breaking point, but the marriage was ending. Ann and Augie were essentially separated, living apart in the same house since Augie could not afford to move out. I kept their situation to myself, never revealing their plight to mutual friends or to our sons until years later when the divorce had long taken place.

I was affected by the dissolution of the marriages I saw crumbling around me, and not for the first time realized that despite an initial commitment between partners and a declaration of shared goals, marriage was often a fragile institution, especially in these rapidly changing times.

Back to School—At Last!

By early summer 1972, I was enrolled for the September term at the university as a fulltime undergraduate, with about two years' worth of college courses to my credit. Having made several false starts on a college degree over a twenty-one-year period, my plan was to take all the courses I could handle each semester until I'd completed my BA, most likely in Spanish literature.

The sixties upheavals on college campuses had brought about serious change in what was considered a legitimate course for credit. I was ready to take advantage of every loophole that would move me quickly toward graduation, though my old-fashioned, traditional notion of concentrating on rigorous academic content was always my first priority. I combined the work in my chosen field of linguistics and Spanish literature with a few courses of dubious value, such as "Feminist Action" which involved meeting in the dorm room of two female students where, after a brief lecture on feminist issues, the class time was entirely taken up with complaints about the unfairness of life and problems with sexist classmates or professors. In an earlier era this course would have been a typical, after hours, dorm bull session; it might better have been titled "Bitching and Moaning 101."

One complaint from a student in this course that diverged from purely feminist concerns was the new attitude in responding to criminal behavior on campus when race was an element. When one of the women described a dangerous assault by an acquaintance that she had fought off to avoid being raped, we all responded with outrage. Yet when asked if she had reported the assailant to the campus authorities she remarked, "I couldn't do that. He's black." A similar response was made by two students who said they were upset that their stash of pot had been stolen from their dorm room by two women down the hall. We assumed they could not report the crime because of the drugs involved but they explained that the ones who stole their property were African American students and they wouldn't dare make a fuss about it for fear of being labeled racists. The code of silence in these matters was something I would hear about frequently in the following two years. As an older student among much younger women, I noted that the code of selective silence applied equally to African Americans and to a newly labeled group, "Hispanics," minority groups of special, protected status.

My sons and my husband adapted well to my new schedule and the responsibilities they had to assume. I had time for most of my classes and for studying and research during the day when the boys were in school, but I had two evening classes that left David to supervise dinner, clean up, homework, evening activities, and bedtime. This is not to say that there were no complaints but they mostly gave me—Mom, the Student—enthusiastic encouragement. They enjoyed the funny stories I would bring to the dinner table about the more outrageous behavior, dress and (censored) language of students and professors. How they laughed when I related some of the idiocies in the lectures from "The Struggle for Food," a Mickey Mouse course designed to provide science credits for nonscience majors.

Career Shift

During my first full semester of studies I made a dramatic change of direction in my career plan, which for many years had been to major in Spanish with the intention of becoming a teacher of Spanish language and literature. However, an exciting new movement had begun in the Spanish-speaking communities, starting in Florida and the southwestern states in the late 1960s and now had arrived in the northeast. Owing to the large increase in immigrants from the Caribbean and Latin America, the sorry plight of non-English-speaking children in U.S. public schools was now labeled a civil rights issue. A series of measures were enacted to address the special needs of these children, from the 1965 Civil Rights Act prohibiting national origin discrimination, to the creation of an Office of Bilingual Education in the U.S. Department of Education, and the Transitional Bilingual Education Act passed in Massachusetts in 1971.

Earlier generations of immigrant children had been accorded no special treatment. They were expected to "pick up" English and learn their school subjects willy-nilly; if they failed, they would drop out of school at age fourteen or sixteen and take up unskilled jobs. The current wave, mostly Spanish speakers from Cuba, Mexico, and Puerto Rico, would be treated to an untested education experiment that became law, with my own state of Massachusetts leading the way. And I, a grownup immigrant kid myself, became imbued with the zeal of discovering a vocation: to help other immigrant children.

The Bilingual Education Imperative

Simply put, bilingual education presumed that children should be taught their school subjects, including reading and writing, in the language they already know—Spanish, for instance—while gradually adding lessons in English. The theory of using the two languages proposed these benefits: children would not fall behind in learning their school subjects; they would learn English and soon be able to do all classroom work in English; the transition from being taught in Spanish to being taught in English would take a period of three years; and the children would acquire a high level of self-esteem from seeing their native language respected in the classroom. The self-esteem factor was considered most important or, as put by "educrats" at the time, "if a kid feels good about himself/herself, he/she will do well in school."

Revolutionary, all this, and immediately appealing to me for two reasons: I would apply my fluency and literacy in Spanish in very practical ways, and I would be giving immigrant children the urgent special help not given to my generation of immigrants. I transferred my major to the School of Education for training in Spanish bilingual education and English-as-a-Second-Language (ESL) teaching.

For a comprehensive treatment of the way bilingual education developed over time, the politics of Latino empowerment and the corrupt practices I observed in this field, as well as an extended description of my experiences in the School of Education at the University of Massachusetts, Amherst, I refer the reader to my first book, *Forked Tongue: The Politics of Bilingual Education* (Basic Books, 1990; second edition 1996). Briefly, the School of Education at UMass in the early 1970s was considered among the most innovative, futuristic, cutting-edge places in the country. Given the sudden availability of federal grants for bilingual teacher training, the University was in a position to bring visiting lecturers to campus, essentially *creating* this young field of study, and to offer scholarships to students from across the country.

I now knew how to scam the education system for my own purposes. In addition to the courses with solid academic content, I piled up extra credits in such courses as volunteer tutoring in a school with Italian immigrant children in Springfield, and giving weekly lessons in English in the home of a Puerto Rican family in Holyoke. It was in the latter project that I was paired with another student, Claudia Lombroso, for the weekly drive to Holyoke, where each of us would visit a separate family in the same tenement building to give them English lessons. My tutees, the Santiago family, became very dear to me because their situation reminded me of my own early childhood days in Newark. The young couple had three small children; only the oldest girl was enrolled in school. Manuel worked in a gasoline station, and Tonita was a fulltime homemaker. Although the family spoke Spanish, the parents were working on their English, eager to see their children learn the language in school as quickly as possible.

My lessons for Tonita focused on familiar nouns for household items, family, clothing, foods, and the phrases that would be useful in shopping, doctors' visits, school meetings, and social conversations. She was an avid learner and a pleasure to teach. We moved from simply reciting to relating actions to words as a means of making the language immediately useful. For instance, a dialogue about food and good nutrition lead to an impromptu cooking lesson, using the ingredients for making oatmeal cookies that I brought from my own kitchen. The Santiago family visited my home one Sunday afternoon, a mutually enjoyable visit that became an annual event at Christmas time for several years.

The chance partnership with Claudia in the spring semester of 1973 was providential. She is the great-granddaughter of the late-nineteenth-century Italian scientist Cesare Lombroso. His international fame rested on his theory of phrenology and criminal behavior: that violent criminals shared similar knob-like formations on their skulls and could in many cases be identified by their skull shape. In the course of driving back and forth to Holyoke, Claudia and I had long conversations about our Italian backgrounds. Claudia explained that her grandparents, also scientists, lived in Genoa. They had sent their children, including her father and his family, to Boston just before World War II. Once the war started, the grandparents were not able to leave and, as Jews, they survived by being sheltered by an Italian family in a small village until the war was over. Grandmother Silvia Lombroso published two books that Claudia gave me to read: *Case di Sogni, Case di Mattoni*, about her early years as a young bride in the Lombroso family, and *Si Puo Stampare*, about her family's experiences during the war. I found both to be excellent accounts, comparable in literary quality to Carlo Levi's fine novel about fascist Italy, and I promised myself I would translate them some day for an American audience, a promise I have yet to keep.

A Difficult Summer

From late May to September, David and I were free to travel with our sons. We planned a family summer in Europe, renting for July, in Rome, a furnished apartment from grandmother Lombroso, and for August, obtaining the use of a house in Keele, England, while our friends would be out of the country. Putting these two arrangements together, and with cheap charter flights available, we anticipated a combination of high culture—museums, classical ruins—and the family's enjoyment in spending a month each in two countries we loved. In our minds, the plan was failsafe—but, ah! what fools we mortals be, said the Bard, wisely.

Perhaps I've made this observation before but it is worth repeating: whatever wisdom we gain from life experiences, no matter how well prepared we are for similar circumstances, when next we step out on what we think is familiar ground, there will be new lessons to learn and daunting situations not anticipated. And so it was when we arrived in Rome at the beginning of our European summer.

The Lombroso apartment, though gloomy and lacking natural light, was on the ground-floor of a building on Piazza Adriana, facing the River Tiber and Castel Sant'Angelo, with the Basilica of St. Peter and the magnificent Piazza San Pietro two blocks behind us, a perfect spot for walking all of the *centro storico*. Whatever possessed us to think that our sons would just amuse themselves on the streets of Rome while David and I spent part of each day on our own work, he on a scholarly article, I on an independent study in astronomy for which I would gain course credits at the University? They had no friends in the city, and Roman traffic is so heavy and erratic that we needed to accompany the boys to parks and other amusements. They soon became sulky and difficult, especially Tom and Dave, our teenagers. After a day trip to Tarquinia to see the Etruscan antiquities, and a few attempts at recreational outings in the Villa Borghese, we decided we all needed a few days out of the city. We rented a car and drove to Positano on the Amalfi coast for a beach holiday at our favorite little family-run hotel, Villa Franca. Here, indeed, we all reveled in the beauty of this ancient mountainside town. The beaches, categorized "topless" in some areas, riveted the attention of the two teenagers. Climbing up and down the mountainside was a welcome change from the urban streets.

Back in Rome, cheerless dispositions resurfaced. We enrolled six-year-old Steve in a summer nursery school for two weeks, which was a real trial for him since he did not speak the language of the other children, though he did like the Italian pasta lunches. Though Tom and Dave were good companions who shared many similar interests, this was a particularly poor time to sequester them in each other's company. We sent them off to the American Embassy's Fourth of July picnic for U.S. visitors, to the pool at the Hilton Hotel, a long bus ride from the center of town, and devised as many family activities as we could, but every day had its glum overcast mood.

One evening, Dave set a can of Coca-Cola on one of the window sills and when he accidentally knocked it out of the window, he climbed out and jumped down to retrieve it. To our horror, he landed partly on one of the pointed spikes of the wrought iron fence surrounding the building. He limped back in, his foot leaving a trail of blood on the marble steps in the lobby. Dave needed medical care immediately, and we had no way of finding a doctor at that time of night. Fortunately, a large clinic with a brightly lit sign for its emergency room, *Pronto Soccorso,* was located a short walk from our apartment. We were promptly seen by a doctor on duty. I described the accident and, after cleaning the wound, he advised a tetanus booster shot but did not recommend stitches. He bound the wound and sent us on our way. We could not hail a taxi to take us such a short distance to the apartment, and Dave has never forgiven us (in jest, of course) for making him walk home with his wounded foot.

One natural phenomenon that captured the interest of all of us was the news that a solar eclipse would be clearly visible over Rome in a few days. The *Rome Daily American* newspaper gave explicit instructions for viewing the eclipse without harming one's eyes, by constructing a cardboard screen with a pin-dot hole through which to view it. This especially appealed to me as I would write up a short essay for the astronomy course I was doing. We all felt like privileged, amateur scientists peeking through a cardboard frame at this glorious event in our solar system and even recorded it in a photograph.

Our time in Italy ending, we took the short flight to London, boarded the train to Stoke-on-Trent, and picked up a rental car for our month in the Adams house. Once again our expectations were dashed. We believed that once settled in a town Tom and Dave knew, where they had classmates with whom they had attended school for a year, and sports facilities galore—from soccer fields to cricket pitches to a gymnasium—they would now take the initiative to entertain themselves. It was not so simple, we discovered. We had been away from

Keele for three years and the boys resisted calling their old friends—we had to lean on them to do it. Once again, they seemed to be stubbornly locked into a self-enforced isolation, though with plenty of play areas around them. We tried to design a daily schedule that would allow me a few mornings in the library and David some half days for his work while we expected the boys to find their own amusements. One day, I lost all patience when I saw Tom and Dave taking turns riding the single bicycle in circles around the perimeter of the house, round and round and round. Something had to change or we would just be miserable together the entire month. It was time to drop our adult work and embark on some serious sightseeing. This became a source of tension between my husband and me. He agreed to two days in London to attend a cricket match and explore the Greenwich Observatory. Beyond that, he insisted on focusing on his own work and would do no further traveling.

I arranged two trips with the boys that turned out really well. First we traveled by train to Gloucester, staying in an old coaching inn, visiting the cathedral, and making the pilgrimage to the ancient ruins at Old Sarum and Stonehenge. In 1973 it was still possible for tourists to stroll among the massive structures, now forbidden by high fences. We were immensely pleased to walk among the stones, pondering the mysteries of the Druids who accomplished such engineering feats but left no written language.

For our second trip, as our month in England was more than half over, we went to Scotland to explore Edinburgh and environs. We were seasoned veterans of rail travel, yet we didn't anticipate a situation that would have seriously delayed our arrival at our final destination. At the stop in Glasgow, the train dropped half its cars. We were finishing lunch in the snack car at the rear of the train when the announcement reached us that only the first dozen cars of the train would now be proceeding on to Edinburgh. Yikes! All our traveling gear was ten cars up ahead—we would be stranded in the Glasgow station with nothing, not even our tickets. We made a mad run for it and just managed to hop on the last car as the train started. Three days exploring Edinburgh's castle, the homes of literary figures, and some of the countryside passed swiftly and we all looked ahead to York, where we would be met by Dad Porter for a day of sightseeing before heading back to Keele. We greeted each other warmly and the boys were full of stories, eager to tell their father everything they'd seen. The next day, August 9, we took a small cake on the train with us to celebrate Steve's seventh birthday on our way back to Keele.

David's Traumatic Experience

We were making the best of a summer that had been unwisely planned and that we now knew would have been better spent at home. I had completed all the written essays for my astronomy course, and David had done a modest amount of literary research, yet there was still tension between us. On our first evening after returning to Keele from York, we left the boys with fish and chips and a favorite sports quiz on the telly and drove to a local pub for dinner. Try as we might to be our old companionable selves, conversation lagged. Rather than enjoying this as a time to relax, to relish the aspects of British life our family so enjoyed, and to anticipate getting back into American gear, we were afflicted with a poverty of imagination. We could not know that this was the last evening we would succumb so easily to simple boredom or minor concerns: A near disaster lay immediately ahead of us.

Not long after I'd fallen asleep that night, David woke me suddenly. He was clearly alarmed and in great pain. He said, "My God, I feel as if my head is exploding. I've got the most splitting headache of my life." Knowing my husband as the least given to exaggeration and never one to complain about pain, I took his statement seriously. But beyond a few aspirin, which did little to lessen the pain, we could only wait until morning for further help. David was reluctant to call a doctor on a Sunday, so it was another day of severe head pain to get through. The boys were advised to keep their voices down in the house and the sound on low on the telly; David was ultra sensitive to noise. By the time a doctor from the University Health Service examined my husband twice during the following week, and the stronger pain medication she prescribed had made no improvement, we were both quite alarmed. After her second examination and a repeated testing of his reflexes, she announced, with great care, that her preliminary diagnosis would be that David might be suffering from meningitis. She recommended that he be taken to the nearby Royal Staffordshire Infirmary in Stoke-on-Trent for testing and treatment, and she made arrangements for an ambulance.

Our sons had been subdued and cooperative for days, knowing that something was very wrong with their father's health. When they saw him taken into the ambulance on a stretcher, I did my best to calm their fears. I followed the ambulance in my car, arriving at the hospital at the same moment, walking along into the emergency entrance with him. I expected that, as is the normal routine in American hospitals, we would have to satisfy paperwork rules to get David admitted, especially since we were not British citizens but visiting tourists, but that was not the case. As my husband was wheeled in, I stepped up to the desk to show the registrar our passports and our Blue Cross and Blue Shield card. With a brisk wave of her hand, she motioned me aside saying, "Go ahead, luv. See to your husband. See that they take good care of him."

The crisis of David's serious illness posed a dilemma for all of us. We were due to fly back to the states in ten days, with both Tom and Dave scheduled to begin soccer team practice and classes a few days later. The specialists at the Royal Staffordshire Infirmary scheduled a series of tests to determine the cause of David's near paralysis from the constant pain. It would take several days to diagnose the illness and to determine whether surgery or medical treatment would be required. They could not tell me at this point how long my husband would be in the hospital or what further care he'd require before he could travel. I made a decision for the whole family, and David agreed to it, though he was so weak that he could barely focus on the discussion.

For everyone's benefit, Tom and Dave should fly home on August 25 as scheduled, so they would be home to go back to school, Tom in tenth grade and Dave in eighth. I would enroll Steve in the Keele village school, freeing me to spend as much time as possible at the hospital.

He and I would remain in Keele where our hosts, the Adams family, had just returned from their summer travels in America and urged us to stay on. My brother Anthony and David's sister Marge agreed to meet our sons at the airport in New York and deliver them to Amherst, where our next door neighbors, the Campbells, would look after them until our return. I knew our sons were in good hands back home, and would be well occupied with school, much better for them than sitting in Keele for an unspecified number of days or weeks with little to do. My one fear was that they might never see their father again, if he were to take a turn for the worse, but I pushed that thought away.

The mass of details to be arranged in just a few days for the boys' departure would have been impossible had it not been for the help of Keele friends, Colin and Mary Bonwick. As an economy measure, we'd included our three sons on my passport. Now we needed to get new passports just for Tom and Dave, so they could reenter the United States without me. The nearest consular office was in Liverpool, an hours' train ride away. We had new passport photos taken, and the U.S. Consulate agreed to issue a new passport on an emergency basis. Colin Bonwick took us to the Stoke-on-Trent station and picked us up later in the day. The charter airline company approved the two boys' travel and cancelled the flight for the rest of us, to be rescheduled at a later date.

Tom and Dave visited their father in the hospital one last time and at 4 AM the next morning Colin took us to the earliest train to London, where we made a connection to Heathrow Airport. We arrived at the gate only to discover that all the passengers had already boarded, but an intrepid airline employee commandeered a motorized cart, took Tom and Dave and their bags and charged out to the plane, just before the stairs were due to be removed. They made it! I started back through London, on a brilliant, sunny morning. As my taxi circled Buckingham Palace, with tourists gaping at the Horse Guards on parade, I was momentarily stunned by the thought that we, as a family, might not ever again enjoy such scenes together.

Arriving in Stoke-on-Trent, I went directly to the hospital where the doctors treating David were scheduled to talk with me about the test results. With three specialists in attendance, Dr. Gydis Danta, a neurosurgeon from Australia, gave me the opinions of the group. Meningitis had definitely been ruled out. David, it appeared, had suffered a subdural hematoma, which they described as the bursting of a blood vessel in the brain. This was not caused by trauma but was most likely due to a birth defect in one of the blood vessels, which had suddenly broken open, flooding his brain with blood, the pressure causing the intense pain. The normal course of this incident would be for the tiny break to close itself, for the bleeding gradually to stop, and then the pain would decrease. Another option would be to operate to remove the blood, but the conservative course recommended by Dr. Danta was to let the healing proceed naturally without resorting to an invasive procedure. The decision was up to me. Neither option was guaranteed to produce full recovery, each had its risks, but on balance, the cautious course got my approval. They would monitor David's progress daily and consult with me in the event that his recovery took any abnormal turns.

My first responsibility now was to reassure Steve about his father's health and help him adjust to a strange school in the village—to at least give him some semblance of normalcy and some classmates to distract him. We fell into a routine with the Adams family. Steve and the Adams children were in school from 8 AM to 3:30 PM. After helping with chores, I would make two visits a day to the hospital. I talked with Tom and Dave in Amherst a few times a week, giving them the good news that their father was slowly improving.

David would be in the hospital two weeks longer, becoming more and more his normal self as the pain gradually receded. He had lost a great deal of weight. Dr. Danta spoke with us before releasing David from the hospital. The prognosis was excellent. Brain incidents of this sort are considered one-time occurrences, thus allaying the fear that it would happen again. David's traumatic experience had not produced any lasting effects, no diminished mental capacity, no blindness. He should spend at least another week or more at rest before attempting the flight back to the United States, and should schedule annual check-ups with the appropriate specialists back home to make certain that all was going well. No disabilities—how incredibly fortunate we felt when we heard this wonderful news.

The Bonwicks were going to France for a few weeks, and they urged us to stay at their house for David's recuperation period when he was well enough to leave the hospital. This quiet row house on the edge of the college campus suited us perfectly. There was an outpouring of good wishes from friends and acquaintances, some offered to have Steve play at their homes after school, others to help with shopping or do any chores we might need done. This was the warm community we had become so fond of when we had thought of moving our family there permanently. Our families back home were greatly relieved to hear the good news and looked forward to our return, especially Tom and Dave.

And what of the Royal Staffordshire Infirmary and the payment for two weeks of intensive care? On the day I was to take my husband home, I went to the office to get a bill for David's care. To my astonishment I learned that I owed nothing, it was all taken care of by the British National Health Plan—no need to fall back on my American health insurance. I thanked them heartily for their good services. A year later, Dr. Danta was in Boston for a medical conference, and he called to ask about David. We invited him to our home. What a kind human being, a professional who extended himself beyond expectation. He wanted to see us and to assure David again that his health was completely restored.

Coming home took an exhausting two days. We arrived in New York during a heavy rainstorm and were met by two Amherst friends, Jules Chametzky and Jo Haven, who had volunteered to drive us home, an eight-hour round trip for them. Tom and Dave were subdued in greeting us, their worry over their father's health immediately apparent. Steve was so happy to be home again to take up his normal life as a second grader at Crocker Farms School, where he was warmly welcomed by his teacher and classmates.

I had registered by mail for the fall semester at the university. It was essential that I not give up a semester's work if I expected to graduate by the following summer. My husband had arranged for his classes to be covered by English Department friends for the first few weeks—he adamantly refused to take a semester's leave. In fact, he was offered a "Handicapped Parking" sticker so he would have a shorter walk to his Bartlett Hall classrooms but turned it down. Clearly, it was of great importance to David not to be seen as an invalid or as in any way of diminished capacity. He navigated slowly around campus at first, but gradually regained his strength and normal pace of activities.

The high level of worry for David's recovery prompted my parents to accept our invitation for the Christmas holiday, something they had never done, preferring always that we drive to New Jersey to be with them. Frank and Lucy rode the train to Massachusetts and spent three days with us. My father's greatest delight was in sitting before the open fireplace and feeding in logs. They had never had a house with a fireplace since leaving Italy, where the fireplace had been their only means of heat. It was such a joy for me to be hosting my parents for the Neapolitan Christmas Eve multi-fish feast, and to see their appreciation that our family was observing one of their most cherished holiday traditions. How fortunate that we had this enjoyable holiday together, for it would be my father's last.

David regained his energy through the fall months but seemed unable to convince himself that he had truly survived the brain episode and that it would not recur. We drove to Boston for special tests and a consultation with an eminent specialist who urged David to engage in his usual physical activities, but to avoid strenuous sports such as tennis for a year or so. He encouraged us to travel abroad again, if we so desired. This seemed daring to me, but my husband decided it was just the thing to do. We made arrangements through our niece Wendy Philipp, who had grown up in the Bahamas, to take a five-day trip in January to Harbor Island, a place recommended by Wendy's family. The mini-vacation was planned on an impulse, an action David believed was essential to regaining his confidence in traveling.

Student Teaching

For my last semester in the School of Education in spring 1974, I began my required assignment as a student teacher in a second-grade classroom in the Holyoke Public Schools bilingual program. Holyoke, once home to large Irish immigrant and French Canadian immigrant communities, had declined from a textile and paper goods manufacturing city to a place of blighted, abandoned buildings and a growing migrant Puerto Rican community beset by poverty. Entering the classroom on the first day, I found two teachers seated at the front of the room, chatting, while the twenty or so students were busy at their desks with a writing exercise. Assuming that the teachers were preparing lessons, I approached to introduce myself. What I overheard, before I started to speak, was a discussion of the events on the previous day's TV soap opera. Both women continued dissecting the plot until a student approached the desk to say, "Meesy, I finish my paper." He was handed another sheet of paper and told, "Do another one." What the child had completed was a sheet covered with letters of the alphabet with spaces for the students to copy each letter several times.

I observed that this stultifying, repetitive exercise was just a strategy to keep the children occupied before the official start of class. In fact, a year earlier, as a volunteer tutor in a classroom in the neighboring city of Springfield, I observed a tired teacher close to retirement age who employed the same mind-numbing exercise, to my great dismay. But these two young women in the Holyoke classroom, one of whom was a graduate of Smith College, should have been showing enthusiasm, energy, and a more imaginative approach to teaching. Far from giving me good practical experience in a bilingual classroom, my five months in the West Street School made me think often of scenes from Jonathan Kozol's book *Death at an Early Age*, his account of blighted urban schools and their impact on children's lives.

With two full time teachers (and my modest assistance), a classroom of half English-speaking children and half Spanish-speakers should have been an ideal situation for providing the rich learning environment these children from disadvantaged families sorely needed. Instead,

I saw a mediocre performance by two teachers who did not convey any excitement about the joys of literacy, numeracy, science, art, or anything else. The school principal, a nonentity who inspired no one to excellence, must have been appointed through the old-boy network that rewards seniority rather than educational leadership. Among the more shocking events of my time there: the blinding of two pet rabbits in a third-grade classroom by a boy who sharpened his pencil and gouged out their eyes when the teacher stepped out of the room; the flooding of several classrooms when neighborhood boys vandalized the school one night by turning on faucets in the bathrooms on each floor; the deliberate upending of a fish tank in a kindergarten room, leaving the dead goldfish to be found by the children after outdoor recess. Destructive acts of cruelty they were, but even more shocking to me was the atmosphere of bored resignation by the staff, regimentation of the students to get them through the school day, and a uniform state of low expectations.

My Father's Death

During this student-teaching semester, I received the news in mid-March that my father was seriously ill and would have to have surgery. On a weekend during a severe snowstorm, we traveled to New Jersey to be on hand for the postoperative consultation with his doctors and to be helpful to my mother. My father was found to have pancreatic cancer. Dr. Filipone, the specialist who performed the surgery, informed us that Frank's condition was fatal and that no cure was possible. He advised us to help our mother consider two options: keep him at home where, with the help of medication, he would be fairly comfortable but slowly waste away, or take him to Memorial Sloan Kettering in New York City for chemotherapy treatments that would be very hard to take in his weakened state and would require his hospitalization. The first course would probably give him about three months at home, allowing him many occasions for visits with all of us. The second option would subject him to pain and suffering, far from home, and might extend his life an extra few weeks at most. Our mother was paralyzed with indecision and turned to all of us for advice. All of us but Domenick, who could always be counted on to oppose the majority, counseled our mother to do the humane thing and bring Frank home. We promised to do all we could to help her, and that was the decision she made.

David and I told our boys the sad news. We would now make several trips to Livingston, New Jersey, sometimes all of us, sometimes only me, while Grandpa was alive. In fact, every other weekend for the next three months, we did just that. On several weekends, I left school on Friday afternoon and rushed to New Jersey by train. I helped my mother and father with chores, taking my father to the doctor on a few occasions, taking my mother out for a break from her role as full time caretaker. At my mother's strong insistence, my father had not been told of his fatal condition. We all had to join her in the charade of keeping up his spirits about his recovery.

One weekend in late May David and I made the visit together and offered to drive my parents to the Jersey shore for the day. My father was very pleased and asked, "Let's go to Long Branch. I want to stop and rent a place for this summer for me and your mother. We can go there for a week, but we have to give them a deposit now. We had a lot of good times in Long Branch when you kids were small." My father asked us to take him to his favorite place on the boardwalk, a Nathan's Hot Dog diner for lunch. It was deeply disturbing to see my father's weakened condition and to keep up the pretense that he would be recovered by summer. We stopped at a house with a rental sign, and talked with the owner. I was ready to hand over a check for the fifty-dollar deposit when my mother took me aside, out of earshot, and whispered angrily, "Your father is not going to live 'til the summer. Don't give the lady a deposit." I argued that it was a small price to give my father a semblance of normalcy, to let him continue thinking he was making plans for his future. She was adamantly opposed. And so we did not arrange the summer rental, to my father's mild disappointment. Although the outing lifted my father's spirits, I was left with the impression that my mother had gotten one tiny bit of revenge for all the years when he had so sorely mistreated her.

In the last weeks before my father's death on June 24, his weight loss and low energy level curtailed any activities outside the house. He became increasingly quiet, but good-humored whenever anyone visited him. My mother was obsessively concerned that he would die while they were alone at home. Dr. Filipone, the surgeon who had operated on my father, kept in touch with my mother and, on one occasion when I was there, he came for an impromptu visit. He reassured my mother that she was keeping my father comfortable in his last days and that he would have my father brought back to the hospital when his condition could no longer be handled at home. That an overworked surgeon would take the time to pay a home visit to my parents was a great kindness. As the son of Italian immigrants, he confessed a special understanding and concern for Lucy and Frank.

On our last weekend visit, we found my father in Saint Barnabas Hospital, where we each spent a few moments with him. He was conscious and clear in his speech, though one could read the realization in his eyes that he was relapsing and lacked the will or physical strength to carry on. Four hours later we arrived in Amherst, only to be met with a telephone call informing us that my father had died an hour after our visit. He was not yet sixty-six. We would need to return to New Jersey the next day for the wake and funeral. My sister's house became the focus of funeral-related activities. As is their custom, friends began delivering food for the family gatherings between visits to the Ippolito Funeral Home, where the wake was held in our old Italo-American neighborhood in Orange. The coming together of brothers and sisters, nieces and nephews, and their wide circle of friends reminded me vividly that, as the only one who lived far away, I lacked such a strong, cohesive community in my Amherst life.

One small incident puzzles me though. On the morning of the funeral, at the last viewing before the coffin would be closed, my mother cried out mournfully, "Frank, why did you leave me? You're going away and I'm here by myself." The sentiment did not startle me but the fact that she cried out in English. I expected that in this moment of deepest distress she would revert to her most familiar language to express strong emotions—Italian.

Wake and funeral were conducted with dignity and my father was buried in the double plot they had purchased in Gate of Heaven cemetery in East Hanover. On returning from the cemetery, we had to take our leave. Lucy would now begin her solitary widowhood. My sister and three brothers all lived nearby, but she would be alone for the first time in her adult life. She was far more resourceful than we had expected. Within a few months, during which time my sister and brothers were wary about who would have to have Mom move in with them, Lucy regained her composure, enrolled in driving school, applied for a job in a local supermarket, and announced that she would stay in her own house. That my mother, at age sixty-three, who had never taken one English-language class and with only four years of formal schooling in Italy, would pass the New Jersey driving test the first time around— both the road test and the written test—is a testament to her incredible native ability and her stalwart will to achieve. She understood very well that in a suburban town there could be no mobility without her car, and she demonstrated her capacity to cope with the new demands in her life. Not that she would relinquish her role of Neapolitan martyr, The Widow, for that was second-nature to Lucy. She must never let us think she was too happy lest we stop feeling guilty about not doing enough for her.

A Stressful Summer

Though our sons were happy at home at their various sports, day camps, and neighborhood activities, the summer of 1974 was not a happy one for David and me. Tensions centered on our incompatible views of how my new teaching career would affect the family. He feared I would be away from home and mostly distracted by my job, unable to give him and our sons the attention and care they needed. I believed myself capable of handling it all, with some cooperation from them. The boys would all be in school while I was teaching, and I would be home in time for their after-school activities. We were in a state of limited communication; David resented whatever I did, such as work toward completing the last course for my undergraduate degree, and spend time applying for a teaching job in one of the neighboring cities. He guarded his own time for research and writing, refusing to go on any family trips. It was left to me, again. I wangled a visit to Lake Garfield with our friends, Dean and Alice Allen, and a few days at the Jersey shore with my brother Anthony's family, where our sons always enjoyed being with their cousins.

One outstanding event of the summer that brought us all together was the evening of August 9, a great moment in American history. There would be a speech by President Nixon that could well deliver the culmination of the entire Watergate imbroglio. David and I had focused intently on every single moment of the despised Nixon's machinations—the investigations, the hearings in Congress—and now the scoundrel was ready to make an important announcement. It happened to be our son Steve's eighth birthday, and our nephew Mike Philipp, an undergraduate at the university, and our friend Nonny Burack were both present for the speech. David brought out a huge piece of cardboard on which he wrote our guesses as to what Nixon would say, to wit: (1) he would say he was resigning, (2) he would announce that we had just attacked Red China, or (3) he would declare martial law and the dissolution of Congress, declaring himself President for Life. Fortunately, Nixon did the honorable thing and resigned, which produced great glee and much shouting of our approval.

In mid-August I was notified that I been granted my bachelor's degree in liberal arts, *magna cum laude*. Since I had completed my studies during the early summer after the graduation ceremonies had been held in May, I missed the excitement of joining my fellow graduates, in cap and gown, marching up to the stage to receive the diploma. Still, it was a moment of great personal satisfaction in our immediate family. By the end of the summer, after interviews in three school districts, I was hired as a Spanish/English Bilingual teacher in the Springfield Public Schools, scheduled to teach in the Armory Street School, about a half-hour's drive from my home in Amherst, at a starting annual salary of $8,300. David and I barely talked as Labor Day weekend signaled the opening of the school year, he nursing premonitions of a chaotic household, I feeling uncertain of my role as a forty-three-year-old "new" teacher.

A Profession at Last

September 1974 brought the heavy hand of Judge Arthur Garrity down on the urban schools of Massachusetts, principally Boston and Springfield. Due to the growing racial imbalance in the Boston Public Schools, a case to desegregate the schools had made its way through the courts. The resolution was to force citywide busing of students, meaning that African American students from Roxbury and Jamaica Plain would be bused to South Boston and white students from that traditionally Irish neighborhood would be sent to schools in which the majority of students was black. The protests and demonstrations by South Boston families and their sympathizers, sometimes violent, were to be the focus of evening news programs for years.

When I reported to the Armory Street School, the principal assembled the staff and announced that classes would be delayed for two weeks in order to comply with the court order requiring the entire student population of the city to be reassigned to achieve racial balance. New bus routes would have to be designed. Springfield's public schools were already 75 percent integrated, but Judge Garrity did not find that sufficient and ordered students bused away from their neighborhood schools to achieve 90 percent integration. The population of Springfield is majority low income, about 25 percent African American, 25 percent Puerto Rican, and the rest of Italian and Irish derivation. All the students were now to be uprooted from their neighborhood schools and made to travel across the city each day.

Armory Street School alone, though it was sited in a low-income neighborhood of mixed ethnicity, must now monitor students arriving in fourteen different buses and see their own students living nearby dispersed throughout the city. This widespread upheaval took a heavy toll that first year of desegregation, disorienting children and disgruntling teachers and parents. What we did not even foresee was the fact that in a few years, as the population demographics changed and more white families moved out to the suburbs, students would again have to be transferred in pursuit of an elusive goal: balanced skin color in each school. The failure of busing to result in higher academic achievement for African American children was soon obvious. Years later in an autobiography of William Bulger, longtime president of the Massachusetts Senate and outspoken foe of busing, Professor Christine Rossell, the expert who had played a critical part in convincing Judge Garrity that the desegregation plan was necessary, was quoted as saying, "I was wrong."

As student reassignments were completed, teachers were instructed to plan lessons and prepare classrooms. I now learned that I would have no classroom of my own. As the one "Bilingual and English as a Second Language" teacher in the school, I would give tutorials in a large closet where a table and six chairs were set out for me. The students would all be fifth and sixth graders who had little or no knowledge of English. Also, I was assigned to teach part of every day in the kindergarten classes where I would give some instruction in Spanish (on the basics of letters, numbers, colors, size, and so forth) and some lessons on the English language. It was a confusing assignment and I felt little confidence in my ability to make it work.

A further source of anxiety was the relative newness of bilingual teaching and the almost total lack of textbooks and teaching materials in Spanish and English suitable for the different grade levels—we were in uncharted territory, with only vague guidelines from the central administration. This separation of certain students from their classmates a large part of the school day didn't make sense. It took the better part of two years for the other teachers and the principal to regard me as a professional whose work, although substantially different from that of the typical classroom teacher, merited respect. They could not begin to understand why I was to teach all the subjects to our fifth- and sixth-grade Puerto Rican students in Spanish, or why I would spend time with kindergarten children speaking to them mostly in Spanish, when the stated goal of the bilingual program was to help these children learn English as quickly as possible! I would ask myself the same question in a few years, and the answer—that I should be teaching them in English—began a new chapter in my career.

The first few weeks of school for our family was a time of adjustments, and our sons handled it well. David seemed to be holding his breath, suspending judgment on whether my having a fulltime job would yet cause insurmountable problems. Toward the end of September, while David's mother was spending a few weeks with us, we were invited to go away for the weekend by good friends, an overnight trip to Cape Ann. David Leeming we had known since our days in Istanbul, and when he returned to America and took up residence in Connecticut with his wife and children, we reestablished a close friendship. The Leemings knew about the tensions over my new job and devised this weekend to give us a change of scenery. It was exactly what we needed. We knew the boys would be fine with their grandmother, and we even arranged for our nephew, Mike Philipp, a student at the university, to drop in and make certain that Bertha Porter and the boys were okay.

We met David and Pam in Concord for a quick tour of the Ralph Waldo Emerson home, left one car parked there, and put ourselves in the hands of our friends, who gave us a delightful tour of Salem, Swampscott, Marblehead, and other scenic spots on the way to Gloucester and Rockport, where we walked the magnificent rocky shore. That weekend with our friends was the catalyst that banished the anxieties between us, just as the Leemings had intended. We enjoyed their good company, and really relaxed with each other. On Sunday morning, when we left the hotel to take a stroll down Green Street to Pigeon Cove harbor to watch the fishermen unloading their lobster catch, we noticed a "For Sale" sign in front of a tall, narrow house. On an impulse, we jotted down the realtor's phone number. The house appeared to be over a half-century old, set on a hill over the harbor, giving the promise of good ocean views from all its windows. The idea of once again owning a summer place took our fancy, and especially appealing was the prospect of having a house within easy access—a mere two-hours' drive—rather than the long seven-to-eight hours of travel to the old place on Nantucket Island. And my new salary would make this investment fit our budget.

Number 6 Green Street, a handsome old, three-bedroom house in good condition, had a few quirky features. On descending the basement stairs to check out the oil-burning furnace, we found the house to be solidly anchored on bare, massive boulders. In the narrow garden toward the rear of the property were two small buildings—a garage with storage shed in the rear, and a classic, two-seater outhouse in pristine condition, complete with little lace curtains on the window and a collection of ancient *Policemen's Gazette* magazines. Every window in the house facing east and south provided a fine view of the rocky Atlantic coastline and the distant Gloucester lighthouse. The house had one serious drawback: it was located around the corner from the Pigeon Cove Tool and Die Company, a drop-forge plant producing heavy mining equipment. Since the Civil War years this factory was the main employer in the area, so its heavy thudding noises that started at six every morning and lasted until four every weekday afternoon were tolerated by the neighbors. Had it not been for the factory, a house on Green Street would not have been on the market for the modest $38,000. price. Weighing all the pluses and minuses of the property, we decided to buy it. In mid-December 1974 we took title, and contracted with George Witham, a local builder, to make two improvements to the house: add a second full bathroom on the second floor and raise the roof on the attic to make it into a single master bedroom with a balcony that would allow us to capitalize on the magnificent views.

My husband loves to tell everyone he meets that the one other benefit of my starting to work full time was my announcement that I would treat us to a season subscription to the Metropolitan Opera in New York. It was a chance conversation with an Amherst couple, serious opera lovers, which implanted the idea of purchasing one subscription to the opera season and dividing up the series between us. This allowed us each to attend four performances and, at a cost of twenty-two dollars per ticket, the total charge was within our means. We were giddy at the prospect of hearing four operas every year! Arranging a responsible, mature babysitter for the day was not difficult. Leaving Amherst at 7 AM, arriving in New York by 10:30, allowed us to make one brief visit to a museum or art gallery, get a quick lunch at O'Neal's Balloon or The Ginger Man near Lincoln Center, thrill to the opera performance, and get back to Amherst by around 9:00 PM, an exhausting but totally delicious day.

The 1974–75 school year was full of professional anxieties for me. At age forty-three I was learning how to be an elementary school teacher with an unusual "bilingual" twist, carving out an unknown role among co-workers who were skeptical of what I was doing. Gradually, as I earned the trust and respect of the fifth- and sixth-grade teachers and the principal, by my second and third years at Armory, the classes with the older students took the shape I determined would serve them best. Students who enrolled in our school without a full knowledge of English were assigned to me for two to four hours of the school day. I finally secured my own classroom, a solid base of operations for our special lessons. The most radical change I made in my "bilingual" teaching assignment after the first year, with the support of Jim Moriarty, our school principal, was to focus on intensive lessons in the English language for the older students. Rather than teaching all the subjects in Spanish during the hours these students spent with me, we employed all the newest strategies for learning school subjects and English simultaneously—using film, games, songs, building a classroom grocery store for lessons in nutrition and math, doing science experiments, and acting out simple plays. My lessons in the kindergarten classroom also focused on English-language development, using nursery rhymes, songs, and children's classics to teach basic school vocabulary, reading and math.

One year at Christmastime I defied the district rules in the name of cross-cultural understanding. My older students learned a few classic English Christmas carols and also practiced, with rhythm instruments, the traditional carols of Puerto Rico. We were given permission to do a serenade tour of all the fifth- and sixth-grade classrooms. I countered the mild objections of the principal by declaring that this activity fulfilled important goals of the bilingual program: demonstrating the students' English fluency, promoting understanding of the students' Puerto Rican culture, and developing their self-esteem. Who could object? But that was 1978. Today such an activity in any public school would absolutely not be allowed—thank you, ACLU.

As time passed, my teaching job proved manageable and satisfying. Arriving home soon after the three boys gave us time for chores, homework, Tom and Dave's after school sports, and an evening meal together. It was not the Beaver Cleaver household, to be sure, but our teenage sons were not making our lives too miserable, and Steve was an easy-going child. Our next-door neighbor Edie Campbell offered to lend us an upright piano that a cousin was discarding, if we would pay for the moving of it. We took it and Steve began piano lessons with Jean Tucker down the street. He also joined the Cub Scout troop and played in the Amherst Youth Soccer League on Saturday mornings. Tom and Davey, at right and left guard, were stars on the championship soccer team at the high school, and we attended every game. At season's end, there were such high spirits among the parents that we decided to organize a celebration for the soccer team, a pot luck supper at the American Legion Hall, with food prepared by the families. After supper and humorous speeches, the boys on the team did the clean up. It became an annual event for several years, until it descended first into a pizza party and then went out of style.

Another Loss

In February of 1975 we received an urgent call from my husband's sister Dud in Batavia, New York, where Mother Porter was visiting. It appeared that she had suffered a massive stroke and was in the hospital. Before we could even prepare to make the seven-hour drive to see her, she died. David was terribly saddened not to have been with his mother at the end. We all loved Bertha and took comfort in the fact that she had had a long visit with us in Amherst a few months earlier. The trip to Elba for her funeral was a strained occasion because there had been a breakdown in communications between the two halves of the family over Roy's divorce—Dud and Roy on one side, David and sister Marge on the other. However, everyone was civil and Bertha's eighty-five year sojourn on this earth was duly honored by all her children and grandchildren. Our sons enjoyed the two days with their Porter cousins. From the first day I met Bertha Porter in 1956, she showed me unfailing respect and love, which I returned in kind. I was moved by her independence of spirit and her wonderful sense of humor.

A Graduating Senior Son and Rockport Summers

A major event in the spring of 1975 was Tom's performance on the national PSAT exams which placed him as one of nine Amherst high school students who were National Merit finalists. Tom's keen mind in both verbal and mathematical spheres was long known to us, but it was wonderful to have his above-average ability confirmed by the objective tests. Tom, if asked at that time, would probably have said that the most exciting event of his sixteenth year was his evening at a Led Zeppelin concert, in person. It was what Tom wanted most for his sixteenth birthday. Good father that he is, David ordered tickets for the February 4 concert on Long Island, a five-hour drive from Amherst. Tom, Dave, and their father left in late afternoon, with a heavy snowfall predicted. The concert was spectacular, and David said later that the marijuana fumes reaching their high-balcony seats were almost overpowering. They had to drive home slowly on the snow-clogged roads, arriving after 2 AM. The experience so impressed Tom that he declared he would take up the acoustic guitar and form a rock band of his own, giving both parents shock tremors that he might decide to "tune in, turn on, and drop out."

Our nephew, Michael Philipp, completed his undergraduate degree in art history at the university and announced he would be married shortly after graduation in May. As he was marrying Sher, his college sweetheart from Magnolia, a seacoast town near Rockport, we were happy to combine the wedding weekend with a visit to our soon-to-be remodeled summer home. The wedding was quite a departure from what we expected from the very prosperous Philipp family of Ridgewood, New Jersey. Sher's family hosted a wedding reception in their garden, after a ceremony at the local Methodist Church, with home-made sandwiches, potato salad, and a modest wedding cake. It was a warm, family event that the Philipp crowd carried off with great aplomb. Mike and Sher were gorgeous, he in a white three-piece suit, open-necked shirt, à la John Travolta in *Saturday Night Fever* and she in her simple cotton gown with flowers twined in her beautiful cascade of honey-hued hair. They dazzled us.

Mike and Sher surprised their families with their determination to take up the counterculture life style in toto: vegetarians, they would live in a little house in the woods with a kiln in the front yard where Mike would fire his ceramic ware and Sher would deliver two beautiful boy babies at home with the help of a mid-wife. Their simple lifestyle lasted five years until one evening, when they dropped in for a beer. Mike announced to Uncle Dave and Aunt Lee, "I've been accepted for graduate study at the School of Business Administration at UMass. I'm going to get an MBA in international banking." Wow, what a sharp turn that was. To their great credit, Mike and Sher handled the move from backwoods academia to fast track Goldman Sachs and beyond without faltering. This amazing couple figures later in my story.

Our visit to number 6 Green Street during the Philipps' wedding weekend revealed that George Witham, the local builder we contracted months earlier to make improvements to the house, had actually done nothing. David called George and had what he thought was a serious discussion with him. But it was not serious enough. George assured Dave that he was ready to start very soon, stressing that the work must be completed before the end of June so we could move in for the summer. "Yes, sir, yes, sir, you'll find it all done in plenty of time," said the native to the outsider. My husband was inclined to be indulgent of the local ways, and we foolishly took George at his word. On the second of July we packed the car with our family, our cat, Steve's friend Aaron Stern, clothes, books, games, and groceries, and started out for Rockport. Imagine our utter disgust on arriving to find the installation of a second floor bathroom barely started and nothing yet done to build us a third floor master bedroom. All the ground-floor furniture was stacked in the living room, as we had left it in December. We called George Witham to task, we were furious. George had the gall to suggest that we could just camp out here for a while until he finished. Unimaginable! We turned around to drive back to Amherst, threatening George with a lawsuit. We lost any chance of being in Pigeon Cove, Rockport, and the work was not finished until the end of August, giving us only Labor Day weekend there.

During the summer David took Tom on a tour of colleges including Johns Hopkins, Georgetown, George Washington University, and Yale, which gave them an opportunity to spend a few companionable days together. In early October we took a family drive to Hamilton College, my husband's alma mater, for a football game weekend and a visit to the Psi U house, where we were warmly welcomed at the fraternity house cocktail party. Tom liked the campus quite a bit, though he did remark later, "Dad, the guys at Psi U drink a lot, don't they?" Our son was yet to discover the ways of college men—and women. Tom applied to six colleges, was accepted at three and finally chose to attend Hamilton, a school that turned out to be exactly right for him.

Fall 1975, Tom's senior year, brought the premier performance of the rock band he had organized with high school classmates Joe Keenan, John Cellura, Gil May, and Dave Weidenfeld. *Kiss of Fire* played its first paid engagement for an Amherst High School dance and David and I announced that we would be there. Tom told us to please stay far in the background of the gymnasium and absolutely not stand near the bandstand and "dote." This was all new territory for us, and we complied with the rules. Dave, on the other hand, had remained faithful to his cello lessons and his participation in the high school orchestra. A strikingly handsome boy, Dave attracted girls more easily and began socializing at a younger age than Tom. Both boys were actively involved in a variety of after-school activities—music, sports, art—and each had an assortment of good friends.

Certainly they pushed for greater freedom than we were prepared to allow. We enforced what we considered reasonable hours for coming home from high school dances and parties on the weekends, and since Dad had to give them rides, our rules prevailed. They did sneak over to the university on occasion to play the arcade games and probably did other things we never learned about. One Friday evening, not long after my husband had dropped Dave at the junior high dance at St. Brigid's Church Hall, he called us to say, "I'm not feeling well. Can Dad come and get me?" Dave's experiment with a friend's marijuana had not been pleasant, and he needed us to come to the rescue. Our two persistent fears as the boys entered their mid-teen years, based on what we had observed in the families of friends with slightly older children in the 1960s, were the serious risk of heavy drug use (drugs were easily available in our college town) or of the boys running away to join a commune. Somehow, our close monitoring of their activities and friends did not push our sons in either of these dreaded directions. The fact that neither brother decided, for instance, to drop out of school to become a rock musician, although they both organized rock bands in high school and college, is another thing for which we are devoutly thankful. But looking back on it now, our fear of that scenario grew more from our response to the "dropout culture" than from our either of our sons' penchant for joining it.

The 1975–76 school year centered around Tom's activities as a high school senior and the tremendous intensity with which Tom and Dave played varsity soccer for their Amherst team, which won a state regional championship. My husband had taught the boys the joy of sports from their very early years in our own backyard, and gradually encouraged them to participate in team sports; he still maintains that valuable lessons are learned there, no matter what the sport. Being a proud spectator at our sons' baseball, soccer, hockey, track, and other events gave me special pride, but with a distinct disappointment that, as a young girl, I was never allowed such an experience.

We were very pleased that Tom chose the college that his grandfather, Roy Avery Porter, and his father David Thomas Porter, graduated from in 1913 and 1950. As time for the Amherst High senior prom approached, Tom invited his girlfriend Anne Feaster to be his date, and I went with him to the nearby tuxedo rental shop where he chose a powder blue number with navy velvet trim—quite dashing for the time. Tom's class prom was held in the Top of the Campus Center at UMass and the big "after party" took place in the Quonset Hut bar and grill on Route 9 in Hadley, one mile out of town, followed by early morning breakfast at the McManus Diner. The trend in later years has been to more elaborate and costlier high school proms with measurably worse behavior.

That summer was our first in the Rockport house, providing us the excitement of exploring a new part of the state and the satisfaction of introducing relatives and friends to the beauties of the rocky coast and the charms of nearby Gloucester's large-scale fishing fleets and its art colony. Our Green Street neighborhood was decidedly working class and that suited us just fine—no having to carry on academic chit-chat over the back fence. Our boys took turns inviting classmates to come for weekend visits. My brothers and sister and their families came up from New Jersey. Our visitors were most amused by the two-seater outhouse, which we left exactly as we found it, lace curtains and all. Most afternoons we bicycled to the nearest sandy beach in town or walked the half mile to nearby Rocky Neck, an area of enormous boulders, to climb and watch the sea crashing on the glacier-smoothed rocks, a place to investigate the tiny sea life in shallow pools—a perfect spot where we enjoyed dozens of picnic suppers each summer. The third-floor bed/sitting room with its small balcony became the place where we could occasionally retreat to enjoy a cocktail before dinner. David worked mornings on his literary research and writing at the tiny Pigeon Cove Library, which was mostly deserted, and joined the family later in the day. The only unhappy lad was Tom, whom we had persuaded to find a job in a Pigeon Cove restaurant for the summer to earn money for his coming expenses at Hamilton. He did not want to be away from Amherst, but there had been no work available in town and he understood the need for his earnings. Even with both David and me earning teacher's salaries, and a scholarship offered by Hamilton College, the tuition of $7,300 for the year was a stretch for us.

It became our established pattern to find a tenant for the Rockport house from September through June to help pay the mortgage, taxes, and insurance. The first year we rented to the Carrolls, an attractive family with three young children. When we arrived at the house for the summer of 1976, Joan met us and explained that she and her husband had separated and she just couldn't meet the last month's rent. But she would be willing to trade the $600 for a watercolor of our house, which she would frame nicely for us. We accepted and still have the lovely painting hanging over our living room coach.

Our second year tenants, two young women school teachers, convinced us to allow their pets, two cats, against our better judgment. On our arrival the following summer, we found the house infested with fleas. Our first day in residence, David went down to the basement to check on the hot water heater, and when he looked down at his feet, he saw his white socks turn to black as the resident fleas flocked to attach themselves to this new host. Thrifty as we were, we could not afford to call exterminators but instead found the best product in the hardware store and studied the directions carefully. A poisonous gas canister was to be placed in a central area on each floor, including the basement. Once the toggle switch was turned, the canister would release a mist of chemicals fatal to fleas. Once David placed the canisters and turned them on, he slammed the door and came running out to the car, ready to drive to the beach. Curses, the car keys were up in the third floor bedroom. Quickly he dashed up the stairs for his keys and shot out of the house even more rapidly, hoping he had not breathed in too much of the noxious air. This would not be our last adventure with the rental of our summer home, but we became practiced in coping, since it was the only economical way to carry the expenses of two houses and our family.

If I were to ask our sons what they remember as most pleasurable about the Rockport summers, I suspect Tom and Dave might cite Tim Halpin's visit, when they spent hours in the shed constructing and painting a floating shark's fin that they put in the ocean near the crowded beach to frighten everyone who had just seen *Jaws.* Steve, who invited the most friends to stay with us, might most prize the day trip to Boston to see the "Tall Ships," sailing ships from many countries, gathered to celebrate the bicentennial year of our country. For David and me, the most incredible achievement of the 1976 summer full of visitors, picnics on the rocks, and lazy afternoons on the beach, was the arrival of a letter from Maude Wilcox, managing editor of the Harvard University Press, announcing that they would publish not one but two books that David had submitted for consideration: a book on Ralph Waldo Emerson and a second book on Emily Dickinson's poetry. What a coup! We were in academic Seventh Heaven. The publication of his first book by Harvard was a high honor to start with. This new development would have large implications for David's career opportunities in the near future, bringing research grants, job offers, and invitations to speak all over the world.

Reflections on Teaching in General

In my personal view of our six summers in Rockport, the biggest boon was my privilege, as a teacher, of having ten precious weeks free of professional work. This is a fair place to interject a little realism about the mythical plight of teachers, the poor overworked, underpaid slaves in our public schools. In the three decades since I entered the teaching field, teachers' salaries across the country have increased dramatically, though there are disparities between the wealthiest states that spend the most per pupil on public education (New York, New Jersey, California, Connecticut, and Maryland), and the poorest states that spend the least (Mississippi, Alabama, and Louisiana). Productivity as far as student academic achievement has not improved in tandem with the high investment in salaries. If anything, student performance has declined and the gap between the highest achievers (Asians and whites) and the lowest achievers (African Americans and Latinos) has widened.

Since the doom-saying report of 1983, *A Nation At Risk,* was published, many strategies have been touted to stem the tide of mediocrity in the performance of U.S. schoolchildren except that of increasing the "time-on-task" for students, that is, extending the hours and/or days of actual schooling to make our schools competitive with the rest of the developed world[7]. Today, 2008, on the thirty-fifth anniversary of that report, teachers' unions are desperately fighting to keep teachers from being evaluated in part on their students' achievement, on whether the children are learning anything.

In Massachusetts, teachers are closely supervised by the school principal for their first three years, with scheduled classroom observations and a written critique. In Springfield we were required by union contract to attend a number of teacher-training sessions after school during the year. At Armory Street School, we were required to leave detailed lessons plans on our desks before dismissal on Friday afternoon. Some elected to take graduate courses in the summer months or evenings during the school year, to accumulate credits for a master's degree and higher salary scale. Once passing the magic third year, with good evaluations on file, a teacher automatically earned tenure in the fourth year of teaching and was no longer bound to attend training sessions. Raises in salary occurred annually according to seniority and advanced degrees, by union contract, and we all moved in lock-step toward retirement—no one accorded a higher salary for meritorious teaching or being denied a raise due to truly substandard teaching— and certainly no one feared being fired. It is not a formula for inspiring extraordinary performance.

First to Leave
In the fall of 1976, Tom's leaving for Hamilton College at the young age of seventeen opened the first of three successive gaps in the fabric of our family. Dave was noticeably quiet in the first months after his brother's departure. Though pleased to have a bedroom to himself for the first time, he missed Tom's company at school, in team sports, and around the house. We all felt the absence of Tom's exuberant personality, his enthusiasms, his wild dashes up and down stairs, and I missed the soft strains of "Stairway to Heaven" emanating from his bedroom at 11 PM on school nights when I would stop in to say "good

night." Cleaning out Tom's closet I committed the unpardonable sin, the inexcusable. Finding a shoebox full of carefully catalogued baseball cards, I remembered an announcement on our local radio station's Swap Program that an Amherst man was interested in buying such collections. Without consulting my son, I sold the whole set for $35. When I called to tell Tom of this bonanza, he surprised me by his explosive reaction. He was terribly hurt at my callous disregard for his property and said so in the strongest terms. *Mea culpa, mea maxima culpa.*

Tom adjusted well to life in his freshmen dorm and the various campus activities, as we noted on a visit during Parents' Weekend in the fall. Communications between us were almost entirely conducted by letter, since telephone calls were an expense we could not often indulge. In fact, we concocted a little stratagem for outwitting the telephone company. Each time Tom returned to college after a visit at home, we wanted to know that he had gotten back safely as he would be traveling by train, bus, or some friend's rattletrap car. Tom would call the long distance operator and place a person-to-person call to our number, asking to speak with Ralph Emerson. Whichever of us answered the phone would recognize this coded message and answer, "I'm sorry Mr. Emerson isn't here, he's gone to Harvard for the week." With this ploy, there was no charge for the call and we would know that Tom was back at school.

The year ended on a very pleasing note when we accepted an invitation to spend the Christmas holiday with my brother Anthony's family in Livingston, New Jersey. The three days together gave our children enough time with their favorite cousins, and for David and me to engage in unhurried discussions with Anthony and Dee, each of whom was pursuing an interesting career, my brother rising rapidly in the ranks of high administrators at NBC-TV and his wife now operating a successful real estate company. On the last day we took a trip to the Statue of Liberty and Little Italy, bringing my mother along for the treat.

Lucy, the indomitable Lucy, was making the best of new her role. After my father's death, she continued to work in the deli department of the Shop Rite Supermarket, principally in the catering section. She enjoyed showing off her high energy level, rarely taking a coffee or lunch break, and her skills in arranging food and serving customers. She loved to tell us anecdotes about the poor performance of the younger workers and the foolish expectations of customers who seemed to have no idea of how to organize a meal. My siblings and I were insensitive to how very much our mother was starved for appreciation, how desperately she had missed the approval of my father during all the years of their marriage. I'm ashamed to say that we all teased her a bit about her experiences at Shop Rite, and sometimes, especially from my brother Domenick, the banter was not good-natured but had a vicious edge.

Now, at age sixty-four, Lucy was contacted by Dr. Loren Rosenberg, an allergist in town who had recently been widowed when his forty-three-year-old wife died of cancer, leaving him and their three sons in need of help. The doctor asked her if she would consider being their housekeeper, from 2 to 6:30 PM each day. She was to be on hand when the three boys returned from school, take them to music lessons or sports, supervise their homework, and prepare dinner for the family. She would then leave. The salary he offered for the part-time position was decent and the hours were shorter than the long shift at the supermarket. Wisely, Lucy accepted the offer. She worked for Dr. Rosenberg and his family until her real retirement in 1984, after suffering a minor fall and a broken wrist. She was treated with the greatest respect by the doctor, his second wife, and his sons, and was included in all family observances as an honored guest. While it lasted, it was a mutually agreeable arrangement, and later Lucy benefited from her relationship with the doctor when she needed advice and referrals.

In early 1977 David was approached by the head of the English Department at Purdue University, urged to consider a position as full professor there, and invited for a campus visit to give a guest lecture, meet the faculty, and see the town of West Lafayette, Indiana. As the date fell during my February winter vacation week at school, I went with him. Purdue was impressive, the English Department faculty members who entertained us were very welcoming, and they responded with enthusiasm to David's lecture. It was an opportunity for a hefty salary increase and the move to a more prestigious university, but taking ourselves to Indiana—to the banks of the Wabash—was just not appealing. David was recognized now as a first-rate scholar, and he would soon be wooed by Washington State University, the University of North Carolina, and Dartmouth College.

While in West Lafayette, I learned that my mother had been taken to the hospital for abdominal surgery. Instead of flying back home with my husband, I took a flight to Newark where my brother Frank Jr. took me directly to the hospital to spend the evening with my mother. She was happy to see me but not very alert; she was just emerging from anesthesia. Still, we were content to sit together late into the evening. Returning home the next day, I had missed a visit with our son Tom who was home briefly to observe his eighteenth birthday. He was good-natured about it, having had a visit with his father and brothers. The pattern of my travels to New Jersey by then was well established. I would pick up and go—by bus, train, plane, car, with or without my husband and children—whenever I was called. I felt obliged to do the traveling since, as the oldest child, I had always had an overdeveloped sense of responsibility, and also because I was the only one of my siblings to have moved away from New Jersey from the day I married. Today, in the new millennium, I still compulsively make the effort to travel to New Jersey for family events and feel deeply sad that my sister and brothers are not inclined to return the courtesy, always finding excuses not to make the trip to Amherst.

Summer of 1977 was relatively problem free until mid-August when our son Dave was seriously injured in a league soccer game. The Amherst group had formed a summer team of young men who loved the sport, and arranged games with other teams in the Pioneer Valley. We were watching the game one early evening when Davey, dribbling the ball toward a goal, collided with another player. We all heard the crash, a sound like a pistol shot. It was immediately obvious that this was no minor accident but a bone-jarring, possibly serious leg injury. The other player was not injured, but Dave sustained damage to his left knee that required surgery and two months on crutches. Gone was the dream of playing on the excellent soccer team his senior year of high school. He recovered full use of his knee in time, but no longer had the speed that made him such a great runner in all the sports he enjoyed.

Irreparable Loss

November brought us one of the deepest tragedies ever to be visited on our family. Our good friends from Istanbul, Mary Alice and David Sipfle, wrote to say they would be in the East to see their daughters, one at Bryn Mawr and one at Middlebury. David was the professor at Robert College who had strongly influenced my husband's decision to become a college professor; Mary Alice was my best friend in Istanbul. They were now both teaching at Carleton College in Minnesota. We invited them to spend Thanksgiving weekend with us. It was a thoroughly satisfying three days, though Tom and Dave were rather shy around Ann and Gail Sipfle who were a few years older and seemed more sophisticated.

On Saturday morning, after a special breakfast to celebrate Ann's twentieth birthday, the Sipfles piled into their VW, heading to Vermont to drop off Gail at her dorm before taking Ann to Pennsylvania. Driving north on Route 7, a two-lane road, at sunset, a pick-up truck driven by a man who had been drinking heavily, crossed the median line at high speed and plowed into the left side of their car. David, the driver, and his daughter Ann who was sitting behind him, were seriously injured, though they were wearing seat belts. Mary Alice and Gail suffered multiple injuries but nothing serious. Passing motorists called the police and the entire family was taken to the nearest hospital in Rutland, Vermont. The next morning, as soon as she could find a telephone, Mary Alice called us with the horrible news and to ask if we could drive to Rutland. As the least injured, she was responsible for talking with the police, filling out hospital paperwork, and coordinating the diagnoses and treatments prescribed by various doctors who were on hand when the family was admitted.

We left our sons to see to themselves and drove to Rutland, David and I canceling our teaching for the following day. In consultation with the lead doctor who was treating the family, we learned that David Sipfle had suffered a broken jaw, two broken arms, two broken legs, broken ribs, and that his injuries, serious but not life-threatening, would require long hospitalization and a long recovery period. Ann Sipfle, who was in intensive care next to her father, was in the greatest danger. From her seat in the middle section of the car, she had been crushed between the heavy luggage behind her and the back of the front seat, with the seat belt contributing to severe internal injuries. Every effort was being made to ease her pain and to determine the best course for operating to repair the damage to internal organs.

After collecting the handbags, wallets, and essential items the police had retrieved from the badly smashed car, and making phone calls to relatives of the Sipfles, to the girls' schools, and to insurance companies, we left for home, promising Mary Alice that we would return on the weekend. And so we spent the next three Sundays at the hospital, visiting with the family, running errands, and trying our best to raise their spirits. On each visit we were dismayed to find little improvement in Ann's condition. She was immobilized, but happy to see visitors. The Sipfles had brought in additional specialists to consult on her condition and were confident that she was receiving expert care. Moving her to Boston or New York was considered too risky.

On Christmas Eve, as our family sat waiting for me to serve dinner, the phone rang and as soon as I heard Mary Alice's voice I understood the news would be bad. Ann had died that afternoon. They would need us to rescue them from their desperation, and the lead doctor had asked that we take the whole family out of the hospital for a few days. When I turned to the family from the kitchen doorway, they immediately guessed the news. In my distress, I dropped the huge platter with our dinner on the floor. There was little appetite anyway, and we turned instead to preparing the house for our three guests, especially David Sipfle, who was still in casts and needed a wheel chair. Friends agreed to have our sons spend Christmas Day and an overnight with them.

Bringing David, Mary Alice, and Gail back to Amherst with us allowed their grieving to proceed in greater privacy, with close friends around, and away from the scene of so much pain. Those few days bonded our two families together, though it would be three decades before the Sipfles would be ready to talk with us about Ann's death.

The Sipfles spent another month in the Rutland Hospital before David was sufficiently recovered to allow their return to Northfield, Minnesota. The young lout who had caused this tragedy was found to have been driving without a valid license, and to be a repeat offender for driving while drunk. The authorities did not charge him with vehicular homicide or any such criminal charges, noting that it would be a difficult charge to prove since Ann had lived for four weeks after the crash, and who could be sure that it wasn't the fault of her hospital care. The Sipfles sued the VW automobile company over the seat belts, which appeared to be the culpable factor in Ann's internal injuries, and were awarded a substantial settlement. After different periods of therapy, they finally all recovered their capacity for physical activities, skiing, tennis, and running, but the loss of Ann cast a pall on each of them that is still subtly apparent.

Second Son to Take Wing

Spring 1978 engaged us all in special activities around Dave's senior year of high school, with letters coming from the schools he had applied to and which of those offered acceptances (University of Pennsylvania, Brandeis, Hamilton—not Brown), and the typical round of plays, concerts, and parties that characterize academic social life. Dave was dating one of the beautiful Stein twins, Suzy, and, like his older brother, he had organized a rock band, this one called *Rainbow Bridge*. The local newspaper featured a photo from the ARHS senior prom of Dave and Susie—she in demure white, he in his grandfather Roy Porter's cutaway and striped pants from 1913. I had started graduate classes in the evenings toward a Masters degree in second-language teaching, my husband was busy with his teaching and the writing of his Emerson book; Steve was following in his brothers' footsteps with high grades and a talent in sports, but with the added facet of becoming a serious piano student.

Summers in Rockport did not appeal to Tom and Dave, who finally convinced us that they should be allowed to find jobs and stay in Amherst on their own. Reluctantly we gave in. Our sons understood that they must work summers and secure on-campus part time jobs to help pay their college expenses. Both Hamilton College and the University of Pennsylvania offered some scholarship aid, and our modest family income entitled us to low-interest loans that would be paid back after they graduated. Not one of our sons was given a car of his own, not in high school or in college, a situation that would be considered positively primitive in new-millennium middle-class families. Of course, the use of one of our two cars was often a contentious issue but not exceedingly so. They were able to travel from college to home and back by train or bus and we felt fortunate in being able to give each one a second-hand car on their graduating from college, when they left to find work in distant cities. Our family priorities had always been skewed towards making the most of our combined incomes for overseas travel, cultural activities, and good schools—not in extravagant clothing or expensive furnishings.

Driving to The University of Penn campus at the end of August with Dave's luggage and paraphernalia for his entry into life as a freshman, and for the beginning of soccer-team training, we had a felicitous family reunion with my Uncle Michael and his family, who had settled in Philadelphia several years earlier. They invited us to dinner at their apartment near the city's Museum of Art, whose long stairway featured in the famous *Rocky* films. Dave and Steve were charmed with Uncle Mike and Aunt Mary, whom they had hardly ever seen before, and with my cousins Rosalie and Gloria. What a pleasure for me to see that Uncle Mike was as sharp and witty as ever, regaling us with family anecdotes. They expressed satisfaction at Dave's choice of UPenn and encouraged him to drop in to visit. Gloria, a rabid sports fan, promised to call Dave whenever she had spare tickets to local sports events, and did so on several occasions. The next day we moved Dave's things to a fourth floor room in an old dorm building and bade him a teary goodbye. Now reduced to the small number of three at home, it was a harder adjustment for all of us than when Tom had left. We soon acquired and welcomed a temporary boarder, Paola Miccinelli, the daughter of our good friends in Milano.

Paola, at twenty-four, had completed the equivalent of a master's degree in biology at the University of Milano and wanted experience at an American university as a research assistant or lab technician. Since we had met Paola years earlier when visiting Italy and felt she'd be companionable addition to our family, we agreed to have her live with us and arranged her connection with the Biology Department. As an adult Paola had developed into a statuesque beauty with a very pleasing, good-natured personality. Her English, learned from British teachers, was fairly fluent though accented, and rather formal for American daily life. She quickly became ingrained in our daily routines, helping with chores, bantering with Steve at the dinner table, and amusing us all with her stories of the amazing sights and behavior she witnessed on the university campus. She would often start a story with the statement, "I cahn't believe it." Whenever she called us on the phone she would announce, "Hello, I am Paola," which always amused us.

Dave's letters home revealed a less than happy life at UPenn. He was assigned a tiny single room—no roommate—in a dorm building populated by upperclassmen. Most of the students were from the metropolitan New York/New Jersey area and would leave the campus every weekend. Classes were interesting, but the freshmen soccer-team experience was disappointing, and there were no organized social events in his dorm. Until late October, when Paola took a trip to Washington, D.C., and stopped to visit Dave overnight on her way back, we had no idea just how unhappy he was. She told us that Dave was so sad that he might want to drop out, which is just what our son announced to us when he came home for Thanksgiving weekend. It presented us with a dilemma—did our son need help to adapt better and not surrender too soon to the impulse to bolt, or should we support him in his intentions?

The fact that Dave's high school sweetheart, Suzy Stein, was still here in Amherst, probably subtly influenced his decision as well.

We went to work to present Dave with a compromise solution. After many telephone calls to college administrators and dorm counselors, we secured a change of dorms for the second semester. Dave would be lodged in a coed dorm full of freshmen and sophomores, with a young couple who lived in the building as resident counselors who ran a full social program of weekly brunches, films, and other events. We urged Dave to remain at Penn, give the new dorm a try for one semester, and not to drop out in mid-year. We would help him apply to other colleges for the following year, if that was still his intention. To our immense relief, he agreed.

On the other campus of interest to us, Tom, in his junior year at Hamilton College, was in full stride, academically and socially. He was elected vice-president of his fraternity, Psi U, the residential club of which his father and grandfather had been members. Tom's rock band, *Rogue,* played for college dances, and he formed friendships that would be long-lasting with several of his "brothers." Tom's years at Hamilton coincided with the "merger" of Kirkland College, an independent school for women on "the Hill," and Hamilton forming one coed college. Kirkland had been started in the late 1960s but within the first dozen years was on financially rocky ground. Due to the trend away from single-sex colleges, the incentive for Hamilton and Kirkland to join forces was obvious. Since they were located in such close proximity, students would take classes together. Owing to Hamilton's solid financial status and its preeminence as a highly regarded small college for over a century, the newly combined college would retain Hamilton's name. Strange as it may seem, Kirkland students were harshly critical and seemed not to understand that the choice was between joining Hamilton or being closed down. They were not only angry about the Hamilton connection but fostered a climate of nasty attitudes toward the college's male students. It was a very uncomfortable transition for all concerned and certainly marred what should have been achieved with greater grace and good will.

We decided to take a weekend trip to Hamilton to visit the campus with Paola to show her what an American college is like. In Milano, where she had completed her university studies, as in other Italian cities, students live at home and attend the local institution of higher education. There are no dorms, clubs, sororities, fraternities, campus centers, infirmaries, counseling centers—in short, students attend the lectures that interest them and, when they feel ready, choose to sit for exams in their field of study. Visiting Hamilton proved of great interest to Paola, who found the campus setting beautiful and marveled at the range of student activities beyond the classroom. We attended a cocktail party and dinner at Psi U, a performance of the Sam Shepherd play *The Tooth of Crime*, starring Tony Goldwyn and featuring Tom Porter's rock band, visited the campus center, art museum, and new science building. Steve was with us, and he opted for a side trip to Cooperstown the next day to visit the Baseball Hall of Fame and to view the site of Nathaniel Hawthorne's *Leather Stocking Tales*, which made for a well-rounded, all-American weekend.

Christmas 1978 presented us with the first opportunity to stage a reading of *The Nativity Play of the Shearmen and Tailors of Coventry* (dating from the fifteenth century) in our living room. When we lived in Istanbul we had been invited, along with most of the American community at Robert College, to join Professor MacNeil and his wife for their annual Christmas Eve reading of this play; a few of us were selected to read the parts of Mary, Joseph, the shepherds, kings, and so forth, and all of us sang the traditional English carols that interspersed the story. David and I treasured the memory of these readings and obtained a copy of the play and its musical score from friends in Washington. Though my husband was aggressively agnostic in matters of established religion, he admitted his cultural roots in a Christian tradition and agreed with me that the play reading would be a felicitous celebration of the season. For our first attempt we invited Amherst friends, an eclectic gathering of Christians, Jews, and nonbelievers to participate with us, a custom that we still observe thirty years later.

David made a few remarks about the history of the play and how it was read by members of the craft guilds from the back of a wagon dragged into the center of Coventry. Dean Allen accompanied the carols on the piano, and the reading began with suitable reverence, no smirking, wisecracks, or silliness allowed. At the end, we all rose to sing the final carol, "Adeste Fideles," in Latin and English, and then spontaneously applauded. On to the refreshments, homemade pastries and eggnog. Since that first reading we have missed only one year, the time when our sons could not be at home with us. We have held family readings, with participation by any willing guest in the vicinity, in Cervinia, Italy, Washington, D.C., Boston, and Singer Island, Florida. Though only our son Tom is a baptized Christian, all three sons and their spouses/partners/friends are devoted to the annual event on Christmas Eve afternoon.

Disillusion With My Field

With the start of 1979 I continued my after-school and evening classes to complete a master's degree; the last few courses I needed were in socio-linguistics, statistics, and measurement of cognitive development. I could not escape my growing disillusion with bilingual education. Not one of the theories had been borne out in five years of classroom work. The problems with the experimental theory were now obvious to me and to many of the teachers with whom I worked, but there was no public complaint, and the University of Massachusetts teacher training in bilingual education was as firmly entrenched and as politically unassailable as ever. In fact, a further dimension was added, the requirement to call our field Bilingual/Bicultural Education, mandating the teaching of each child's "culture"—opening the door to another time-wasting piece of foolishness.

I base my critique of bilingual teaching at that time on my five years classroom teaching in grades kindergarten through sixth grade, my research in graduate school, and the experiences of bilingual teachers with whom I compared notes:

a. Teaching Spanish-speaking children in Spanish most of the school day for three years does not help them learn English well enough to do their schoolwork in English.

b. Hiring Puerto Rican teachers, many of whom could not speak English, as "bilingual" teachers in Massachusetts does not promote the learning of English.

c. Segregating limited-English students by language and ethnicity most of the school day for several years does not promote higher self-esteem and may reinforce feelings of inferiority by being kept out of the mainstream of school life.

d. Taking time out of the school day to teach the "culture" of Puerto Rico to a Puerto Rican child defies reason and deprives those students of time better spent on math, science, U.S. history, art, music, or more English-language lessons. Families maintain traditions distinctive to their ethnicity at home—this should not be a responsibility of our public schools.

e. No educational initiative should be above critical review, but this program was above reproach, with even constructive criticism viewed as racist or nativist, thus frightening off anyone who might dare to voice an alternative opinion.

Oddly enough, the Puerto Rican parents whom I interviewed when they arrived to enroll their children in school had no interest in the idea of *la educacion bilingue*. By law we were required to describe our program to the parents (which I did in Spanish) and obtain their signature on a consent form, thus locking their children into three years or more of bilingual—meaning mostly Spanish-language—instruction. The parents would almost always say something like this: "Okay, teacher, that's nice. But I want my Jose to learn English. I want him to do good in school and grow up to have a better life than me." It was not the parents who wanted a two-language education for their children, but the Latino leaders who were ramming through laws in other states to mandate this untested experiment that had no research evidence to support its value. The parents were wiser than their "leaders."

To do my best for these needy families, I soon designed my own supposedly "bilingual" schedule of instruction, with the tacit but wary approval of our school principal. With my older students, fifth and sixth graders ages ten to fourteen, I used the two-hour block every morning (designated "Language Arts") as the time for intensive teaching of English language—speaking, reading, writing—a practice that would advance their ability to use the language as quickly as possible for learning school subjects in English. And they made remarkable progress. But this was in defiance of state law, which would have had me teaching the language arts only in Spanish. Similarly, when I met with these students in an afternoon block devoted to math/ science/social studies, I moved as quickly as the students' performance allowed from teaching the subject matter in Spanish to giving the lessons in simple English. It is amazing how soon students understood enough vocabulary to do science experiments, math problems, and history lessons in English. The transition from learning in their first language to learning in their second language, given this kind of special help, was a marked success. Once recognizing that the bilingual idea had failed our students, I began my private rebellion against the state bureaucracy. I knew that in giving my students strong fluency and literacy in the common language of our country I was giving them the best preparation for further schooling and the chance to avail themselves of educational opportunities that would lift them out of poverty.

Other Outposts

In the spring of 1979, Paola left us to return to Milano and to prepare to marry her fiancé, Vittore Rizzi. Immediately after their wedding ceremony in June they left for a village outside Bujumburu, Rwanda, where they would live for eighteen months, Vittore helping to build a school and Paola teaching teenage children science. It was Vittore's choice to serve in Italy's version of the Peace Corps rather than serve eighteen months in the military.

At the same time, my husband was offered the exchange teaching position at the University of Kent, Canterbury, England, for the 1979–

80 academic year. He accepted. We would take Steve with us and enroll him in the local grammar school for his eighth-grade year, David would lecture at the university, and I would concentrate on further graduate study toward the doctorate. We would all enjoy the benefits of living in England again. The Springfield Public Schools granted me a year's leave without pay, on condition that I would return to my teaching duties in the fall of 1980. Both Tom and Dave were well settled in their respective colleges and would enjoy spending the long Christmas holiday vacation with us in Europe.

Dave applied to transfer to Brandeis University for his sophomore year and had been accepted. We received happier letters in the spring semester after he'd moved to the new dorm at UPenn—he was making friends, enjoying the camaraderie in his building, and exploring the many aspects of big-city Philadelphia. But on an evening in late May Dave arrived home for his summer vacation with a very attractive young woman, a fellow student with whom he had hitched a ride home, and who would be going on to Vermont. After she left, we asked about Dave's plans for the fall and he nonchalantly announced, "Oh, I've decided to stay at Penn." Just like that, his school life had been quietly settled to his own satisfaction—and to ours.

For the first time, I was able to take part in the commencement ceremony at the University of Massachusetts, where I was awarded the Master of Arts degree. The summer flew by as we made preparations to leave for a year in England, finding an academic family to rent our home, securing a house to rent in Canterbury, and searching out a school for Steve. Rather than fly to London, we decided that Steve was the only one of our boys who had never experienced an ocean crossing by ship, since his voyage on the *Cristoforo Colombo* at the age of eight weeks did not count. Ocean liners for the Atlantic crossing had almost entirely gone out of business, ceding to cheap airline fares. We found a Polish Ocean Lines ship, the *Stefan Batory*, which would sail from Montreal and take us right up the Thames to London's Tillbury Dock. The University of Kent would send a faculty member to meet us for the drive to Canterbury and arrange for our luggage and my new toy, a bright yellow motor scooter, to be transported to our new digs, a neat brick row house at 45 Cossington Road.

Several days before we were due to sail another tragic accident afflicted the family of close friends. Kathy Silva, twenty-year-old daughter of our Nantucket Island friends Alby and Jane, and one of our son Dave's best friends, was killed in an auto accident on Labor Day weekend. Grandfather Silva asked us to accompany Kathy's best girlfriend, her college roommate Lisa Mascis, on a private flight to the Island, which he arranged. The weather was blustery and the young girl flying with us was repeatedly nauseous on the bumpy flight, but that was nothing compared to the terrible sadness of seeing Alby and Jane's grief, their utter devastation at the church service, and the laying to rest at the Quaker Burial Ground. We mourned with them for their unbearable loss.

The six days at sea provided a soothing balm, a restful period in which to pull ourselves together after the funeral. The accommodations on the *Stefan Batory* were far from luxurious, but we were delighted to be on board, ready to make acquaintances, enjoy the bracing walks on deck, the good if unimaginative meals, and join in the evening entertainments. Among the many Canadians on board, we struck up a friendship with two women going to England for graduate study: Kathy Nielsen, an attorney from Vancouver, and Dorothy Wigmore, an industrial engineer from Sudbury. We would see them several times during our year in England. The chef produced a marvelous cake for David's fifty-first birthday on September fifteenth. Mary and Douglas MacCay, an academic family headed for the University of Nijemegen in Holland, struck up an acquaintance with us. Doug had started a detective novel set on a Polish liner. He later confided that he introduced a couple in the first chapter, two people curiously like David and Lee Porter, who, having succumbed to strychnine-laced Martinis, would be the first murder victims. That novel never did find a publisher.

Arriving in Canterbury we were greatly impressed with its cathedral, the charming neighborhood where we were subletting a furnished, three-bedroom house only a short walk from the town center, and the knowledge that we were ideally situated to travel to London by train, or to France and Holland by ferry across the English Channel from nearby Dover. The University of Kent where David would be teaching was located high on a hill overlooking the city and easily accessible by public bus. We decided to rely on public transport and my scooter.

Steve was enrolled at the prestigious Simon Langton Grammar School for Boys. We took Steve to meet the headmaster, obtained information about the courses he would take, and about buying him the school uniform. Our son left for his first day of school the following Monday in a maroon blazer, gray trousers, white shirt, and maroon and gold striped tie, looking very much the English school boy. The standard curriculum for eighth graders included literature, maths, French and Latin, history, two periods of science, religion, art, choir, and games (physical education), plus after-school sports. In the first few weeks, Steve adapted easily to the demanding schedule and announced that he had been selected to be on the first string football (soccer) team, a sport at which he excelled and loved playing. Soon, his manner changed perceptibly. No longer was he a gregarious, cheerful lad but very quiet on his return home and morose each morning at the prospect of going to school. We finally coaxed him to tell us why he was so unhappy. Steve was reluctant to share his misery with us, and to this day we do not know details of the cruel hazing incidents, but we learned that Steve's classmates were so nasty in their behavior that he decided on two defenses: he would no longer eat his lunch in the school cafeteria but in the library, by himself, and he would not play on the school soccer team. He did say that he was unmercifully teased about his American accent and, as the only student in the school who was not a native of Canterbury, he was the object of this kind of scorn as a "foreigner."

We were stunned at his account. My husband and I made an appointment with the headmaster to discuss the problem and also had an informal talk with the games master who coached the football team, to see if they would do anything to improve the situation. Neither was in the least concerned and subtly hinted that we should all just get along with it. Not one boy extended a welcome, invited Steve to visit after school or on weekends—our lovely son who had always had so many friends and playmates was in this school a pariah. We were approaching the Christmas holiday break by this time, and we offered Steve the option of leaving the Simon Langton Grammar School and transferring to the nearby Comprehensive High School for the rest of the school year. To his credit, Steve decided he would stay and make the best of it, even joining in such events as the Christmas choir concert because, as he said, no one could resist the chance to sing in Canterbury Cathedral. We did our best to make his year in England an interesting one. We found an old piano on loan and a music teacher nearby for weekly lessons, and bought sheet music for some of the popular songs of the day, which Steve learned to play and I would sing along. Almost every weekend we took a sightseeing trip, either to London or in the surrounding Kent countryside.

While Steve found the ambience at his school quite cold, my husband experienced a tepid reception at the English Department at the University. What a total difference from our arrival at Keele ten years earlier, where we had been so warmly received by campus families. We soon learned that in England northerners are more open and friendly while southerners are extremely reticent and conservative. In the entire year in Canterbury we never received one invitation to the home of a colleague, and we decided that our revenge would be to give a huge drinks party for the entire English Department at Christmastime. One of the wives had the cheek to say to me that it was unfortunate that Steve had a place at the Simon Langton for the year, since it was depriving a local lad the opportunity. I responded that back home we welcomed a visitor from another country as an enriching opportunity for our own students. My husband gave his usual best effort to his teaching and tutorials, but found both his colleagues and his students to be of less than stellar quality, several rungs below the capability of the University of Keele community where he had taught in 1970. His only bright intervals were in the company of Professor Jeffrey Meyers, another American at Kent for the year. Jeffrey, his wife Valerie, and their daughter Rachel became our best friends, with many an evening of riotous laughter together over takeout Tandoori chicken from the local Pakistani restaurant.

And how did I spend the year at Kent? Sad to say, I was rejected by the university and driven away, rather rudely. I had made an appointment with the head of the Linguistics Department and asked permission to audit one or two courses, not for credit mind you, just to guide my reading in the field. As the wife of a visiting professor, I assumed the approval for my sitting in on a few classes would be easily granted, as it would have been at the University of Massachusetts. Instead the man was visibly uncomfortable, avoiding eye contact and barely willing to speak. Finally he informed me that it was probably not such a good idea: It would burden the instructor to grade my exams (I had no plans to take their exams), and my sitting in the classroom might deny the place to some local citizen who might—just might, mind you—suddenly decide to audit Advanced Phonetics or Applied Sociolinguistics. I understood that I was not wanted, so I jumped on my yellow motor scooter and sped off toward home.

London Times

David commiserated with me, agreeing that there was a provincialism at Kent that we had not found before in England. What a blessing for me that they turned me away! I took a wild chance and telephoned Professor Basil Bernstein at the University of London, whose works in language acquisition I had read. When he answered the call, I put my case to him directly: that I was in England for the year, wished to sit in on some graduate courses in linguistics, pursue my doctoral studies, and do independent research in second language acquisition. He was absolutely charming and replied, "Why, that is quite possible, luv. Come ahead and talk with Professor Josie Levine who will square you away here at the Institute of Education's Department of English as a Foreign Language. Perhaps you might be coaxed into giving us a lecture or two on the subject of your work." How refreshingly generous! It was all the encouragement I needed.

The following day I took pen and notebooks in hand, boarded the train for the seventy-five-minute ride to London's Victoria Station, and began my travels on the underground to Russell Square and the university. Professor Levine helped me identify the courses best suited to my subject, gave me credentials to use the library, the Language Research Center, and the Students' Union, and informed me of the office to contact if I wished to visit any London schools as part of my research, all for the humble sum of ten British pounds for the year, amounting to twenty-two American dollars..

Thus began for me a period of concentrated study and a broad exposure to language policy issues in many countries. The Brits have been in the business of teaching English and training teachers of English for centuries, and routinely bring linguists from around the world to London. I sat in lecture halls and graduate seminars where the newest theories and practices in language acquisition and language teaching were presented. At first, I made two or three day trips a week to London, returning in time for dinner with my family. Then I developed a friendship with a Canadian woman who had a small apartment near the university, and she invited me to stay overnight and sleep on an air mattress on the floor of her living room. This suited me even better since I could then make one trip a week and fit in all my work in two full days, leaving my readings for Canterbury. We Porters were all more or less comfortable with our situations now and enjoyed referring to ourselves as "The Cossington Road Three." Riding my little yellow motor scooter into the center of town to do the grocery shopping at the local Marks and Spencer or Tesla made me feel quite young and adventurous. Tom had given me a bright green tracksuit to wear on my scooter, saying, "You don't have to go jogging in this outfit, Mom, it's for hanging out in the singles' bars."

Weekends were for exploring. In late fall we planned a trip with our Canadian friend Kathy Nielsen to walk Hadrian's Wall, the Roman structure built in the early second millennium to keep out the barbarians (Scots) from invading Roman Britain. On two blustery, wind-swept days we hiked along some of the remaining parts of the walls, stopping often to view the fresh, green countryside on both sides and to contemplate what a Roman soldier on those ramparts, far from home, would be thinking. Each evening we returned to the little Hadrian Inn in the town of Wall, to sit before the open fireplace with drinks, enjoy a hearty English dinner, and retire early. Steve counts that weekend as the best time of his entire year in England. We ended the hike across country at Newcastle-upon-Tyne, where we took a train back to Canterbury, happily exhausted. Early the following morning, November 4, 1979, as we listened to the BBC at our breakfast table, we learned that a terrorist mob had stormed and taken over the U.S. Embassy in Teheran. Little did we know that the hostage taking would be the dominant event in world news for the next 444 days, ending President Carter's political career as a result.

Christmas brought our two sons from their colleges to spend the vacation abroad with us, and a happy reunion it was. We took the local train to Dover, got on the ferry to France, and then on to Milano for an overnight with our friends, the Miccinellis. They had offered us the use of their apartment in Cervinia for Christmas, complete with skis, boots, and ski clothing. Our friends the Sipfles with daughter Gail would be joining us in the Alps for the holiday, staying at a little inn near us. True to form the Miccinellis had organized our one day in Milano to include a visit to the church housing Leonardo's *Last Supper*. The painting was in very poor condition. It would be carefully restored several years later when the beauty of this masterpiece would again be on view. We were delivered early the next morning to the bus for the ride to Cervinia (known as the Matterhorn on the Austrian side of the mountain), at 18,000 feet the highest village in the Alps.

We took delight in those five days, having all our sons with us, and the Sipfle family as well. Traveling as a group now was no longer the chore it had been when our boys were very young and needed to be carried or pushed in carriages, had to have diaper changes and bottles of milk. Now, *they* hoisted the suitcases on to buses and trains and generally helped get *us* around. We went off on individual activities during the day, down-hill or cross-country skiing, sitting in the coffee bars ogling the young in their ski suits, and later gathering for dinner, good conversation, and games in the evenings. Waking up the first morning to fifteen inches of new snow just made the beautiful sight from our windows absolutely perfect. Christmas Eve I put together a simple dinner in the tiny, galley kitchen before our Nativity Play reading; Christmas Day we were guests of the Sipfles for a more festive meal at their inn.

All went well but for an incident on the last day that might have ended fatally. Dave, Gail and Steve, who had taken a few ski lessons the previous winter, rented skis and rode up on the lift to Monte Rosa in mid-afternoon. By the time they waited their turn on the lift, and arrived at the top, they did not understand that it was the last trip of the day and they missed their chance to ride back down. They were now at the top peak in the Alps, not one of them an expert skier, and they had to make their way down. At first, their descent did not seem daunting, but as the light began to fade, the air became hazy with ground mist. Now they had to be extra cautious to avoid slipping over into a crevasse. Gail had a particular problem as her glasses kept fogging over and she was very nearsighted without them. Somehow they made their way down, returned the skis and arrived home late, overcome by the realization of their close call with death. When they told us how it all came about, I said to Dave, "But Dave, you only had a few ski lessons many years ago, how could you dare go up to the highest mountain in the Alps?" He then admitted quietly, "Mom, I didn't take ski lessons—that was Tom. I never had a lesson until yesterday. I had no idea we were going so high or that we couldn't just ride the lift down." The unusually quiet demeanor of the three skiers that evening amply demonstrated their relief from the tensions on the mountain. The rest of the trip was uneventful with an overnight stop in Torino, and two days in Paris before bidding goodbye to the Sipfles and boarding the boat train back to England.

Dave left for Philadelphia shortly after New Year's Day, and Tom stayed on for an additional three weeks to do an independent study on an aspect of Christopher Marlowe's plays. One day he borrowed my motor scooter to take himself to the Simon Langton School, where he had made an appointment to visit, since he had read letters that told of his brother's unhappy experiences there. Steve greatly enjoyed the company of his brothers and we were all sorry to see Tom leave. However, we soon had other company from Amherst. Charlene and Byron Koh and their three children were arriving for the semester, and we had found a house for them to sublet, quite near us, from January through June. Both Byron, a professor of literature, and Charlene, a theater critic on National Public Radio, were incurable Anglophiles who wanted their children to have the experience of living abroad. Scott (fifteen) and Blake (twelve) would attend the Comprehensive School, and Erin (nine) was enrolled in the primary school. Blake was our son Steve's good friend from home. The arrival of the Kohs improved Steve's life immediately.

From January to June the daily rhythm of Canterbury life went smoothly. Steve excelled in all his school subjects, David won respect for his teaching, and I found the London University experience even more useful than I had anticipated. In addition to lecture notes and the research facilities where I gathered material for what would become my doctoral dissertation, I visited schools that enrolled substantial numbers of foreign-born, non-English-speaking children, and interviewed educators from African and Asian countries for their views on education programs for language-minority children. After giving a guest lecture on the theory and practice of bilingual education in U.S. public schools, I was questioned by a school administrator from Nigeria who said, "What you've described is incredible to me. You are doing the opposite of what we believe is best in our country. We have dozens of tribal languages spoken and we are bringing all students to a high level of proficiency in English as the unifying tongue of public schooling. It seems to me you lot in the U.S. are creating problems for yourselves by trying to teach children in all different languages. Quite amazing!"

On two occasions I spent a day observing classrooms with large proportions of non-native speakers of English—Pakistani, Greek, Italian, and Portuguese children. When I mentioned to the headmaster that we in America would place these children in different classes where they would be taught in their native language part of the day, he was astounded. "But why? You would take them out of their neighborhood? The parents here would never allow it. The children are all expected to learn English in a regular classroom with English-speaking classmates. We give the Pakistani parents free use of the school on weekends for a little Gujurati language and culture program they handle themselves." When I tried to explain that we now moved children out of their neighborhood schools to achieve racial balance, as a civil rights matter, the headmaster threw up his hands in exasperation, unable to imagine such a situation in multiracial, multiethnic London.

I discovered a prime example of a misguided language experiment when I accepted an invitation to visit a school in Bedford, an industrial city north of London. Handsome, young Arturo Tosi, a linguistics researcher at the university, intrigued me with his description of a mother-tongue program for Italian immigrant children of mine workers who had immigrated to Bedford after the second World War. Arturo himself had designed this educational initiative, an attempt to teach the second generation—the children of the original immigrants—the southern Italian dialect of their parents. What Arturo believed was important was preserving the Sicilian dialect for communication between parents and children, and later teaching the children standard Italian for literacy purposes. All of this was being attempted during the school day, which meant that blocks of time were taken away from the already heavy English curriculum in order to teach a non-standard dialect. Arturo held the strong opinion that this would give the children greater self-esteem, which would lead to improved academic performance[8]. One of the serious drawbacks to this plan was the resistance of the Italian children who wanted no part of being singled out as "different." Born in Bedford and already fluent in English, these children wanted to be full participants in school-day lessons with their pals, not set apart in order to retain their foreignness. I came away from Bedford with the impression that this experiment would not last because it had minimal support from the families, no interest from the children, and was of little practical value. It called to mind the efforts being made in Wales, the Irish Republic, and other places to revive languages and dialects that had little everyday use but that roused romantic excitement in linguists.

Best Part of Canterbury Year—Italy!

The grand adventure for the Cossington Road Three came in the long spring vacation when my husband was invited by United States Information Service (USIS) to give lectures in Palermo and Rome. The British schools give students long Christmas and Easter vacations, about three weeks each, and a shorter summer break, and this fit our plans very well. But the day before our flight to Rome, Steve fell ill with a high fever. It appeared to be nothing more than a flu or cold symptom so we took the chance of starting out anyway. With Steve taking aspirin and sleeping most of the time, we flew to Rome, picked up a car and drove as far south as Positano the first day, stopping, as usual, at the Villa Franca. The following day's drive took us to the end of the Italian peninsula, to Porto San Giovanni and the car ferry to Messina. From there it was a harrowing two-hour drive in torrential rains to the city of Catania for an overnight stop. By now Steve was feeling much better, and by the next morning he had a normal temperature.

Italy's major cities were still suffering attacks from the radical Red Brigade terrorists—not on government buildings but on banks, corporate headquarters, and other targets. Near our hotel in Palermo the presence of armed soldiers standing guard in front of public buildings was frightening. We walked by each machine-gun-toting young soldier, careful to do nothing suspicious. A week later, when David was giving a series of lectures in Rome, the body of Prime Minister Aldo Moro was found in a car parked in front of the Palazzo Antici Mattei, the building housing the Centro per Studi Americani, the very building where my husband taught his seminars. Since that time the site has been marked with a plaque, and flowers are placed on the sidewalk at that spot by Romans and visitors.

The Sicilian part of the trip allowed us to take Steve to places we had visited with his older brothers when he was a baby, like the climb up Mt. Etna, but also to stop and see Maria Stanganella, the woman who had been his nursemaid and our housekeeper when we lived in Catania in 1966 and 1967. Maria was thrilled to see this tall, friendly thirteen-year-old boy, the baby she had lovingly cared for. Steve was pleased to meet her and to see how much the visit meant to her. Our sons have all returned to Sicily on their own in recent years, revisiting the eastern coast sites of Greek temples (Segesta, Selinunte), Roman amphitheaters (Siracusa, Taormina), and even the little village of Acicastello and the hillside apartment where we lived—all this a testament to their high tolerance for nostalgia.

On our way north, after David completed his week of seminars in Rome, we followed an eastern route in order to visit the magnificent hill town of Urbino, home of the Duca di Montefeltro and the painter Raphael, drove to Ravenna to pay homage at the tomb of Dante Alighieri, and proceeded to Venice. The ancient Pensione Seguso accommodated us for two days, and it was a joy to introduce our young son to the delights of Piazza San Marco and Harry's Bar (for future reference). We arrived in Milano on Easter Sunday to stay at the Miccinellis apartment while they were out of town. Strolling through the city center we were alarmed to note that every shop, museum, and restaurant was firmly closed—what barbarian would be out in public on Easter Sunday when proper Italians must surely be at home with their families? Finally, on a quiet side street, we discovered a small restaurant serving Sunday dinner, and I remember it best as the first place we were introduced to the delicious dessert called tiramisu.

Franco Miccinelli, ever the well-organized host, had left instructions for his personal driver to take us to the airport the following day for our flight back to England. The driver gave us a brief account of the threats made to businessmen in Italy in those days. As Franco was a high-ranking executive of the Siemens Corporation, an electronics and communications technology company, he was at risk at being targeted by the Red Brigade terrorists. Each day, the driver informed us, he would call for Franco at a slightly different hour, and he would take a variety of routes to the office. Of course his wife and children were also trained to follow certain safe procedures when in public places. It had been a stressful few years for the family because of these risks and an unfair burden to be borne by such good, truly decent people. The Red Brigadists and their comrades, the Baader-Meinhof gang in Germany, would not be subdued for several years yet, ultimately succumbing to state terror tactics coupled with the loss of sympathy from the general population, combination that made the anarchist criminals vulnerable.

On our return to Canterbury we were busy with the chores of finishing up Steve's school work, my research at the University of London, and David's teaching duties at Kent. We would be leaving a few weeks before the official close of the spring semester at the University of Kent to be home in time to attend Tom's graduation ceremony at Hamilton College in late May. Although my husband had made arrangements for his last few classes to be covered by colleagues, had collected final papers and prepared to turn in final grades for all his students on time, there was a last minute fuss by the administrative office. It was not enough that my husband had taught three times as many hours as the young man who had gone from Kent to Amherst to teach in David's place—the university wanted to exact its last pound of flesh. My husband refused to be cowed. We left a country we love dearly, but with no affection for Canterbury.

Tom's Commencement
Driving to Clinton, New York, with Dave and Steve for the Commencement weekend gave us a special thrill. Our first-born, Thomas Avery Porter, would be the third in the family to graduate from Hamilton College, and the third member of the same fraternity. Tom and his band entertained us a rock concert outside the Students' Union. Since neither his father and grandfather distinguished themselves for their musical talent, Tom's musical ability may be inherited from my side of the family, or so I choose to believe.

Arriving back in Amherst with a bachelor's degree in the liberal arts focused on literature, Tom decided to take a summer course in computers at UMass while living at home and actively pursuing job possibilities in Washington, D.C.. We were delighted to have all three sons with us, though we were slightly uneasy about Tom's serious girlfriend, Debbie Cohen, and the possibility that he would decide to marry her before leaving for D.C.. We were fond of Debbie and had met her parents, Haskell and Lois Cohen (he a mathematics professor at the university), but we thought the two were too young to settle into married life. Apparently our concerns were ill-founded; Tom soon made clear that he would be embarking on his first job at Ross Perot's Electronic Data Systems corporation, with fraternity brother Aaron Reed sharing his apartment.

Job-hunting for Mom

My teaching job in the Springfield Public School System awaited me in the fall, but I began scanning ads in the Boston and New York papers on the chance there might be a suitable administrative position in my field. In the July 4 Sunday *New York Times* I happened on an ad that looked perfectly suited to my education and experience, Coordinator of Bilingual and English as a Second Language Programs for the Newton, Massachusetts, public schools, in charge of overseeing the special programs for kindergarten through twelfth grade and supervising a teaching staff of two dozen. Applicants were required to have a master's degree in the field, bilingual teaching experience, and fluency and literacy in Spanish, Italian or Chinese. I literally jumped for joy when I read the ad aloud to my husband. This was the opening I had hoped for, an opportunity to extend my ideas beyond the one classroom, to shape policy in a city famous for its excellent school system. My qualifications suited the job perfectly, and my fluency in two of the three languages exceeded their requirements. The one drawback was the distance from Amherst, ninety miles, making a daily commute unrealistic. My husband and sons all urged me to send a letter of application. As David has often advised me in situations like this one,

"Do it. If you get it, you can either take it or not. If you don't get it, there's nothing to decide."

Soon after writing to Newton, I received a call inviting me to an interview. David and I drove to the city and, even with map in hand, were lost for a half hour, making me late for my appointment with the interviewing committee. Compounding this misstep with another foolish error, I walked by mistake into the conference room where another applicant was being interviewed and was asked to please wait in the hall. Finally it was my turn to face the dozen or so teachers and administrators brought together to question candidates. I moved into the conference room with a good deal of confidence. I actually enjoyed the opportunity to describe my background, teaching experiences, knowledge of second-language acquisition and bilingual education, and my recent studies at the University of London. In exchange I learned that the Newton schools enrolled about 350 limited-English students from thirty different language backgrounds, though the largest groups represented were speakers of Italian, Spanish, and Chinese. I came away from the interview with a feeling that I had presented myself well. I had few illusions about my chance of being offered the job. The conventional wisdom is that no one finds a good position by answering a newspaper ad, that ads of this sort are placed to satisfy equal opportunity laws, and that there is almost always an inside candidate who has been groomed for the job.

A week later, a second call came, informing me that I had been selected among the seventy-five applicants to appear for a second interview, this time with the superintendent and his team of top administrators. What excitement in our family. Our son Tom offered to drive me to Newton and we arrived on time, now being familiar with the route. My meeting with Aaron Fink, the superintendent, Norm Colb, assistant superintendent for curriculum and instruction, and personnel director Tom O'Connor focused on the philosophy of bilingual education, my understanding of state and federal laws in this area, and my professional ideas on the best approaches to educating immigrant children in our schools. To my immense relief,

I discovered that the Newton leaders agreed with my views. They, too, were committed to giving non-English-speaking children special help in mastering the English language, thus providing them access to equal education opportunities. This wealthy community was known for generous spending on its schools and for doing more than was required to promote equal opportunity for minorities.

Now that I was being seriously considered for the job, it was time to sit down with the family for a practical discussion of the logistics of my working far from home. In 1980, the commuter marriage was rare. In our case, Stephen, who was entering ninth grade, would be the only one of our sons living at home, with Dave at the University of Pennsylvania for two more years and Tom settled in Washington, D.C., for his first job. With my husband's teaching schedule, he would be at home by mid-afternoon on most days, available to give Steve rides to team practices, music lessons, and whatever came up. My workday would be from 8:30 AM to 5:00 PM and include evening meetings with the school board or parent-teacher meetings in various schools. A daily two-and-a-half-hour drive in each direction (allowing for rush-hour traffic) was not feasible. I was reminded that our good friends Kathy and Charlie Knight had settled in Newton when they moved away from Amherst and, on an impulse, I called to describe my situation and ask about their house and its occupants. By great good luck, Kathy informed me that two of their children would be leaving for college in September, Nathanial to Oberlin and Jenny to Bryn Mawr, leaving only high-schooler Lucy at home—and two empty bedrooms. I asked if they would like to have a boarder and Kathy responded immediately, "Yes, indeed."

At the end of July I received the offer. Would I accept a salary of $28,100 (more than twice my teaching salary of $12,000 the previous year), to start on September 1, and would I be available to spend at least three days in Newton for orientation in late August, at a generous daily stipend? The offer was better than I had expected, but the most satisfying note to me was Superintendent Aaron Fink's comment, "Lee, we know you will be coming to Newton, leaving your family during the week. We are comfortable with your leaving early sometimes or arriving late on occasion. Your competence will not be judged by the number of hours you sit at your desk. Your performance will be evaluated on the basis of what you accomplish, sometimes working sixty hours a week and sometimes only thirty hours. Helen Randolph commutes from her home on Long Island and it is working out very well." That cinched it for me. Aaron Fink's terms made good sense.

In order to make my absence on weekdays as easy as possible, we devised this schedule: I would leave home very early Monday morning, stay in Newton until Wednesday; leave Newton mid-afternoon on Wednesday, arriving in Amherst in time for dinner with Steve and David; return to Newton early Thursday morning and come home late Friday afternoon. This would give me three nights in Newton to work late or attend meetings, and four precious nights in Amherst. The Knights agreed to my plan to live in Jenny's old bedroom at the modest charge of $125 per month. I would bring my own food and use the kitchen for breakfasts, and occasionally for dinners. Having known the Knights when Charlie taught n Amherst for several years and our children were playmates, we were very comfortable with each other.

The last professional errand to carry out involved the Springfield Public Schools. My year's leave without pay to go to England was over and I was scheduled to return to my teaching position. When I met with assistant superintendent, Tom Donohue, to tell him of the promotion I was offered in the Newton Public Schools, he made me a gracious offer. "Rosalie," he said, "we have valued your bilingual teaching. Certainly you should take a more challenging opportunity. But it's hard to predict how the job will turn out, and whether you will find living away from your family to be too much of a burden. Why don't we extend your leave without pay for one more year? If by next spring you are happy in Newton, just write and let me know. If not, and you want to return to your teaching here, we'll be ready for you." I thanked him warmly for giving me such a solid, fall-back guarantee.

Everything conspired to make this dramatic step as easy as possible. There was no professional risk involved. As my husband said, "If you go to Newton and do a great job, you'll continue there with all our blessings. If you don't like the work, or your colleagues, or the commute, then leave at the end of the year. No harm done. It's a worthwhile experiment and we'll handle it. Not to mention the salary!" No woman in my Pedalino family had ever dreamed of doing anything so outrageous as to live in another city, away from husband and child, part of every week. This opening came at the most suitable moment, after ten years of feminist advocacy for liberation, and my husband and sons were strongly encouraging me to take it. I was supremely ready and willing.

CHAPTER 9

My Turn: The Newton Decade

New beginnings, the excitement of a truly radical change in my life—professionally and personally—produced feelings of euphoria tempered by a slight ambivalence, the natural reaction to stepping up to a much larger career challenge. I had never held an administrative position. How would I learn the intricacies of recruiting, training, and supervising twenty-five teachers and assistant teachers; the budgeting process; managing a special program in a dozen schools throughout the city? And how would I adapt to a very prosperous community that expected high student performance in exchange for the high level of funding given to the schools every year? Certainly I had qualms about meeting Newton's expectations.

I n the three days of orientation with my immediate superior, Norm Colb, Assistant Superintendent for Curriculum and Instruction, I learned much about the Newton's non-English-speaking students. In addition to the mix of languages, the socioeconomic mix was quite varied: about a third of the students were Italian and Chinese children of working-class families bordering on poverty; another third were the children of scholars visiting in the U.S. for a year or two, or the children of diplomats and businessmen—a well-off and well-educated group; and the last third were refugees, mostly from Southeast Asia, who had suffered war and oppression in their native lands, many of the children having missed years of schooling.

I was, of course, interested in knowing why the person who had held the job before me had left. It appears that my predecessor, the program coordinator for several years, had so alienated the administration and half the teaching staff that he was given an ultimatum—resign or be fired. No details of the crisis were revealed to me, as was proper. When I was escorted to the office that would be my work place, Norm Colb introduced me to Mary McGowan, the department secretary, and asked her help in directing me to the files and records I should study. When Mary opened the file drawers, they were empty. Norm was astounded. "Where are all the student records, test scores, enrollment figures, state reports of the past five years?" he asked Mary. The poor woman was exceedingly embarrassed. She said, "Mr. Shea decided he would get rid of them all, and let the new person start afresh." Norm was furious; the idea of destroying school records is not only unprofessional but illegal. We would now have to reassemble data on the three hundred or so non-English-speaking children, which would make my job much more difficult than anticipated. On my first day in the office I learned of one more departing action by my angry (and, apparently, immaturely vindictive) predecessor. When a Vietnamese parent called the office to make an appointment, he heard no normal recorded voice—only a long series of chicken noises, cluckings, and shrieks. It took a few days for this outrage to be discovered, deleted, and replaced with a proper message. Imagine the reaction of parents who called to enroll their children in a Newton school.

One more damaging legacy of the former administrator's style was a badly divided teaching staff. Half the teachers and aides were so incensed by the rampant favoritism he displayed that they would not talk to the others. At our first faculty meeting of the entire staff I realized this unhealthy situation needed my prompt attention.

Driving home to Amherst at the end of my first full week, I was bursting with odd anecdotes to tell my family. As I entered the kitchen, I found that my husband and son had almost finished preparing a simple dinner. The doorbell rang and a young teacher arrived, just dropping in to say hello. We offered her a glass of wine, and she sat with us for a while as I regaled her with my adventures. I was so self-involved that I did not notice how silent Steve and his father had become. Finally David said, "Are you not aware that your son has been waiting to talk with you? Can you just give your family, who have not seen you in three days, a little of your attention?" I was devastated, and humbled at my insensitivity. The young woman had the good sense to leave immediately, and I apologized to Steve and his father. The hard-learned lesson—to curb my enthusiasm and be thoughtful of others—has never been forgotten.

New Skills for David

The domestic arrangements and the commuting schedule turned out to be suitable to our individual responsibilities. David's teaching, administering of the graduate program in the English Department, and his writing—each a part of every day—easily fit into a schedule that allowed him to be at home by late afternoon. Steve, a varsity soccer player, stayed at school until 5 PM every day for team practice. Father and son would be together for dinner every evening, and each would repair to his own desk for class preparations or homework until bedtime. At first they thought they would go out to dinner on the nights I was not at home, but after a few tries the novelty wore off. Waiting in line for a table and for service at the local Chinese restaurant, while enjoyable on occasion, was not the way they wanted to spend every dinner hour.

My husband asked me to start writing out some simple recipes that he and Steve could prepare together, and that proved to be a success. The first recipe was for making roast chicken, which began with this essential step: "Remove chicken from freezer in the morning and leave in kitchen sink to thaw." David, who had never shown interest in or helped with kitchen chores, discovered the relaxing aspects of cooking a simple dinner while sipping a cocktail. He was amazed to learn that cooking a piece of meat or fish, a potato, and a fresh vegetable for two people could actually be done in twenty to thirty-five minutes while listening to National Public Radio. Over the span of the Newton years, my husband amassed a collection of simple recipes he took pride in.

Steve was very happy back in Amherst, among his normal circle of friends again, after the year in England. The Simon Langton Grammar School experience quickly receded from his consciousness. Music lessons continued, with a new teacher who gave him more rigorous works to master. Between schoolwork, sports, music, and just hanging out with friends, his time was well filled. I asked my son one evening, "Steve, do you feel bad about my not being here with you and Dad every single day?" He answered, "I really don't, Mom. Some of my friends don't see their parents who are divorced as much as I see you. And I get to spend a lot of time with Dad when you're not here. We get along just fine."

David was working on his third book, *Dickinson: The Modern Idiom,* for Harvard University Press. While his analysis of Emily Dickinson's poetry placed him in the first ranks of Dickinson scholars, he was also recognized for his work on other American and British writers and as a voice in the new schools of criticism. He was now in demand to speak at conferences. With the enthusiastic support of the Five College Consortium (Amherst, Mount Holyoke, Smith, and Hampshire colleges, and the University of Massachusetts), David organized the first Emily Dickinson International Conference. Scholars from Japan, Austria, England, Finland, France, Italy, and from several American universities came to Amherst for the mid-October weekend when the autumn leaf colors would be at their brightest. Conferences of this sort rarely interest the mainstream news media, but as luck would have it, the *New York Times'* literary critic, James Atlas, was on his way to Vermont for the weekend and he decided to stop in Amherst and interview my husband. Atlas arrived at our house in the early evening tired, rumpled and in need of rejuvenation before heading to the opening session. He declined the offer of our shower, but instead washed up quickly and went out to the back yard, sat on our old wooden swing and shaved with his battery-powered razor. It amused us to see the well-known writer from New York being so nonchalant. Both the *New York Times* and later the *International Herald Tribune* published his lovely essay about David and his work with the conference, "Emily Dickinson in the Ascendant," quite a coup.[9] David's invitations to the international group of scholars soon led to his being invited to speak in other countries, a not unanticipated outcome.

Shaping a Teaching Team
Meanwhile, back in Newton I worked long hours each week getting to know the depth and breadth of my responsibilities. The Bilingual/English as a Second Language Program existed as a separately administered entity in the school district, had its own budget, hired and evaluated its own teaching staff, and handled the enrollment and records of all students who arrived in Newton's schools without a full command of the English language. In 1980 there were three major language groups—Italian, Spanish, and Chinese (mostly speakers of Cantonese), with small numbers of children from twenty-seven other language groups. By state law we were expected to teach all school subjects to the children in the native languages of the three large groups, as well as to give all three hundred students English language lessons.

Massachusetts also required that each child receive lessons in the history and culture of his or her native land; the purpose of educating these children "biculturally" was to keep them from losing touch with their family culture. This idea was totally unworkable as well as harmful to the best interests of the children. On the first count, no school district in the country, no matter how great its financial resources and how dedicated its teaching staff, could possibly create a curriculum of weekly lessons in the history and culture of thirty different countries, to be taught at every grade level. Family, religious, and social centers in the different communities had always borne this responsibility. As for the value of promoting the culture of the native lands during school time—taking time away from academic work and from the important obligation to help these students learn about U.S. history and culture so they would rapidly adapt to being Americans—it just didn't make any sense.

From the very beginning of my work in Newton, I understood the almost boundless opportunities for becoming a recognized voice in education reform. Newton prided itself on being an educational leader, an innovator, and it nourished with approval its staff members who achieved state or national recognition. For one example, Jonathan Kozol, the angry chronicler (in *Death at an Early Age*) of the depredations of urban schools, had once taught in the Newton North High School[10]. Seeing the administration approve of designing a program that would depart from Massachusetts' regulations but still give immigrant children greater opportunities for academic success, I seized the chance to make the evolving Newton program the subject of my doctoral dissertation. Bringing together my graduate work at the University of Massachusetts and the previous year's research at the University of London, I proposed a model program—a new hybrid focused on rapid second-language literacy—to my graduate advisor, Dr. Gloria de Guevara, who readily approved. When I discussed with my husband the prospect of going forward with the dissertation, he gave me this advice: "My dear, you've already achieved academic distinction and the boys and I are very proud of you. Many graduate students complete all their course work but fail to write a dissertation. You are certainly capable of doing it, and this will place you in an even more exclusive club—the small circle of those who complete an earned doctorate. Do it!"

The challenge in making a success of the Newton job had a few daunting aspects for an outsider: first and most essential, creating a flexible program that the superintendent and school board wanted—and this rested on my gaining the cooperation of the teaching staff and the support of school principals and administrators; second, learning to navigate the shoals of political alliances among Newton's ethnic, religious, and cultural leaders; and third, gaining familiarity with Newton- and Boston-area geography in order to visit schools and attend state meetings, which meant driving around with a map in one hand. I developed my "management style" entirely from intuition based on work experiences in New York, the organizational demands of childrearing, and the planning I had done for our family to travel and live in different countries. My immediate superior, Norm Colb, gave me useful information and tactful advice, together with frequent helpings of encouragement. In the three years we worked together, Norm never attempted to micromanage my role, but merely exerted subtle guidance and let me work out the details of administration. He was an excellent mentor.

As a result of dozens of interviews with school principals, parents, and teachers, I began to understand the scope and failings of this department. My predecessor had employed a laid-back manner, mostly leaving teachers to fend for themselves in their individual schools. After a half-dozen years of his supervision, there was no evidence of a well-thought-out plan for what was to be taught to immigrant children at each grade level, or what language-teaching strategies or textbooks would be most effective, or how to evaluate how well the students were progressing. The philosophy and goals of the Bilingual/English as a Second Language Program had never been clear to teachers, parents, or the community at large.

Developing a cohesive department out of an assortment of individuals who saw each other once or twice a month and barely understood or trusted each other was an undertaking that had to be approached with care. As a newcomer to the city and its schools, I had much to learn. It took meetings at each school with teachers and administrators, from the preschool through grade 12, to get a firm understanding of each situation and to assess how our efforts could be improved. Monthly meetings were scheduled to engage the entire staff in a review of the latest in language-teaching theories and practices, and to explore some of the legal issues in our field; these discussions led us to define what we wanted our work to accomplish. It was the beginning of a master plan that would be explained within the Newton schools and at regional meetings in the greater Boston area. In the process of discussing our work together, we became better acquainted.

Thinking that members of our program would benefit from some informal socializing with their colleagues, I hosted an annual Christmas cocktail party for staff and spouses and an end-of-the-year picnic, gatherings that became annual traditions. At first, these were stiff, dutiful get-togethers, but in time they became quite enjoyable. I instituted a practice of funding attendance at national conferences for three or four teachers each year, with the understanding that they would bring back valuable information, new teaching texts, and effective strategies we all could learn from. Teachers were encouraged to give presentations at TESOL (International Teachers of English to Speakers of Other Languages) or MATESOL (Massachusetts Teachers of English to Speakers of Other Languages) conferences, to become educational leaders themselves. Since our MATESOL organization was dominated by university professors, I started an annual day of workshops in Newton, open to all Massachusetts English-as-a-Second-Language teachers, and entirely focused on new ideas in working with students in grades K through12. This became a popular event that attracted a large attendance from the Boston area, and gave pride to our department.

Weeding Out the Chaff
While all this was taking place, I became concerned about the status of two teachers in our department. There was a suspicion among the staff that some of their colleagues were not qualified to teach, and some indeed were very poor at their work with students. First was the case of Carmine T., an Italian bilingual teacher at Newton North High School who was hired in the early years of the program when almost all the non-English-speaking students were from Italy. His master's degree from Middlebury College was legitimate, but the written evaluations of his work in the classroom were barely adequate.

In consultation with the high school principal, it became obvious that we had a dilemma. Italian-speaking students had dwindled to less than a dozen, and the growing population of non-English speakers were from Indochina—Vietnam, Cambodia, and Laos. Carmine insisted he had no responsibility for teaching the Asian students, that he was only obliged to teach the Italian speakers. His student roster included the same dozen students registered for three separate classes: Italian bilingual, Italian language, and Italian culture. We could not support a fulltime high school teacher with only twelve students when most teachers were handling four classes a day with twenty to thirty students in each class.

I explained to Carmine that he was obliged to teach more classes, perhaps working part-time in two schools. He refused and threatened to go to the teacher's union to complain, expecting to browbeat me into backing down. Carmine had been one of my predecessor's preferred pets. Clearly he had not been warned that insubordination is not tolerated. At the end of my first school year in Newton, the situation with Carmine had deteriorated to the point where I was ready to recommend that he be let go. To my astonishment, he decided, at the last possible moment, to resign. Apparently Carmine had come to realize that he wanted a change of career. I met him a year later at an elegant Boston North End restaurant where he was the maitre d' and we actually had a very pleasant exchange.

A second case was brought to my attention a year later. The Director of Personnel (now called Human Resources) had reviewed the file of one of my teachers, Guido F., when he applied for a higher salary level based on having completed a master's degree. Normally such a request would be granted as soon as a transcript was provided from the university where he studied. But he submitted records from a correspondence school that had no fixed address and could not be reached by telephone. In short, it had all the earmarks of a phony diploma mill. This occasioned a closer scrutiny of Guido's entire personnel file. When Guido was hired he claimed to have taught for a few years in Italy before arriving in the United States. On reading the documents carefully I discovered what other administrators had apparently missed—if indeed he had taught in Italy, he would have started when he was eight years old.

Questionable credentials aside, I had observed some resentment among the other teachers that Guido, making different excuses each month. never attended our department meetings. When I spoke with Guido about this he admitted he was working a full forty-hour week at the Raytheon Company after leaving school at 2:30 each afternoon, and therefore could not be available for any after-school responsibilities such as parent conferences, department meetings, or giving extra help for students. Since he was the highest-salaried teacher in our department, this dereliction of duty raised hackles. Once the man's dishonesty was revealed he decided to resign and concentrate on his job at Raytheon. His departure greatly raised morale among the teachers.

These two troublesome situations should have been handled equably years earlier. I partly blame the timidity of some school administrators but also fault the rigid support of teachers' unions, even for demonstrably inept, underperforming teachers. Not ridding the profession of its worst incompetents is dismaying to hard-working teachers, but—far worse—it damages children.

Our First Joint Foreign Lecture Tour

In early September 1981 David received an invitation to go on a two-week lecture tour to Finland and Norway on behalf of the USIS. (This division of the U.S. State Department arranged both for American professors to go abroad as guest lecturers and for foreign scholars to speak in the states.) He sent an inquiry to USIS on my behalf, asking if they wanted me to accompany him on the tour and give lectures in my specialty—second-language acquisition and immigrant-education policies. They replied immediately that four places in Finland were interested. I applied for ten days leave without pay, which was granted. Aaron Fink, Superintendent of the Newton Public Schools, took me aside to commend me: "Lee, Newton has produced a number of nationally recognized educational leaders. It's an honor for us that you are becoming such a voice in your field that USIS invites you to go abroad. Just between us, if you need an extra day or two over there when the lecturing is over, just take it."

Anyone who has worked in U.S. public schools will understand how rare such an attitude is.

And so it came to pass that Rosie Pedalino from South Day Street, Orange, New Jersey, entered a new dimension of professional activity—the opportunity to join the class of academic global voyagers. Most satisfying of all was the joy of traveling with my husband—not certainly as his equal, since his scholarly achievements far outshone mine, but not as the wife/handmaiden/child-minder either. This would be the first of several lecturing trips we would take together for USIS (later renamed USIA, United States Information Agency) to Japan, Turkey and Italy, and which I would later take alone to China, Israel, and Bulgaria.

To Finland with Love and to Russia with Trepidation
We left Boston on Finnair for a grueling eighteen-hour flight to Helsinki. Our contact at the U.S. Embassy, Marjatta Nikkanen, called for us early the next morning—no allowance for jet lag—with our fellow-traveler Robert Gross, an Amherst College professor of American Studies. We four would be traveling together from Helsinki to Tampere, Turku, and Yvaskilla over the next ten days. Mid-way in that period, David and I flew to Oslo, Norway, where he gave a guest lecture at the university. There we were warmly entertained at a faculty reception, and even managed to squeeze out an hour for a visit to the Munch Museum.

From my graduate studies, I had read the works of several Finnish sociolinguists, and the occasion of my trip allowed me the rare chance to meet Haakon Ringboom, Nils Enkvist, and Kari Sajavaara for brief talks and the promise to correspond later. Finland has long experience with a Swedish minority population over the issues of native-language maintenance, assimilation and second-language learning. As in the United States and other immigrant-receiving countries, the issues are contentious. Some linguists take a strong position in favor of maintaining each child's native language through the first eight years of schooling as a human right. At an international conference in 1995, Finnish language expert Tove Skutnabb-Kangas attacked the United States for our teaching of the English language to immigrant children, calling it an act of linguistic imperialism and a civil rights violation. It was my impression, from her writings and speeches, that the fiery Skutnabb-Kangas was motivated more by socialist/Marxist theory than by a practical concern for children's survival and achievement in new environments. For her the idea of "assimilation" through acquiring the common language of one's adopted country is the most repugnant idea of all. Clearly, I am not in that camp.

The whole Finnish tour was successful and Marjatta gave the U.S. Embassy a very positive report. We got along very well in our travels by car and train as far north as the Arctic circle. Returning to Helsinki, we were invited to the home of a university professor for a classic evening of steaming in a sauna, gentle lashings with birch twigs while running thought the snow, and afterward a supper of Finnish delicacies with their best Vodka. Truth to tell, the notion of getting naked with Bob Gross and the others in a steam bath really did not appeal to us. Call us cowards, but David declined the invitation, citing a previous dinner appointment. Instead we had a quiet dinner at a restaurant overlooking the Baltic Sea, with a novel dessert: cloudberries dotted with heavy cream—luscious golden globes we had never heard of or tasted before. Our first joint lecture tour taught us that we would hardly ever have any time alone together. At every stop, we would do our work and be entertained by groups of local academics for lunch, dinner, breakfast, tea, whatever—all very enjoyable, to be sure, but at the end of two weeks we would be pining for a meal alone.

The occasion of being in a place so close to the Soviet Union, a mere overnight train ride or one-hour flight away, gave us an opportunity that was too good to pass up. Before leaving the states we had applied to the USSR for a tourist visa, hoping to spend a three-day weekend in Leningrad. We would not have dreamed at that time that the city originally known as St. Petersburg would revert to its centuries-old name a few short years later. In 1981, Westerners could not simply decide on the spur of the moment to enter the Soviet Union. Our visas allowed us to visit only the one city and leave within three days.

At the airport our small overnight bags were carefully searched. The customs officers concentrated most on perusing our books and magazines, to see if we had any scraps of secret messages or writings of a subversive nature. After exchanging U.S.-dollar traveler's checks for rubles at the airport bank, we rode our assigned bus into the city. Leningrad, with the River Neva running through it, reminds me of Rome, that other grand, sprawling once-imperial city. Majestic as we found the city, the daily life going on around us seemed quite subdued, gray-tinged by the dire shortages.

Our hotel was huge, impersonal, and dull by Western standards. Long gray corridors were monitored at each end by a dour woman who sat at a desk and asked all the guests to show their papers; we saw the same scenario when (several times) we mistakenly got off at the wrong floor. The dining room where we were to take all our meals was a huge cafeteria—no going out to different restaurants to sample local delights. (Soviet gastronomy, as we knew it from the cafeteria, was not about to win any prizes. We found the same array of foods at every breakfast, lunch, or dinner: many cold meats, cured fish, pickled vegetables, borscht, heavy breads. But, of course, we were not there for the food.) At our first lunch we were approached by a friendly young man who asked to sit with us to "practice his English." Somehow, this same young man was always near us and I'm positive I once spotted him boarding the same bus we were riding on. It would have been normal at that time to have had a "minder," since U.S. tourists were closely observed. We had been warned not to carry contraband—blue jeans, perfume, cigarettes—and not to dare to change money on the Black Market, meaning with a person on the street.

We did get to spend some hours at the Hermitage, the former Winter Palace of the Czars, which cannot be compared to any other museum in the world for its architectural beauty and the wealth of art on view. An evening at the Opera, where we sat on delicate gilded chairs in the fourteenth row of the center orchestra to take in a magnificent performance of *Eugene Onegin*, cost us six dollars a ticket. As we waited for the first act curtain, I accidentally pushed the woman in the seat to my left and to apologize, I said "Affedersiniz,"—excuse me, in Turkish. I don't know what impulse made me do it. But immediately, a young man seated behind us leaned over and said, in English, "Are you from Turkey?" David and I talked to the young man who identified himself as the son of a professor at Robert College. What an incredible coincidence! We found that we had many friends in common. This brief encounter only added to the pleasure of the entire evening. On leaving the theater we were in a large crowd waiting to hail the infrequent taxis when a policeman singled us out and asked, "American?" When we answered, "Yes, da," he whistled for the next taxi cruising by, and when it stopped, he ordered a young couple out and waved us in. We were humiliated, but did not have the words to object, so we just said "Mockba Hotel."

I believe I speak for both David and myself when I say that the most heart-rending part of our visit to Leningrad was the half-day tour of the Summer Palace at Peredelkino. The summer retreat of the Czars was interesting, of course, but most of the guide's concern was to show us the sites of the World War II battles when the city was under siege by the German Army for eighteen months. The suffering of the Russian population from cold and starvation when supplies could not get through enemy lines, and the deaths of millions of civilians during the siege remain a horrible example of inhumanity. That the Russian Army was finally able to drive back and crush the German invaders is a marvel of modern warfare. The bravery and steely stoicism of the Russian people who survived Stalin's reign, during which tens of millions died, and of those who survived perhaps that number of dead again under the Nazi invasion, was crucial to the remarkable rebuilding of their country after its near total destruction during the war years. At the time of our visit in 1981, the Soviet control of Eastern Europe seemed permanent, and our few days' experience in Leningrad added to that impression.

One afternoon we walked through parts of the city and came upon the one remaining Christian church open for visitors as a museum, St. Stephen's. We visited the fabled GUM department store, a sad example of how few consumer goods were on sale. Russian-made arts and crafts could only be purchased at the *Berioska*, the foreign-currency shops open only to visitors. Spotting a line of people waiting to enter what looked like a tea shop or café, we joined them, only to discover when we reached the front of the line that it was an optometrist's store. Lines outside stores were quite common, and street-corner vendors attracted immediate crowds whether they set up to sell apples or nylon stockings: everything was in short supply. Though we were approached half a dozen times, we turned away anyone wanting to sell us rubles, and a good thing we did as we were now certain that we were being followed.

Arriving at the Aeroflot terminal for our short flight to Helsinki and then the connection to Boston, we were separated at customs. I was motioned to step aside while David was asked to follow the guard into a side room. Our luggage had been thoroughly searched and we had accounted for the rubles we had spent and assured them we had none left. My anxiety level rose as the minutes went by and my husband did not reappear. Surely the NKVD could not suspect an innocent English professor of being a spy. At last, David emerged, a bit pale but relieved to have gotten through the close questioning and the examination of everything in his pockets and billfold. Once cleared for departure, we held tightly to each other throughout the flight until we landed in free Finland, very happy to have been in Leningrad but even happier to be out of there.

A General Perception to Correct

The twelve-day tour over, it was time to concentrate on my work. One issue that became important from my early days as an administrator was to correct the perception of non-English-speaking students as being disabled or mentally retarded. One of the public relations goals in my field—not just in the Newton schools but across the country—was to clarify the difference between our students who only suffer a temporary lack of the English language as opposed to children with learning disabilities, physical, emotional, or mental limitations, or other conditions that impair their ability to learn.

Education bureaucracies identify children as falling into certain categories and assign them to the care and responsibility of one special program or another—with the best of intentions, that is—to give them special help tailored to their particular needs. In recent decades, federal and state legislation has created these niche settings with their own rules for identifying their client populations of students, their own special funds, their own special teachers, and their own tests for progress. Since the early 1970s, the three largest special programs for students are Title I for children of poverty who are below grade level in reading and math; Special Education, for children with learning problems; and Bilingual Education for non-English speakers.

One day I was called to a meeting with my superior and with the director of Special Education. I was informed that since our limited-English students were educationally disadvantaged, our department rightly should come under the Special Education umbrella. I objected immediately and forcefully with the following response: "Making such a change would be the most demoralizing action for everyone—students, parents and teachers. Across the country, we are working mightily to make everyone recognize that our children are not mentally retarded or disabled. They are only temporarily lacking in a sufficient knowledge of English, a situation that is remedied in a few months or a year or two. *These children are not permanently disabled.* Since the creation of IQ tests in this country in the early twentieth century, it has been a struggle to separate those who have learning problems from those who do not yet know the language in which the test is administered."

The two administrators were stunned at the passion of my reply. I made one more plea, an important point: "Consider the teaching of limited-English students as best compared to the teaching of foreign languages, that is. French, Spanish, Latin. We are teaching our students a new language, English, to prepare them, as rapidly as possible, to handle academic subjects taught in English, and to have social conversations in English with classmates and teachers. We are language teachers and belong with the other subject matter specialists, not with Special Ed." The issue was referred to the superintendent, as a policy matter, and to my immense satisfaction he saw the logic of my arguments and decided in my favor.

This issue was not a small matter with me; it was part of my intention to radically reverse the bilingual education idea. From its inception, this special program required a separate education for non-English speakers, segregating them by language and ethnicity from their English-speaking classmates most of the school day. In the model I proposed in my doctoral dissertation and which was now in full operation in the Newton schools, limited-English students were given intensive English-language lessons from one to three hours each day, depending on their age, and included in regular classes the rest of the time. The goal was to give them a double advantage: special help part of the day, and as much exposure as possible to English speakers. The research literature is full of evidence that children in traditional bilingual programs tend to remain educated apart in native language classrooms for years. As the Newton model was to demonstrate and document, our students overcame their lack of English in an average of one to two years, giving them early access to educational opportunities. And the high school graduation rate for children who entered the Newton schools without a sufficient knowledge of English was phenomenal for this population: less than a 1 percent dropout rate.

Coming Out of the Bilingual Closet—and the Consequences
When I began promoting these new ideas at regional meetings of educators, it did not go unnoticed. At a Boston gathering of language teachers, I presented a description of Newton's innovative approach. In the audience I saw Mr. Ernest Mazzone, State Director of the Bilingual Education Bureau, who was paying very close attention to my remarks. To Mr. Mazzone I was a heretic. In this politically ideological field, apostasy is not tolerated.

A few weeks later, I successfully defended my doctoral thesis at the University of Massachusetts. After accepting everyone's good wishes, I was taken aside by Dr. Gloria de Guevara, my thesis advisor, and told the following: "Rosalie, you should know that an attempt was made to have your dissertation dismissed. The head of the Bilingual Bureau called Professor Luis Fuentes here at the University. He told him that your dissertation would be damaging for bilingual education and that it should be thrown out. I asked Luis if he had read your work and if he had any specific questions about it, but he had not. I told him that your work was well documented and well written and deserved to be published, even if I did not agree with all of your conclusions. While Luis could attend your oral defense, I cautioned him that it would be ill-advised to come and make a scene, as he threatened to do. I tell you this in private, Rosalie. Given the politics in this field, I cannot involve myself publicly in the situation."

The ensuing conversation with my husband, sitting on our wooden swing in the backyard, unleashed the emotions I had held in check through the afternoon. Knowing of the threat robbed me of the sweet triumph I had worked so hard to achieve, to be the first in my family to attain a high academic degree. My husband was outraged. He wanted to lodge an immediate complaint with the dean at this attempt by a state official to violate academic freedom, and also to excoriate a faculty member who had tried to pressure my thesis advisor to suppress scholarly investigation. Once we both calmed down, we agreed that it would be best if I myself reported the situation to the Dean of the School of Education, Dr. Mario Fantini. When I met with the dean, he commiserated with my distress and promised to personally handle the situation. But he did nothing. He did not take any steps to deal with this attempt to censor my work—and thus allowed this corruption of academic integrity to remain a dirty secret. More outrageously, he recommend Luis Fuentes, a man lacking in academic credentials or publications, for tenure the following year. My advisor, Dr. de Guevara, a respected professor, was not reappointed to an academic position but was transferred out of the School of Education and into administrative work.

I felt it was my duty to report the event to my superior in the Newton Public Schools. Norm Colb was furious and immediately said he would lodge a complaint with the State Commissioner of Education. Again, I counseled the cautious route of keeping things quiet as being in the best interests of the Newton Public Schools. My judgment in both cases was entirely wrong. Two years later, in a vindictive move, the Massachusetts Department of Education launched a massive investigation of Newton's bilingual program, bringing the weight of the bureaucracy down on us, with a public relations blitz that saw headlines in local newspapers decrying Newton's "denial of the civil rights of its bilingual students." To Newton's credit, Superintendent John Strand, every member of the school board and the parents of the bilingual students rose in support of our excellent educational program, with statements to the press and calls for a fair reporting of our students' achievements.

As one of the dozen most respected public school systems in the country, Newton's voice would not be easily dismissed or subordinated to the likes of Ernest Mazzone and company. We fought back the requirements for "documentation" with tons of reports testifying to everything they requested and more. The siege lasted five years and resulted in Newton's losing a small amount of state funding for each year that our program was judged to be "out of compliance." The crux of the matter was this: although Newton's bilingual students registered better academic performance than any other group in the state, and the district spent more on its bilingual program than any other district, and the parents publicly declared that they wanted exactly this kind of program, the state monitors declared that our "innovative, alternative approach" was not legal, that there could be no deviation from the regulations. Long after we proved that we were doing more—and better—than any other district for these children, the state Department of Education quietly reversed its opinion (when nobody was looking!) and informed us that we were now "in compliance." And we had not made one change—they were just tired of carrying on the over-heated supervision of Newton.

The public nature of the dispute had several unintended consequences for the bilingual bureaucrats. Newton gained renewed public attention as a place where new ideas were being tried successfully and where non-English-speaking children were valued and helped. My name became synonymous with antiestablishment efforts in this highly contentious field, and opportunities came my way to publish articles and to serve on national advisory boards. What amazed and pleased me the most was the fact that I had not been fired from my job outright—that the Newton community recognized and valued the philosophy and practical outcomes of the program I had crafted with the efforts of a fine teaching staff.

A Quarter-century to Celebrate

Once the intense hurt of the doctoral dissertation imbroglio wore off, our family celebrated the new Dr. Mom. Topping this off was a planned trip in July with our three sons to celebrate Mom and Dad's twenty-fifth wedding anniversary. My husband, sons Dave and Steve, and I would fly to Italy for a few days in Positano at the little old family hotel we had discovered in 1959. We would meet Tom in Rome and all go to Ancona to board a Turkish ship for the three-day voyage to Istanbul. We wanted Tom to see the place where he was born, and all the boys to have at least an acquaintance with the Istanbul area that meant so much to their parents.

The 1982 voyage was a success. Landing in Rome and picking up our rental car on an early Sunday morning, we expected a quick two-hour drive to Positano. We had not anticipated the number of people who would be heading for the Amalfi coast, especially not every German tourist dragging a boat trailer. The drive over the narrow, switch-back mountain roads took almost nine hours. At one point as we drove through a tiny village, barely moving for minutes at a time, when my distress at not finding a public bathroom became acute. I jumped out of the car and knocked at the door of a modest little house that fronted on the road. I pleaded with the woman who answered the door to allow me to "use the facilities." (How critical the ability to speak the language!) She immediately invited me in and showed me to the bathroom, walking past the family who were seated at their Sunday dinner. When I emerged and explained how badly the traffic was backed up, she and her husband graciously invited our family to join them for dinner. With regret I declined, and thanked them warmly for their kindness. Outside, I found our car had not moved but ten feet.

Being in Positano again was pleasurable, but much more thrilling was our being in Italy at the time of the World Cup Championship games in which the Italian national team was featured. Our sons, all soccer players and fans since early childhood, were excited at being here for the semifinal match between Italy and Brazil. Our little hotel did not have good television reception. so we went to a café nearby to watch the match. There, in a smoke-filled room, sitting among dozens of village men, we saw the remarkable victory of the Italian team. Greater moments cannot exist in this soccer-mad country, and we have been there enough times to see it verified. Everyone erupted from the café, young men leaped into their little Fiats and began driving up and down the mountain roads, blaring their horns, shouting with glee. Soon from our hotel porch, we heard what sounded like thunder but was actually the shooting off of old cannons from a nearby village—a joyous outpouring.

Tom met us in Rome and the next morning we boarded the Turkish ship in Ancona with our friends, David, Mary Alice, and Gail Sipfle. The brightest single event of the voyage was watching Italy play West Germany for the world soccer championship—on a tiny black-and-white TV in the ship's bar—surrounded by dozens of young men drinking and smoking and cheering. Our two families were the only ones that rooted for Italy's victory, since most of the people on the ship were Turkish workers based in Germany heading home for vacation. The Turkish ship was a disappointment—the air conditioning stopped working after the first day, some toilets did not flush—but we seasoned travelers did not let these irritations impede our delight in revisiting Athens and the Acropolis, Izmir and the Dardenelles, and the beautiful approach to the magnificent "Sublime Porte."

Traveling as an adult family was a novelty. Our sons schlepped the luggage, hailed taxis, and took care of the many detailed arrangements that kept us moving. Being in Istanbul with the Sipfles made the visit much more enjoyable as well. Jo Greenwood, a family friend who had settled in Turkey for life, offered us the hospitality of her home, while the Sipfles stayed at the Bebek Hotel in the village at the foot of the Robert College hill. I believe we succeeded in giving Tom, Dave, Steve, and Gail an acquaintance with the beauty and the historical importance of this crossroads of the ancient and modern worlds. We introduced them to the Near East, with the hope that they would all return on their own, and most have.

The trip was a whirlwind showcasing Istanbul's treasures. We toured the Sultan's Topkapi Palace, the Blue Mosque and Hagia Sofia. For sentimental reasons, we made a trip to the Amiral Bristol Hastahanesi (the Admiral Bristol Hospital) where Tom was born; the Protestant cemetery where good friends Keith Greenwood, Dave Garwood, Hillary Sumner-Boyd, and Lee Fonger are buried; and a visit to the Theodorus Hall apartment on the college campus where we lived for two years. As typical tourists, we rode the ferry boats from Bebek into the city, and then up the Bosphorus towards the Black Sea, picnicked at Kilyos, shopped in the Grand Bazaar, and sampled the world-class Turkish food at Pandeli's in the Spice Bazaar and at Abdullah's. Our last adventure, just before leaving the city, was too drive over the new bridge connecting Europe, on the western side of the Bosphorus, with Asia on the opposite side. This marvel of modern engineering, spanning the body of water near the site of Lord Byron's swim across what he called the Hellespont, proved to be a terrifying experience. Finding ourselves in the extreme right lane of the three lanes heading east, we were buffeted by high winds and by the immense lorries driving past us on our left, with only a low parapet on our right, not anything that would keep us from tumbling over the edge if a passing vehicle crowded us. Arriving on the eastern shore at Uskudar, our whole family was so shaken that it took all our courage to turn around and drive back over the bridge.

Our departure from Istanbul by air was ordinary but for Steve's sudden illness on the plane. He was overcome by nausea and fever, perhaps from a sudden onset of stomach flu or a reaction to his rich lunch at the Liman Lokantasi, the charming restaurant near the port. Arriving in Rome to change flights, we checked in with a medical assistant at the Pronto Soccorso but decided it would be best to go on to Milano where we would be staying in the home of friends and could easily get a doctor. A few days of rest restored Steve to good health. Soon it was time for Tom and Dave to take the train to Rome and fly home. Steve, age sixteen, was not burdened with job responsibilities, and could remain with us for another week in Italy.

We had planned a leisurely drive down the western coast, skirting Genoa, viewing the *Cinque Terre* towns of Portofino, Santa Margarita, Lerici (site of poet Shelley's drowning), the marble hills of Carrara, and stopping for a few days in the Medieval walled city of Lucca. We chose this city because it is not overrun with tourists, even in midsummer, but also because one of the teachers in my department urged us to see her cousin, Gil Cohen, who had bought property near Lucca and moved to the area permanently. Not only was Lucca visually and historically fascinating, but we discovered two new friends in Gil and his partner, Paul Gervais.

Gil and Paul, Massachusetts lads, had bought a 60-acre property of olive trees and grape vines with a villa commanding a magnificent vista over the village of Massa Maccinaia and across the valley. Both house and lands had been sorely neglected. It was their intention to restore the villa, gradually, to its original beauty and to regenerate the crops. We were impressed by their intelligence and good humor, as well as their realistic assessment of the long road ahead to research the work and materials, and to find the skilled workmen to do the essential projects of restoration. Both were becoming fluent in the language and ways of Italian society. Truly, we found each other instantly *simpatici*. They won our hearts with a simple but elegant luncheon on our last day in Lucca. In the garden behind the villa was a stone structure, perhaps at one time a family chapel, with moss-covered walls and a trickle of clear water streaming down the rear wall. On a hot summer day, sitting in that sylvan shade, and being served a lovely frittata, green salad, crusty bread, and a chilled white wine—what bliss! It was the first of many happy visits with Gil and Paul, both in Massa Maccinaia and in the United States.

A Fairly Normal School Year

Celebrations and travels behind us, we returned to our school and work responsibilities—David to his university teaching and work on the Emerson book, Tom in D.C. forging his career at *National Geographic*, Dave finishing his senior year at the University of Pennsylvania, and Steve in his junior year at Amherst Regional High School where, in addition to his classes and varsity soccer team activities he added high school theater. Steve volunteered to be the accompanist for the rehearsals and performances of the high school musical productions, which involved him with the "arty" crowd. I started my third year in the Newton schools with confidence that the work of our department was now understood and accepted by the school community and parents, leading to higher morale among teachers. We were no longer viewed as a separate, mysterious group of marginal "helpers" but as an integral part of the education process in each school, the language teachers who gave new students a rapid mastery of English to prepare them for full participation in the academic and social life of the classroom.

The fall semester passed without incident and we celebrated the holidays with our three sons. Dave brought a sweet girl named Suzy Arlen to spend Christmas with us. On Christmas Eve, Dave and Suzy arrived in the kitchen with a little bundle which was held out to us as an early present. Dave said, "We want you and Dad to have this kitten to replace our cat that was hit by a car last summer. We got it from a family in Hadley." I was aghast at the nature of the gift and said, as tactfully as I could, "My goodness, that was a nice idea, Dave, but we just can't have it. You'll have to return it. You know that we're all leaving for California the day after Christmas and there will be no one here for ten days. Who will take care of the kitten?" I know that I disappointed my son, but I was just being practical. I hope he forgave me a long time ago.

The trip to Los Angeles was our first visit to the West Coast. My husband was invited to present a paper at the meeting of the Modern Language Association, the annual gathering of English professors where they'd impress each other with their erudition, interview for jobs, and to do whatever people do when they are away from home at a convention. Dave, Steve, and I went along for the sight-seeing in Los Angeles and San Francisco. Tom had to go back to work. L.A. did not impress us, although we enjoyed the Getty Museum in Pasadena, a stroll down Rodeo Drive to window shop—not a movie star in sight—and a drive along the coast. Courtesy of my brother Anthony's position at NBC-TV, we had studio passes to attend a taping of Johnny Carson's television show in "beautiful downtown Burbank." As David had to spend a few more days interviewing candidates for positions in the English Department at the university, the boys and I decided to take the "Starlight Express," an eight-hour train ride along the coast from L.A. to San Francisco; David would fly up and join us later.

We made the most of visiting all the traditional sights and quite enjoyed the ethnic Chinatown and Italian neighborhoods, riding the cable cars, and going to the Top of the Mark for a cocktail on New Year's Eve. On our last day we took a short train ride to Palo Alto to meet an old, dear friend from my RCA days, Ward Gebhardt. Ward had moved into the new technologies of transistors and computers in the early days, making a huge success in business. We had corresponded over the years and he invited us to stay at his home overnight, and offered to take us to the airport early the next morning. First we were given a guided tour of the beautiful Stanford University campus, then driven to the Gebhardt home in Redwood City to meet Mary and the two children. The Gebhardts gave us a companionable close to the West Coast voyage.

Two events of the spring semester I remember as being especially important: Dave's graduating from UPenn with a bachelor's degree in American Studies, and my being offered a promotion. Living in an academic setting, I have mostly divided my years into fall semester, spring semester, and summers, and the mindset is still there, still the way I organize my memories. Dave's commencement ceremony was an occasion to gather in Philadelphia. Uncle Michael, Aunt Mary, and cousins Gloria and Rosalie and her husband Stephen, were invited to have dinner with us. They had all been kind to Dave while he was a student in their city, and we asked Uncle Mike to choose an Italian restaurant in the south Philly neighborhood. The Osteria Romana, decorated in typically garish Italo-American style but with excellent food, turned out to be perfect for this family fest. Uncle Mike suggested we start with the house specialty, Pasta Tricolore, a plate holding a small sampling of three pastas sauced in the colors of the Italian flag—the red ziti, green pesto fettucine, and the white gnocchi in gorgonzola cream sauce. It sounded corny to me, but I trusted the fine palate of Uncle Mike. It was not only delicious but introduced us to a new form of pasta that immediately entranced my husband—gnocchi! My husband declared to the whole table, "I'll run away with the woman who can make me gnocchi like this!" We all laughed, but David's little joke led to my serious pursuit of gnocchi recipes on two continents.

Toward the end of the school year, I was invited to the office of the Superintendent, John Strand, who was completing his first year heading the Newton Public Schools. He informed me that Norm Colb, my beloved mentor and the Assistant Superintendent for Curriculum and Instruction, would be leaving to take the top position in the Mamaroneck, New York, schools. This announcement was a deep disappointment to me, as Norm was a man I admired professionally and personally. The much greater shock came when John Strand said, "Lee, you've done a tremendous job in a difficult situation, bringing together a fine teaching staff and providing leadership throughout the schools and community for a better understanding of your students. You have earned the respect of your peers, the other subject-matter coordinators. We have not found a suitable candidate to fill Norm's position for this fall. I would like to offer you the position of acting assistant superintendent for the coming year. That will give us time to conduct a national search for a permanent appointment. You will have had some experience in the job, and you may want to apply for it. If not, you can return to your old job a year from now. I'd like you to take a little time to think this over but please keep it confidential."

What an incredible opportunity! Why I and not one of the other coordinators who had so many more years of administrative work in Newton? I was reeling over this new development and could hardly contain myself when I called my husband that evening. He was immediately thrilled at the prospect. On arriving home for the weekend, I found a large cardboard sign on the front door, proclaiming my promotion to the world. Father and son were excited at the prospect and certain that I could handle new responsibilities, not to mention the prestige and substantially higher salary I would earn.

A week later, I accepted the appointment. English teacher Marcia Ratner would be acting head of the Bilingual/ESL Department for the year, a choice I heartily approved. My salary would be raised a whopping 25 percent. I would move into Norm Colb's corner office and inherit the very efficient Anna Berardi, Norm's secretary. One condition for my accepting the position was the understanding that I would not have to give up the two-week lecture trip to Japan in October. At the request of a Japanese professor, USIS had invited me to give a series of lectures on English-language teaching and do observations at several schools.

Norm gave me a brief orientation on the major responsibilities but mostly cautioned me to be sensitive to the various constituencies—the school board first and foremost, school principals, community groups that helped the schools in various ways, and the mayor, for instance. In addition to being charged with planning the supervision of professional staff and the development of curriculum standards, I must be alert to the politics of keeping good will for the schools, not the easiest part of the job. As the newest kid on the block, with only three years on the staff, I dreaded the reactions of the coordinators, for I had now been promoted over all of them. My fears were unfounded. Whatever they thought, this group with whom I had met weekly for three years, greeted my appointment warmly. My perception is that the seasoned, politically astute group did not consider my temporary appointment as a threat. Certainly I would be smart enough to realize that I should not expect it to be a permanent position. It was simply John Strand's way of gaining time to attract a real star to Newton.

My colleagues on the Bilingual/ESL staff were pleased at my temporary good fortune. My appointment was confirmed by a school board vote in midsummer. My group was very happy for the upgrade, believing that I could probably do even more good for the non-English-speaking students in my higher position. I kept my own nervousness to myself, considering the fact that I had never taken one university course in curriculum development or in the intricacies of evaluating professional staff. Everything I knew in these areas I had learned through observation and practice. What I knew about human relations was not from textbooks but from the trite but true "life experiences." I embraced the challenge of mastering yet another set of circumstances, for which I had meager training, with aplomb!

Years later, in September 2006, my son Steve called to say he has just been hired to join the Music Department staff at Phillips Andover Academy. He reminded me that in the spring of his junior year of high school, in 1983, while I was considering whether to accept the promotion in Newton, I learned of the six-week, summer chamber music program at Phillips Andover. I urged Steve to audition for a place. He was not enthusiastic about it at the time, wanting to just hang around Amherst for the summer. But he did apply and was accepted. Steve now tells me, "Mom, that turned out to be such an important summer. Besides enjoying the school and the musicians I played with, I met a wonderful teacher from Oberlin College who influenced me toward a career in piano performance. It was a good thing you made me do it!" We both laughed at the memory and the fact that he would now be teaching at that very school.

A Promotion and a Very Tough Year

The summer of 1983 was a stressful time for me. I was training Marcia Ratnor to head the Bilingual/ESL Department and was simultaneously involved in a round of meetings with Superintendent Strand's new management team—Vincent Silluzio, budget and finances, Tom O'Connor, personnel, Betty Quinn, secondary schools, Earl Hines, elementary schools, John Cullinane, special education services—and system-wide curriculum and instruction was my responsibility. Our areas overlapped and lines of individual accountability were not always clear. Earl, Betty, and I were new to our positions, and John Strand had only been in the Newton system one year, but we were all keen to work together smoothly and present a positive front.

In a wealthy school district like Newton's, it is not lack of funds that preoccupies everyone but the manner in which money will be spent. A new administration must first gain the trust of the professional staff—teachers, principals, support personnel—and convince them that their work is valued; it must decide which innovative ideas will be supported and encouraged, and it must be effective in presenting the governing school committee and the mayor with programs and budgets that will gain acceptance, albeit through long negotiating sessions. Promoting harmonious relations within the system that educated 10,000 children was as important as the need for good public perceptions of the quality of education for which Newton parents paid high taxes.

I failed one test in the very first few weeks in my new job. Son Dave was exploring the possibility of finding a teacher-aide position, to give him a year's experience in the classroom before deciding on teaching as a career. Since the Newton Bilingual/ESL Department often hired teaching assistants fresh out of college, and a few young men had held these positions at our high schools with good results, I suggested to Dave that he apply to Newton as well as other districts in the Boston area. Marcia Ratnor interviewed Davey and offered him a job at Newton North High School to help in the ESL classroom.

A week later I was summoned to John Strand's office where he informed me that my son could not be hired because it would be seen as nepotism. I was stunned. The possibility had never crossed my mind. John tactfully explained that although I was not directly doing the hiring, Marcia Ratnor reported to me, and Dave Porter's being offered the job presented a conflict of interest. I felt humiliated for my poor judgment. John did offer a small sop: Dave could apply to be a substitute teacher and once on the approved list, he would be called when needed. Since he would not be on the regular staff, this would be permissible. Since my son had already moved to Boston in anticipation of the Newton job, I was terribly disappointed for him and for my own stupidity. Dave had little choice but to accept the less attractive offer, but the experience of being a substitute in different schools, trying to teach different subjects at different grade levels several times a week was not one that inspired him to pursue a teaching career. At the end of the school year, he chose to go back to Philadelphia and enter the field of journalism.

Many worthwhile projects were initiated or continued under my direction, among them a research study on restructuring the junior high schools, training for department heads and principals on improving teacher evaluation, a system-wide effort to narrow the achievement gap between African American students and white and Asian students, expanding the training of elementary-level teachers in the Newton Advanced Challenge curriculum (it was Newton's version of a Gifted and Talented Program). However, the single initiative that dominated the year for all administrators was the recommendation from the superintendent that we close two school buildings due to declining enrollments in the city. Nothing will so urgently galvanize citizens into action than the threat of shutting down their own neighborhood school.

The 90-year-old Hyde School in Newton Highlands and the Meadowbrook Junior High School were targeted. The compelling reason was the drop in student enrollment over several years, with these schools not making full use of their classroom spaces. John Strand's rationale was sound: better to close two buildings and save the costs of heating, repairing, and maintaining the structures, which instead could be profitably sold for apartment developments and make a handsome profit to the city. The resulting savings to the school system would be used to support teachers' salaries and special programs. No teachers would be dismissed, and students would be accommodated adequately in nearby schools. For the entire school year, until the school committee voted its decision in the spring, our administrative team was engaged in public discussions and meetings several evenings a week to present demographic and financial data to the public. Nevertheless, the neighborhood activists waged a sustained and sometimes vicious campaign to keep the schools open, and it was wearing on all of us. In the end good judgment prevailed and the buildings were slated for closure, but not before a lot of emotional posturing and ranting and raving had been on display.

One project I was assigned, a small effort that I (wrongly) expected to carry through with a minimum of fanfare, particularly stands out in my mind. Our driver education program, in place at the two high schools, provided a short course in the state's motor vehicle laws and, for a small fee, road lessons in actual driving—both were necessary parts of preparing high school students to obtain their licenses. For some years there had been complaints at the high schools that going off on road lessons during the school day caused students to miss some of their academic classes. In surveying how driver education was being handled in nearby, comparable high schools, I discovered that other districts had removed driver ed from the school-day schedule, cut the driver ed teacher position, and contracted with an independent agency to provide the same service to all interested students after school, at a lower cost than the schools charged. I prepared my presentation for the school committee, confident that my proposal would be easily accepted. It would save the district about $55,000 per year, not a negligible sum at that time.

Arriving at the evening school committee meeting, I found a surprisingly high turnout of citizens. From the whispering among the people sitting around me, I soon understood that a large group of activists had been assembled to "save driver ed." When I made my presentation, the Chairman asked for public comments, and thus began an unending number of speakers who made impassioned pleas for keeping the program as is, for the importance of keeping the teaching position for kindly Bob who had been saving the lives of Newton youth for years, and on and on. There was not one substantive argument offered for the status quo, but when the school committee members voted they turned down my proposal by a wide margin.

This was one more lesson for me: Politics trumps good management every time, and elected officials rarely ignore public demonstrations of large groups of aroused constituents. Interestingly, the driver ed teacher's job was not threatened again until 2005, when a high school student accused him of making sexual advances during the road lessons. Bob was put on leave while the charges were being investigated and, though the girl's accusations were proven false, he retired, bitterly resentful of his treatment by the school district. Only then, twenty-two years after my original proposal, did Newton decide to turn driver ed over to an outside agency. This little vignette serves as one representative example of the inefficient ways in which public schools are run.

Japan Interlude

In late October, David and I embarked on a two-week lecture tour for USIS, stopping en route in Hong Kong overnight. Louisa Lok, the Chinese bilingual teacher in Newton, had urged me to call on her brother, Cecil Sein, a business man in Hong Kong considering a move with his family to either Canada or the United States. What a thrill to fly into Hong Kong, swooping down rapidly on to what looked like a small airfield positioned between high mountains covered with tall buildings, with the tarmac ending abruptly in Hong Kong Bay. Our plane skidded to a stop just short of the edge! Louisa's brother was a charmer—friendly, soft-spoken, with impeccable British-accented English. He took us shopping, to a dim sum lunch, and then to his family's apartment near the top of Victoria Peak. The view is incomparable. Nowhere had we ever seen such a densely populated cityscape. We both treasured the invitation to meet Cecil's wife Katy and their two children and the unusual chance to visit their home. Many times when we have been entertained by hosts in other countries, we've almost always been taken place to public places.

The following day we flew to Osaka to begin the Japanese tour. We were met by Professor Tamaki Yamakawa, of Osaka University, and two female graduate students who grabbed our heavy suitcases from the airport bus and insisted on carrying them to the Terminal Hotel. Professor Yamakawa and his wife had spent a year in Amherst where we had invited them to our home on several occasions. The young women, Masako Takeda and Hiroko Uno, scholars of American literature, came to the United States often. USIS scheduled David to speak in Kobe, Kyoto, Okayama, and Tokyo. My own talks were given in Kyoto, Nara, Nagoya, and Tokyo, with an all-day visit to an elementary school arranged by Takekazu Ehara, a professor of education at Kyoto University. Everywhere we went, we were escorted comfortably by car, bus, or train (including a ride on the famous, high-speed Bullet Train), and royally entertained each evening at one ceremonial dinner after another. Some of the delicacies I especially savored were the ultra-high-grade Kobe beef we dipped in boiling broth, along with an assortment of Asian vegetables (this is the famous dish *shabu shabu*), and a wonderful whole fish baked in lengths of hollowed out bamboo. But my Italian heart was gladdened at the sight of Japanese businessmen slurping up huge bowls of noodles in a broth with shrimp, spinach, and other vegetables. At every lecture David was presented with a handsome gift, and, a few times, I was included in the gift-giving ceremony. I was impressed by the stylishness of Japanese women and to this day, whether in Europe or the states, it is my observation that the best-dressed women are not from Paris or Rome but from Japan.

Each city provided us with exciting and varied impressions of the nation and of our academic hosts. For me, three occasions stand out. My trip to Hiroshima, alone, since David was speaking at Okayama University that day, is the most wrenching and memorable event of all my travels. Professor Shoko Ito met me at the train and drove me around the city pointing out such important local spots as the baseball stadium, home of the Hiroshima Carps baseball team. We then joined a bus tour of the important sites related to the atomic bombing in 1945. We were first shown the memorial at Ground Zero, the skeletal remains of the building at the epicenter of the atomic blast, and the huge grassy mound beside it where thousands of remains were stacked and covered with earth. Our next stop was the museum that catalogues the horrors of the city's complete destruction with survivors' accounts and photographs. A photographic record of the later progress of the radiation sickness suffered by the survivors was unbearably hard to look at. I was the only American on the bus tour made up entirely of Japanese tourists, and I felt horribly chastened.

The most warmly pleasing experience in Japan was the overnight visit with Takao Furukawa and his family. We had not expected such familial hospitality. Takao had spent a semester at UMass in Amherst and had been our welcome guest on several evenings. On our arrival late in the afternoon, we met Takao's wife, Sumiko, and their two high-school-age daughters, both intent on doing homework. The older daughter, with her mother's help, was composing an essay about the novel they had just read, *The Diary of Anne Frank*. The Furukawa home was located out in the country, near the city of Okayama. A modest place, sparely furnished in the Japanese style, with a tiny ancestor's shrine in the corner of the living room, this home introduced us to a custom we'd never before encountered: at bedtime, the dining table and chairs were removed, and we were given thin straw mats to spread on the wooden floor, two pillows, a tumbler of water, and two glasses. I still cannot understand how we slept comfortably and awoke without stiffness the next morning. Takao's pride and joy were the vegetables he was cultivating in the small garden plot he owned nearby. Apparently the luxury of a garden is rare in this densely populated country.

Professionally, my day at the Saho Elementary School in the lovely city of Nara reversed many of my stereotypical ideas about Japanese education. Among public educators in the Unites States it is widely believed that Japanese schools are too regimented, that students spend long days in rote learning, doing boring, repetitive lessons—nothing to compare with the child-centered, innovative, creative days enjoyed by American school children. For shame, that we should be so provincial. My colleagues in Newton blithely dismissed the fact that on comparable measures of math and science learning, for example, Japanese students at eighth-grade level are generally among the top performers, while U.S. students score near the bottom, year after year. However, on the accompanying survey of student evaluations of their own achievement, U.S. students score highest in self-esteem while Japanese are modestly near the bottom. Need I say it? Our children, in the decades since the explosive 1960s, have been brought up to feel very good about themselves, even if they do not actually learn very much!

My colleagues excuse poor U.S. performance by proclaiming that in other countries only elite students take the eighth-grade tests while here all students are tested. Not true! By the very strict guidelines of the International Math and Science achievement tests, all the students at that grade level take the tests. I reported back to Newton the following elements in Japan that lead to high student achievement: a long school day (eight hours to our six) and a long school year (240 versus our 180 days), deep societal respect for schoolteachers, a predominant ratio of mothers at home and available to help children with homework, and a homogeneous population with almost no influx of immigrants. Like it or not, these conditions produce a highly educated citizenry.

My visit to the school began at 8:30 AM in the large playground where all children, teachers, and the principal assemble every morning to sing the school song and do calisthenics for fifteen minutes. I then visited a variety of classrooms where I observed small groups of students collaborating on science experiments, young children working on a large art project in a hallway, and an English-language class practicing the song "Little Brown Jug." At lunchtime groups of students, from the youngest (age five) to the oldest (age twelve), whose turn it was to serve the meal, were seen in white painter's smocks with white face masks (for sanitary reasons) carrying large baking pans of food to the tables. No cafeteria workers on hand. The cooks prepared a full meal in the kitchen, the children took turns in serving and clearing away the crockery and utensils (no disposable plastic items here) and the well-prepared, well-balanced meal. I had seen the same routine in our sons' schools when we lived in England—a very civilized practice, teaching children cooperation, good nutrition, and good manners. The afternoon included more class visits and an interview for me, in English, on the amateur radio station operated by students. What a day. By 5 PM, when the last students, left I was saturated with good impressions—the lively children, a school environment highly conducive to learning, the high morale of the teaching staff.

The last few days we spent in Japan were in Tokyo, where David gave lectures at Meiji Gakuin and Tokyo Universities and I gave my last talk at a luncheon of the International Children's Bunko Association. The strange title of this group has nothing to do with our understanding of the crime of "bunko" or fraud. It is a social group of women who have lived abroad for several years and, on their return to Japan, band together to look for ways to maintain their children's fluency in the languages they had learned in other countries. Affinity groups can be assembled for any good or perceived good, or for no good reason in modern advanced societies. The city of Tokyo itself is a marvel—densely packed with the most crowded sidewalks we have ever navigated, and much more civil behavior than one would encounter in, say, New York City, the "attitude capitol" of the world.

We spent our last evening in Tokyo by ourselves. We found a French restaurant that served us a "cooked" meal of Western food. All the lovely banquets of the past two weeks were wonderful, but we were aching for comfort food, and for a *diner-a-deux* during which we could relax and not have to make conversation with others. Our trip reinforced my personal attitude about the two countries that were our deadly enemies when I was growing up during World War II: Germany and Japan. I have visited both countries and have met many of their nationals in our travels. Why do I have a mostly negative attitude toward Germany but a positive one toward Japan? Is it the consummate politeness of the Japanese compared to the hard-edged German manners? I cannot understand my impulses, they simply are so.

On our long flight home, I had a conversation with a Japan Air Lines stewardess that has become one of our favorite anecdotes. I asked the attractive young woman where she would be leaving the flight for her scheduled rest. "Ankaledge," she replied. When I asked what she would do in Anchorage, Alaska, our own stop to change flights, she said with a big smile, "Sreep." Her answers, which perfectly illustrate how the Japanese tongue interchanges the two consonants, *l* and *r*, in their English contexts, may not be funny to anyone but linguists!

Surprise Welcome at Home

Arriving in the Hartford, Connecticut, airport, we were happily surprised to find our sons Tom and Dave there to drive us home. For Tom to have come from Washington, D.C., and Dave from Philadelphia, just to greet their parents seemed unusual. We asked, and learned that the brothers not only wanted to see us but would be attending the high school play that evening, to see their brother Steve perform. What filial and fraternal devotion. Of course, there was a more serious reason, as we soon learned.

Tom said, "Mom and Dad, there's something you need to know and we wanted to be here to tell you. A week ago, Steve was in a serious accident with Mom's new car. He was driving his friends home from school after soccer practice, on South Prospect Street, when a car came up a steep side road without stopping, crashed into the right front of the car, and totaled it. No one was hurt, thank God. We decided not to call you in Japan. You couldn't do anything about it and would only worry. So, Dave and I wanted to be here to tell you." What a shock! My "little red roadster," a new Chevy Chevette hatchback that I'd only had for a few months—gone, never to be seen again. Never mind. We were so grateful to Alex Page, at whose home son Steve had been staying while we were away, for the time and effort he expended on the police and accident reports, and to our two older sons for showing such feelings for their brother. When we met Steve that evening after the play in the high school auditorium, he was quite nervous but we soon set him at ease with our hugs and good-natured teasing.

Life Near the Top in Newton

Back at work, the school year and my role as one of the top administrators became a serious strain on my self-confidence. I missed the easy, trusting, and mutually respectful relationship I had enjoyed with my former superiors, Norm Colb and Aaron Fink. Personally I liked and admired my new boss, John Strand, but I felt a heightened tension among the team he had assembled who, like me, were in new positions and understandably out to prove themselves. As the least experienced administrator, even though I had established a certain amount of credibility in my shaping and improving of the Bilingual/ESL Program, I was always conscious of being a temporary figure in the grand scheme of Newton school politics. Still, my good husband encouraged me to apply for the permanent position when it was announced after the Christmas vacation. I threw in my hat, went through the interview process, but was not offered the job. In some ways, it was a relief. At the end of the school year, I would be back among my favorite colleagues, heading the educational program for which I felt supremely qualified.

There were some lovely highlights in that year of 1983–84. In February we arranged a birthday luncheon for our son Tom's twenty-fifth birthday at Le Relais, a restaurant on Madison Avenue in New York City. Dore Ashton and her family joined us, she being an art historian with whom my husband was collaborating on a project. Steve was accepted at Oberlin College and decided that was where he'd be going to school in the fall. In early spring 1984, I organized a dinner for the professional staff of the Newton Public Schools, with author and civil rights activist James Baldwin as guest speaker, which turned out to be the most popular single event of that school year. We had become acquainted with Jimmy through Istanbul friends; he had spent a few years at Robert College and was now living in Amherst as a Visiting Lecturer in the University's creative writing program. What an evening! Baldwin electrified the audience with his dramatic, free-wheeling remarks on literature, American society, the African American struggle, and his anecdotes about life in Paris and Istanbul—he charmed us one and all with his wit and intellect.

In April I spent my week's spring vacation in Rome with my husband, who had again been invited to give a week of lectures at the Centro per gli Studi Americani. As an early high school graduation gift we took our son Steve. We also agreed to take along our good friend Nonny Burack, and the story of that week in Rome with her is an example of how people you're quite comfortable with on mundane, common turf often surprise you in a more exotic locale.

Nonny, a very bright, very well-read woman, typifies the kind of aging groupie who thrives on the fringes of academia. We met when we both worked in the office of *The Massachusetts Review*. She became a fixture in our household, dropping in for drinks or dinner once or twice a week; we always enjoyed her company, and I even cooked separate meals for her when she became a vegetarian.

We knew Nonny to be a secular Jew—that is, until we arrived in Rome on Palm Sunday, which in 1984 coincided with Passover. As we strolled through the city's Jewish ghetto, she asked me if I thought any of the passersby looked Jewish, and if so would I stop and ask if they knew where any public Seders might be held. "Nonny, everybody here looks Jewish to me," I said. "How am I supposed to know?" We stopped at Da Giggetto for a late lunch, the best-known restaurant in the ghetto, and Nonny again nudged me about finding a Seder she could attend. To satisfy her I walked to a nearby table occupied by a large family and asked, in Italian, "Excuse me, but I wonder, are you by any chance Jewish? My friend is trying to find a public Seder in the city of Rome. Do you know of any?" The grandmother answered graciously, "Yes. We can help you. Call the synagogue and they will tell you the time and place for tomorrow night." I thanked them and reported the news to Nonny.

The next afternoon Nonny urged me to find her a box of matzos, which I did by asking a grocer who handed me a package, saying: "Ah, si, pane degli ebrei (Ah, yes, bread of the Jews)." I couldn't help but think that before the trip she had rhapsodized about the joys of eating bread in Italy. Hadn't she anticipated then that the timing for such an "indulgence" would be wrong? Soon we were on our way to hear an art lecture at the American Academy on the Gianicolo hill, and from there I called the synagogue and got the address of the Seder. Assuming now that Nonny would be happy and anxious to attend the dinner, we offered to call her a taxi. But she demurred, saying. "I don't want to go by myself." Frankly, we were surprised, having known Nonny for sixteen years as an independent soul. Perhaps it was the environment, finding herself in Catholic Italy at the time of Passover, that brought out her identity assertiveness.

A few days later, when we took the train to Lucca to visit our dear friends Gil Cohen and Paul Gervais, I hadn't realized that Nonny's hopes for attending a Seder were still high. Gil and Paul's house was in the middle of a giant restoration project, but they had urged us to stay overnight, although that meant we would be in sleeping bags in an attic room. At the dinner table, just before Paul served us a magnificent roast lamb, Nonny turned to Gil and rather disappointedly asked, "Aren't you having a Seder?" Gil looked startled and quickly replied, "No. I'm sorry, I don't do Seders."

The end of the school year could not come soon enough, the time when I would be released from the assistant superintendent responsibilities, and, by a fluke of contract language, I would have the whole summer free, not be obliged to work my usual month in the summer. In the fall, when I returned to my normal job, my salary would revert to the lower figure, about $15,000 less. I will never forget the telephone call from my husband on the very last night I was in Newton before vacation. He called to say, "My dear, I am so very happy that this is the last night we have to be apart. I can't tell you how much I've missed your company these four years, though I had Steve with me on those three nights a week when you were not here. It's over now, and the coming year we'll be together in Boston, now that I'll be on sabbatical from the university."

Boston Adventure and an Empty Nest

Contemplating the unusual freedom for two whole months, we rented a place in East Orleans on Cape Cod for the month of July, an old house with lots of bedrooms, a nice big lawn for picnics, and a short walk to the beach. Steve and his high school pals came for long visits; Tom and girlfriend Karine arrived for a time; so did my best friend from advertising days in New York, Peg McWhirt—enjoyable house guests all. One weekend with the entire Schleappi family and David and Sonya Sofield visiting, we thrilled to the magnificent speech by Mario Cuomo at the Democratic National Convention and the nomination of Geraldine Ferraro. Dave and I love entertaining and I find it relaxing to be with good friends, good food and drink, and good conversation, even when I'm the one doing all the cooking. The month was restorative. One day an Amherst acquaintance who had a summer cottage nearby called to say she had been collecting mussels on the rocky beach and would we like some? Polly Longsworth's pail of fresh mussels, steamed in white wine, garlic and parsley, made two consecutive lunches.

Now to find a place to live in Boston for the coming year. Dave decided it would be more interesting to live in the city than to move to Cambridge, which would be Amherst writ large. Through *Boston Globe* ads, we soon lucked in on a penthouse condo in Back Bay. The owners were leaving the place completely furnished at a reasonable rent for a two-bedroom, two-bath apartment with an indoor staircase to the private roof deck. We were a short walk from shops, art galleries, museums, and the Charles River. There were two drawbacks: there was no garage (on-street parking by permit meant circling the block many times to find a spot), and it was a fourth-floor walk-up. We took it, and sublet our house in Amherst for the year to a couple of budding academic superstars who would be teaching at Mount Holyoke: novelist and literary critic Brad Leithauser and his wife, poet Mary Jo Salter.

Toward the end of August, we drove with Steve to Oberlin, Ohio. Despite the fact that family connections with brother Roy Porter and sister Dud Pixley had been severed a few years earlier, we decided to call and let them know that we would be stopping in Batavia overnight on our trip west. They warmly welcomed our call and suggested dinner together. Without any apologies or references to past differences, Dud and Roy were happy to see us and to become acquainted with their nephew, Steve. Helping our son move into his freshman dorm on the Oberlin campus, the experience of leaving him so far from home, was sad for us, and for him. We knew he would quickly adapt, make friends, and become comfortable in Oberlin, and he did. Oberlin, with its long history of leading the way in educating women and African Americans since the nineteenth century and its excellent music conservatory. turned out to be exactly right for him.

While at Oberlin, Steve played on the varsity soccer team all four years and we made at least one trip to the campus each fall to see a game. Steve was invited to audition for the conservatory, to be in a five-year, double-degree program that would give him an undergraduate degree in liberal arts and a master's degree in music, but he declined the offer. Knowing that conservatory students spend the majority of their time on music, Steve was not ready to narrow his focus so soon, preferring to have a broad liberal arts undergraduate experience. He succeeded in doing just that, earning a degree with high honors in English, and doing enough conservatory work to merit giving a senior concert performance.

Professionally, David and I were both in comfortable situations. He was on sabbatical leave from teaching for the year, working on a projected television series on language and on a critical piece linking the art of Joseph Cornell with Emily Dickinson's poetry. In connection with this latter project, David was awarded a six-week research fellowship at the National Gallery in Washington, D.C. I returned to work in September in my rightful place as head of the Bilingual/ESL Department. We were both delighted to be living together fulltime again after four years of my commuting back and forth, and to start exploring city life in Boston. We rubes from the hinterland of western Massachusetts walked the city every weekend, marveling at the architecture of Back Bay and Beacon Hill, the sophisticated music, museum, and restaurant scene, the new, posh Copley Plaza shops—it was all we had anticipated. We were off to a good start for a year together but that, alas, was not to be free of tensions.

My husband was due to start his prestigious fellowship at the National Gallery in late September, which would require that he be in Washington some of the time for the following six weeks. We both realized that we would not be together after all, and I did not handle it well. David decided he would fly to D.C. early in the week and return to Boston by Thursday or Friday. An unexpected benefit was the invitation from our son Tom that Dad should share his apartment when he was working in D.C. It was a blessing, not only for the economy of it but more for the two to have the opportunity of spending companionable time together. That I would be alone again part of each week was not what I wanted, so I accepted David's plans with ill grace, childish behavior I am not proud to remember.

The Chinese Coup for Newton

I soon learned that I, too, would be out of Boston that fall. I was included in an official group scheduled to travel to the People's Republic of China in mid-October. A Newton Public Schools delegation was invited to negotiate the first exchange program between a Beijing high school and one in the United States. My part was to give lectures on English-language teaching and visit schools and universities. On this historic trip we worked out the details of an exchange of teachers and students between the Jingshan School in Beijing and Newton North High School: on alternate years, two teachers and four students would go from China to Newton or from Newton to China, spending a period of five months. The Chinese teachers would have the experience of assisting in an American high school, observing our teaching methods, and would chaperone the Chinese students; the students would be fully enrolled in classes and participate in extracurricular activities. One condition we insisted on and the Chinese government finally approved: each visitor would live with a Newton family—they would not be housed together as a group as the Chinese had first demanded.

The first group arrived in Newton in the fall of 1985. Mr. Jou and Ms. Nai Wen, with two male and two female students, adapted to American life fairly quickly. The Chinese bilingual teacher on my staff, Louisa Lok, was a great help as a liaison with the group. Though they were all fluent English speakers, they needed to learn the cultural nuances of life in an American high school. This first round of the exchange was a success but for one incident that might have sunk the whole endeavor.

Ms. Nai Wen was assigned to the English-as-a-Second-Language program at the high school where she helped the two ESL teachers already in place. Also on the staff was a young, recent college graduate, Haig Townsend, who was employed as a teacher aide. It soon became apparent that Nai Wen and Haig were smitten with each other. When I was informed, I spoke to John Strand, who had designed the exchange. John and I were concerned that Nai Wen might run away with Haig or that he might follow her back to China, and that either action would spell the end of the whole program. Some tactful, private talks were held with both young people and they were convinced that for the greater good they should wait until Nai Wen returned to China and correspond with each other until they could plan their future without endangering the exchange. And they did wait, though distance and time cooled their ardor. Haig's impulse to run away to China and be an English teacher gave way to an interest in architecture and graduate studies for a new career. Nai Wen continued with her teaching, married, and started a family in Beijing, having the one child permitted by government edict.

Pedalino Note

My youngest brother, Frank Jr., was married on May 25, 1985, to his second wife, Mary Ellen O'Brien, a rising young executive with AT&T whom he had met when she interviewed him for his job with the corporation. Mary Ellen represented the exact opposite of his first choice for a wife in his hippie days—Gloria, the Chicano/Cherokee wild woman who had given our family an overdose of *agita.* As the oldest of nine children in a close-knit Irish Catholic family— her father an attorney, her mother a realtor, Mary Ellen and her family represented solidity and a level of normalcy Frank had not much experienced. I made a special effort to initiate a friendly relationship, even traveling to New Jersey for her bridal shower.

Their wedding in the O'Brien hometown of Mendham was a truly happy event with all Pedalinos in attendance but one. Frank invited me, as the eldest sibling, to give a short reading at the wedding Mass. My biblical selections were the usual exhortations to newlyweds, except that I began by noting that May 25 was especially auspicious since it was also the birthday of Ralph Waldo Emerson and our son, David Lawrence Porter. The only sad note was that our brother Domenick was not invited. Frank had not forgiven Domenick's rude behavior at the family party for our mother's seventieth birthday a few years earlier—his refusal to be in the family photograph, his telling the photographer that he no longer considered himself a part of us. We were embarrassed in front of our guests, and then, rubbing salt into the wound, Domenick later refused to pay his share of the luncheon party. But in spite of our pleadings with Frank not to leave his brother out—and I won't say that we didn't have reservations about this being a suitable occasion for their reconciliation—Frank was implacable. He would not risk Domenick's making a scene at the wedding reception.

Professional Honors

In June of 1985 I received a call from the U.S. Department of Education in Washington asking if I would accept an appointment to the National Advisory and Coordinating Council on Bilingual Education (NACCBE), a group charged with advising the U.S. Congress. The three-year appointment, providing my background check proved adequate, would involve approximately four meetings a year in D.C. to hold hearings, gather data, and make an annual report to congress on the national status of this educational initiative. The Newton School Board approved, though we were all surprised that, as a good liberal Democrat, I would be chosen by Republican William Bennett who was then Secretary of Education.

In that same month David received word that he was one of four professors selected for the honor of Outstanding Teacher of the

Year. The University's annual recognition of faculty carried with it a year's stipend for scholarly pursuits and release from all teaching and committee responsibilities. After the celebrating was over, we had our first discussion of the next year's living arrangements. Truly, the year in a Boston apartment had not been satisfying for my husband. Yes, we were together, we explored the marvels of Boston, Cambridge and environs; we did a lot of entertaining and enjoyed the cachet of living in a penthouse. But my husband really missed living in a house with the convenience of a garage and the "burden" of a garden to plant and grass to mow. On hearing the wonderful news that he would be on leave for a second year, I assumed that David would stay in Boston with me in the same apartment. He was absolutely stunned at my assumption and told me I was selfish to expect him to make the sacrifice for a second year, to expect him to stay away from his scholarly connections in Amherst. I was just as surprised at his reaction, and just as angry that he would condemn me to another year of commuting.

We both learned something about commuter marriages: each year has its own set of problems, and the longer the commuting goes on, the more stressful it becomes. Neither of us would budge at first, but soon I caved in, gave up the lease on the apartment at summer's end, and found a room to rent from one of my co-workers. Leaving St. Botolph Street on the day I removed our last few possessions from the apartment, I sat in the car and wept for the seeming unfairness of it all.

My friend Mary Kay rented me a bedroom in her apartment with a shared bath and kitchen. Somehow we misunderstood each other about the living arrangements. I knew I would be in the apartment three nights of the week and in Amherst all weekends. She didn't expect me to be underfoot so many week nights and thought I would use the apartment more on weekends when she often left town to ski or travel. Neither of us was comfortable, but we tolerated it until I moved back to live with my friends, Kathy and Charlie Knight, midway through the school year. Even living in their attic was preferable to being where I really felt unwanted.

Villa Serbelloni—The Rockefeller Connection

In spite of the commuting disagreement, the closing months of 1985 yielded one of the most exciting, nay, glamorous events of our entire married life. David had applied for a residency at Bellagio, the Rockefeller Conference and Study Center at Villa Serbelloni on Lake Como, Italy. When he received the invitation to spend six weeks at this plush retreat, from mid-November to the end of December, of course he accepted. The Rockefeller Foundation invites a dozen scholars in a variety of fields to work on some worthwhile project of their choice while enjoying magnificent seclusion and freedom from domestic chores, all expenses provided, with spouses and partners included in the package. David was working on a piece of writing that could be reasonably completed in that six-week period. I could not absent myself from work for that long, but I requested a three-week leave without pay between Thanksgiving and Christmas; I would go to Bellagio and begin work on a book. Newton being the enlightened place that it is, granted me leave. Our three sons did not need our supervision; Tom was working in D.C., Dave in Philadelphia, and Steve was in his sophomore year at Oberlin.

David left for Bellagio and was immediately charmed by the villa life. Each scholar had a private office with telephone, computer, and supplies. Breakfast and lunch were informal affairs; at dinnertime scholars (and their spouses or partners) were seated in the magnificent formal dining room according to a plan that changed each evening. Cocktail hour on the loggia preceding dinner lasted only long enough for everyone to have one very small cocktail before the drinks cart was whisked away. Since the scholars arrived on a staggered schedule, the faces changed every week or two.

The scholarly and social ambience of the villa was further diversified by the arrival of larger groups scheduled for two or three day conferences. The conference attendees took their meals with the resident scholars and the residents were free to sit in on the discussions if they chose. In the short time I was there, I sat in on a session on Southeast Asian political developments since Vietnam, and another on nuclear nonproliferation. Residents were free to set work aside and take in occasional local sightseeing, although trips away from the study center for overnights or dinners were frowned upon. One did not need to turn in a log of hours worked or a finished product at the end of the stay, but all were encouraged to send copies of resulting published works to the villa's professional library.

To prepare for my departure to Italy, I had daunting responsibilities. We had contracted to have the interior of our house painted while we were away, and I did the necessary moving and storing of things in preparation for the painters. The weekend before leaving, I bought, wrapped, and labeled all the Christmas gifts, piled them on a table covered with a large cloth to protect them from paint dribbles—all this so they would be ready for our return home two days before Christmas. I had applied for a job as a lecturer at Holyoke Community College, close to Amherst. Although it paid much less than Newton, it would allow me to live at home again. I went to the campus for my interview, returned to Newton, tidied up my office, and left for the airport—ready to collapse. On arriving in the Milano airport the following morning, the day before Thanksgiving, there was my sweetheart David looking for me through the crowd, flanked by the chauffer who would drive us to the villa.

It was a glorious reunion and we spent the evening alone, catching up on each other's experiences and on some much-needed snuggling. The next morning I met the merry scholars at breakfast and was informed that there would be a croquet game at noon, with champagne, at the foot of the hill near the lake. Among the fascinating people with whom we formed lasting friendships, starting from the croquet game/champagne event, were: the artist Sigrid Burton and her husband Max Brennan, an architect; the sociologist Joyce Gelb and her husband, an attorney named Joseph; the sociologist June Nash; a psychiatry professor, Jack McDermott, and his wife, a botanist named Sally; and the feminist literary critic Carol Schloss.

I was invited to join a few of the women in planning a Thanksgiving pageant for that evening. My contribution was to make paper Pilgrim and Indian hats to be worn by various speakers who would make historical (and amusingly irreverent) speeches for the occasion. The pageant, performed after a sumptuous *tacchino* dinner, amused us; my part was to recite, in Italian, a brief account of my homeland's contribution to the American Thanksgiving, namely, Cristoforo Colombo's little sailing trip, made some centuries before the Pilgrims washed ashore at Jamestown.

Those three weeks were pure magic. As soon as the holiday celebration was over, I had a blunt talk with my husband. He had actually expected that I would use the time to relax, socialize, read, and just enjoy the surroundings. I, however, had a serious purpose in mind. I was determined to outline the main elements of a book on the politically controversial bilingual education field—issues of language, culture, identity, nationhood—and perhaps even to write the introduction and one chapter. David, to give him the immense credit he deserves for understanding my ambitions, gave me his complete approval and requested a typewriter and supplies for me. I would work in our bedroom while David "commuted" to his office on a wooded hillside nearby.

Our large, well-appointed bedroom in the main house had two windows facing on the lake and mountains. Over the bed was a painting by Canaletto. The bathroom was noted for the unusual design of purple, black, and white tile, and it also had a window overlooking the lake. The room was notorious among Rockefeller fellows as the place where President Kennedy slept (with a well-known beauty, not his wife) when he visited the villa overnight after a conference in Switzerland.

Like the official "fellows," I set to work each morning and managed four to five hours of uninterrupted writing until lunchtime. Afternoons were for hiking the villa grounds, exploring the village, or taking short trips on the *vaporetto* to villages/castles/churches across the lake. We did not leave Bellagio except for one weekend, when we traveled to Milano where our friend Franco Miccinelli had managed to secure a pair of tickets for us to attend *Aida* at La Scala, with Luciano Pavarotti singing the lead. Knowing how demanding Italian opera fans are, we both held our breaths when he sang the first big aria in Act I, "Celeste Aida." The audience rose as one to applaud with loud cries of *bravo, bravissimo!*—reassuring us that our instincts were correct. Luciano was at his peak.

Two important influences affected my work and future while at Bellagio, both resulting from my sitting in to listen at the conferences. The conference on Southeast Asia, a decade after the end of the U.S. involvement in Vietnam, included a few Vietnamese generals, Russian military leaders, and American representatives from the Pentagon and U.S. State Department. As I sat in the large, magnificent library, listening to the speakers drone on and viewing a perfect scene of green hills, snow-capped mountains, and the confluence of the Como and Lecco Lakes below, I was struck by the incongruity of the seminar topic, the setting, and the attendees. Dashing back to my room with an idea, I quickly wrote a short essay that raised question about why Cambodia had not been invited to participate, which I sent off to the International Herald Tribune in Paris, the most widely circulated English language newspaper in Europe. A few days later, they called the villa to see if I was actually there and to verify that I had written the piece, promising to publish it very soon—my first piece of writing published in a recognized newspaper[11]!

The other piece of good fortune occurred during the nuclear nonproliferation conference. At lunch I happened to sit next to one of the participants, Joseph Nye, a Harvard professor and the former under-secretary of defense in the Carter administration. He turned to me and asked, "What is your project here?" When I said I was working on bilingual education he said, "I'm a good liberal. I want to see immigrant kids get the help they need. Tell me in twenty-five words or less what I should think about bilingual education, what are the issues." Gulping for an instant, I answered him with a very short explanation. He seemed satisfied and turned to talk to his seat companion on the other side.

His question and his avowed interest, as a well-intentioned person not well-informed on education issues but wanting to know more about this topic, shifted my book in a different direction. This would not be a book for teachers or school administrators to hash over the best ways to educate non-English-speaking children. There must be a larger audience among the general public for a wider ranging presentation that would encompass what problems had brought about the new education laws, why was it all mired in the politics of language and ethnicity, and what would be the future implications for the country as a whole and for the (then) three million children involved. I was just beginning to outline the scope of the book and write the introduction, when my chance conversation with Joe Nye turned me in a new and ultimately more productive direction.

A Zany Weekend

In late January 1986 our family came together from several directions for several days in Washington, D.C. The account of that weekend is memorable because it describes the lengths we would go to just to *be* together, but I remember it also because the day on which I flew home coincided with one of the sad events of the late twentieth century.

This was the plan: David would give a guest lecture in Raleigh at the University of North Carolina and would stop in D.C. on his way home for a weekend visit with Tom; Steve, with the offer of a ride to D.C. from Ohio friends, decided to make the trip and join them; I would arrive in Washington on Saturday, two days in advance of a National Advisory and Coordinating Council on Bilingual Education meeting I was scheduled to attend, and take my part in the family-weekend adventures.

A blizzard in Amherst—followed by ice, followed by a January thaw—caused flooding in our basement the day before I was due to leave. This required turning on the sump pump every two hours to get rid of the water. In spite of all this, I was determined not to miss out on being with my family. Early Saturday morning I drove two hours to Framingham State College for a meeting of bilingual program directors, to "show the flag" for Newton. Returning to Amherst, I realized the basement flooding problem would be disastrous if I left it unattended for three days. Inspiration! I called one of Steve's friends, high school senior John Fortescue, and offered to pay him to stay in our house overnight and keep the sump pump running—he accepted. I arrived in D.C. just in time to see the play Tom had gotten tickets for, *Secret Honor*, a one-man play about Richard Nixon, our favorite villain, whose disgrace we had much desired. Looking back on that weekend, it seems a bit over-determined and frenzied, but it's indicative of the efforts we all made to coordinate our often disparate agendas.

Leaving D.C. on January 28, the scene in National Airport was one of silent grief, a sign that some terrible tragedy had occurred. Every single traveler was focused on the overhead television monitors. I stood with the others to watch the repeated scenes of the Challenger spaceship exploding, and the replays of the happy crew boarding the shuttle—haunting visions.

At home again, I received a disappointing notice from the search committee at Holyoke Community College: of the two finalists for the position of Lecturer in English as a Second Language they had chosen Mrs. DeMas, not me. In retrospect, my failure to assume that position and move back to Amherst was better for my fast-developing career, but at the time it seemed unjust. Not only were my credentials more than adequate for the job (B.A., M.Ed., and Ed.D. degrees in ESL; fluency and literacy in Spanish) but I had experience teaching in the Puerto Rican community from which most of the students came. Mrs. DeMas had a master's degree in psychology, no course work in ESL, and no experience teaching in the field. Clearly, as a woman from Puerto Rico, she was chosen for her ethnicity. I filed a hiring bias lawsuit with the Massachusetts Commission Against Discrimination which would take years to resolve. In the meantime, Mrs. DeMas did not succeed in the job and was eased out in less than two years.

Newton Under the Gun

Spring 1986 brought a dilemma for the Newton schools. While the Newton program for non-English-speaking children gained attention for its student successes, and the teaching staff earned praise from

Newton parents, our good work was not lauded by the State Department of Education. Notice was given that an audit of the bilingual program would be initiated, with a team assigned to a week in Newton to observe classrooms, interview staff and parents, and review data. We teachers and administrators understood that this level of scrutiny would have been more than enough to examine a district ten times the size of Newton. We saw it as an attack on the one alternative program in the state that diverged from state law and documented student achievement superior to that of the state-sanctified bilingual programs.

Twelve educators arrived, carried on their bureaucratic duties, took reams of notes, and left to assemble what would surely be a critical report. One member of the team happened to be a congenial colleague who told me that the group had been instructed to look for every shred of possibly damaging practices, as Newton must be brought to heel before it gave ideas to other school districts. For two months after the site visit, we did mountains of paper work, responding with haste to all requests from the state office. We expected a report that would acknowledge the good work being done—the high level of spending on bilingual students, for instance, or the qualified teachers, or the high achievement most students made in school subjects and English language learning in two years (versus three to six years in standard bilingual programs), the very low school dropout rate, or high parent satisfaction. We expected some credit for good work and some criticisms for areas to be improved. We completely misread the script.

On a late Friday afternoon, the superintendent's office received a call from a *Boston Globe* reporter asking if it was true that Newton was denying the civil rights of bilingual students. Apparently, before the report was received in Newton, someone at the State Department of Education leaked its report on the audit of Newton's bilingual program, accusing the district of noncompliance with state and federal laws. The wording of the report was harsh, calculated to cause the greatest harm to the reputation of a public school district nationally renowned for excellent schools and for its programs for minority students. The local press was not kind.

Newton's defense in the press, in meetings with community groups, and with the state bureaucracy was to reiterate the facts: yes, our program was an alternative that we considered allowable under state law, it was the kind of program the parents wanted, and it was showing success for the students. The teaching staff was seriously disappointed at the public spanking, but gallantly soldiered on, with strong support from the school board. Thus began a sparring match between Newton and the State Department of Education that created extra work for teachers, the loss of some state funding while the program was under the "noncompliance" edict, and the cost of projects such as the translation of our Handbook for Bilingual Parents into six languages—Mandarin Chinese, Italian, Hebrew, Spanish, Japanese, and Vietnamese. For years those translated handbooks were offered to every family enrolling their non-English-speaking children in our schools, but few ever took them. In fact, many families included one parent who knew some English, others brought along an English-speaking friend or relative when they came to my office.

In April a bill was submitted in the legislature, proposing a minor change in Chapter 71-A, the Transitional Bilingual Education Act. This new law would allow alternative programs and called for annual testing of students to measure English-language and subject-matter learning. For the first time, I drove to Boston to speak at a public hearing on the bill. To my surprise there were hundreds of demonstrators outside that beautiful, Bullfinch-gold–domed State House, with signs protesting "Don't End Bilingual Education." Busloads of school children and their parents had been brought in for the demonstration on this school day, and television cameras were filming the event. Inside, in the hearing room, there were more school children and teachers. I signed up to testify in favor of the bill and took my seat, next to a group of first-grade children. I asked their teacher why the children were not in school and she answered, "Oh, they are here to learn about democracy." Six-year-olds should be learning to read and write, I thought to myself.

Only two or three citizens were on the list to speak in favor of the bill; the major part of the day would be taken up by speakers against any change in state law. As a measure of how well our students were learning English in their bilingual classrooms, I offer one anecdote. I stood before the legislative committee and gave my three-minute speech in favor of change. The entire group of high school students sitting in the balcony stood and cheered when I finished. Then their teachers shushed them by telling them (in Spanish) that my remarks were not to be favored, and the students all stood and boo-ed! That these high school students could not understand enough English to know what argument I had made is a sad commentary on their schooling.

Soon after the committee hearing, it was determined that the bill would be referred for further study. Translation—nothing will be done this year, the bill is dead. I wrote an op ed piece for the *Boston Globe* decrying the political paralysis that allowed a failing program to continue to the detriment of 45,000 students in Massachusetts schools.[12] For the next several years, I made repeated appearances at the State House or sent statements in support of legislative reform of bilingual education, but no bill was ever voted out of committee.

On the positive side that spring, the first contingent from Newton was ready to leave for Beijing. Both students and teachers had studied Mandarin intensively to prepare for life in China. They carried off this novel opportunity with great fortitude, very little complaining of home-sickness, no dropping out—all persevered through the whole five months. For Newton students from upper-middle-class homes, living with a family in a tiny, two-room apartment where a bath or shower was not possible even once a week took some adapting. None of the host families owned a car. The normal means of transport was the bicycle, joining in the daily fun of cycling Beijing with a few million others. They survived, returning home with a deeper understanding of that country than the typical American school exchange that lasts two or three weeks. Newton is proud that this exchange is still in effect in 2008, though it was cancelled for a few years during the turbulent times of the Tiananmen Square pro-democracy demonstrations.

Porter Summers

Our summers now were centered in Amherst, where Steve would be home from Oberlin, and Tom and Dave would often visit. David and I began thinking about Nantucket again as the place to search for a summer getaway and the idea immediately appealed to the whole family. Coincidentally, we learned that David's brother, Roy had retired from work as an investment broker and had settled on the island to be near his adult children. We looked at a few properties, and met with Roy, who volunteered to look after the place for us if we bought on the island again.

Through our good friend Jane Silva we found an affordable cottage in Pocomo, a little settlement on the harbor, seven miles out of town. Though it was just a tiny two-bedroom cottage with attached garage, and sited on a narrow piece of land, it was right on the water. With some cleaning up and fixing up, it would serve. The current owners lived in Michigan and were eager to sell the place, as is, old furniture and all. Our offer was accepted and Jane, as the agent, delivered our buy/sell agreement and picked up the deposit check for $25,000.

The conniving that went on around that property purchase resulted in our losing Jane's friendship for several years. Apparently the owners received a higher bid for the house and called to say that they were no longer accepting our offer because the real estate agency Jane worked for had never been commissioned to sell it. Horrors! We were taken aback by the unscrupulous action and notified the owners that we would sue them if they did not honor our agreement, for which we had paid a deposit.

Our lawyer initiated a law suit against the Michigan couple, and within a few weeks they came around. The suit was dropped, they honored our contract to buy, but insisted on one condition: there was to be no realtor's commission paid to Jane because her agency had acted without authority. We accepted, believing we could settle with Jane personally. I made several attempts to call her at her winter home, and left messages for her. Unfortunately, Jane's father was dying, and she was so taken up with family affairs that she never received our messages. When she read about the sale in the Nantucket newspaper she was angry, and rightly so, and called us to say as much. Our explanations by phone and in an apologetic letter David wrote to her were not accepted. We would not see our friend for seven years.

In spite of these real estate shenanigans, we each carried on with our work. My spare time was devoted to the book manuscript, which was progressing very slowly. An Amherst friend told me about the Bunting Institute at Radcliffe College, a research institute for women in midcareer that provided a year's fellowship at the Radcliffe/ Harvard campus with an office, research facilities, and the networking opportunities at this most elite of elite universities. It sounded much too grand for me, but I brought it up with David, who gave me his usual advice, "Do it. You are working on a good project—timely, socially important, controversial. You may well be accepted, but you won't get anything if you don't try for it." As a veteran writer of grant applications, he helped me put together a convincing appeal. I enlisted the support of three excellent referees: Professor Christine Rossell, head of the Political Science Department at Boston University, Dr. Adriana de Kanter, policy analyst at the U.S. Department of Education, and Dr. Esther Eisenhower, director of English-teaching programs for the Fairfax County, Virginia, Public Schools. The fellows selected for the 1987–88 academic year would be announced in the spring of 1987.

Steve's Semester Away from Oberlin

On Thanksgiving Day, while at dinner at my sister Francesca's house in New Jersey, we were called to the telephone. It was Steve, calling from Oberlin. My husband was on the phone quite some time and returned to the table looking worried. Our two older sons were with us, and we all excused ourselves from the table. David told us Steve was in a panic, something was causing him great anxiety, and he wanted to leave school for the rest of the year. David announced that he would go to Oberlin the following week for a good talk with our son.

The source of Steve's problems was never entirely clear to me. I did not question him too closely at that time, telling myself that I respected his privacy. Now in his junior year, Steve seemed to enjoy the academic course work and his piano study, the camaraderie of the soccer team, and a lively social life. David's talk with Steve revealed that he was determined to leave Oberlin for a while. My husband's first suggestion was a semester of study abroad but Steve rejected that, saying, "Dad, I've been abroad so many times while I was growing up, it really would not interest me." Rather than just doing nothing for a half year, or taking a menial job, my husband suggested that Steve take his "semester abroad" in Amherst—come home, and take classes at the University of Massachusetts, so that the semester would not be a loss and he could return to Oberlin in the fall and graduate with his class.

Steve liked the plan. Giving himself the distance and time away turned out to be healing and productive. He was able to take advanced courses—Paul Mariani's graduate seminar in modern poetry, Kathy Swaim's graduate course in Milton, and piano study with Estela Olevsky, the internationally renowned concert pianist. We treasured the rare privilege of having Steve at home with us for several months. Once our sons left for college, they would not live at home with us again, and, with the exception of Tom, who more than a decade hence would come back to Amherst with his second wife and their children, they made their homes and families and careers in other cities.

The first half of 1987 was uneventful, the usual commuting routine for me, but with a more comfortable living arrangement where my husband occasionally made the trip in midweek for an overnight in Newton, saving me a round trip to Amherst. We found a furnished apartment in Chestnut Hill, a corner of Newton on the boundary line with Boston, allowing us to do a little entertaining, or have overnight guests now and then. My occasional suggestion that David spend the weekend in Newton with me seldom met with his approval. He really preferred to be in Amherst and would not compromise, putting up instead with my sulks.

Rumania, Sicily, and Turkey

The United States Information Service (USIS) wrote to David and me, asking if we would be available to go on a rather demanding two-week assignment. They had a request from the University of Palermo for me, and from several colleges in Romania for David, plus invitations for both of us to lecture in Turkey. We were experienced in the ways of academic speaking and traveling and especially thrilled to go back to Turkey. USIS pays all travel expenses and provides a very small stipend. It was another adventure of the kind we love to embark on, confident that we would meet our professional obligations, knowing we would enjoy the ancillary benefits of traveling together.

David left for Romania in early April, to give lectures in four cities including Sighisoara, the home of Count Dracula. He found very receptive audiences of faculty and students eager to hear about American literature and new trends in critical theory. Under strict Russian rule for so many years, there had been little access to current Western writing. At a gathering after one of his lectures, a young professor slipped a scrap of paper into his hand and whispered, "This is my sister's address in the United States. Please call and tell her that you saw me and that I am well." He hid the note carefully so it would not be discovered when he left the country. Incidents such as this made my husband impatient with the lauding of all things socialist/communist by his university brethren. Under forty years of Russian rule, Western tolerance for free speech rights was completely absent in that part of the world.

David flew to Rome to meet me, then we'd be off to Palermo. While strolling along the Tiber, talking over recent events, I stepped into a pothole and twisted my left foot severely. Limping along, we made our way to a meeting at the American Embassy to receive our travel documents and schedules and were on our way. Walking was painful with my swollen ankle, but we managed. We were met at the Palermo Airport by a represented from the U.S. Consulate in a chauffer-driven car. Once seated, we were informed that the car was bullet proof and would be driven at high speed to the hotel in mid-town. We thought this was excessive protection for two American teachers and laughingly said so. But we were informed that the recent activities of the Mafia against Italian authorities and business leaders—the shootings and kidnappings—were a serious threat in Sicily. We were only there for two days, but walking around the city was frightening. At many street corners and in front of every bank and government building, soldiers with submachine guns were stationed, some looking quite young and inexperienced. We always smiled and tried to look as benign as possible when we walked by them. ·

The great excitement of our brief stay in Palermo came when our son Steve telephoned to say that he had received a call from the Bunting Institute at Radcliffe. When he told them that I was out of the country but that he was responsible for taking my messages, they informed him that I was offered a fellowship for the 1987–88 academic year at Radcliffe/Harvard with full privileges but no stipend. They would need my acceptance or refusal within the next ten days. It didn't take us but a minute to tell Steve to call the Bunting and accept for me. The opportunity of a full year to work on my book among other women scholars—and with the prestigious Harvard connection—I simply could not turn this down. We would manage family finances without my Newton salary for a year, now that we had only one son needing his college tuition paid.

From Palermo we flew to Istanbul. Checking into the Bebek Hotel at the foot of the Bogazici University campus, we were dismayed at the accommodations, a damp bedroom with shared bathroom that had not been recently cleaned. The heavy rain and muddy streets further lowered our spirits, but we called two American friends, Joanne Greenwood and Carol Fonger, who promptly came to Bebek; we found a table at the old Gunes Lokantasi for drinks and swordfish kebab. Just their company and the familiarity of the justly famous Turkish cuisine restored us completely. Two days later we picked up a rental car for the drive across the Bosphorus and on to Anatolia, where I was scheduled to speak in Izmir. Our schedule allowed us to drive to the Dardanelles, take a car ferry across to Çanakkale, and stop for a half-day's visit to Troy, the fabled site of the *Iliad* and ancient Greek history.

On the car ferry we noticed a large group of high school students with their teachers. As we sailed across the straights, the teachers led the students in a group sing. To our surprise, the first song was "Old Macdonald Had a Farm." Arriving at the entrance to the excavations of ancient Troy, we were alone except for a bus load of Japanese tourists whose attention was riveted on a massive wooden statue of a robotic-looking horse. This creature, meant to represent the Trojan Horse, was in the worst taste. However, the site was quite impressive. We wandered around the dig, studying the layers upon layers of city streets that had been uncovered. In its time, Troy was a seaport but is now located far inland as the port was silted up, and the Aegean is barely visible on the horizon. Rounding a corner to the place where the amphitheater had been restored, we were pleased to see the students from the car ferry. We joined the group, who were now seated and listened to a dramatic reading of *Oedipus the King*, declaimed in Turkish, by some of their classmates—it was so very appropriate.

The sight that moved us deeply was the view of Gallipoli and the sentiment carved into the mountainside, words of Kemal Atatürk, the father of modern, secular, democratic Turkey. The World War I battle of Gallipoli pitted the combined British, Australian, and New Zealand forces against the last holdouts of the Ottoman Empire. The superior Western forces, however, were pinned down on the beach while the smaller Turkish Army occupied the mountaintop. Months of fighting resulted in the deaths of thousands of ANZAC soldiers, many more from dysentery than from firepower, and the battle was lost to the Turks. The terrible toll in lives on both sides elicited Atatürk's memorial statement: "We mourn all the dead on both sides and we honor all mothers of these brave soldiers."

We had never been to the city of Izmir (formerly Smyrna), a bustling Turkish commercial and tourist metropolis sitting on a marvelous curve of the Mediterranean. Both evenings there we took long strolls along the waterfront, found little outdoor cafes, and feasted on the fresh fish grilled at tableside. My assignment was to give two lectures on new strategies in English-language teaching to groups of high school and university teachers. Both gatherings were well attended and followed by long question-and-answer periods. I was amused at the end of the second event when the moderator, a courtly, stylishly dressed, elderly gentleman gave me a gift (an antique copper vessel), a letter of thanks, and a little kiss on the cheek. Zounds! I could not imagine any male academic in an American university being daring enough to make such a gesture. I took it for the warm expression of appreciation it was meant to be.

Our lecture tour nearly completed, we flew to Rome for David's last two lectures at the Centro per gli Studi Americani. Pleasant as it was to be in our favorite European city, even briefly, we were both focused on getting back to the states to begin reorganizing our lives. On our last morning in Rome we went to a coffee bar for breakfast. As is the custom, you pay the cashier first, obtaining a chit which you then take to the counter to get the coffee and pastries. David paid for two café lattes and two pastries, feeling confident of his Italian for this simple task. We stood before the baked goods and, pointing to the croissants, he said, "Due cornuti." The bakery clerk gasped and stared at him, totally confused. I noted my husband's mispronunciation and quickly spoke the correct word for croissants, "corneti." My husband had asked for two cuckolds.

Much family excitement over the Radcliffe appointment for Mom, memorialized in cement by my husband, who carved this message into the wet cement of our garage floor, "LP—RG 1987–88," Lee Porter, Radcliffe Girl. That piece of graffiti is still in plain view twenty years later. I requested a year's leave without pay for professional activity, not neglecting to point out the glory that would reflect on Newton from my fellowship. Nothing impresses people in the Boston area more than a connection with Harvard, no matter how many degrees of separation.

A grand offer came my way from a wholly unexpected place, one that I would have accepted in a second, even giving up the Radcliffe fellowship. On an evening in late May I received a call from the Deputy Director of the Office of Bilingual Education and Minority Languages Affairs (OBEMLA) in Washington. Anna Maria Farias had attended several of the meetings of the National Advisory and Coordinating Council on Bilingual Education (NACCBE) and been an advisor to our group. She would be leaving OBEMLA in a few months to return to a Texas law practice, and she was sounding out candidates for her job. She had been favorably impressed with my work on the council. Anna Maria wanted to know if I would consider the appointment and assured me that my resume was excellent and my background check had been favorable. Would I consider moving to D.C. for a year or two? Giving Anna Maria my word that I would consider it and respond in a few days, we ended the call.

My husband was elated at the prospect, for he loves the city of Washington and had often said that it would be so interesting to live there. Before I had the chance to call her back, Anna Maria called me to say, "Rosalie, I'm so sorry to have to say this. We really want you for the job and thought we could make you the offer, kind of informally, but we can't do it. The problem is that you're not Hispanic." Boom! The old, ethnicity bomb exploded over me once again, the ugly underside of affirmative action, or rather what sociologist Nathan Glazer labeled by one of his book titles, *Affirmative Discrimination*.[13]

Nantucket Again

Our two summer responsibilities were to fix up the little shack we had bought in Pocomo and to find an economical pied-à-terre for me in Cambridge for the coming academic year. The first task turned out to be far more onerous than we imagined. Arriving on Nantucket in mid-June, we were met by brother-in-law Roy, whose news was not good. "The carpenters who built the porch on the cottage did a really nice job but I had a call at six this morning that there was a fire in the kitchen. It was put out, but there's a lot of damage to the kitchen and a heavy smoke smell throughout. You probably won't be able to stay there for a while and had better find a room in town." We drove out to Pocomo to see the damage and get a first-hand report from the workmen. The crew leader gave us an unlikely sounding story. Somehow a fire had started spontaneously in the kitchen, but when it reached the ancient hot water heater the tank had burst, leaking gallons of water that simply put out the fire. The kitchen was in a terrible condition: stove and refrigerator damaged, floor singed and cracked, hot water heater beyond repair, smoke stained walls. The carpenters had done some minimal cleaning up but the rest would be up to us, and a terrible job it was.

We rolled up our sleeves and began the work that would take up what we had expected to be our vacation. When I called my brother Domenick to tell him of our misfortune, he asked, "Have you filed an insurance claim yet?" It made us feel pretty foolish, not even to have thought of filing a claim with our homeowner's policy. Removing appliances, scouring walls, laying new linoleum, sorting out the old furnishings left by the former owners for disposal at the dump—in two weeks we had the place clean enough for us to move in. Once in situ there was much more to be done to make the place even minimally habitable, inside and out. I sewed curtains for the windows, arranged our second-hand furniture from Amherst, and repaired window screens. Outdoors, the grounds had not been cared for in several years. Around the path to the beach and around the cottage, there was a heavy overgrowth of hedges and vines covering a bumper crop of poison ivy, all needing urgent clearing. An unattached, single-car garage was filled with broken or partially rotted implements, an old rowboat that would never float—all to be disposed of at the town dump.

Sons Steve and Tom came to Nantucket for a week of really heavy work on the grounds. Chopping the overgrown foliage was hard work and we all wound up with poison ivy. Steve's visit was also marred by the infamous New England micro-bugs called "no-see-ums" by the natives—tiny, black insects that sting and arrive in their millions in early summer. Bad enough that Steve was sleeping on the living room floor, but even worse was the nightly bug attacks that our ancient window screens could not protect us from.

Enter Paige Thompson

Following Steve's visit, Tom arrived with his serious love, Paige Thompson. We had met Paige, who worked with Tom at *National*

Geographic, a year earlier on one of our D.C. visits and had invited her to spend Easter weekend with us in Amherst. Paige, a very bright, attractive, long-haired blonde California girl, had a breezy manner. This week together on Nantucket would give us a chance to become better acquainted. The outcome was not what anyone anticipated.

Paige grew up in Long Beach, graduated from the University of California at Santa Barbara with a major in sociology. She had married her college sweetheart, a young man raised mostly in Brazil, soon after graduation. Paige counted her participation in the "Semester at Sea" program as the highlight of her college years, studying and living on a ship and visiting Asian and South American countries. When she met Tom at work, her marriage was already ending in divorce. On first meeting Paige we were not aware that she had occasional bouts of anxiety, which she managed with medication and regular therapy sessions.

Our first surprise, considering how hard we were all working on the house and grounds, was that Paige occupied herself with the Iran-Contra hearings on TV, for hours, as we went about our chores, not offering to help in any way. For the first few days, Tom took Paige out every afternoon to show her the island, to look up old friends, to dine in one or another little favorite place. On their second-to-last day in Nantucket we planned a dinner on our new porch. David prepared the charcoal burner for grilling steaks, I did the rest of the meal, we had a cocktail, and we waited for Paige to come out of the bedroom. Tom went in to talk to her a couple of times. Finally it was dark, hours past the time for dinner, and Tom and Paige now appeared. She made no apology. We were so embarrassed at her rudeness, momentarily stumped. Then my husband addressed Paige directly, saying, "Do you know that we've all been waiting for you? We just don't understand why you would treat us this way!" It was a rare confrontational moment for my husband, who has managed to conceal his temper on many family occasions. Paige mumbled an apology, and Tom was desperately unhappy to be torn between his parents and his lover. A mostly silent dinner was quickly consumed, and Tom and Paige left to go into town. We soon went to bed and had no further discussion of the event.

The next morning Tom and Paige came to breakfast, and he announced he had taken Paige to the grounds of the historic old windmill where he proposed marriage and that, to his great joy, she had accepted. We hugged and kissed and congratulated them both and invited them to a celebration dinner in town that evening. We welcomed our prospective daughter-in-law warmly and left the island the next day. content with the work done on the cottage.

Settling in at Radcliffe

Steve returned to Oberlin for his senior year in September and David and I adapted to a new living arrangement. The Bunting fellowship expected scholars to reside in or near Cambridge, make use of the research facilities at Harvard and Radcliffe, and benefit from the formal and informal contacts among the fellows. Each week one of the fellows would give a presentation of her project to the community at large. The day after each lecture, a "brown-bag lunch" for all fellows gave us the opportunity to discuss the presentation with its author; it was a good forum for constructive criticism. The Bunting director organized a series of dinners, with one fellow at a time inviting a few members of the Harvard faculty to be her guests. We were often invited to the Kennedy School of Government when some eminent lecturer would be speaking. My two favorite evenings were one with Geraldine Ferraro and one with the witty William Bulger, then president of the Massachusetts Senate.

To benefit from all these activities, I could not just stay in Amherst and write. We agreed that I would need a little place to stay in overnight, once or twice a week at most. From a note on the Bunting bulletin board, I found what was really an illegal "studio apartment." A Radcliffe professor had fixed up a ground-level room under her house, with a sleep sofa, a tiny student refrigerator, a two-burner hot plate, and a bathroom with shower. With its own door set a few steps below the sidewalk, the separate entrance gave privacy. The day that David brought me from Amherst with my very few personal belongings to move in, we spent the night together in my new digs. It was not yet apparent that my husband and I had very different expectations about how we would live that year. I imagined that David would be as intrigued with Harvard as I was and would enjoy spending an occasional night or weekend in Cambridge with me in our tiny nest. He, for his part, believed that I was so tired of the years of commuting that I would never want to be away from home. We each misjudged the other badly, and it made the year less of a success than it might have been.

Once through the orientation, I focused most of my time in Amherst for writing, and one or two days in Cambridge for library research, meetings, presentations, and special events. How I reveled in the many informal discussions with the other women, professionals in such a variety of fields: artists, writers, literary critics, sociologists, scientists, historians—a rich coterie of accomplished women. I could hardly believe I was in their midst and might dare to think of myself as among equals—it was a pretty heady notion.

For the first month or so, David and I were compatible—until the afternoon I arrived in our kitchen to blurt, without thinking, "Oh, so-and-so is going to be speaking at the Kennedy School tonight and I really wanted to stay over ..." My husband took immediate umbrage. He became very angry and accused me of not wanting to be with him, and brusquely said that this year was not turning out as he had hoped. I tried to placate him but, it was soon apparent that my remarks had aroused very strong feelings simmering just beneath the surface. It was the second weekend in October. From that day on, through so many happy and unhappy events that fall, my husband barely spoke to me. And for the rest of my Harvard year, he spent one night with me at the apartment, an occasion when he was in Cambridge to have dinner with a Japanese scholar. That hurt.

Tom and Paige made a trip to Positano for "a prenuptial honeymoon," as they were planning a quiet wedding ceremony that fall. A terrible tragedy occurred when Paige's ex-husband committed suicide and was found by his parents on their return from Brazil. Paige was called on to help with the funeral arrangements. Tom and Paige met their responsibilities in the situation, but it took a severe emotional toll on Paige. They delayed their wedding plans until Thanksgiving and limited the guests to the two immediate families and Paige's best friend. We arrived in Washington with Bill and Sally Thompson, Paige's parents, for the Thanksgiving-morning ceremony held in the garden of the County Courthouse in Alexandria, Virginia, the very same place where David and I were married thirty years earlier. A judge performed the ceremony, and we all repaired to Tom and Paige's apartment, there to join in preparing the turkey dinner while the two families became acquainted. The weekend was enjoyable, the Porter brothers made handsome speeches, and my husband and I had gotten past the silent angry period, which had been unknown to the others, and were back to our normal good relations.

The day before our trip to Washington, it had been my turn to speak to the Bunting community (and several visitors) about my project at Radcliffe. My lecture was televised for the institute's archives. The quality of the questions and comments at the end made me certain that I had explained the issues clearly in what is a contentious but little understood area of public education. The subject of my book seemed to resonate with an intelligent adult audience.

We were a small gathering for Christmas. Tom and Paige began the very sensible pattern of alternating holidays between the two families, and this was their year to be in Long Beach, California, with the Thompsons. At our house we did the usual play reading on Christmas Eve afternoon, enjoyed our traditional Neapolitan Christmas Eve dinner, and spent the peaceful holiday missing Tom but quite happy with the company of Dave and Steve.

The day after Christmas I went right back to work, knowing that the time remaining on my fellowship might not be enough to finish the entire book. It was my third and last year on the National Advisory and Coordinating Council on Bilingual Education in Washington. The council's major project for the year was to analyze the available research on bilingual education and produce a report for the U.S. Congress by June, with recommendations for changes in the national Bilingual Education Act which was up for reauthorization. My role as coeditor of the report was useful as the data gathered fit right into one of my book chapters. By midwinter I addressed the need for finding a publisher for my manuscript, and here the Bunting connection proved invaluable.

When I first conceived of the book idea a few years earlier, I had sent an outline to two publishers; both turned it down. One of the services the Bunting Institute provided was access to the Harvard network of publishers interested in scholarly works. I was advised as to which publishers and editors would be most likely to want to see my manuscript, and on how to draft a good approach. The expert advice, plus writing my letters on Bunting Institute letterhead, resulted in a few meetings with editors. In a month's time, I had a letter from the president of Basic Books, a division of Harper and Row. Martin Kessler, the president of the publishing firm, wrote to say he was interested in my book and would like to meet to discuss a contract. He would be in Cambridge to meet with Professor Derrick Bell at Harvard Law School—would I be free for a drink at the Commodore near Harvard Square? Nothing could have stopped me from being available! We talked briefly and he offered me a contract to deliver a completed manuscript by spring of 1989, one year hence. My book would come out in spring 1990. Before signing I needed to review details about royalties, marketing, and advertising. The advance was a very modest $6000, half on signing and half on publication, but being published by Basic Books was what mattered. Now I had the best incentive to finish the job on time.

The special circumstances of my family, the family David and I had created and nurtured, were invaluable in my ability to strive for greater heights of achievement. I never discount the unearned blessing of good health as one of the foundations for good work. My husband's encouragement and professional help is no small thing, either. From the beginning he has read and edited everything I write, a practice he continues to this day. Had he been a businessman or scientist or in some other profession, I would not have had the help of a scholar and writer living in my own home. As for our sons, all had survived not only the normal perils of growing up in a permissive college town, and were unscathed by the disruptions to their social and school lives during the years we had taken them to live in foreign countries. Through it all, we had developed a close, loving family. Now that our sons were adults, each pursuing a career far from home but close to us with weekly letters and telephone calls, they were a source of satisfaction and not a drain on our energies. Not that their lives and ours were problem free, far from it. But when I reflect on my own growing-up years, with the turmoil and unhappiness of my parents, their difficulties in adapting to American life, and the burden on us to rise above poverty and beyond their parochial ways to establish our own identities—I count my experience as a parent to be much happier and less stressful.

Two Interruptions: First Bulgaria, Then Berkeley

My work schedule was even more frenzied in the second half of my year at Radcliffe. Daily writing was the chief focus, hardly ever interrupted. However, two exciting prospects came my way: an invitation from USIS to go to Bulgaria for two weeks in May to give lectures in four cities; and my first opportunity to be an expert witness in a high-profile court case on behalf of the Berkeley, California, Unified School District. Both opportunities appealed, the first for the adventure of going to another Communist country, the second would provide a valuable chapter for my book and enhance my national stature in my field.

Within the space of six months, roughly from March through August, our family activities would include: the sale of the Pocomo cottage when a sudden offer came out of the blue; the purchase of two tiny, newly renovated beach bungalows in Wauwinet, both of which would need furnishing; two weeks in Bulgaria; a trip to Oberlin College for Steve's graduation; a week in Berkeley, California, to prepare for the court case; and a two-week vacation in Lucca with Steve and Dave. It was definitely over the top but here's how it was all done.

USIS asked me to enlist another English-teaching specialist to go with me to Bulgaria, and I suggested a professional friend, Jill McCarthy of Newton. We left Boston together for the long flight to Sofia. No lecturing trip abroad, before or since, was as poorly planned or wasteful of our time as the two weeks in Bulgaria, and from the first day there was an uneasy atmosphere. On our arrival we waited a very long time before a young university student showed up, identified herself as our guide, and took us to an ancient, dilapidated car, whose driver would chauffeur us to our hotel. (The young woman and driver would continue to deliver us to our various scheduled appointments, but since we had been warned not to make critical comments in front of them, our conversations would remain stilted.) After checking in to our hotel, we asked our young guide where we could get a little lunch—we were famished, having been en route for most of two days with only random snacks at odd hours, and the hotel dining room was closed. She offered to accompany us on our search, and so the three of us walked two or three miles along tree-shaded city streets, until we could barely walk any further. We finally asked again if she knew where the nearest restaurant might be and were shocked to learn that she, a nineteen-year-old woman, had never been to a restaurant, that she'd been helplessly looking around hoping to find one. By now the hotel kitchen would be setting up for dinner and we returned there, foot sore and thoroughly puzzled.

The following morning, we were taken to the U.S. Embassy to meet with the USIS officer who would give us our schedule and contact names for the next two weeks. After waiting well beyond the time of our appointment, we were taken to his office. We soon learned, by the man's boorish behavior and slightly veiled hostility, that he had not been properly advised of our visit and had had to put together the lecture schedule very quickly, although this did not excuse his behavior. He did not rise to greet us or ask us to be seated, so we sat ourselves and made our polite introductions. He sipped from a can of Diet Pepsi throughout our conversation and never offered us anything; he gave us a sketchy outline of where we would go, what our audiences would expect, and then said he had another meeting to go to. Consequently, between the hastily organized lectures and the inexperience of our assigned guide, Jill and I were often confused as we traveled from Sofia to Plovdiv to Burgas, never knowing what we would find.

The absolute test of our patience occurred during the eight-hour drive to Plovdiv, where we were to visit a highly regarded high school to meet with teachers and observe classrooms. On arriving at the school parking lot, we were surprised to see not one car in sight. After ringing the doorbell several times we were finally met by a dapper man in a double-breasted navy-blue blazer, hair slicked back like a B-movie gangster, who identified himself (in an elite British accent) as the principal of the school. He welcomed us, and as we walked to his office, we noticed that there was no one in the halls or classrooms. "Ah," he smilingly pointed out to us, "the whole school has gone on a field trip today." We could hardly hide our dismay. He explained that communications with USIS had not been handled well; he apologized and then served us tea accompanied by a long-drawn-out description of the superb English teaching in his school. What an overbearing windbag!

We did have some useful meetings with teachers at other times, though, and there were brief opportunities for admiring the historic sights and the natural beauty of the countryside. As on my earlier visit to Leningrad, there was a sense of suppression, of grayness, of a static society. Our student guide gradually became more comfortable with us, especially when we were not with the driver. She began to ask us questions about life in the West. On a train ride one day, she suddenly blurted out, "Tell me about Freud." I had recently read parts of a biography of Freud and related the facts I had learned about his life and work, and I asked why she wanted to know. She said shyly, "We are not allowed to read Freud. I am studying psychology and I wanted to know about this man. Please don't tell anyone that I asked you." Of course we promised to be discreet. She also mentioned that there were so many American writers whose names she had heard but whose books were forbidden. We could none of us have imagined in the spring of 1988 that the Berlin Wall would be dismantled the following year and the Soviet Union would dissolve soon after, bringing freedom for Eastern Europe in short order. Bulgaria's abominable dictator, Ceausescu, would be summarily executed.

On the flight home, Jill and I wrote our report for USIS. We decided to be candid, though tactful, about the poor organization of our visit by the local USIS office at the embassy. We provided information about the good language teaching we had observed and made a plea for contributions of books for Bulgarian libraries, especially in American literature. The country, under Soviet rule since 1945, had only allowed the study of the Russian language until the 1980s, when English language teaching was introduced, hence the scarcity of texts in English.

Frantic is the only word to describe my return to the states. Landing at New York's Kennedy Airport, I took a bus to Hartford, Connecticut, where my husband met me for the hour's drive to Amherst. There we prepared for the ten-hour drive to Oberlin the next day, to attend the commencement activities. Tom and Dave joined us in celebrating their brother's completion of his undergraduate studies. Steve was awarded a bachelor's degree with highest honors in English, although he'd taken many music courses and had given a senior recital at the Conservatory as well. On the warm sunny day, as the graduates were slowly filing up to the stage to receive their diplomas from the University president, our family was grouped under a shade tree. Tom spoke to me privately with this suggestion, "Mom, I've read your book manuscript and what you've done so far is just terrific. I have thought of a title for your book that I think conveys the central meaning of the work. How do you like this? 'Forked Tongue?'" It took me no more than a few seconds to recognize the absolute rightness of Tom's idea. "You've got it! That title is going to make the book! This is it. *Forked Tongue: The Politics of Bilingual Education*.' Thanks a million, my dear son." Tom was prominently acknowledged for his sensational idea when the book was published.

The day after commencement, I left for Berkeley, California, from Cleveland, while my husband helped Steve pack all his belongings for the trip home to Amherst.

In Support of Berkeley

My involvement in the Berkeley case came through my colleague, Christine M. Rossell, at Boston University. She is a recognized expert in school desegregation and, at that time, one of the few researchers to have written in critical terms about bilingual education. Christine was first to be hired as a consultant to the Berkeley schools in a lawsuit brought by a group of parents (*Teresa P. vs. Berkeley Unified School District*). She called to ask me if I would be willing to join her as a prospective expert witness on behalf of Berkeley. I had no idea what such work entailed but Chris gave me a quick orientation. The legal team representing Berkeley, Tom Donovan and Celia Ruiz, would defend the school system.

A public advocacy group, Multicultural Education and Training Advocates (META) sued Berkeley on behalf of Teresa P. and a dozen other students, alleging that (1) the schools were not giving enough special help in the classrooms and (2) not teaching enough hours in Spanish or Chinese, and (3) that the students were being denied an equal educational opportunity. California had no law requiring bilingual teaching, but META was claiming discrimination under federal law. Berkeley must prove in court that student's rights were not being denied, that non-English-speaking children were receiving as good as or better an education in the Berkeley schools as in other California districts. The real crux of the case was an attempt to force Berkeley to do much more native-language teaching than the district believed to be helpful to the children, a naked attempt to get through the courts what was not required under state law.

Studying the documents in the case, data on students' achievement, high school dropout rates, and the depositions of school administrators, teachers and parents on one side, and bilingual education experts on the other side, I soon became convinced that I could make a vital contribution to Berkeley's side of the case and agreed to be an expert witness.

Our attorneys had organized my days in Berkeley efficiently, giving me the broadest view of the school programs for limited-English students. I observed classrooms at the elementary, middle school and high schools, some for Spanish speakers and some for speakers of Mandarin Chinese, visited the after-school tutorials, interviewed teachers and school principals. I learned that Berkeley paid close attention to the preferences of the students' parents. In the second-grade "Chinese Bilingual Classroom" I observed a reading lesson in English to second graders, all obviously Asian. She occasionally interjected a word in the Chinese dialect of the students to help explain some element of the story they were reading. After class, the teacher explained to me that the Chinese parents had insisted that their children be taught in English and that the native language be used as little as possible in the classroom. The "Republic of Berkeley," long known for its worship of self-expression and self-determination, would not refuse such a strong request.

At the middle school and high school, I observed classes for the Spanish speakers who were well advanced in learning English but still needed some help. The amount of Spanish used in classroom instruction was determined by the needs of the students. The Latino parents, for the most part, had not made demands on the schools. How the lawsuit got started, I could only speculate. However, as I have since had the experience of investigating and taking sides in over a dozen law suits, it generally begins with one or two disappointed parents who connect with an advocacy group like META that rounds up a few more with grievances and starts a class action. The advocacy group has nothing to lose but its time. When they bring a suit against a school district, if they win, the defendants must pay their legal costs. If they lose, they pay nothing. Since advocacy groups are privately funded by individuals and well-intentioned foundations (read Ford and Rockefeller here), they operate with impunity. Their aim is to coerce school districts to do what the advocates want, out of fear of crippling legal expenses. Some districts settle the lawsuit by hiring more teachers, revising the curriculum, or doing whatever is demanded of them. Oddly enough, when districts fight it out in court, they almost always win. META almost always loses, but it keeps on truckin'.

Berkeley's national reputation rests on the university's radical leftwing image and the upper-middle-class professionals that seem to make up the entire population, but it actually has a large working-class population of African Americans and recent immigrants, both groups over-represented in the poverty camp. As in many urban districts, the academic achievement gap between minorities and whites and Asians is wide, and is reflected in the higher level of school dropout rates for minorities. Again, as in other concerned communities, the schools are committed to reducing the achievement gap, to providing extra help to give minorities the opportunity to improve their learning. Berkeley provided before-school and after-school tutorials for high school students, summer school enrichment, an impressive array of extra help. When I visited an after school program where undergraduate students from UC Berkeley came to tutor high school students in math, science or English, I was met with an unusual sight. In a large auditorium, about eighty students were studying, each with a tutor. Every single high school student was Asian. I asked one of the monitors, "Are there no Latino kids coming to the tutorials?" The answer was, "No. We've made several approaches to the parents but they don't seem to be interested. Some of them have said the kids get enough English during the school day."

The best evidence for the good work being done in Berkeley was in the data on the performance of non-English-speaking students after one, two, or three years in the local schools. The administration reported test scores, report-card grades, and promotion rates, and compared these data to non-English speakers in similar districts in California. Berkeley's students were performing academically as well as or better than most other districts. Students who were getting much more instruction in Spanish were not doing better than the Berkeley kids. There was no reliable data to use against the Berkeley program, and that contributed to the outcome of the case. The differences between the bilingual education advocates and the English-teaching advocates were ideological and pedagogical. Factual data favored our side.

At the end of the week, the two Berkeley attorneys confirmed my appointment as an expert witness. In addition to traveling expenses, I would be paid an hourly rate for my time in Berkeley and for studying documents sent to me by the attorneys for the duration of the case—a modest $125 per hour, but as a novice that seemed generous to me. For testifying in court, I would be paid at a higher rate.

Home to Amherst again and off to Nantucket Island to transport a truckload of old furniture and to buy whatever else we needed to outfit the two bungalows. Dave's brother Roy, who was working for Marine Lumber Company, the only "department store" on the island, helped us buy basic things such as mattresses and lamps with his employee discount. In a week we had done the work and prepared to leave for Italy. Dave and Steve met us at Boston's Logan Airport for the flight to Milano. We picked up a rental car and drove the long autostrada route past Genoa and the coastal towns, finally arriving in Lucca in late afternoon. Our friends Gil and Paul had offered to rent us their guest house in the garden behind their villa for two weeks. After the grueling drive we were desperate for a swim, and the four of us just dropped our bags, put on bathing suits, and jumped into the pool. Just standing on the edge of the pool, feasting on the view across the valley to the Tuscan hills, was balm for the weary. Now we were ready for a different kind of feasting. We drove to the next village where the local grocer had started a family restaurant in his backyard. On this our first visit as diners—we knew Giorgio as the grocer—we were famished and asked for his suggestions. He offered us a sampling of three dishes for our *primo piatto*, a Tuscan vegetable soup and two different pastas. "Si, si!" we all agreed. And it was one of those simple but memorable meals. Over the next few years, Giorgio's backyard restaurant expanded. On our last visit we found a huge mural of an improbable Hawaiian scene tacked on the back wall. No longer the little family *trattoria*, it was a disappointment.

Dave and Steve took the long train ride from Florence to Sicily to revisit the places Dave remembered from our year in Catania when Steve was just an infant. They managed to fit in Agrigento, Siracusa and Taormina, as well as a visit to our old apartment in Acicastello, in three days. Though neither of our sons is fluent in Italian, when they went to the old hilltop apartment they were able to convince the occupants that they had lived there as young children and were invited in for a visit.

This was one of their chief interests in making the trip, and we were happy to know that they cared so much about the Sicilian connection. On their first morning in Taormina, the hotel waiter brought their continental breakfast. Steve thought they had brought him tomato juice from the color of it, and that it was an unusual breakfast drink. When he tasted it, he had his first acquaintance with the sharply tart taste of blood oranges.

All in all, they enjoyed their week with us, and we were sorry to see them leave for home. During the entire time in Lucca I worked mornings on my manuscript. Afternoons we would sometimes go with Gil and Paul to look at property, since we were still on the quest of finding a small farm house for our future retirement years. Our two friends were generous with their time and advice. They also announced to us, soon after we arrived, that they would not charge us rent this time because the guest house was much in need of repair, and it did not seem fair to make us pay for the substandard accommodations—what an unexpected boon.

One of the quaint customs of the village of Massa Macinaia, at the foot of the villa drive, was the annual Sagra dei Funghi, the three-night festival celebrating porcini mushrooms. We'd not ever been present at any village event such as this one. Every evening the local townspeople set up long trestle tables and chairs under strings of colored lights. At dusk a small band would strike up popular tunes as the ladies began ladling out substantial portions of pasta with mushroom sauce, salads, bread, and wine. We bought tickets and joined the diners one evening. We learned that villages throughout the country have their own *sagras*, celebrating their specialties—game, cheeses, prosciutto, even one for gnocchi! My husband still wants to find that town. The only discomfort for those three nights was the very loud music so near to our bedroom windows but we would not begrudge the locals their fun.

The approaching end of summer, after our return to Amherst, meant bidding the Bunting Institute goodbye. What an exceptional experience, to have shared the companionship of so many talented women, to have enjoyed so many professional and personal chats on

so many occasions, a soul-satisfying year. Dr. John Strand, Newton
superintendent, left his position while I was away to join an educational
consulting firm in New York City. The new superintendent, Dr. Irwin
Blumer, could not have been a greater contrast to Strand. From our
first meeting in the hallway of the administration building when I
introduced myself and explained my position, he impressed me as cold
and unapproachable. That turned out to be an understatement.

Closing the Newton Chapter

September 15, my husband's sixtieth birthday, coincided with a trip to
San Francisco to testify in federal court in the Berkeley case. David went
with me to celebrate his "big birthday" out there with our son Steve,
who had moved to San Francisco after college and was now working as
a paralegal. Steve seemed a bit lonely in this new city, and we admired
his courage in striking out on his own, so far away from family.

I gave my testimony on behalf of the Berkeley schools. It was
exciting and slightly daunting to be in a federal courtroom, awaiting
my turn. When the Berkeley attorneys conferred with me later that day,
they both said that the case looked promising so far, and that witnesses
on our side were doing a first-rate job. Steve and I treated Dad to a
birthday dinner at the Zuni Café. Tom Donovan, the lead attorney
for Berkeley, and his wife Shirley joined us the following evening and
took an interest in our son. They were kind to Steve on a number of
occasions during his two years in San Francisco. In fact, we developed
a cross-country friendship with the Donovans that lasted several years
beyond the trial. Tom was appointed to a judgeship in California,
shortly after the Berkeley case.

Our commuter marriage arrangement, now in its ninth year, was
descending into an almost intolerable situation, but neither of us was
ready to call it quits. David had signed on to an early retirement plan
offered to full professors the previous year. Any professors signing an
early retirement agreement would have a salary increase for the last three
years of teaching, which would boost their pensions; they then would
retire at age sixty-two rather than at sixty-five. We knew then that he

would stop teaching fulltime at the end of the spring semester of 1990, two years hence. Since federal laws forbid forcing tenured faculty to retire at any age, this incentive program gave productive scholars the opportunity to leave the classroom and focus on research and writing, while freeing up those large salaries to use in hiring junior faculty.

Since I had been a stay-at-home mom for several years entering the teaching profession at age forty-three, I had only accumulated twelve years of contributions to the state teachers' retirement plan. On investigating the pension situation for my own salary and years of participation, the prudent thing would be for me to work another three years, but that prospect was very unappealing. David and I needed to give some serious attention to this topic.

The atmosphere in the administrative offices on my return to Newton had changed. With a new leader, a not-so-subtle shift in loyalties was readily apparent. Superintendent Blumer's management style was coldly formal, his personality short on warmth or charm. I had witnessed one "changing of the guard" when John Strand arrived in 1982 to replace Aaron Fink, but that had not produced such anxiety as the present change of leadership. Perhaps it was my being away a whole year that gave me a more critical view of the jockeying for power among the administrators, the obvious toadying around the new chief. Perhaps I was so caught up in the challenge of resuming my job responsibilities as well as devoting every spare minute to working on my book manuscript that I felt distanced from what had once been an all-absorbing position. I was uneasy with Irwin Blumer, and harbored the nagging sense that he did not value my work or the effective job being done by my teaching staff.

In our one brief meeting during the fall, a get-acquainted twenty minutes to provide him with the general philosophy and background of the Bilingual/English as a Second Language department, he stunned me by saying, "Most Newton bilingual kids really don't need this. They could probably get along just as well without this special program, but we have to follow state law." He informed me that some of the teachers on my staff, the Chinese bilingual teacher, for instance, were reportedly not up to the job—a harsh judgment from a newcomer. I defended Louisa strongly as one of our more competent senior teachers who had taken graduate courses in our field, and who worked far beyond her normal duties in maintaining active relations between her school and the Chinese parents. Blumer just seemed to be negative on anything to do with my department for reasons I could not fathom.

By December, I knew that I could not complete my book manuscript by the March deadline unless I took a short leave. I requested a two-month's leave without pay and it was granted. This would give me from Christmas until March 1 to do nothing but write. Our holiday guests that year included Tom and Paige as well as Paige's parents, who were coming to Amherst to stay at the local inn for several days. And a joyous celebration it was! Dave and Steve were delighted to have Paige for a sister. The Thompsons were genial company. Bill was especially happy to be back in Massachusetts with the chance to revisit his alma mater, Springfield College, and the Basketball Hall of Fame. Steve gave me two gifts to keep on my desk to inspire me in my writing chores (and they are still here): a copy of Shakespeare's sonnets with a beautiful filial inscription, and a copy of Spy magazine's collection of photographs, "Separated at Birth," to keep me from getting too pompous or terminally serious.

Those two months proved to be the most productive, and a time of unalloyed pleasure in our closeness for David and me. It would have to hold us in good stead for the chaotic and occasionally deeply unhappy times that followed. Every day, by 9 AM I would be in the tiny fourth bedroom upstairs that had become my "office," descend for lunch with David, return to work and write until 5 PM. We would have a drink together while I made dinner, and we'd talk about our day. Just the novelty of having every meal together with no trips or interruptions soothed our bruised relationship. My husband's editing of each chapter, with rigorous attention to the logic, argument, continuity and style of each section—and no tolerance for generalizations, unsupported conclusions, or banalities—made my rewrites far better than I could have done on my own. Eighteen years later, it pleases me to note that, as I have become a more experienced writer, David's remarks on my written pages have gradually declined in number to almost zero. He is still the ultimate authority I consult.

The work was completed and a good first draft sent off to Martin Kessler at Basic Books in March, as per our agreement. While I was on leave, Stephanie Cohen, a teacher on my staff, was recruited to carry on my duties for the eight weeks. Superintendent Blumer had a plan to reduce administrative positions and he asked Stephanie at a meeting of department heads if, in her opinion, my job could be done as a half-time position. Feeling pressured by Blumer, she replied without thinking, "Yes, I guess so." It was some time before this exchange was related to me as an example of a really treasonous act on Stephanie's part. I met with Stephanie, who was contrite and totally apologetic, bursting into tears. She had not meant to convey to Blumer that my responsibilities were so scant that a half-time person could handle things, only that she was doing the minimal while I was away, not all the work I carried on—the supervision and evaluation of teachers, the contacts with the state education department, the meetings with parent groups, the gathering, analyzing and reporting of student achievement data. In other words, the multitude of activities I pursued Stephanie did not carry forward during my short leave. But the damage was done. At the end of the school year my position was reduced to half-time department head and half-time supervisor of special education for bilingual students, the monitoring of referrals for learning disabilities and other educational deficits. It was a crippling blow for me, as if all the years of hard work I had done to make the Newton program locally successful and an increasingly recognized national model no longer had any value.

During my summer vacation, I had met with Martin Kessler at Basic Books. My manuscript had been accepted with few suggestions for changes but with a note that I should do a little more writing to link the chapters together. As Kessler put it, "We're not publishing ten thirty-page essays but a work that needs a little more continuity." Having done my best to follow his recommendations, I was eager to know if the work was now considered publishable. Kessler's first comment was, "You're a fast learner." Yes, the manuscript was acceptable but I would have to meet with a copy editor, with the marketing people, and help the publisher with potential advance readers who could contribute a blurb for the book jacket—all crucial to the end product. While I was chatting with Charlie Cavaliere, the copy editor, he excused himself for an important call. I could not help overhearing the name Joe Nye, and as the call was ending I asked Charlie if I might speak with Mr. Nye. This coincidence was too good to pass up. "Joe Nye, do you remember a conversation we had at the Rockefeller Institute on Lake Como, when you gave me some advice about my book? Well, here I am with the book about to come out. And I understand you have a book with Basic also!" He laughed and shared my pleasure at the coincidence, saying it augured well for both books.

Now that we had a summer place on Nantucket again, we struck up a new relationship with my husband's brother Roy—he would be our agent on the island for the summer rental of our two cottages. We would share the work among the three of us, I making up ads for the local newspaper and keeping the cottages adequately furnished with linens, china, and other household items; David would handle the finances; Roy would meet tenants on their arrival, take them to Wauwinet, show them around and arrange for the cleaning between tenants. He would report to us any signs of damage. The two little cottages we had bought were newly renovated, one with three bedrooms, one with one bedroom, sitting side-by-side in a semicircle of beach bungalows facing a sand dune and the ocean. Our fondest times were the occasional week when our whole family could be there together. The rest of the time we did our best to find tenants, to help us cover the mortgage payments and other expenses. Once certain that my book was to be published, I hired Nantucket photographer Beverly Hall to take my picture for the book jacket.

Returning to Newton in September, with a much heavier work load and the ignominy of having my salary reduced, was depressing. My status as a "ten-month administrator" had also been cut back to a nine-month teacher's schedule, also as a cost-cutting measure. I had originally been hired to work at least one summer month due to a heavy schedule of interviewing families of new students, supervising an ESL Summer Program, and planning teacher placements for the coming year. The families of bilingual students were highly mobile, arriving from many different countries, moving from one city to another. From year to year, the teachers in my department sometimes had to be assigned to different schools, changes that were highly unpopular. At one of the early meetings in the new school year, I lost my temper at the carping and complaining about new assignments and blurted out to the staff, "What are you complaining about? I have had my responsibilities doubled and my salary reduced by $6,000 for the year. None of you have lost any of your pay." I knew immediately that I had overreacted and I apologized.

The strain of this my tenth year of commuting was becoming unbearable, and my husband and I agreed that this was absolutely to be the last year. We would both retire in June 1990. I could not bear to hang on for the two years that would have increased my retirement income. Our combined retirement incomes would have to suffice.

In October of 1989 the San Francisco earthquake caused us severe anxiety until we got news that our son Steve was safe. I watched the network news after dinner every evening and saw scenes of the disaster. David telephoned me immediately to say that he had tried to reach Steve's office but it was after hours and there was no answer at his home phone; in the days before cell phones, of course, what we today take for granted—instant communication—did not exist. It was late that evening before Steve was able to get a call through to his father. He had had a frightening experience. The earthquake tremors began as he was leaving his office building shortly after 5 PM. He stood watching as the sidewalk throbbed slightly, and pedestrians became alarmed. People poured out of the office buildings, walking frantically away. He lost hope of getting bus transportation and feared the subway would be dangerous. In fact, it had shut down. So he walked with the crowds hoping to escape the downtown area and find their way home. It took him five hours to trek across the bridge to Oakland and to his apartment. Along the way he was horrified at the sight of the bridge that had buckled, pitching several cars into the water. The experience left Steve so shaken that it soon resulted in his decision to move back East.

But soon there was good news from California: the court ruled in our favor in the Berkeley case. The Berkeley Unified School District was officially confirmed in its right to continue the way it was educating non-English-speaking children. The results in student achievement were the essential proof and the judge found no grounds for requiring Berkeley to add more teaching in Spanish or Chinese or any other language. It was a great victory for our side and a smart slap in the face for META, the advocacy that had brought the suit. The California Legislature had allowed the bilingual education law to lapse in 1986, giving each district the right to design its own program. META's attempt to force its agenda on the Berkeley schools did not succeed. In spite of this court ruling, the bilingual lobby of activists, teachers' unions, and professional organizations would keep the pressure on school districts for several more years. The decision carried only symbolic importance for Newton since Massachusetts' bilingual education law was not affected by the ruling, but it did lift our spirits.

As for our three sons, each in his own way was pursuing his goals. Tom and Paige were enjoying their work at the offices of *National Geographic* television, and had bought a home in northwest Washington, a house that resembled our Amherst home except for the price, which was thirty times what we had paid for ours twenty years earlier. Dave had settled in Philadelphia, making a career in sports writing. He worked part time for the *Philadelphia Inquirer* and for a radio station, and also wrote freelance articles for magazines. Steve was having his "after-college fling" in San Francisco, but would move back to the East Coast the following summer. Having no college tuitions to pay now meant that we could help our sons in other ways. For example, we loaned Tom part of his down payment on the house, and began to help Dave and Steve with their college loan payments, since they were not earning big salaries.

The New Year began with the heightened excitement about the end of my commuting days and about seeing my book in print within the next few months. My Newton position was advertised in the trade press and the district received many applications. Ten candidates were interviewed, and the job was offered to Jill McCarthy, my colleague on the Bulgaria expedition. I heaved a sigh of relief, believing that the program I had worked so hard to develop over ten years would be in very capable hands.

Meeting the demands of my increased job responsibilities had become manageable, thanks to the help of an excellent secretary and my own determination to streamline some of the practices of the office. Through January and February I stayed late many evenings to proofread my manuscript, check footnotes, citations, and the index. I was a fledgling author, too unsophisticated to appreciate the excellent marketing and support services of a good firm such as Basic Books. They secured blurbs for the book jacket from prestigious names, sent out dozens of review copies to their contacts in the media, and did much to promote a book on a little-understood social issue.

Forked Tongue is Published

By early spring, when advance notice of my book appeared in the publisher's catalogue, the media machine took me in tow. Soon there were telephone calls by the dozens each week from radio and television stations clamoring for interviews. The media attention was dazzling, but I soon understood that the radio stations would call anybody to fill in their time. Typically, the interviewer would know nothing about the issues. My chance to speak would be limited to a single sentence or two in response to a silly question from the announcer, sandwiched in between ads for used cars or a celebration of National Condom Week. The satisfying interviews were those I did on stations affiliated with National Public Radio. For example, the Boston public radio station offered me a two-hour slot on David Brudnoy's evening program, an opportunity for an intelligent discussion with a knowledgeable host.

I was inspired to attempt an op ed in a large-circulation newspaper when I learned that Noah Epstein, the author of an important early critique of bilingual education, was an editor at the *Washington Post*. Looking back now, I marvel at the incredible chutzpah of my action. I telephoned Mr. Epstein, introduced myself, said I was a fan of his book, and that I would like to submit a piece I was writing on the bilingual education controversy, since my own book would soon be out. He responded politely that the editorial department could well be interested and gave me a direct link to the appropriate editor.

I sent my article to the editor of the Sunday *Washington Post* opinion page with a cover letter about my conversation with Epstein. Two weeks later, the editor called me to say that he would like to publish my piece with some changes. I expected he would want it shortened, but he surprised me by asking that I expand the article to about twice its current length, and could I have it ready within the next few weeks. What an incredible stroke of luck—the *Washington Post* article would appear the very week that my book came out, and the article would be syndicated in a number of newspapers across the country.[14]

It was Mother's Day weekend, an occasion when my brother Anthony hosted a pancake breakfast for Lucy at his home in New Jersey, inviting my brothers, sister, their spouses and their children. When Domenick and his wife leafed through their copy of the Bergen County newspaper, they were excited to see my name on an editorial essay reprinted from the *Washington Post*. They brought their copy of the newspaper to the breakfast and called me from Anthony's house to tell me how proud they all were of my accomplishment. Truly, it was one of the rare times when all my siblings and my mother took unalloyed pride in a family event, without an iota of rancor or anyone's attempts to disparage the honor.

There were great personal and professional disappointments that spring as well. The pressure mounted daily and made me testy and easily temperamental. I received a call from the Massachusetts Commission Against Discrimination (MCAD) about my complaint filed in 1988 alleging that I had been discriminated against in the denial of a position at Holyoke Community College. Mr. Douglas Sweet, the MCAD administrator who called me on June 12, 1990, said, "Dr. Porter, we find no cause to rule your complaint to be a case of discrimination. As a white, middle-class person, you must be prepared to give way to a minority to be given an opportunity like this." The outrageousness of this was so indisputable that I totally lost my temper and said, "You son-of-a-bitch. How dare you lecture me. How dare you tell me that a woman from one of the wealthiest families in Puerto Rico who has no credentials and no experience for the job, should be favored. I came to this country as an immigrant child in a family destitute throughout the depression. I worked in a factory and went to school at night, and you're telling me that I should be generous and step back so that this "minority" person can take a job for which she is totally unqualified?" Mr. Sweet was cowed but unwilling to concede any error. He simply informed me that I was free to bring suit in civil court, at my own expense, but not through MCAD. I have never forgiven the agency and will never get over my bitterness over the incident.

Family Dilemma

Now I must find the strength to write about the most difficult situation my husband and I have ever confronted. In early April I was scheduled to speak at the international TESOL (Teachers of English to Speakers of Other Languages) conference in San Francisco, and David had made plans to go with me so he could visit our son Steve. On a Friday evening I arrived in Amherst for the weekend to be met by a look of such utter misery on my husband's face, an emotional intensity I had never seen before. In a soft, subdued voice he said, "I have a letter here that you must read by yourself. I'm going for a walk and we'll talk when I get back. I think we've been expecting something like this."

Steve's letter, a long thoughtful explanation to us, revealed that he is homosexual, that he had been aware of his natural inclinations for a long time but had been reluctant to tell us. His move to San Francisco had been a determination to find his own way, away from the close family setting. Now he wanted us to know him completely and accept this part of his character. He had decided that the occasion of our being in San Francisco for a few days would be the ideal time for us to come together. He also informed us that he had been romantically involved for some time with a fellow paralegal, Justin Lopes, a young man from New Bedford who was sharing his apartment and whom he wanted us to meet.

By the time David returned from his walk, we looked at each other in agony, hugged, and cried. I had not honestly suspected Steve's sexual orientation to be what it is. He had such good friends in high school, had been a very popular guy with boys and girls, it seemed. College life, as much as we knew of his time at Oberlin, revealed the same pattern—a very popular young man. The fact that he had not brought a serious girlfriend home to meet us did not raise any troubling signals for me. My husband, who had lived alone with Steve through his high school years, had on one or two occasions taken Steve to task for the seemingly "girly" behavior of one or two of his friends. I had overlooked my husband's annoyance, advising him not to overreact.

What were our very first two concerns, on learning about Steve, which we voiced to each other immediately? AIDS, of course, and the fact that our wonderful, sensitive, talented, loving son would not have a family, not have the chance to be the fine father he could be. And why should one of our sons be homosexual, what had we done that had brought this about? The natural reaction to this revelation was to look for a cause, among the various bits we knew about the subject—was it a genetic condition from birth, did my absence from home during Steve's high school years make it happen, was it something about the way we two parents conducted ourselves that had an effect? Our sons knew that we were completely comfortable with homosexual and lesbian friends and acquaintances. But being on very friendly terms with several gays was not the same as finding one of our sons in their camp. And how would we handle this news? Among our Amherst friends, Steve would find easy acceptance, but for the Pedalino family it would be the ultimate scandal, far worse than any transgression yet imagined. What about the Porters, Philipps, and extended family members?

Having exhausted the beginning of this subject, we were concerned to talk with Steve and reached him late that evening. David spoke first, reassuring our son of our love for him and our earnest wish to come to terms with what had been a shock for us. I gave Steve the same assurances. I think my husband believed, in the unbearable emotion of the moment, that if we gave Steve all our love and support he might be able to overcome this alternative sexual identity. This conversation could not cover all the thoughts we three were struggling with, and we agreed to talk again. In the next few days, David decided that he simply was not up to going to San Francisco to face the situation. Of course, Steve was hurt. I left for San Francisco alone, not for the excitement of being recognized professionally by my colleagues for my book, but with a heavy heart, determined that my time with Steve would be the entire focus of the next few days.

After putting in the obligatory appearance at the TESOL conference, I turned to my son, to acquaint myself with what had been his life in the past two years—and not the abridged version. I met Justin, a pleasant, friendly young man, visited their apartment in Oakland, went shopping with Steve in Berkeley, anything to pass the time together as naturally as possible. One afternoon I had tea with Steve's friend Catherine McLean, who lived nearby. Catherine was working for Planned Parenthood, living with Chris Jonas. She and Chris had been two of Steve's closest friends at Oberlin. Catherine was taking a brief work break while considering what career to pursue. She later decided to go into medicine and is now at the Centers for Disease Control in Atlanta. Catherine encouraged me to talk, to cry, to say it all, everything that worried us about Steve's life. She is a wonderful woman whose empathy and nonjudgmental manner was what I needed. She made me believe that we would overcome this temporary distress and, good family that we are, we would be comfortable together once again. She was right, of course, but it would take us several years to reach that stage. Steve's brothers were totally supportive from the first instant. In fact, I remember Tom's comment to us, "Mom and Dad, Steve has my unqualified love and respect, and always will have."

How ironic that at the moment of my reaching unimagined success as a professional woman, to the immense satisfaction and pride of my immediate family, David and I felt such devastation over Steve's news. On my return from San Francisco, relations were strained between us, my good husband having a more difficult time accepting Steve's situation, I trying to be the bridge over the gulf between father and son.

We had to get on with the book-related activities planned by the publisher. In late May, there was a book signing at the Jeffrey Amherst Bookshop that was very well attended by friends and colleagues from both the university and Amherst College. But the book signing that gave us even greater joy was the event at the Bunting Institute at Radcliffe. To be feted on the Radcliffe/ Harvard campus was to have reached the pinnacle of academic celebrity. The Bunting Institute hosted a cocktail party and invited scholars and personal friends of mine, as was their custom. David and I made plans for dinner with our good friends from Amherst, Sonya and David Sofield, who took us to the Four Seasons Hotel in Boston. In spite of the secret cloud hovering over us, we savored the moment to the fullest.

To celebrate my retirement from Newton, we rented a stone farmhouse near our friends, Gil and Paul, in the village of Compito for the month of July. Dave and Steve would fly to Rome with their father to see a couple of World Cup soccer games in Rome and Florence; I would join them a week later. Our Dave was writing sports articles freelance and planned to write some pieces from Italy; Steve had just returned to the East Coast and had not yet found a job. He was happy to make the family trip with us and, on my arrival in Rome, I found David and our sons handling the strained situation quite well. No one was completely at ease, but we made much of our enjoyment of soccer, and of the exuberant excitement of the Italian fans. Steve stayed on for another week after his brother left, and moved with us into the Compito cottage, just outside of Lucca. We did not initiate any serious discussions with Steve but neither did we discourage him from bringing up the subject. By tacit agreement, it was a topic we would reflect on now and consider for further discussion later.

The remainder of our time in Compito was restful, easing the strain of the past year and my exhaustion—physical and emotional— of recent months. We took day trips to Bagni di Lucca, Montecatini Terme, Viareggio, Pisa, and our favorite Etruscan village of Volterra; we shared some dinners with Gil and Paul and the Martinis, our local Italian friends, and sat under the sun-dappled pergola on our front lawn, reading. One afternoon while we lingered over a late lunch in Gil and Paul's garden, Steve called us from the states to tell us that there was a grand surprise waiting for me at home, something to do with my book. "Is it a review in the *New York Times?* What is it?" I could not pry the information out of him. He assured me that it was something terrific. Just days earlier I had done an hour-long interview by phone with Richard Bernstein, who was writing a feature for the *New York Times* Sunday Magazine. On returning to America I was told the secret, and it was much better than a book review. The *Times* Sunday Magazine had used my name and a sentence from my book as the subject of their double acrostic puzzle! For Sunday *Times* crossword puzzle lovers like me, it doesn't get any better than that.

After the Italian interlude, August was mostly an unpleasant month. Steve found work in Boston as a temporary office worker and a cheap apartment in a dilapidated building near Fenway Park. We helped him move into the fourth-floor walk-up. He could afford nothing better but pointed out the one good feature of the place: from one of the windows he had a view of Fenway and could actually hear the roar of the crowds when the Red Sox hit a homer!

I felt obliged to give Newton a few weeks more work in August, although my replacement was already in the office. When I had first arrived, ten years earlier, I had found almost nothing to guide me—no written description of the program, or of the staff or of the students enrolled for special help, nothing. I was leaving a well-organized enterprise, with a teaching staff recognized as educational leaders, and a city-wide community convinced that we were giving non-English-speaking students in the Newton schools the best opportunities. Still, I found it difficult to detach myself from Newton, to walk out of the building for the last time. Ten years of excitement, drama, tears, triumphs—it had become my identity. It makes me uncomfortable now to realize that I dragged out my departure days longer than necessary, making my husband even unhappier with me.

On the hot day in August that I packed my car with books, files, computer, and personal belongings and drove home to Amherst, I was unprepared for the level of hostility I found. Trucks were parked in our driveway where a crew was digging a swale around the house, a deep trench that would be lined with gravel and filled in, to allow the run-off of underground water from the hillside behind our backyard. It would save us from floods in our basement after heavy rains and from having the backyard a soggy, spongy swamp through most of the summer. David was watching the workmen and barely bothered to look my way. There was no warm greeting, in fact, he would not speak to me. I had parked my car at the Campbell's driveway next door and said I had a lot of things to unload. No response. To my acute embarrassment, my husband stood with his back turned as I made trip after trip from car to house carrying heavy loads. Norm Campbell, whose offer of help I declined, watched from his screened porch, puzzled I'm sure at my husband's unnatural behavior. Thus began what would be a long and often painful period of adjustment.

Section IV

Transformations, Resolutions

Chapter 10
Winding Down

The challenge in concluding the description of my life, which I'm still energetically living, seems especially difficult; the most recent years have been my most frantic, with more involvement in public activities, more complicated situations to handle with our sons, and still more issues to be resolved between my husband and myself.

What major lesson have I distilled from the past four decades of feminist activity? Without a plan for my marriage and career, I followed the path of mid-twentieth-century wives—work until marriage, be a stay-at-home wife and mother during the child-rearing years, and take up volunteer or paid work outside the home (or further studies) gradually, as the children grow up. Completing my undergraduate degree at age forty-three and beginning my first job as a professional at that age had benefits I did not appreciate enough at the time.

What I learned dovetails with the choices being made by some young career women today, but I still think it's important to emphasize this lesson. Interrupting a career to devote time and attention to child-rearing allows well-educated women the opportunity to return later to their original profession or to a new one with renewed vigor, and the accumulated life experiences can enhance decision making. Instead of being at the burnt-out end of a few decades of work both inside and outside the home, a woman reentering the labor force in her third or fourth decade, full of new enthusiasms, fosters the desire and capacity to carry on for another two or three decades. At seventy-seven I am still lecturing, writing, and advising schools, families, government agencies on policies affecting immigrants—and fully savoring the satisfaction in being active and useful.

The years of my life since 1990 can be organized into four main categories: the long-delayed problems between David and me, which we confronted and eventually resolved; my professional work in the United States and abroad that created a "whirling dervish" character to our home life; the young adult lives of our sons, their marriages, divorces, careers, moves, and children—in other words, their shifting burdens and relationships; and the closing of the circle—our reactivating friendships with people we had been close to in our youth in Turkey, Sicily, England and many parts of the United States, and with some Porter and Pedalino relatives, a rich bounty.

The Marriage: Getting in Synch—Again

From the August day in 1990 when I arrived home, finally breaking free of my Newton life, I found that I was trespassing on the boundaries David had created during our ten-year commuter marriage. Without my having noted the fact, he had taken over the entire first floor of our house—living room, dining room, TV room, study, all but the kitchen. His books, folders, files, and notes festooned every table, chair, every flat surface, leaving me no space for the materials I had brought back from Newton. Having been alone at least three nights a week for years, David had become addicted to eating his dinner on a tray in front of the TV news programs. After one day at home, I made my plea for having our dinners together away from the evening news, that we would be healthier and happier not watching and listening to the horrors of the world but giving our attention to discussions of our own. That was an easy victory.

The more difficult adjustment was in our now sharing the house, both of us working at home. I was relegated to making a guest bedroom upstairs into a "study," where I set up my computer, telephone, fax machine, and file cabinet. One drawback was soon apparent: with my own telephone line upstairs, I found myself racing up the steps to answer it whenever I was out of the room. Requests for information from state or federal officials, interviews with reporters, graduate students wanting leads to research—often these calls would come from the West Coast while we were in the middle of dinner or later. The interruptions were a provocation to David, who became resentful. For my part, I smarted at having such a small, inconvenient space for my growing work commitments compared to my husband's continued expansive use of the large work areas on the first floor.

The early 1990s were blighted by a mismatch of aspirations. My husband expressed his desire for certain changes in our lives, some minor and some major: upgrade the kitchen, live in Washington, D.C., move to a different house in Amherst, live in Rome. But when I made these things happen, or set out to see that they would, he insisted they really weren't what he wanted at all, or else their inconsequential nature never addressed the deeper problems we faced. Trying to effect these changes consumed our relationship for the better part of six years.. David was reacting, perhaps, to the separation of our ten-year commuter marriage, to the fact that I had gone off on a great adventure and he had held the fort at home. He could not admit such a negative attitude because he had been consistently supportive of every career move I made, and had taken genuine pleasure and pride in my every achievement. Still, the negative impulses must have lurked beneath the surface, for they were manifested on a number of tense occasions.

Washington, D.C.

The three events that produced the greatest tensions and unhappiness involved changing our domicile. In our younger lives, we had, as

I've described earlier, taken our family to live in other countries for extended periods. We had always overcome difficulties and made these times valuable for the whole family. I assumed we were still able to carry off such transitions. When I was approached in the late 1980s for a possible appointment to the U.S. Department of Education in Washington, D.C., David had been enthusiastic about living in that wonderful city. In the early 1990s, it became essential that I open an office in D.C. in order to build the non-profit Institute for Research in English Acquisition and Development (READ). David agreed to the plan. I found an apartment to lease from academic colleagues, and negotiated an office space, at a very modest rental, in the offices of a large law firm with rooms to spare. We drove to D.C. at the end of August 1991 and were warmly welcomed by our son Tom and his wife, Paige, who lived not far from our apartment in the northwest part of the city.

David helped move my gear into the office. I went to work immediately, full of the excitement of finding funding sources for READ, visiting government agencies that provide research data, and initiating contacts with academics in my field, especially at Georgetown University. My days were full and I was overbearing, wanting to tell all *my news* every evening. We had a good social network of friends we'd known in Istanbul who had relocated to D.C., and my work gave us an entrée to political gatherings, such as a cocktail party sponsored by U.S. English, one of the oldest and best-known organizations that work toward supporting English as the official language of the country, where we met Senator Eugene McCarthy, one of our heroes from the 1960s. The two greatest joys were being near our son Tom, whose work at the Discovery Channel intrigued us, and the access to so much great art and history in the D.C. museums and area.

I had expected David to make his own connections with scholars at area universities and among the museum people he had worked with in the recent past. He did not initiate enough activities of his own, seemed to begrudge my time at the office, and soon began to hint at a disaffection with city life, especially the inconveniences of living in an apartment. We had not lived in D.C. more than a few weeks when the gathering storm broke. We were out for a stroll one early evening, when David told me the wonderful news that he had been nominated for an honorary doctorate at Hamilton College, his alma mater, to be awarded the following spring. I congratulated him on this signal honor, but soon launched into a long tirade about the two READ board members who had caused great damage to the organization and about the problems I faced replacing them. David had finally had enough. He grew angrier and angrier as we reached home, accusing me of being obsessed with my work and my new-found fame to the point of neglecting him completely. In an unusual fit of temper, he shouted that he was completely fed up and would leave early the next morning to return to Amherst. I was horrified and begged him to stay and let me make amends, but to no avail.

Our separation lasted three weeks, the unhappiest time of our entire married life, as we have agreed since. It also shocked our sons, but their responses to both of us were warm and supportive. Since Tom and Paige lived nearby, they were especially solicitous and helpful while I was in the city without a car.

One day David called me to say that he had been so lonely and unhappy with himself that he had had a counseling session with a local psychologist, trying to come to a better understanding of our situation. He knew that he wanted us to be together again and asked if he could come back. I immediately welcomed his return, and we vowed we would be more thoughtful of each other's sensibilities. As it turned out, we both returned to Amherst at the end of October.

For my part, I had decided that residing in Washington was not healthy for our marriage. I found a former colleague, Gary Imhoff, who did freelance work for different foundations, and hired him as executive director of the READ Institute for one year. I would be in close contact, and Gary would carry on the work of raising money, recruiting new board members, establishing connections with academic researchers in our field, and planning the launching of a scholarly magazine. I already knew that from January through June of 1992, David and I would be living in Rome, where I had been granted a Fulbright Lectureship by the U.S. State Department. I counted on Gary to hold the institute together until my return from Rome, when I planned to devote my professional time to READ again—although not from Washington, D.C.—and he succeeded in doing just that.

At year's end we all gathered at Tom and Paige's house for our Christmas celebration, a rather subdued time for David and me, our manner with each other still somewhat tentative. We would be leaving for Rome in early January. On our last day in Washington, we visited the National Gallery to enjoy a lecture by Renaissance historian Simon Schama on the approaching 500th anniversary of Cristoforo Colombo's European discovery of the new world and to marvel at the exhibit of art, science, and literature of 1492 Europe, Asia and Latin America—what a tribute to man's creativity and energy in three major centers of that period's known world. Not a bad way to leave America for a sojourn abroad.

Roma—*Citta Aeterna*

It was David who had urged me to apply for a Fulbright lectureship in the field of English-language teaching and to request an assignment in Italy. As always, he encouraged my professional endeavors, and yet he was still affected by the strains of our commuter marriage. Perhaps he hoped the situation would fix itself if only we could recapture the joys of our early travels—but then again, was he willing to disrupt his own schedule to suit mine?

The Fulbright announcement came to us in the fall, when we were at our worst period of distress about our marriage. We put the issue aside for a few weeks until David announced he would definitely go with me to Italy. He was delighted that I had been awarded the plum position in Rome. On our arrival, I reported to the U.S. Embassy for three days of orientation, and David went in search of housing for our six-month stay. He found us a short-term spot in a good location while we searched for a more permanent place. We walked over to a little trattoria, Piccolo Arancio, to celebrate having arrived. I was exhausted and feeling the first twinges of the onset of a flu virus, which left me bedridden for the next several days.

We were staking out new territory. Every previous residency abroad had been David's professional appointment, and it had been my responsibility to make the domestic arrangements. Our roles were now reversed—but not completely, since I still did all the household chores, cooking, and laundry, and I made the travel arrangements when necessary. My lectureship duties included occasional trips to other cities to give presentations to groups of English teachers, as well as a full schedule in Rome. Our temporary apartment on Corso Vittorio Emanuele sat between the popular Pizza Navona and the Campo de' Fiori, the outdoor marketplace renowned not only for its choice produce but for its vivid displays of flowers. We were in the *centro storico*, within walking distance of the city's best coffee bars and bakeries, and, of course, its major attractions—from the Vatican and St. Peter's Basilica to the Forum, the Coliseum and the Trevi Fountain.

My work days, when I was not out lecturing somewhere in the city, were spent partly at my desk at the USIS office at the American Embassy and partly at home. David established a routine of going out for the *International Herald Tribune* and *La Repubblica* newspapers every morning, and occupying himself later with scholarly reading at home or on literary activities at the American Studies Center. Our routines varied from week to week, fitting in visits to museums, ruins, and cathedrals whenever possible. On Sundays we adopted a leisurely practice of viewing art works in the morning, followed by a mid-day dinner at a local restaurant and a walk along the Tiber. We developed a close friendship with the director of the USIS office at the Embassy, Dolores Parker, and her husband Jack, a retired military man, and would sightsee with them at nearby out-of-town places that could easily be reached by car in an hour or so, such as Ostia, Todi, or Orvieto.

Soon a realtor turned up what was described to us as a furnished apartment on Via del Bosco, a quiet little side street off the heavily trafficked Via Nazionale. When we looked at the one-bedroom apartment we remarked to the owner that it was almost entirely bare of furniture, but he promised to deliver all we would need within a week or two at most. We agreed to rent the apartment, furnished, for the next six months. The owner of the building in which we were staying temporarily, the charming Signor Caroselli, said he was sorry to see us go and hoped we would return in the future. We moved to our new digs and discovered on the first morning that there was almost no natural light in any of the rooms; overhead lights would have to be on at all times. During the next few weeks we spent hours on the telephone and in person, pleading with the owner to bring in some furniture. We had a bed and a kitchen table with two chairs, one rickety love seat in the living room, and one lamp that we perched on an upended suitcase— and here we were paying a very high rent. My husband finally said, "This is ridiculous. Let's go see Signor Caroselli and find out if we can take a long-term lease on the apartment in his building. If he says yes, then we'll just move out and not even tell this con man who hasn't dealt honestly with us." It worked! Caroselli was delighted to have us back and gave us a discount for staying four months. We borrowed the Parkers' car, packed our belongings and, in two trips, moved everything back to Corso Vittorio Emanuele. We wrote a letter to the owner of the dark apartment, enclosed the key, and mailed it to him, with a copy to the realtor. *Finito!*

The rest of our time in Rome passed for the most part pleasantly. All our sons came to visit at different times (this apartment had a sleep sofa in the living room) and reveled as always in the city's magnificence. We took each of them on day trips to Orvieto to see the Cathedral and to Montepulciano for a little wine-tasting and buying. When Dave and Steve came for a week, we took them to their first opera performance in Rome, *Tosca,* then on a walking tour of the three places in our neighborhood where the opera is set: Act I, the church of Sant' Andrea della Valle; Act II, Palazzo Farnese; and Act III, Castel Sant' Angelo. We spent Easter weekend in Lucca with Gil and Paul; visited many new cities when I had lecturing dates in Pescara, Monte Cassino, L'Aquila, and even Taormina, Messina, and Catania in Sicily.

But the greatest thrill for both of us we owe to the happenstance of our brief stay in the neighborhood of the dark apartment. One day we found a flyer under our door announcing that the Pope would be celebrating Mass at the tiny church around the corner on the second Sunday of Lent. Apparently it is the custom for the Pope to go to a different neighborhood church each Sunday of the Lenten season. As residents of the neighborhood, we were invited to attend the Mass and we did, together with two non-Catholic American friends.

Pope John Paul arrived in a small motorcade, and once inside the church he slowly made his way, walking alone, up the central aisle, stopping at left and right to greet and kiss the elderly, stooping to pat children on the head. When he arrived at our aisle and took my hand, I was so overwhelmed with the intensity of his charisma that I blurted out, "God bless you." One second later I blanched in horror—I had blessed the Pope! He nodded and fixed his eyes on David who was standing beside me. My husband swears that the Pope gave him a secret message of approbation in that glance, something like, "I know you're not of my crowd but you are a good soul nevertheless." Pope John Paul celebrated Mass, gave a most inspiring sermon on making amends to the Jews and establishing better understandings between religious groups, and left, as soon as the Mass was over, with a minimum of fuss—nothing like his appearances at St. Peter's where tens of thousands would be in the audience. My husband, an un-baptized, life-long agnostic, was deeply moved by Pope John Paul and remained his admirer until the Pope's death.

David was invited to give guest lectures in Rome and in Bari and to speak at an American literature conference in Portugal. The trip to Portugal, unfortunately, coincided with my scheduled lectures in Sicily. We went to Taormina together, traveling with Phil and Irene Leonardi, who had been in Sicily with us in 1967, but David had to leave for Lisbon in the middle of our time there, much to his disappointment.

Once my lectures were done, the Leonardis and I spent a few days revisiting favorite places and marveling at the enormous development up and down the east coast, new high-speed highways, hotels, housing, resorts. The little trattoria in Acitrezza, next to the birthplace of Sicilian writer Giovanni Verga, where our two families had gone for an occasional seafood lunch in earlier times at a cost of about six dollars per couple, was now transformed into a chic, upscale restaurant where businessmen met and where our one lunch there cost us about a hundred dollars apiece. In the evening, walking down the main street of this once-sleepy coastal town, we were assaulted by the loud pounding of rock music emanating from the shops and the roaring of cars full of young people driving up and down this street—what had become of the evening *passegiata,* the leisurely stroll typical of small town Italian life? It had been replaced by "progress."

All in all, our time in Rome mended the wounded feelings of the Washington, D.C., fiasco. David adapted to apartment living and we both managing without a car, except on the occasions when we used the Parker's. These inconveniences were greatly outweighed by the daily thrills of life in this city. Riding the crowded buses was not one of those thrills, but it did provide occasional laughs, especially on the day we boarded the infamous #64 bus to go on our weekly marketing trip. Tourists to Rome were warned to be especially careful on this bus route between the Termini Railroad Station and the Vatican since it was the popular venue of gypsy pickpockets. We were jammed tightly together when my husband felt a light touch in the area of his trouser pocket, just as we were trying to exit the rear of the bus. After stepping down, David felt in his pocket and said, "Oh, rats, they got our shopping list!"

Toward the end of our time in Rome, Dee Parker, having received good reports on my work, invited me to return for another six-month lectureship the following year; in fact she even proposed that I stay right on for another eighteen months, but I turned that offer down on the spot. When I brought up the opportunity of another Rome residency with David, he agreed to consider it. I did, however, accept a special assignment to go to Israel for three weeks of lecturing in August.

Knowing that our time in Rome would only last six months, we treasured each week. Soon enough it was time to leave for the states and the Hamilton College commencement activities where David would be awarded an honorary Doctor of Letters degree. Working on his speech was a steady preoccupation. David appreciates the college, not only for the excellent education he received and the good friendships formed there but also because his father, Roy Avery Porter, was a 1913 graduate, and our son Tom, who was graduated in 1980, had spent four supremely happy years there. In late May we flew to Clinton, New York, to join our three sons, and David's sister Margery Philipp and husband Bill, for the weekend festivities. I cannot imagine anything more personally gratifying than being recognized with highest honors by one's peers, surrounded by a loving and admiring family. David's address to the graduating seniors was a triumph, combining the right mixture of intelligence, poignant sentimentality, and sharp wit—he made us proud.

My Israeli Junket

Settled again in Amherst, we were gradually achieving a comfortable *modus vivendi,* each pursuing separate daily routines and yet accommodating the other's foibles. I was tremendously excited at the prospect of returning to Jerusalem, which we had visited in 1958 when the city was divided between Israel and Jordan, with U.N. forces patrolling the demarcation line. The opportunity to see more of Israel was very appealing. On the lecturing program with me was the University of Georgia professor John Algeo, editor of the *Dictionary of American Idioms.* Our seminar at the American Cultural Center in Jerusalem would be attended by thirty-five high school English teachers; a USIS memo of July 1992 described the group as follows: "Israel's geographic and demographic patchwork, with kibbutz, and village, religious Jews, Arabs, Druze and Bedouin all represented."

Let no one imagine Israelis as slackers. Our work days began at 7:30 AM when we were picked up at our hotel; we took a long mid-day break from about 1 to 3 PM for lunch and rest; then work resumed until about 7:30 PM. My room on the tenth floor of the Sheraton Hotel, with a balcony facing the magnificent honey-hued walls of the Old City and the golden Dome of the Rock, was inspiration enough at the end of the day, and I spent happy minutes feasting on the view. The summer heat was bearable by early evening and I enjoyed strolling the busy streets, observing the natives, snacking on street food, and then I returned to the hotel to prepare lectures for the following day.

We were allowed two free days. The Algeos and I hired a car and guide to take us on a tour of northern Israel including Haifa, Caesarea, and any number of archeological sites of interest. On our other free day, Martin Quinn, head of USIS at the American Embassy in Tel Aviv, guided us on a walking tour of the Old City. Revisiting the most holy places of the Jewish, Christian, and Moslem religions was even more impressive than my earlier experience in 1958, knowing that conflicts over this central bit of real estate are yet to be resolved. After an exhaustive tour, we were driven to a small restaurant where our host, Mr. Quinn, assured us that the neighborhood should be safe for his car. Apparently on the Sabbath, ultra-religious Jews in some sections of the city would express their intolerance of drivers by stoning passing cars or vandalizing a car once parked. We were spared the experience.

The crowning jewel of my two weeks was the chance meeting with one of Israel's iconic figures, Dola Ben-Yehuda Wittman. On my way to the hotel's welcoming cocktail party, a diminutive elderly woman turned to me in the elevator and said, "You look American, are you?" With that we began an easy conversation and sat together in the lobby for drinks. I explained my work in the English-teaching field and my focus on immigrant education, explaining my own arrival in America as an immigrant child. Mrs. Wittman turned out to be a charming, intelligent conversationalist, but I had no idea of her importance in the history of the Israeli state. She invited me to her apartment in the hotel to examine some of her books and memorabilia.

Dola's father was the Russian Jewish scholar, Eliezer Ben-Yehuda, who immigrated to Palestine with his wife and several children shortly after World War I. His importance to the State of Israel was in his monumental, seventeen-volume dictionary of the Hebrew language, and the even more difficult project of convincing Jewish leaders to make Hebrew the official language of Israel. Until his time, Hebrew was deemed fit only for religious use but not for every day utility. Ben-Yehuda succeeded in effecting that enormous change. The main street in Jerusalem, which I had walked many times, is named for him, Ben-Yehuda Street. The government bestowed on his daughter, Mrs. Wittman, a pension and an apartment in the Sheraton Hotel for life, in recognition of her work in helping with the Hebrew dictionary project. She gave me a copy of *Tongue of the Prophets*, a biography of her father, which I have loaned to many friends over the years.[15] We began a correspondence that lasted several years until her death. My biggest surprise was the day after meeting Dola when I casually mentioned to my class, "I met an interesting woman in my hotel last night and had a delightful visit with her. Her name is Dola Ben-Yehuda Wittman." At that, there was an outcry from several teachers, "You met the daughter of Ben-Yehuda! She never sees anyone, never gives interviews! How lucky you are! Tell us all about it."

Because Israel's population has been largely immigrant since the country's founding in 1948, their experience with assimilating large waves of newcomers should have been a lesson to us in the United States when our own immigration numbers began to soar in the mid-1960s. Israeli schools place new students in regular classrooms and give them special help in learning Hebrew for the first year; it also offers adults the community "Ulpan" classes to learn the language rapidly. Israelis take pride in their government's ability to integrate large numbers of immigrants, whether from industrialized countries such as Russia or from agrarian societies such as Ethiopia and Yemen. They do not share our American angst over preserving each newcomer's native language and culture. Students begin studying a second language, usually English, in the later years of elementary school and by the end of high school most are fluent in Hebrew and one other language, an enviable record.

USIS received a positive evaluation of our seminar by the teachers and administrators at the American Cultural Center, and the Algeos and I prepared to leave. Our driver delivered us to the Tel Aviv airport at 4 AM for the flight to Paris, where we would connect with another to New York. I was presenting my ticket and passport to the agent at the Delta Airlines desk when a loud siren sounded, followed by this announcement, "Leave the terminal immediately. Do not pick up luggage or documents, walk rapidly out the doors and over to the parking lot. Wait for further instructions." I was told to leave everything on the counter and my suitcase on the floor. With the other travelers, I walked quickly to the designated place about a quarter of a mile away. We stood under a starry sky and waited, chatting among ourselves, for two hours until a new siren sounded the "All Clear" and we were allowed to return to the terminal. An unclaimed suitcase sitting in the middle of the terminal caused the alarm. Israel's security arrangements for travelers have always been the most stringent, as I discovered on my first flight on El Al in 1953, and a good thing, too. Today, in 2008, too many are impatient with safety measures at airports—I welcome the efficient screening of people and baggage if I'm boarding a plane.

Once More in Rome

By fall, David decided he would accompany me to another half-year assignment in Rome, given two conditions: that we get the Caroselli apartment again, and that he be allowed to leave before the end of the semester, say by late April. Signor Caroselli was happy to rent to us again, and spending a month in Rome by myself did not trouble me. We had good friends in the city, I would visit my Pedalino relatives again in Avella, and our son Tom hoped to visit me while on a business trip to Nice in the spring.

Our second winter in Rome was much less stressful, not having to search for housing, and being much more familiar with the daily ways of Italian city life. Once again we had the loan of the Parker's car for out-of-town lecturing trips while they were in the states on a six-week leave. One lecture trip north to Perugia and Bologna left us a few free days that we chose to spend in Venice. On arrival the city was blanketed in fog on a cold February day, our hotel was a dump, and we had to find other lodgings. But we are not of faint heart. Strolling the quiet streets after dinner, we happened on a poster announcing a guest concert by the Hamilton College Glee Club and Choir that evening at a nearby church. We found the church in time to hear a fine program, and to greet the students and choir master afterward. They were happy to meet a Hamilton College alum so far from home, and eagerly invited us to their really big performance the next morning, at the Cathedral of San Marco, where they would sing at High Mass. Of course, we attended, and heard as well their last concert in Rome a week later.

Time passed quickly and mostly in happy coexistence, though I occasionally discerned bouts of discontent in my husband. In my view, he did not do enough to make his own time more interesting, to contact other scholars for a chat over coffee or lunch, though he has a number of acquaintances among Italian academics and Americans living in Rome. It is just not his way. He enjoys social occasions and intelligent conversations immensely, but rather than initiate things he relies on me to do it. Every once in a while David would complain a bit too much about the annoyances of city life, about being like the old retired men he saw on the streets of Rome, and so on. One day, as we were waiting for a taxi to pick us up in front of our apartment building, my resentment at his carping reached its limit and I blurted out, "How can you stand there and complain when we are so damn fortunate to be living in this magnificent city, a place you've always said you love? We're blessed with good health and energy, a good living situation, our kids back home are all okay, and every time we walk out of this building we can expect to be thrilled by artistically pleasing sights. Please, try to be more upbeat and don't let the minor stuff spoil our days." My outburst left David in a reflective mood for some days.

The fortunate timing of the annual international convention of English teachers to be held in Atlanta in April provided the impetus for planning the rest of the spring semester. I was scheduled to give a paper at the convention, with the government paying my travel expenses to the United States and back to Rome. We decided to fly home together for Easter weekend. Then I would go to Atlanta and from there back to Rome to finish the last month of my contract with USIS. Our sons would be with us for Easter and, for a family treat, we bought the wonderful Roman bread rolls called *rosette* at our local bakery on the morning of our flight, as well as a kilo of fresh *gnocchi*.

Returning to Rome alone was exciting for me. I relished the work days and planned to make use of my free time to visit any masterpiece of Roman art and architecture that had eluded us so far. On the day I arrived at the apartment I noticed an unusual gathering in Piazza Navona, right behind our building. After unpacking, I walked back there and found folding chairs set up by the hundreds throughout the piazza, a speakers' platform already occupied by notables. I took a chair and was handed a program. It was the annual celebration of the founding of *Aeterna Roma*, the city's 2,746th birthday. The speakers declaimed in Latin on the glory that was the Roman Empire. I listened, bemused, as I could only guess at the meaning not having studied Latin. This was followed by choral and instrumental selections of Cimarosa, Wagner, Respighi, and Beethoven, with readings from Italian literature—an amazing offering to citizens and tourists alike. I felt truly welcomed back to Rome.

My routine varied little, though freedom from the responsibility of preparing meals, doing laundry for my husband, and adjusting my daily schedule to his allowed me a little self-indulgence. Living a few steps from the Campo de' Fiori open-air market, I often walked around the piazza in early evening, bought a slice of pizza to eat while sitting at the feet of Giordano Bruno's statue, and was content to watch and be amused by the passing crowds. Now that Romans had become enchanted by the American novelty they called "lo 'take-out'" there were a number of small places from which to buy simple meals to take home, sometimes a more appealing option after a long day of traveling and teaching than waiting until 8 PM for a restaurant to open. The only frightening aspect of living alone in our apartment building, something that had always made us both anxious but now held greater anxiety for me, was the elevator. As is customary in European buildings, the first floor is the one above the ground floor. Thus our apartment on the fourth floor was really what we would call the fifth floor in America.

We could and actually did walk up and down the staircase when the elevator was out of order, but it was an inconvenience, especially when carrying heavy packages or suitcases. On a few occasions the elevator had stopped between floors and left us stranded for some time until we could get it to move again. My greatest fear, the whole month I lived there by myself, was that I would be trapped in the elevator over the weekend when the shops on the ground floor and the offices on the first and second floors were closed, and no one would know that I was in trouble until Monday morning. In the era before cell phones, this was a possibility but, thankfully, the dreaded elevator breakdown did not occur.

Early in the year I had sent notes to my brothers and sister and close friends to say that I would be in Rome alone for a month in the spring and would welcome visitors. No one accepted my invitation except a colleague from Massachusetts who spent a week with me, enjoying city sightseeing and tagging along on two lecture trips out of town. Having good company for a few days was fine, but not essential. A few times a week David would telephone to hear about my adventures and to catch me up on family affairs. I left Rome at the end of my time there with a sense of satisfaction—in the work I had done, with the opportunities I'd taken to visit my Luciano and Pedalino relatives, and for the friendship formed with the Parkers, whom we would see again in the states. All in all it had been two gratifying half years. My husband and I resumed our companionable Amherst life together without considering any moves for a few years—at which time we would go through another major upheaval.

The Institute for Research in English Acquisition and Development (READ)

The READ Institute had lain mostly dormant while I was in Rome but now needed my serious attention if it was not to die the death of many small think tanks for lack of funding and serious, visible activity. The other burgeoning claim on my time came from the requests for my help as an expert witness in court cases involving two very different areas of contention—education problems of non-English-speaking children and education problems of children who had been exposed to lead paint. READ would occupy front and center of my attention for the entire decade of the 1990s, but the expert witness work is still an active part of my life today; I have given testimony in federal court on behalf of the State of Arizona as recently as 2007.

The READ Institute was founded in 1989 with a grant from U.S. English of $250,000 meant to cover its first two years of operation. Its first director, Dr. Keith Baker, was to initiate research on effective programs for immigrant children, distribute practical information to public schools, appoint a board of directors, and start fundraising to keep the institute going. Dr. Baker, a highly respected researcher at the U.S. Department of Education, invited me to be on the board in 1990, shortly after the publication of my book, along with two Californians, Dr. Robert Rossier and Dr. Fred Baughman. Nearing the end of the two-year U.S. English grant money, we called for a board meeting to assess the work done to date. It was readily apparent that Baker had not come close to fulfilling what had been expected of him—no new research studies, no publications, and no fundraising. We were alarmed by the seeming inactivity of the only paid staff member (aside from a part-time secretary). As far as we could ascertain, the institute's money had gone largely to Baker's salary, with a raise he voted in himself.

Subsequent discussions with Baker indicated his reluctance to take up fundraising, and he seemed to have no plan to step up the speed of scholarly work. Finally, as president of the board of directors, it became my responsibility to inform Baker that we would terminate his three-year contract at the end of its second year for nonperformance of duties. An ugly situation developed, resulting in a lawsuit against READ. The board stood firm and unanimous in refusing to pay Baker a year's wages as a settlement when he had essentially already depleted the READ funds. Our attorney negotiated a settlement in which READ paid Baker a modest severance, and both parties—he and the READ board—agreed to keep the incident private, a nondisclosure pact. We abided by the agreement. Baker did not. He vented his anger against me personally, in interviews and in published articles. Though READ was largely impoverished, we could now start rebuilding.

Small nonprofit research and advocacy organizations start up by the thousands. Few survive even to the five-year mark. Fund raising is the largest preoccupation, but equally daunting is finding people with experience who are willing to work for little or no salary at the beginning, and actually deliver a product to interested parties who may then invest in the organization. U.S. English would not soon advance us new grant money, since READ had produced nothing 1989 to 1991, the two years of their large investment. Having put the Baker problem behind us, we were ready to move ahead on all fronts. I judged it was most urgent that we commission and publish a piece of research that would be of immediate practical use to schools and would quickly establish our *bona fides* with potential funders. With the agreement of the board, I engaged Professor Russell Gersten at the University of Oregon to do a study on the El Paso, Texas, school district's English Immersion program for non-English-speaking students. Gersten and his team completed the report and it was published under the READ Institute imprimatur in March 1992[16]. The grant to Gersten and printing costs just about depleted the READ bank account, but it was a wise step. Our study showed clear advantages for Latino children in giving intensive lessons in English from the first day of school. The report received critical attention in the education press and began to establish READ as a player in the contentious field of immigrant education.

I moved the READ office to my home in Massachusetts, to save the expense of renting an office in Washington, D.C., and accepted the appointment of Executive Director as well as board chairman. For several years I would shoulder most of the work of READ, briefly as a salaried director but mostly on a pro bono basis, only being reimbursed for travel expenses and for doing specific work such as directing a research project or editing the *READ Perspectives* scholarly magazine. Through a combination of luck, networking, and long hours of grant writing and telephoning, we found organizations and individuals willing to support our work.

My favorite story on the vagaries of fund raising involves my meeting two men at a cocktail party sponsored by U.S. English in the spring of 1991. The host welcomed me with the comment that he had just heard about my book, *Forked Tongue*, and was most interested in reading it. He identified himself as having come from Germany as a young child, and professed a continuing interest in the betterment of education for immigrant children. He was a successful advertising executive and author of a number of best-selling "how to" books, he said, and I targeted him as a potentially large grantor to READ. Soon I was introduced to another gentleman, an international investment banker, who also evinced an interest in *Forked Tongue*. He wanted to know what I had been doing since the book's publication, and I told him about READ Institute's endeavors. He scribbled his telephone number on a business card and invited me to "get in touch, and send me a copy of your book." From his off-hand manner I didn't think contacting him would amount to much, but I wrote to both men anyway, sent each a copy of my book and with it an appeal for funding to support the work of READ. Three weeks later, as my husband and I opened our mail over lunch, I found a letter from the banker with a check enclosed. In my excitement, I said to my husband, "Dear, I have a contribution of $1,000 to READ. No, wait a minute! It's a check for $10,000 from the banker I met a few weeks ago! He liked my book and is willing to help our work." Not two days later, there was a small package in the mail from the advertising executive. I fully expected that this would be another contribution. Instead, there was a short note thanking me for my book, wishing me well, and enclosing a copy of *his* latest paperback with a title something like this: "How to Get Along with Your Neurotic Dog," one in the series that also psyched out neurotic husbands, wives, in-laws, bosses—ad infinitum. What a disappointment, and what a lesson—I had incorrectly judged the two men's intentions.

The goals of READ as established by the board were: to sponsor original research or review newly available studies on successful programs for non-English-speaking children, and to make this data available to school districts, policy makers, and the media through the publication of a scholarly magazine. In reality, finding the funding, locating the scholars, and doing the public relations to get visibility for READ proved challenging, even with the active help of the board members and the occasional assistant I could lure into working for a very small stipend. We hoped to build a strong list of subscribers. The first issue of *READ Perspectives* came out in the fall of 1993, and the last one in 2001. Each issue featured an array of articles addressing such topics as "The Languages of the United States: What is Spoken and What It Means," "The Labor Market Effects of Bilingual Education Among Hispanic Workers," "Findings of the New York City Study on Bilingual and ESL Programs," "The Cost of English Acquisition Programs," as well as detailed descriptions of successful programs in El Paso, Texas; Bethlehem, Pennsylvania; Seattle, Washington; and Dearborn, Michigan, to cite a few. The magazine, of which I was editor, gained respect for READ and is widely cited by graduate students and scholars, though we never did raise the number of subscribers to a satisfactory level.

Midway through the READ Institute years, I was fortunate in finding the perfect person to take over most of my administrative work, freeing me to spend more time on writing, public speaking, and expert witness work in court cases. Norma Campbell McKenna, the daughter of our next door neighbors, was born in 1962, the year we moved to Amherst. Norma had been at home raising two young children, but in 1995 she was ready to find part-time work. Our interview was unusual, since we had known each other all of Norma's life. We both wondered if we could indeed work together, and decided to give it a try. Norma's earlier work in publishing was relevant, and when I described the variety of tasks in the READ office, she was highly enthusiastic about the job. She exceeded my expectations. Our collaboration was entirely congenial, and we worked together until the READ Institute was merged with the Center for Equal Opportunity in Washington, D.C., in 2000 and relocated there. Together we built a small but respected research institute whose work was to point the immigrant education field in new directions; we succeeded in keeping our nonprofit organization going for an unusually long period of eleven years. Norma then returned to graduate school and took up her real love, being a school guidance counselor; I concentrated more fully on my secondary occupation.

Detour: On Being an Expert Witness in a Different Arena

My experience as an expert witness in the Berkeley, California, court case that ended with a positive verdict for the schools in 1988 (*Teresa P. v. Berkeley Unified School District*) was an exhilarating event in my professional life. This led to my involvement in several law suits of a related nature, briefly described in the next chapter. How I became a sought-after witness on the effects of lead-paint exposure on children's educational potential is quite an unusual story.

In the spring of 1991, my book had been out for a year and had received dozens of reviews in the print media. The radio and television interviews I gave focused critical attention on the issue of the poor quality of education for immigrant children. I was invited to address a breakfast meeting of the Boston Municipal Research Bureau. At the end of my talk and the question period, a young woman dressed in a smart sun-yellow suit approached me, briefcase in hand, and introduced herself as Maris Abbene, an attorney with the prestigious Bingham, Dana, Gould law firm. She was holding a copy of my book and made a most unusual request, "Dr. Porter, we represent a number of defendants in a class action lawsuit concerning lead-paint exposure of young children. Having looked into your background and experience, we believe you can be of expert help in our case. As it happens, we are meeting with all our clients today; some have traveled across the country for this meeting. If you can spare a few hours, which we will pay you for, will you come to our law offices with me now? We will send you home by limo when our meeting is over." I could not imagine what possible expertise I might have for their case, but I was assured, as we were chauffeured across town, that it would all be explained at the meeting.

Once arriving at the law firm's opulent offices overlooking Boston harbor, I was introduced to the dozen principal defendants sitting around a massive oval table: representatives of Sherwin-Williams Paint Company, the national association of paint manufacturers, the local owner and landlord of the apartment, and the local attorneys handling the case. The plaintiff's lawsuit was brought in the name of Carmen S., an 18-year-old Puerto Rican woman who had been exposed to lead paint as a very young child in the apartment her family was renting. She had received treatment at a Boston hospital and had tested lead-free from then on. The attorney who filed the civil suit for millions in damages claimed that because of her childhood exposure she had attained lower educational achievement than might have been possible and her future earning potential was harmed. The defendants' attorneys wanted me to evaluate the case and give an opinion, possibly in court, as to whether the young woman's achievement was affected by her lack of English language skills, the family's poverty, and other distressing problems, as much as or more than the early lead exposure. They questioned me closely and at the end of the hour decided to retain me. I offered to review the documents in the case before committing myself.

Soon I was ensconced in a company limousine, directing the driver to take me to the Steinway Piano Company showroom on Boylston Street. Before hopping on the Peter Pan bus for the two-hour ride home to western Massachusetts, I wanted to share the delight of this unexpected splendor—a ride in a limo!—with my son, who was working at Steinway. From the backseat I picked up the car telephone, called Steve, and asked him to come out to the front door in a few minutes to meet me. He gave a start when he saw a liveried driver open the rear door and his mother emerge—my Cinderella moment. As we walked to the bus depot, Steve roared with laughter when I told him how I had been "kidnapped" from the breakfast meeting and transported to the highest plateau of Boston legal activity.

This lawsuit led to my involvement in a dozen more cases in Massachusetts, Connecticut, and New York. Once having been identified in court documents as an expert in my narrow specialty, attorneys with similar cases sought my services. All the cases presented some variation on this set of circumstances: one or more children exposed to lead paint, usually in poor neighborhoods with substandard housing, were diagnosed and treated in local hospitals. Attorneys specializing in lead paint obtained lists of patients and contacted the families to initiate lawsuits on their behalf. It was my task to determine, after a close review of all the documents, if my advice would be useful. In the case of Carmen S., I considered her school records, health records, family circumstances; I was also allowed to interview the young lady, in Spanish and in English. Carmen started school in Boston with no knowledge of English and very poor preparation for school. She was raised in poverty and suffered the trauma of seeing her father shot outside a bar over a drug deal. Yet in spite of all these disadvantages, she had earned high grades, was considered a leader and a model young woman in her neighborhood, graduated from high school and was enrolled in a community college. She was articulate in English and Spanish. Carmen was an exemplary woman who had achieved much more than might have been anticipated. How could one judge that the brief bout with lead had adversely affected her? Would she have been a Harvard student if not for the lead exposure? Most cases I testified in had similar basic elements, though Carmen's accomplishments were the most impressive.

Not one of the cases I was involved in actually came to court for trial; each one was settled with a privately agreed-upon payment to the families and their attorneys. This was my first experience with the tort-lawyer tactics of finding potential plaintiffs—whether their cases have merit or not—and filing lawsuits against a wide array of defendants that extended way beyond the building owners who had the primary responsibility of having lead paint removed from the premises. The tactic was to find the defendants with the deepest pockets—the paint companies, for example—even though they had stopped producing lead paints decades earlier, and any others even minimally connected to the issue: sue them all for enormous amounts and expect that the fear of a ruinous trial verdict would coerce a settlement. Contingency-fee agreements with their clients often result in attorneys reaping large fees and the clients getting relatively small sums.

An example of the most ill-founded case I ever encountered, one which was dismissed by the court as lacking merit, involved a Haitian family with three young children. All three had lead exposure and treatment. The eight-year-old and ten-year-old were struggling academically, not surprisingly, since they had moved from Boston to Haiti and back twice, had barely learned English, and were living in poverty with a single mother. But it was the youngest child's case that was the heartbreaker, the case that did not go forward. The six-year-old boy suffered a leg injury that became seriously infected. He was taken to the hospital with a dangerously high fever. Doctors diagnosed a life-threatening infection and recommended amputating the injured leg; the mother refused treatment and brought her voodoo priest into the hospital room to use his magic, which made no improvement. The doctors became so alarmed that they applied to court for an immediate ruling allowing the boy to be treated, which was granted. The leg was amputated, the boy recovered, but the long period of high fevers affected the functioning of his brain. The child was left severely learning-disabled, a condition that was not related to his mild exposure to lead paint at the age of one, hence the reason why his case was dismissed.

The lead-paint cases occupied a third of my time throughout the 1990s, then diminished. Either all the clients had been found and legal remedies pursued, or there was no longer a need for an education expert. Although I can judge my participation in these cases to have been peripheral, I gave long hours to studying documents, submitting opinions, and preparing for testimony in court. I was compensated for all this but never informed of the out-of-court settlements. Now it was time to shift gears; I needed all the time I could find for my work with READ Institute and for testifying in court cases in the bilingual field.

And, no doubt, there were the demands of my gradually extending family—whose problems, resolutions, pleasures, and satisfactions I will take up again at the close of my story. First I'll devote a chapter to the reform movement I participated in and led, and explain the role I play even today as an advocate for immigrant children's education.

CHAPTER 11

Legal and Political Advocacy for Immigrant Children

Fast Forward: Election Night 2002, Park Plaza Hotel, Boston
In a modest hospitality suite reserved for monitoring the initiative ballot Question 2, "English for the Children," people began to gather in the early evening to watch the voting results on the three television monitors, to kibitz, to work the room—all typical of election-night socializing. Two floors above, Republican candidate for governor Mitt Romney, his staff and family, had a much larger suite for what they hoped would be a victory celebration. My husband and I drove to Boston in the late afternoon, walked into the rooms devoted to the referendum question, ready for a late night of flashing election returns. We were here to savor the outcome of eighteen months of intensive campaigning. Having failed for fifteen years in my efforts to get the Massachusetts Legislature to change a state law and improve the education of immigrant kids, I became a political activist, taking the question to the people.

With the "English for the Children" campaign, we put this question directly before the voters—do you want immigrant children to be taught English as soon as they enter our public schools? Seems like a non-issue, right? Who in the early twenty-first century would even question whether to teach immigrant children the common language of the country? Yet for thirty years the wrong-headed idea that children should be taught in two languages had been the law in Massachusetts and several other states, in spite of its poor results. The effort to reverse this 1971 Massachusetts law was up for a public vote, and results would be reported in hours.

By late evening, with most districts reporting, Question 2 was estimated to have won passage by no less than 68 percent of the voters, in a gubernatorial election year when turnout is heavy.

My God, we've done it, I thought! The people of smart-aleck Massachusetts, home to Harvard and MIT, most liberal voters in the known world, have defied the elites—multiculturalists, academics, ethnicity promoters, most politicians (except Romney)—and voted overwhelmingly for a return to sanity by getting rid of the ineffective "bilingual" education. What a satisfaction for the three of us who led the campaign, and how devoutly I desired this outcome. To win in my home state, after helping the same campaign to succeed in heavily immigrant California with 62 percent of the vote in 1998, and in heavily Latino Arizona with 64 percent of the vote in 2000—how sweet it was!

Next morning upon entering the hotel elevator, we found the entire Romney family on board. Without hesitating, I introduced my husband and myself to the governor, congratulating him on his election and adding, "Governor, I believe our landslide victory on Question 2 worked in your favor—helped you rack up a bigger positive vote. What do you think?" He graciously introduced us to his family and responded, "Oh, yes, indeed. We benefited from taking a strong stand in favor of helping immigrant kids in our schools." With that we arrived in the lobby where reporters and TV cameras were clamoring for the Romneys' attention. David and I quietly left the hotel.

Legal Advocacy for Immigrant Children—State and Federal

Over the past twenty years, I have been called on to testify as an expert witness in a dozen or more cases involving the education of non-English-speaking children—immigrants, migrants, refugees—from the first case in Berkeley, California, in 1988 to my current (at this writing) testimony in Tucson, Arizona, in 2007. While each case has its own particularities, most can be clustered into one of the following categories: in the Berkeley (1989) and Seattle, Washington, (1995) cases—where the school district defended itself against the imposition of native language teaching for its students, a practice the schools had found to be segregative and educationally ineffective—I testified on behalf of the school districts; in the cases of parents and citizens suing a state authority or a school district to force the teaching of English—*Bushwick Parents Organization vs. State of New York Education Department* (1996), *Carbajal vs. Albuquerque Public Schools* (1998)—I testified on behalf of the families; in the cases on mandated state testing of all students in English and math, including immigrants—*California State Department of Education vs. San Francisco Unified School District* (1998), *G.I. Forum et al. vs. Texas Education Agency* (1999) and *San Francisco Unified School District et al. vs. State Board of Education* (2000)—I testified on behalf of the state and in favor of including all students in state tests. All but one of these cases were judged in favor of the side I supported—the good guys.

One case that fit into none of these categories was the situation of a six-year-old African American boy entering kindergarten in his neighborhood school in Oakland, California, in 1998. Mr. Louie, the boy's father—a disabled Vietnam War veteran who had sole custody of his son—visited the school and learned that it enrolled a large number of Chinese children in kindergarten. The bilingual teacher taught in a Chinese dialect more than half the day, with English lessons part of the time. Mr. Louie, stating the obvious fact that his son already knew English, requested that his son be assigned to a school where all the instruction would be in English, believing that his child was not well served in the neighborhood school.

The school principal refused his request, and tried to convince Mr. Louie that his child would be enriched by learning in two languages. When Mr. Louie appealed to higher authorities, he was told that his son could go to another school but the city would not provide transportation. The boy was too young to travel by public bus in the big city by himself; having no car, Mr. Louie sued the Oakland Unified School District, and I gave a deposition on his behalf (*Travell Deshawn Louie vs. Oakland Unified School District*, 1998). Coincidentally, just a few years earlier a group of African American parents had filed complaints against the San Francisco school district when, against the will of the parents, their children were assigned to schools with large enrollments of Spanish-speaking students "for racial balance." The parents, whose children were lagging in English reading and writing through first and second grade because they were being taught in Spanish half the school day, objected so strenuously that they finally succeeded in having their children assigned to all-English-instruction classrooms.

The massive efforts undertaken from the 1950s onward to desegregate public schools along racial lines, and the programs starting in 1968 to provide special help to children lacking English language ability intersected in a contradictory way. While educators worked under court orders to achieve racial integration in the schools, the bilingual education movement promoted the segregation of language minority students for most of the school day. This program separated children by language and ethnicity for three to six years in a subsidiary, mostly inferior system, and generated a new bureaucracy that would not easily admit failure or allow change. In spite of the money invested, most of the reliable research studies published by state and federal agencies over three decades reported two devastating outcomes: no observable benefits to years of native language instruction either for learning the English language or for learning school subjects taught in English. But these were the exact goals of the legislation and early court cases—that children who entered our schools without English would, with a few years of extra help, become fluent and literate in English and able to do regular school work in English with their classmates.

To modify, overturn, or significantly change this failing program has been my life's work from the 1980s to this very day. The READ Institute's mission was clear and focused: to find reliable research on successful programs across the country, and publish this information in our scholarly magazine, *READ Perspectives*. At first my advocacy for change in Massachusetts was modest. Each year I urged the legislators to modify the existing law by allowing special English-teaching programs, but every bill attempting to change the law was shelved and killed.

From 1985 to 1988 when I served on the National Advisory and Coordinating Counsel on Bilingual Education (NACCBE) during William Bennett's term as Secretary of Education, our group advised the U.S. Congress to change the formula of 96 percent of federal funding going to bilingual programs and 4 percent to English language programs (referred to as "alternative" programs). We achieved a modest change in the formula: on reauthorization of the Bilingual Education Act in 1988, federal funding for English teaching programs would be raised from 4 percent to 25 percent, hardly reason to break out the champagne. Promptly after this small change, Congress decided to cancel the National Advisory Council, most likely on the advice of the Hispanic Caucus.

A small core of academics, teachers, parents, and social activists working on behalf of immigrant children began to grow, individuals and groups that challenged the conventional wisdom on bilingual teaching. Certainly the work of READ played a part in informing the public and connecting reformers to each other's work. Press accounts of the lawsuits filed throughout the 1990s generated more public dialogue and an insistent demand for change. The reform movement began to capture the attention of the popular media, with favorable editorials in many leading newspapers and weekly magazines. But the bilingual education bureaucracy remained largely unmoved.

For example, in California, the state with 47 percent of the 3.5 million non-English-speaking students in the country at that time, the law imposing bilingual teaching had lapsed in 1987. In 1993 the state published a research study reporting that twenty years of bilingual teaching had produced no evidence of improved academic performance and that children were being kept in bilingual programs, long after they had actually learned English, in order to receive extra state funds for these students, funding they would lose once students were judged to be "English proficient.[17]" In spite of there being no state requirement and no evidence that it had ever produced good results, the California State Department of Education still forced the continuance of bilingual programs, threatening any districts with loss of funding.

Fairfax County, Virginia, and Others Stand Tall

The Office of Civil Rights (OCR), enforcement arm in the U.S. Department of Education, did its part, initiating legal action against districts to force native-language teaching, even though there has never been such a mandate in any act of Congress. School administrators know that fighting a federal agency, no matter how strongly they believe in their cause, is a long, debilitating and costly battle. The OCR's aggressive actions sometimes succeeded in wearing down the districts under scrutiny, but when opposition is sustained, as in the Fairfax County, Virginia, Public Schools, the good guys win.

For five years, from 1975 to 1980, the Fairfax County Public Schools, tenth largest school district in the United States, was under observation by the OCR for a civil rights violation—for allegedly not providing an equal education to its language minority students. The director of special programs for Fairfax County schools, Dr. Esther Eisenhower, argued the realities of the situation: Fairfax enrolled five thousand children from seventy-five different language backgrounds. To even consider finding a staff of teachers able to teach school subjects in all the languages, to find textbooks in all school subjects in those languages, defied reality. Instead, Dr. Eisenhower had designed an English teaching program, trained teachers, and developed a wealth of materials in all school subjects to produce rapid English-language learning and the integration of the non-English-speaking students into regular classrooms within an average of two years. She kept concise data of student achievement, and she arranged for OCR monitors to observe classrooms, interview teachers, parents, and administrators. Finally, OCR informed Fairfax officials that the agency pronounced the special English program acceptable and a model for the country, an amazing and well-deserved outcome. (Information supplied by Fairfax County Public Schools ESL Department.)

In addition to Fairfax, the school districts that fought against heavily restrictive state laws and the intrusive actions of bureaucratic agencies— Newton, Massachusetts; Berkeley, California; Seattle, Washington; Bethlehem, Pennsylvania; Dearborn, Michigan—succeeded in giving immigrant students the best educational opportunities and reporting evidence of student achievement: high levels of grade promotion, lower rates of high school dropouts, and rapid mastery of the common language of school and community.

These districts shared common traits: strong commitment to equal educational opportunities for minorities, strong belief in the ability of immigrant children to succeed, consistent efforts to keep immigrant families informed and supportive of the school's goals, and a willingness to try new ideas that show promise at the risk of incurring bureaucratic censure. In Berkeley, the district was courageous enough to fight a lawsuit rather than accede to unreasonable demands—and they won; in Newton, the district resisted the state's displeasure for five years, losing some state funding, but eventually gained accreditation. In every case, the top level leadership—administrators and school board members—were the crucial element, giving teachers and parents of immigrant children the necessary support.

Had the original state laws given schools the flexibility to try different approaches, to report on what works best, and to allocate equal funding to different options, I do not believe bilingual education would have been so politicized. Had our legislators had more backbone, paying attention to the facts showing poor results for bilingual programs, they might have amended the laws to allow a choice of teaching methods, or they might have killed bilingual programs outright after a decade or two. Instead, politicians either neglected the calls for reform or caved in to the politics of ethnic identity whenever the issue was raised, failing to take action for years.

Here is a good local example from my state. In 2002 I met with former governor Michael Dukakis (and a Democrat candidate for president in 1988) to enlist his support for the referendum question before Massachusetts voters. Mike pulled a copy of my book from his shelf and said, "Rosalie, I read your book and you can see all the scribbles I made in the margins. I have to apologize to you for not taking action long before you wrote this book. Back in the early years of bilingual education, when Massachusetts was the first state to start this program, I was proud of what we were doing for immigrant kids. You know, my family came from Greece. But then I went to visit a school in Springfield and sat in a couple of bilingual classrooms. I was shocked to see that during the whole class, the teaching was entirely in Spanish. I said to my aide, 'when the hell are these kids going to learn English?' But, sorry to say, I never did anything about changing the state law—I just had too many other things on my plate." In spite of my initial dismay, I sincerely lauded Mike for his candor.

Revolt of the Latino Parents—First Brooklyn, Then Los Angeles
Immigrant parents, as a rule, are respectful of school authority and reluctant to question the advice of teachers or administrators. When they are advised to place their children in classrooms where they will be taught in Spanish to help them learn English, they ask no questions and give their approval. Working-class parents with little education defer easily to the "wisdom" of teachers, as did my own parents when I was enrolled in my first American school. But experience has taught Latino parents a bitter lesson about their misplaced trust. Two groups of Latino parents became disillusioned with bilingual education at almost the same moment and decided to fight. Their stories are amazing. In both cases, the communities were fortunate enough to find an advisor to help them fight for their cause. In both cases it was an activist nun.

The Bushwick Parents' Organization, Brooklyn, New York

In September 1995 a lawsuit was filed in State Supreme Court against the New York State Commissioner of Education by the Bushwick Parents Organization representing 150 Latino families with children in the Brooklyn public schools.[18] The complaint charged that, "... because the children of its members routinely remain segregated in bilingual education programs in excess of three years, and in some cases in excess of six years, contrary to State Education Law 3204 (2), these children are not receiving adequate instruction in English, the crucial skill that leads to equal opportunity in schooling, jobs, and public life in the United States."

The parents were being denied their legitimate choice, that is, the right *not* to have their children in a bilingual classroom. When, after several years of bilingual schooling the parents demanded their children be assigned to English-language classrooms, they were again pressured against any change. Fortunately for the Bushwick parents, they found a strong champion in Sister Kathy Maire, an educator and community organizer who helped them obtain the pro bono services of one of the largest and most prestigious law firms in New York City—Paul, Weiss, Rifkind, Wharton and Garrison. It is heartbreaking to read the statements of some of the families involved in this lawsuit, their grievances over the miseducation of their children:

> My grandson was in bilingual education from kindergarten through fifth grade ... He is now in seventh grade and cannot read in either English or Spanish ... We were told that because my grandson has a Spanish last name, he should remain in bilingual classes.
>
> Ada Jimenez, "Trapped in the Bilingual Classroom," *New York Times*, February 3, 1996.
>
> My son is eleven years old and is in the sixth grade. ... He participated in a Head Start program in English before starting kindergarten, but has been in the bilingual

program for six years. ... I have spoken with his teacher
to try to switch him into regular English classes. ... He
is confused between English and Spanish.

Maria Cruz, Affidavit, August 11, 1995)

In her affidavit (February 11, 1995), Sister Kathy Maire tells why these
Latino parents have turned so completely against bilingual and want
their children out of it.

> Within the last two years we have spent a great
> deal of time examining the bilingual program. It
> is not improving the English language skills of the
> students—most of the day teaching is in Spanish with
> a short English lesson for one hour. Many of these
> children were born in the United States and attended
> pre-kindergarten Head Start programs in English,
> but were then placed in bilingual programs when
> they entered the public schools. Parents...discovered
> that their children's performance on English language
> tests were declining...but when they asked to remove
> their children from bilingual teaching ... teachers
> and principals argued against the change ... and the
> parents are unable to overcome the pressure put on
> them by these school officials.
>
> Many of these students graduate from school having
> never fully developed their English language skills, and
> they are therefore unprepared for higher education or
> employment in jobs in which English language skills
> are used.

In 1996 Judge Teresi ruled against the Bushwick parents, stating
that the parents already have the legal right to refuse to enroll their
children in bilingual programs, and his decision was upheld on appeal.

However, two real benefits came out of the effort: successful or not in the courts, the case received wide attention in the New York press and, one hopes, will help stiffen the resolve of other Latino parents. The second benefit was an announcement by the New York City schools' administration that children enrolling in the public schools would no longer be assigned to bilingual classrooms solely on the basis of their Latino last names.

Los Angeles: The Ninth Street School

Meanwhile, in Los Angeles, an angry protest erupted, matching the action in Brooklyn but more forceful and more publicly visible. A group of Latino workers in the garment industry, their children all students at the Ninth Street School, became so incensed at the poor quality of education that they organized a boycott. Keeping their children out of school for a week in February 1996 and picketing the school building was a drastic action that made headlines in Los Angeles and around the country.

Ninety percent of the 400 students in the Ninth Street School knew little or no English when they started school. Their parents formed a community organization, *Las Familias del Pueblo* (The Families of the Community) to provide after-school care for the children. At an evening meeting, when a few parents complained, they discovered that many others had voiced the same concerns to teachers and principal. Their main complaint: that English was delayed for too long, that in the bilingual classrooms their children did not start learning to read and write in English until third or fourth grade. When, at the end of the school year, it was reported that only six students had learned enough English to exit the bilingual program, a rate of less that 1 percent of the enrollment, the fury of the parents led to the boycott.

Episcopal Sister Alice Callahan, a founder of *Las Familias* as part of her work with the poor and homeless, supported the parents in the battle to change the education of Latino children at the Ninth Street School. She bore testimony to the fact that these children spoke only broken English after years in an American school. She was quoted in the *Los Angeles Times*: "What we know is the bilingual system was intended to help children learn another language and maybe it works in some places, but we know our children are not learning to read and write in English. ... And poor kids don't have the luxury of catching up later on."

Sister Alice and the parents are right—every year in a child's life that is misspent in an ineffective classroom makes it that much harder, especially for children of poverty, to achieve a level of education equal with their peers. How that precious, early learning opportunity is wasted is movingly illustrated by a sixteen-year-old student whose comments appeared in the same article. The boy had been in Los Angeles schools since kindergarten and had spent most of those years in Spanish bilingual classrooms. By extra effort on his part, he gained admission to an academically superior "magnet high school." The boy said he is working hard to catch up with his classmates. He said, "I can read, but I can't understand what I'm reading. They never showed me the vocabulary I need now." But why should this bright, well-motivated boy find himself so ill prepared for high school after so many years in Los Angeles schools?

Ron Unz to the Rescue—Three Wins, One Loss
Once the Ninth Street School event made the national news, it captured the interest of a wealthy Silicon Valley entrepreneur and newly minted avenger of public ills, Ron Unz. Having earned a modest fortune, Unz ran for governor of California against Pete Wilson in the Republican Primary of 1988, losing his bid but gaining a respectable 30 percent of the vote. He later funded a referendum to bring election campaign reform to California, which did not succeed. When Unz read about the school boycott in Los Angeles by a group of Mexican sweat shop workers, he found a new mission. Having a background in science and in developing high tech systems, Unz investigated the education issues affecting these children, in California and nationally. His analysis of the situation convinced him that attempting to change laws through

the legislatures and fighting entrenched education bureaucracies would not work.

California Shining—Proposition 227

Unz's idea of the quickest way to effect change to benefit children would be to mount a populist campaign, a state-wide initiative on the ballot of the next California election in 1998. This was an enormous project in a state the size of California, but exactly the right place to stage such a revolt since California has the nation's most ethnically varied population in the country, with slightly more than half of the public school students representing ethnic minorities. One of every four children in California starts school with a limited knowledge of English. If such a campaign could succeed in a state with a high proportion of recent immigrants voting, it could well succeed in other states.

In early 1996, Ron Unz employed his well-honed internet research skills to find the authoritative voices in the country for education reform in this area and came up with the usual suspects: Professor Christine Rossell at Boston University, Linda Chavez of the Center for Equal Opportunity, and me at the READ Institute. In fact, we three had been honored the previous September at a Washington, D.C., press event sponsored by the English First organization, with "Leadership Awards" presented by Representative Toby Roth of Wisconsin for our work on behalf of immigrant children. We were the first to advise Unz on the education reforms that would most help students, while he explored the legal aspects of mounting an initiative in his state and brought his considerable skills in public relations to bear on the campaign. Once the substance of the referendum question had been vetted and approved for submission by his attorneys, he hired local workers to collect signatures to put the question on the 1998 state election ballot. Question 227 was dubbed "English for the Children," an accurate and ultimately popular title that captured the essence of the issue.

Unz put his money behind his mouth, close to a million dollars to cover the signature-collecting, including a very modest $200,000 for radio and newspaper ads in English and Spanish (translations contributed pro bono by high school history teacher Ricardo Munro). California requires certified valid signatures of 8 percent of the voters in the previous election (1994), about 400,000 signatures, to put the question before the citizenry. Unz's goal of collecting 650,000 signatures was sensible, since there are always a number of duplicate or invalid signatures. The marketing of "English for the Children" was brilliantly managed, not so much with paid ads but by using the internet and by personal appearances at hundreds of public debates up and down the state, debates with angry academic luminaries, with doubtful legislators, with teachers' union leaders. Ron Unz is a tireless, focused advocate, and a public figure popular with the mainstream media. The campaign drew a high level of press coverage across the country with hundreds of editorials in the leading newspapers and Unz's appearances covered by cable news channels. Professor Rossell and I played a major role in advising Unz on the key elements of the proposed law of California and our discussions were many. (Due to the difference in time zones Ron's calls often came at inopportune times, unfailingly at dinner hour, or very late in the evening, all the more maddening because he was tenacious in arguing points no matter how long it would take to arrive at an agreed position.)

In March 1998, the prestigious Kennedy School of Government at Harvard University presented a Forum on Bilingual Education, "Is It in Our Children's Best Interests?" Former Senator Alan Simpson introduced the speakers: Ron Unz and I, representing the arguments in favor of Question 227, with a California state legislator and a professor from the University of California at Davis on the opposing side. Moderator Christopher Eddley, a Harvard Law School professor and Clinton appointee to the U.S. Commission on Civil Rights, moderated the discussion. The forum drew a standing-room-only crowd of several hundred, and a very lively question-and-answer period followed our presentations. (David and our son Steve were invited to dinner and the forum—a terrific thrill for me to have them there.)

Heading into the election, California polls showed overwhelming popular support for Question 227, around 70 percent favorable, including voters who identified themselves as recent immigrants. In the last few weeks the big-money ads were rolled out by opponents—a "No" campaign mainly run by teachers' unions, and a blitz of Spanish-language ads on Univision, whose owner, Republican billionaire A. Jerrold Perenchio, hoped to defeat the measure. Of the political leaders in California, not the governor and not the big names in either party supported the initiative. Yet the results were incredibly strong: 62 percent of Californians voted "Yes" on Question 227, though the Latino vote dropped to an estimated 50 percent, according to exit polls.

"English for the Children" was an undisputed victory for the vox populi. The "Yes" campaign carried fifty-six of California's fifty-eight counties. State records on campaign spending report $550,000 spent by the "Yes" campaign (in addition to Mr. Unz's investment) against $4.5 million spent on the "No" side, not counting one to two million in free air time on Mr. Perenchio's television network. Citizens in that most populous state inhabited by a high proportion of newcomers had not been swayed by the negative ads but had viscerally understood how important it is to give children immediate help in learning the common language of the school and of public life and opportunity. My small contribution: an essay in *The Atlantic Magazine* of May 1998, titled "The Case Against Bilingual Education." It appeared on the newsstands just a few weeks before election day.

Arizona Next—Proposition 203

Success in California encouraged a group of political activists and educators in Arizona to get in touch with Ron Unz to enlist his help in staging the same kind of citizens' revolt in this border state with a high proportion of Mexican American citizens. Many parents had already lost respect for the Spanish bilingual programs their children were enrolled in. Under the leadership of Maria Mendoza, Hector Ayala, Margaret Garcia-Dugan, and Norma Alvarez, an initiative campaign followed the California pattern and succeeded in placing the "English for the Children" question before the voters in the 2000 election. I was not involved in the Arizona campaign but watched the reports closely. Would a heavily Latino population show the same desire for education reform—let's say it plainly—would they have the heart to put an end to Spanish bilingual programs? Once again the governor, Republican Jane Hull, Attorney General Janet Napolitano, and the leaders of both political parties opposed the reform question. The "No" campaign spent about $350,000, of which $115,000 was contributed by teachers' unions and $50,000 came from the Navajo community. The "Yes" campaign spent $229,000, Ron Unz contributing $189,000 of that amount, the rest from small contributors. More useful than the dollars was Unz's public relations effort, his success with the mainstream media in getting the issue before the public. Amazingly, the voter turnout was high and the "Yes" vote on "English for the Children" was a resounding 64 percent. It was beginning to look like a tidal wave. (The campaign financing and election results I cite for California, Arizona, and Colorado were obtained from Johanna Haver of Phoenix, Arizona, from her work-in-progress, an unpublished chronicle of the "English for the Children" campaigns.

On to the Commonwealth of Massachusetts
Ron called me soon after the win in Arizona to propose a campaign in Massachusetts and to ask me to be cochairman of the state effort. I responded immediately in the negative. "Ron, the two victories must have unhinged your mind, temporarily. Massachusetts is the most left-liberal state in the universe, it's where political correctness is an inherited gene; it is the state that passed the first bilingual education law in the country, a place full of true believers in the education establishment and inattentive legislators in the State House—groups that will fight hard against change." Ron argued that Massachusetts had to be the next battlefield, that the state was ripe for a ballot question, now that others had succeeded so dramatically in the west. Ron shrewdly gathered the following team to lead the state campaign: as chairman, Lincoln Tamayo, a lawyer and experienced educator in heavily immigrant Chelsea, the poorest city in the state (gotta have a Latino); two cochairmen, Professor Christine Rossell of Boston

University, nationally recognized researcher and critic of bilingual education (gotta have an egghead) and me (gotta have an immigrant and former bilingual teacher). Being well acquainted with Tamayo and Rossell, who are colleagues as well as friends, I agreed to join, and what an exciting eighteen months it became.

In July 2001, having collected a sufficient number of valid signatures to put the referendum question on the November 2002 ballot, we staged a press conference in front of the State House. A few immigrant parents from cities around Boston volunteered to speak, lending their support to "English for the Children." Television, radio, and newspaper reporters gave us good coverage. The presence of Ron Unz attracted far more press than we would have expected, now that his support of similar campaigns in two other states had met with such success. The opposition to "English for the Children" was entirely predictable: leaders of the Massachusetts Teachers' Association (MTA) and the American Federation of Teachers (AFT), academics on practically every campus in the state, most Democrats who make up 90 percent of the legislature, most newspapers, advocacy groups, and ethnic identity promoters. The entire Massachusetts congressional delegation, including the senators Kennedy and Kerry, signed a full-page ad in the Boston Globe urging a "No" vote on the ballot question in the final weeks of the campaign. In Massachusetts, though, we found the first elected public official to speak in favor of our campaign. Governor Mitt Romney was willing to take a clear stand in support of this issue. He would be running for election in 2002, having served a partial term as governor when Paul Cellucci resigned to be the U.S. Ambassador to Canada.

Ron conferred with our team from California, swooping in for an occasional public appearance but leaving us to run the day-to-day activities on the ground. The public relations plan was a simple one: generate as many appearances as possible on TV and radio talk shows, take part in public debates in town halls and on university campuses, give interviews and write editorials for newspapers across the state—all hands-on activities that cost nothing except the time and travel expenses of the three caballeros! Ron offered to upgrade our communications equipment, providing laptops and printers, for campaign use. He also subsidized Lincoln for a year when the Chelsea Public Schools' Superintendent, Irene Cornish, forbade him to participate in the campaign, forcing him to resign from his job. As in the two previous campaigns, advertising would be minimal and concentrated in the last few weeks before the election.

The first half year was not particularly busy with campaign activities, especially since the attack on the World Trade Center and the invasion of Afghanistan concentrated most public attention for several months. We really began to hit the road in the spring of 2002 and discovered, mirabile dictu, that universities would *not* be the natural venues for an exchange of ideas; some schools invited only opponents of "English for the Children" to speak. When "Yes" chairman Lincoln Tamayo called the organizers of a panel discussion at Simmons College to ask for a place on the program, he was told he was not welcome but could, of course, make a comment from the audience. At Brandeis University I was invited to be in a panel discussion where I was the only "Yes" speaker facing five others who advocated the "No" position. In truth, there were several colleges and universities that invited an equal number on each side of the debate, and they are to be applauded: Mount Holyoke, Northeastern, Harvard, and Wellesley (though the crowd at Harvard was the most rude and abusive of any college audience—so much for enlightened debate at our premier university).

The university that disappointed me most was the University of Massachusetts in Amherst, the university where my husband was a much-honored professor and where I had earned all my academic degrees. I learned on two occasions that members of the School of Education invited speakers from across the country to address public meetings on Question 2, but no one who would speak in favor of it. Professor Andrew Effrat, Dean of the School of Education, asked me, informally, to speak at a university-sponsored debate on Question 2, promising details later. As election day drew close, I called him to ask when we would have the debate. Dean Effrat was embarrassed to admit that no professor in his department would debate me. My neighbor,

Hill Boss, an elected member of the town government, asked me if I would speak on the question at Town Hall. I agreed. He called the School of Education and invited Professor Teresa Austin to speak. She found the date free and agreed. Then Hill said, "You'll be in a debate with Dr. Rosalie Porter who is co-chairing the Question 2 campaign and lives here in town." Dr. Austin's stunning reply was, "What? You mean you want both sides represented? Oh, no! No one from this school will do it." Hill was as shocked as I was but even more determined. He found a local educator, a Puerto Rican woman, to be in the debate. We spoke before a large audience, fielded many questions and comments, and embraced in a warm hug at the end. The evening was a success, but the absence of representation by the local university disappointed many in the audience.

The "No" campaign in Massachusetts outspent us, ran ads on radio and TV, and mobilized volunteers across the state. In the last month before election day, lawn signs began to appear. I believe the opposition chose a particularly inadequate slogan for their banners: somber black letters spelling out "Don't Sue Teachers—Vote No on Question 2." The signs looked funereal next to our bright green "English for the Children" posters, but even worse, the slogan was meaningless to the average voter. The "No" people had focused on a small clause in the law to be their battle cry. It is true that the new law allows parents to sue teachers if classroom instruction defies the law requiring English language lessons. In the ten years since this law was first voted in, not one teacher has been sued—but the warning is there.

In the end, we won an amazing 68 percent of the vote in the 2002 election. I wrote an article for our local newspaper highlighting these facts about the campaign: according to the state Office for Campaign and Political Finance, the opposition spent about $725,000 while the "Yes" campaign spent about $425,000; 328 of the 351 communities voted "Yes," and a large increase in the Latino vote was recorded in several urban districts, for instance, Boston, Worcester, and Chelsea. The real story is in the distribution of the majority vote. Elite school districts that have never had real bilingual programs—Amherst,

Brookline, Newton—brought out a vote against Question 2.[19] But the districts with heavy enrollments of Latino children—including Chelsea, Holyoke, Lawrence, Chicopee, and Springfield, the cities where families have had the longest experience with bilingual education—voted in great numbers in favor of "English for the Children."

Colorado Campaign Fails

In the 2002 election in Colorado, the English for the Children campaign suffered its only defeat. The signatures for the referendum were gathered with Ron Unz's financial help, and the language of the ballot question was ruled legally acceptable. Rita Montero, an elected member of the Denver School Board and respected member of the Latino community, led a vigorous campaign. Polls were positive until the last few weeks before election day, when a heavy barrage of negative advertising by an ad hoc group of citizens dramatically turned the tide. The opposition tactic focused its radio, TV, and print ads on one misleading accusation: that the new law would forbid two-way bilingual programs and practically do away with foreign-language teaching. These claims were completely untrue, but they had their effect on voters. The initiative lost by a vote of 55 percent to 44 percent, in this case proving that large sums of money injected into political campaigns sometimes do succeed in spite of popular opinion. One situation particular to Colorado was the fact that the referendum proposed changing the state constitution rather than just overturning a state law, and that is always much more difficult to accomplish.

The battles were now over. Ron Unz's contribution to education reform had run its course. The remaining states with bilingual education laws do not allow initiative ballot questions to be put before voters. However, the people had spoken in a clear, overwhelming majority voice in three important states: California, the state with the largest immigrant population; Arizona, the state with the highest proportion of Latino voters; and Massachusetts, the state that invented Transitional Bilingual Education in 1971. These victories can not help but affect public education across the country. The high rate of immigrant children entering our public schools, now estimated to be five million, in suburban districts as well as big population centers, has made the practical idea of teaching these children English as quickly as possible an unbeatable option. Reports from California and Arizona on improved student achievement through English-immersion teaching are resonating with educators across the country.

Immediately after the California election, legal challenges to Proposition 227, the English Immersion law, were filed by advocacy groups alleging that the new education program would deny the civil rights of language-minority students under the national origins discrimination clause of the 1965 Voting Rights Act. This suit was dismissed in federal court—no civil rights violation was found (*Valeria G. et al. vs. State of California*). Another challenge by the California Teachers' Association alleged that the state could not dictate the language of instruction in the classroom, that not allowing teachers to teach in Spanish was illegal. That suit also failed as the judge reminded the appellants that the state education authority has a clear responsibility to set curriculum policies and expect teachers to comply. I was an expert witness on behalf of the state in both law suits, working for months with the attorney general's office. Challenges were filed in Arizona but did not succeed. By 2002, when the Massachusetts law was voted in, the failed attempts to overturn the law in two other states dampened the desire for a challenge and no law suit was filed.

Perhaps the publication of California achievement data also had an effect. My worthy adversaries in the California academic establishment—the professors Kenji Hakuta at Stanford, Stephen Krashen at the University of Southern California, and Eugene Garcia at Berkeley—all sounded the alarm: once bilingual teaching is removed, language-minority students will fail in their school work. The predictions of an academic apocalypse for one-fourth of the children in California schools did not come to pass. Within two years of the change, the California State Department of Education began reporting higher levels of success in English and math for immigrant children in second grade, and that trend has continued in the higher grades each year. One outspoken convert to the new program was Ken Noonan, superintendent of the Oceanside, California, Unified School District, a district with a high proportion of immigrant, non-English speakers in its schools. Noonan had been a staunch believer in bilingual education, even serving a term as president of the California Association for Bilingual Education. By the end of the first year of English Immersion teaching in Oceanside, he saw a dramatic improvement in children's language learning. Noonan was convinced by his own observations that young children really are capable of learning English quickly, if it is taught to them immediately, without the distraction of being taught in two languages.

Arizona, too, has reported improved student performance both in learning English and doing classroom work in English successfully since the legal change in 2000, according to annual reports from the State Department of Education.

Massachusetts, five years after the change in the law, has yet to publish a full report on how well or how poorly our students are faring across the state, or of making any comparison between English-language learning under the new program versus the thirty-year experiment with bilingual teaching. This is disappointing, but not surprising. Massachusetts did not report on the academic progress of non-English-speaking students even though such accountability was called for in the 1971 Transitional Bilingual Education Act. In the only state-wide report on the effects of bilingual teaching, in 1993, the following statement says it all, "The Commission found that adequate and reliable data has never been collected that would indicate whether or not bilingual programs offer language minority pupils a superior educational option."[20] Since the law was changed, I am informed that most districts are providing English-language teaching programs, though there are still small pockets of resistance, here as in Arizona and California, a nostalgia for the old ways. The battle is not completely over. Education bureaucrats and "true believers" do not "go gentle into that good night" as Dylan Thomas once described a peaceful end, but drag their heels against change.

Meanwhile, Back at the Ranch ...

While all this work was being carried out in the last decade of the millennium and beyond, there were major personal changes in the lives of our nuclear and extended family and some long-overdue resolutions between my husband and me. Having brought my professional activities up to the present, it's time to wrap up the personal lives around me—the chronicle of a love story and a twentieth-century American family.

CHAPTER 12

Resolutions and Rewards

"Time passes, and what it passes through is people—though people believe that they are passing through time, and even, at certain euphoric moments, directing time. It's a delusion, but it's where memoirs come from, or at least the very best ones. They tell how destiny presses on desire and how desire pushes back, sometimes heroically, always poignantly, but never quite victoriously.[21]"

Two Long-festering Problems Solved

During the 1990s, as we entered the fourth decade of our marriage, David and I left two contentious issues unresolved. The first concerned where we would live; the second was religion.

After the mixed success of our earlier sojourns in Washington, D.C., and Rome, there was yet one housing question to be put to rest. David decided we should find a different house in Amherst to make our main residence, something on a quieter street, with a more comfortable arrangement of rooms, and, for my personal stair phobia, a bedroom suite on the ground floor. Indeed our current house, built in the 1950s, needed repairs inside and out.

We began the search for a new one with a local realtor, and it soon became a major source of discord. Over a period of four years we walked through dozens of houses and even made offers on two, although neither was accepted because our bids came in too low. Finally I was forced to admit to myself that David would never be content with any other house in the area—he simply could not contemplate moving. But he could not admit this to himself, and so we kept on looking at houses and he kept finding faults. In the end I broached the subject with David, making this announcement: "We are at odds on this and one of us must compromise. You will never move—you're just downright unwilling to go through the work of sorting your library, academic files, family objects, and junk. Therefore, I suggest we give up the house search. I do not want us to spend the rest of our days together arguing over housing. It's over. We are going to stay in this house, and there are no hard feelings on my part, I really mean it." What a relief to be past that niggling tension. Instead we had some cosmetic work done— floors refinished, rooms painted, an automatic door opener installed in the garage—and agreed to make other improvements as needed. Peace reigned. But the anxieties of the house search had so unnerved me that I almost missed an opening to resolve our old religious problem.

In 1996 I went to the Catholic Newman Center at the university and had a talk with Father Joseph Quigley about the requirements for a marriage ceremony for David and me. Father Quigley, a genial old priest much loved by UMass students, gave me this counsel, "Mrs. Porter, you've come to the right place, and we can certainly give you the Church's blessing. I understand the impediments that stood in the way of your having a Catholic ceremony earlier. At this point in time, however, your husband doesn't have to do much of anything. Obviously he is not preventing you from practicing your religion, you two are not affected by any rules on birth control, and your children are already adults who can make their own decisions about worship. Bring David with you and we can go over this with him." I brought up the subject at dinner one evening and, being overwrought about the house search, or perhaps beginning to experience hearing loss, I failed to hear or register David's answer. I was terribly disappointed, thinking he'd answered in the negative. Some months later I raised the issue again, and David said, "But dear, I said yes to seeing Father Quigley the last time you asked me. Then you didn't mention it again." I almost wept at my own inability to "hear" what had been said.

In August 1996 we took part in a small, private ceremony at the Newman Center. Our three sons each read a short selection from the Bible; our friends, Irene and Philip Leonardi, were our witnesses, and Father Norman Bolton conducted the service, starting with these words: "What we are celebrating today, David and Rosalie, is an acknowledgement of something you have been living for thirty-nine years. It is merely a confirmation, a blessing of your union." It was a moment of pure satisfaction for me, and a relief for all the family. Now I attend Mass on Sundays, with David's sincere encouragement, while he happily enjoys the Sunday morning newspapers and the political talk shows on TV—would that we had come to this amicable solution much, much sooner.

1997 and All That

This is the one year of the decade that, in hindsight, contains the most transitions and upheavals in the lives of our immediate family, as well as a signal honor for me. Marriages and divorces, beginnings and endings, abounded. Dave and his long-time live-in partner Laurie Levin announced that they would marry on June 29 in Philadelphia. We had met Laurie's parents, Betty and Monroe Levin, on a few occasions and found them to be warm, friendly, intelligent people, both involved in the Philadelphia music community. The wedding would be held on the University of Pennsylvania campus, a civil ceremony conducted by a Levin family friend, a local judge. Dave had been working for the *Philadelphia Inquirer* as a sports reporter while building an internet company in Princeton, "Sports Campus: Connects You to the Game." Since Laurie was teaching cello at the Westminster School near Princeton and had many private students in the area, she and Dave were finally ready to leave city life and move closer to their work, giving up the time-consuming commute from Philadelphia. A year later, they bought a "fixer-upper" in a charming old Trenton neighborhood, a narrow, three-story, brick row house that they worked hard to make habitable.

Steve's life in Boston through the mid-1990s was generally satisfying; he worked at the Steinway Piano Company, performing at increasingly popular recitals several times a year, and enjoyed a lively social life with a wide assortment of friends in the Boston area. Steve has a knack for sustaining close friendships with people of different ages, ethnicities, and sexual orientations, entirely comfortable with various social and cultural communities. We had a tacit understanding with Steve that we would gladly attend any event, meet and socialize with any and all of his friends in Boston, but that Steve would keep his gay social life apart from Amherst. This arrangement allowed us to enjoy family holidays, travels and visits together, to help Steve financially when he decided on graduate school at the New England Conservatory, and to show him our love in as many ways as possible. I cannot commend our son enough for his strength of character during those years, his ability to compartmentalize his life in such a manner as to be fully independent yet give us the pleasure of his close friendship and love, allowing us a period of adjustment. Steve completed his master's degree in piano performance in spring of 1998.

Tom and Paige gave us some of the greatest joys and the deepest sadness. They had met when both worked at *National Geographic* television. Tom moved on to senior vice-president at the Discovery Channel cable network, and Paige resigned her marketing position at *National Geographic* when she was expecting their first child in 1993. Carley George Porter was born on Christmas Eve morning 1993, our first grandchild and the happy start of a new generation.

From our first acquaintance with Paige, we'd been aware of her sometimes unusual behavior; she'd withdraw inexplicably from family social events and was often reluctant to join in other group activities. (Paige has a condition diagnosed as bipolar disorder, sometimes making for uneven cycles of highs and lows with no way of calculating how long each period will last.) When Carley arrived, Paige entered her new career as fulltime mother with total devotion. Like any educated, middle-class, first-time mother, she probably read too many of the works on infant care and was somewhat anxious in her new role, feelings I remember well from my own experience. Carley, a healthy baby of serene disposition, gave her parents no cause for worry, breast feeding, sleeping, and growing at average rates. As I had business in Washington several times a year, I extended my stays each time in order to be with Paige to give her support and reassurance, to bolster her confidence and laud her excellent mothering skills.

Carley thrived, and became the darling of us all, parents, uncles, and grandparents. In 1992 Tom and Paige had decided to join St. Columba's Episcopal Church, where Tom enrolled in religious study, which led to his being christened at the same time as his daughter. Our immediate family, including Paige's Dad, Bill Thompson, who came from California, attended the ceremony. It was a secret thrill for me to see one of my sons a baptized Christian, and my visits to D.C. now included Sunday Mass at Tom's church.

Tom and Paige's marriage, however, slowly began to deteriorate. As Paige gained confidence as a mother, she became so over-consumed with maternal duties that she imposed ever more strict controls on Tom's time. Tom's office was a short commute from their home and he was generally home by 6 or 7 PM. He happily took charge of Carley's bath and bedtime routines, giving Paige some time and space of her own. Paige began complaining of Tom's occasional business travel, exerting pressure on him to restrict his time away from home. When Tom decided, for example, that he needed an exercise routine and would work out at a gym on Saturday mornings, Paige objected, claiming this to be "family time," and saying that he should get his exercise during the business days, an unreasonable demand. I cannot say with certainty the reasons why these two became less and less happy with each other, but Tom's increasing disaffection made him vulnerable for a sympathetic, new involvement.

In May 1997 Tom resigned from the Discovery Channel organization in dismay over cut- throat company politics; he negotiated a "golden parachute" for his departure, with the intention of taking a few months' respite before connecting with a new position. On the approaching date of our fortieth anniversary in early August, Tom, his brothers, and Paige and Laurie, conferred several times on where and how to celebrate the occasion. Finally, they agreed on a family dinner in Alexandria, Virginia, at the place where David and I were married in 1957, and invited the Whitmans and Gillards, Washington friends who had lived in Istanbul with us years earlier. At the very last moment, Paige decided she had to get away and left to visit her parents in California, leaving Tom, Carley, and the rest of us. It was a somewhat subdued celebration. We all rallied round Tom and made the best of the weekend, none of us dwelling on Paige's absence. But she had hurt our son deeply.

The Tom and Paige situation would soon reach its apogee of unhappiness, but for the six weeks beginning at the end of August, my husband and I would be out of the country, once more at a Lake Como retreat, once more returning to the Near East.

The Rockefeller Adventure Redux: Paradise on Lake Como

David's 1985 residency at the Rockefeller Study and Conference Center at Villa Serbelloni, where I had joined him for his last three weeks and started work on my first book, was a happy time for us both; we hoped to experience something like it again. So in 1996, when I was encouraged to apply for a Rockefeller residency on my own, I didn't hesitate, even though it seemed an unattainable goal: for every fifteen or so residencies the Rockefeller Foundation awards, it receives over five hundred applications. The project for my proposal was a commissioned piece of writing for *The Atlantic Monthly*. Three heavy-hitters wrote on my behalf: Professor Nathan Glazer at Harvard, President of Boston University John Silber, and civil rights activist and Latino leader Linda Chavez. In January 1997 the READ office manager, Norma McKenna, telephoned me in Florida to say that she had an important piece of mail and had taken the liberty of opening it on my behalf. "Sit down, Lee, before I start. Sitting down? OK, the Rockefeller Foundation accepts your proposal and appoints you to a residency at Villa Serbelloni for the month of September." My shouts brought David to the bedroom door to find me actually jumping up and down with glee. It was a moment of such pure joy—winning such an honor was a high-level recognition for the value of my work, and brought as well the satisfaction of my achieving a prized residency that had been won by my husband eleven years earlier!

One of the valuable perks of being a fellow at the Rockefeller Center, of course, is the allowance for a spouse (or recognized "other") to be in residence as well. David and I became known during our 1998 stay as that rarity, a couple who had each received a privileged appointment. Arriving at the Milano airport, we were met by a chauffer who delivered us promptly to the Villa. The moment of arrival was almost too great a happiness to bear. Gianna Celli, director of the center, greeted us warmly, showed us to a comfortable suite in the main building, and asked, "Rosalie, how does it seem to you, coming back here again, as good as the first time?" I smiled and answered, "No, Gianna, better." And it was! David was assigned a little studio half-way down the hillside, and my study was next to our bedroom, where I could feast my eyes on the sight of the Alps, Lake Lecco, and Lake Como . The Amherst poet Emily Dickinson, who never saw it, imagined this view in her poem written in 1859 (H 12):

> Our lives are Swiss—
> So still—so cool—
> Till some odd afternoon
> The Alps neglect their curtains
> And we look further on!
> *Italy* stands the other side!
> While like a guard between—

The solemn Alps—
The siren Alps
Forever intervene!

Once again we two were caught up in the daily routines, working in the mornings and some afternoons; hiking the long trail down to the village of Bellagio for exercise or taking an afternoon boat ride to some neighboring village to look at art works; meeting for cocktails and dinner with all the residents in the early evening. Catering to our daily needs, the Center allows us scholars to concentrate on our solitary work without domestic concerns, while also providing us with social opportunities for conversation and relaxation. As before, some stars were sprinkled among us, including Susan Sontag, the writer, critic, social commentator, and leading light of New York intelligentsia; Shulamit Aloni, Israeli Minister of Communications and vocal critic of Israeli military actions; and a young Chinese economist, Xiang-hui Li, who introduced us to the word "globalization." On our first weekend the Board of Trustees of the Rockefeller Foundation held its biannual meeting, bringing to our midst, among others: Alan Alda of stage and screen (an engaging, delightful man), Johnetta Cole, a leading African American educator and president of Morehouse College in Atlanta; and Stephen Jay Gould, the Harvard biologist and world famous Darwinian scholar. Not a bad lot to sit next to at meals!

One day, while taking a midmorning café latte on the terrace, I opened a letter from our son Tom in Washington who had this to tell us, "Mom and Dad, I've just had an accident that could have been much more damaging but I'm all healed. A week ago, I was making beef stew and, without thinking, I speared a large chunk of potato, threw it into my mouth and swallowed it whole. It scalded my esophagus and I could hardly breathe. I drove myself to the nearest hospital where I was treated for second degree burns and kept for two nights. The pain was almost unbearable. Then I remembered one of the nursery rhymes you used to read to us, Mom. 'Mr. East made a feast, Mr. North laid the cloth, Mr. West did his best, and Mr. South burned his mouth—while eating a cold potato!'" At this point in my reading, there were tears on my cheeks and I turned the letter over to my husband, who was alarmed. We were horrified at Tom's close brush with a serious disability, relieved that he had not lost his sense of humor, but still shaken.

The month ended all too soon. I fulfilled my obligation to the Rockefellers by completing the article for *The Atlantic Monthly* and sending it off to the magazine before leaving Bellagio. "The Case Against Bilingual Education" would be published in May 1998, one month before the California referendum vote. Interestingly enough, that article has been picked up dozens of times in the past decade for assigned reading in university classes and for publication in text books. Since I hold the copyright, I have earned far more in reprint permissions than the fee I was originally paid by the magazine. In the spring of 2007 a friend noted that my article was among the top five most-read pieces in the *The Atlantic Monthly* online, indicating the essential durability of the arguments I originally advanced.

From Bellagio we went on to Istanbul where David gave two guest lectures at the invitation of our friend, Professor Oya Basak, of the Bogazici University English Department. We had a few days to revisit our beloved Istanbul and see friends of long standing. On our last evening, Oya asked us about a personal matter that had piqued her curiosity for a long time. "You are very good friends of David Leeming, who taught here some years ago at the time when James Baldwin spent several years on campus. We know that David became Baldwin's very good friend and literary executor in New York. Were they lovers?" Oya and David were friends and colleagues, but she was too reticent to ask him directly. I replied, "According to David's own words in his authorized biography of James Baldwin, he says about their friendship, 'we were never lovers.'" From Istanbul we headed back to Italy for a few days in Positano and a chance to see both Luciano and Pedalino cousins in Naples, then flew home to the United States.

Surprising End to 1997

Thanksgiving brought us all together in Amherst—Dave and Laurie from New Jersey, Steve from Boston, and Tom and his family from Washington. It was an unremarkable holiday until the last evening when Tom asked his father and me to take up a serious matter with him. I imagined news of a new job, another child expected, Paige starting back to work—but none of these ideas was even close. Tom's announcement momentarily shattered us. "Mom and Dad, I have to tell you that for the past few months I've been having an affair with a woman I met in my office. Her name is Lisa. Through carelessness on my part, Paige has just found out about it. You both know that Paige and I have been having problems for the past few years. The woman I have been seeing is separated and her divorce is soon to be final. She has two children. We have found each other sympathetic in many ways. But now that Paige knows, things have to change, of course, and I wanted you two to know what's happening."

We were both silent for some minutes. Instinctively, we wanted this not to have happened, wishing that Tom had not been so unhappy as to seek comfort outside of his marriage, but in reality, of course, he had. We asked what he and Paige would do and learned that they would now seek marriage counseling, see their minister at church, and begin the job of rebuilding their relationship. For the short term, Tom promised he would break off his affair, make amends, and work hard to restore a loving partnership. And they began on that hard road. Throughout the following two years, they tried to work things out and went through a trial separation. As spectators, it was a very distressing situation for us to watch. Tom's good intentions often weakened. I make no excuses for Tom. I only gave him my advice on one occasion, strongly urging him not to have any contact with Lisa while he and Paige were attempting to reconcile. I am uncertain whether Tom's brothers gave him any good counsel, though the three brothers are so close it would not have been ill received.

By the beginning of 2000, Tom and Paige's efforts to reunite had broken down completely, and Tom moved in with Lisa and her children in Potomac, Maryland, a half-hour's drive from his former home. In June, David and I traveled to Hamilton College with Tom and Lisa for my husband's fiftieth alumni reunion and Tom's twentieth. We were now becoming better acquainted with Lisa. Soon, Tom informed us that he and Lisa were expecting a baby in December and had plans to marry, but that his divorce was taking longer than expected. My husband and I gave Tom and Lisa our immediate acceptance of their situation. We began visiting Tom and Lisa's home and getting to know David and Addie, her bright attractive children. But my husband and I resolved that we would not abandon Paige who, as the mother of our grandchild, commands our affection. We maintain a long-distance but friendly relationship with her to this day.

Emily Avery Porter arrived on December 8, and we attended her "naming" ceremony six months later, where we learned her Jewish name, Eliana Ahavah. On June 5, 2002, her parents married in a traditional Jewish ceremony, complete with chupah. We are now firmly committed to our daughter-in-law, who keeps a Kosher kitchen and is raising three children within the strong guidance of her faith and close connections to their synagogue, but who remains tolerant of Tom and Carley's Christian beliefs. We have a satisfying friendship with the Perlbinder family, our new in-laws, and are fortunate again in finding ourselves allied with caring people. Tom has made the prodigious leap from being the father of one child to the father of four, and he is up to the challenge. He makes every effort to be with his daughter Carley, sharing her custody equally with Paige.

Tom and Lisa prevailed over the difficulties that face divorced and reimagined families, with these added complications: the nasty behavior of Lisa's ex-husband, who is truculent over every aspect of the upbringing of his children, David and Addie; Tom's good relations with Paige, but her constant need for emotional support, an imposition Tom accepts; and heavy financial burdens. They have overcome major hurdles to form a strong union. Carley has found a loving home with her father's family when she visits, and a solid place among her siblings, with an especially loving little sister Emily.

In 2005 Tom and Lisa moved to Amherst, not three miles from us, thanks to Lisa's being appointed to an administrative position at the University of Massachusetts. Tom is with a local nonprofit organization. We are now truly playing the role of grandparents, up close. Lisa has gained sole custody of David and Addie, who are both flourishing in their new Amherst schools. She loves her job, the town, and the Jewish Community of Amherst (JCA), whose members have already elected her vice president. Tom savors every day in his old hometown after twenty-five years in Washington. Lisa has won our love and admiration for her strong character, loving attention to her children and husband, and the excellent relationship she has with stepdaughter Carley. In September 2008 Carley entered Deerfield Academy as an eighth-grade student and now lives with Tom and Lisa. We count ourselves blessed to have them all near us.

Lucy's Demise

In April 1998, my mother suffered a stroke and was taken to St. Barnabas Hospital in Livingston, New Jersey. When she did not show signs of recovering, not responding to the efforts to bring her out of a coma, we began discussing her long-term care, and the probable need to move her to a rehab center. I made a trip to New Jersey, to spend a few days with my sister, Frances, confer with her and our brother Anthony, who has power of attorney and Lucy's health care proxy. Since our other two brothers, Domenick and Frank Jr., do not talk to our sister, it is really awkward to get anything decided. Knowing of my distress over my mother's condition, our son Steve volunteered to drive me to New Jersey, visit his grandmother in the hospital, and drive my car back to Amherst.

My sister and I sat at my mother's side, watching her breathe normally, hopelessly waiting to see a flutter of eye movement that did not come. She seemed to be peacefully asleep. We stroked her hand and talked to her, as her doctor had advised us to do, on the chance that she might hear us. We reminded her of how alert, competent, and healthy she had been up to the day she was stricken, and our belief that she would recover. I noted that she had just enjoyed a winter visit with us in Florida—how much she loved spending a few weeks in a warm climate while, as she would say with a chuckle, "Everybody in New Jersey is freezing." On Sunday evening, April 19, a little after midnight, the hospital called to tell us that our mother had just died and to give us the chance to see her one last time. We drove to the hospital and wept over our mother's still form, never again to see her beautiful eyes or hear her soft voice.

The grief I still feel for my mother's sad life, for the terrible conditions she lived under and the Herculean efforts she made to better all our lives, and my grief for the wasted opportunities, will never be assuaged. She was forced to marry a demanding and abusive husband, forced against her will to leave her family and country to start a new life in an alien land, bringing to mind these lines taken from Keats' "Ode to a Nightingale": "Through the sad heart of Ruth, when sick for home, she stood in tears amid the alien corn." Lucy often wept in solitude as she was forced to work at various occupations to support a large family and was shown almost no appreciation for her efforts. She survived my father by twenty-four years, but she had been so conditioned by him to hold herself in low regard, never allowed to develop friendships or hobbies or any social life of her own, that she lacked the capacity for learning these skills later. Outside of the world of work, where she found appreciation and approval from her co-workers, she did not see herself as an independent entity but limited herself to relying only on her sons and daughters for companionship.

We tried, especially after she gave up driving her car at age eighty-two, to connect her to the town's Senior Center for weekly shopping trips by van, hoping she would find some congenial elders to socialize with. It was not successful. My husband and I made an effort to take her with us to Italy, to revisit her village and relatives, but she was adamant in her refusal, "It's too late. I should have gone with your father, when we were younger. No, no, it's too late. Forget it." My brother Anthony and sister Frances took her weekly to shop, or to medical appointments, or to an occasional lunch outing. Although they did their best, it was never enough for my mother, who complained of hardly ever seeing any of her children. (That of course was not true!). She had little consideration for the fact that the four who lived near her had fulltime jobs and families. I made three to four trips to New Jersey each year, spending a few days with my mother each time, to take her on errands, out to lunch or dinner. She jealously guarded my time with her, never wanting to spare me any time to see my own friends. She would save her correspondence with government agencies (Social Security, Medicare, City Hall) so that I could handle things she was not certain about. How many times did we visit her safe deposit box at the bank, to pore over her documents and make a list of them? Dozens of times—it was a companionable pastime. She was always so proud to show me her savings in the form of treasury bills, a testament to her thrifty habits, and to remind me that she was saving it all to pass on to us. I urged her spend more on herself but she did not have the habit or the inclination.

For the little real enjoyment Lucy found in her life, I am especially troubled that my brothers, sister, and I were unable to come together to show her our love on her eighty-fifth birthday, a few months before her death. Although we knew she derived the greatest pleasure from seeing us all together—children and grandchildren—on ceremonial occasions, we, my siblings and I, no longer celebrated the major holidays together. For my mother's eightieth birthday I managed to shame everyone into attending a brunch David and I organized in New Jersey, and, reluctant as they were to be in the same room together, everyone attended and made her happy. But when I tried to bring the noncommunicating siblings together again for her eighty-fifth, I met total resistance—for reasons that had been long so ingrained in our adult sibling relationships as to be almost inexplicable. Anthony, the son with the position of greatest suasion among us, chose to absent himself from the effort, saying that he would do something with Mom on his own. And yet, after my mother's funeral, Anthony was the one to arrange a luncheon at his country club, with every single one of us present. Why *then* and not when we could have honored Lucy alive? We were only able to come together publicly for her funeral—*che vergonia*.

To the utter amazement of my husband, given what he'd seen of the Pedalino siblings' "family dynamic," there were no arguments or lawsuits when my mother's estate was settled under brother Anthony's direction as executor, simply an efficient, amicable distribution of funds. David said, "In my family, almost nothing caused strife except differences over money. There are no money problems between you, your brothers, and your sister but you just can't be friends with each other. Our families certainly are different." He's right, of course. The breakdown of civility among my siblings is so well established now that it cannot be changed. It is almost twenty years since we were all on friendly terms and the reasons are at the same time deep-seated and trivial—ancient grudges, feelings of being disrespected, misunderstandings. My stubborn refusal to accept the situation and continue my efforts at peace-making have hurt me deeply and accomplished nothing. I give up. Forgive me, Lucy.

Steve—and Ed

One day in early 2000, Steve brought up a delicate subject when he announced, "Mom, we've had a kind of understanding for the past several years and we've all honored it. I was really not involved with anyone. But now I have found someone whom I care about deeply, and we are seriously committed to each other. I want you and Dad to meet Ed. It's time." I gave Steve my full attention, wanting to know about Ed. "We met through friends. Ed Lee is Korean, he is attending Harvard Medical School and works very long hours. He is a warm, friendly guy who enjoys the social life we have with my friends in Boston. I know you and Dad will like him. There's no rush. We'll get us all together as soon as it's convenient." When I relayed this conversation to my husband, he responded with sincere agreement, "Yes, it is time. Let's tell Steve we want to meet his friend and give him a warm welcome."

Steve and Ed came to Amherst for Easter Sunday dinner in April 2000. Our first meeting with Ed brought us a new individual to enfold in the close-knit Porter family. He impressed us immediately with his open, friendly manner, obvious intelligence, and charming personality. Ed, born in Seoul, South Korea, had moved to the United States for his last two years of high school, living with an aunt and uncle in Iowa. He had a bachelor's degree from Harvard and was nearing the completion of his medical school studies. That day we moved to a new plateau of American family life, having, admittedly, taken a long time getting there. Ed has become "one of us," and we joke about finally having a "real" doctor in the family. It pleases us no end that he is as family-oriented as we all are, completely comfortable joining in our holiday gatherings, including reading a part in the Nativity Play and putting his stocking near the fireplace for Santa on Christmas Eve! Uncle Ed is as natural to our grandchildren as Uncle Steve and Uncle Dave.

In June of 2000 Steve and Ed informed us that they would be moving to St. Louis that fall, where Ed would be doing his residency in radiology at Barnes Jewish Hospital over the next three to four years. We were sorry to see them move so far away but understood the importance of this opportunity. Steve began teaching at Webster University and at the music school connected with the St. Louis Symphony, thanks in part to the connections he made through our great friend from Istanbul days, Professor Sam Grant, a native of St. Louis. The years in St. Louis proved to be an excellent career move both for Ed's future in medicine and for Steve's many opportunities to give concert performances.

The Porter Brothers' Excellent Weekend

The recording of Steve's all-Liszt concert on a CD for commercial use brought him to his home town for a joint celebration with his brother Dave, whose book publication date was March 2001; reviews for *Fixed: How Goodfellas Bought Boston College Basketball* began to appear early in the month. The Jeffery Amherst Bookshop hosted a book signing for Dave on Saturday, March 24, and also featured the sale of Steve's first CD—a double celebration. Steve arranged to give a recital the evening before at the University of Massachusetts. Events such as these get wide local coverage in the media in college towns, bringing out everyone who had ever known or heard of the Porter boys. It was a sensational weekend, capped with a cocktail party at the Amherst College Alumni House. What a display of family pride and joy, community attention for the two lads, and a show of respect for their parents, one of the benefits of living in the same town for forty years. The reviews of Dave's book were uniformly positive and brought him a degree of fame from his appearances on television. His narrative of the point-shaving scandal at Boston College, with bribes, drugs, and a mafia connection, is well told and has "legs." It may yet be produced as a film.

Transitions

Other developments in 2001 would not occasion joy. Dave and Laurie began their married life with good grace, sharing a love of travel, of congenial friendships and good food, of music in various genres from classical to rock; each enjoyed a loving relationship with both families. Their problems were with erratic work schedules, low combined earnings, little job security. At one point, Dave was commuting daily from Trenton, New Jersey, to Stamford, Connecticut, to work for the Professional Team Physicians web site, where he earned a decent salary but spent far too many hours of the week getting to and from work. Their desire for a child was not to be realized and they were reluctant to adopt, leaving the issue unsettled. Through all these problems, Dave had managed to carve out time to research and write his first book.

In early May, Dave confided that he and Laurie might separate. She wanted them to go to counseling, he refused. Once again, we advised caution before making irrevocable changes and urged Dave to make every effort with Laurie to face their differences and try to find ways to restore the harmony they had earlier enjoyed. A family trip to Lucca, Italy, was scheduled for late May, to celebrate my birthday. Our sons have spent a lot of time in Italy and looked forward to this treat. In spite of their difficulties, we convinced Dave that Laurie should not give up the trip. Laurie's mother went with us, to revisit the place where she and her late husband had spent a year studying music in the early 1950s. Our old friends, Gil and Paul, invited us out to their place, to see the restored formal gardens that are the subject of Paul's latest book.[22]

After the trip to Lucca, despite their best efforts, Dave and Laurie did not reconcile and their five-year marriage ended in 2002. An amicable divorce followed, the Trenton house on which they had both invested so much hard work was sold, assets were equably divided; Laurie soon found a new love, and Dave bought an apartment in New York City. His new job as a reporter with Associated Press has broadened his horizons considerably; he now covers all manner of news in New Jersey—politics, crime, government corruption—as well as sports. In 2005 Dave met fellow New Yorker and tennis fan Sally Cooney, commencing a new love with this attractive and talented technical writer. They plan to marry in December 2008.

Steve and Ed returned to Boston in the summer of 2004, when Ed was offered a post-graduate research grant at Harvard Medical School. He has since received a faculty appointment and conducts research in his specialty, pediatric radiology. The move was professionally difficult for Steve, though he is very happy to be near family and friends. The East Coast is overflowing with musical talent, and every teaching job in a college or university brings out hundreds of applicants. It's a tough market, no matter how exceptional one's qualifications. For two years Steve patched together an assortment of part time teaching jobs at community music schools in the Boston area, a discouraging setback after the work he had so enjoyed at Webster University. He is now a fulltime member of the Music Department at Phillips Andover Academy. Steve's true profession is not teaching but piano performance. He gives a dozen or more recitals each year—as a soloist in small venues like the Music on Main series at the First Church in Amherst, for instance, or as a featured accompanist with the Amadeus Symphony Orchestra in London, both in spring of 2008. Steve and Ed are happily settled in Boston and hosted their first Porter family Thanksgiving in 2006. Our three sons and their families live near enough to see each other frequently. That they have such love and respect for one another is our greatest satisfaction.

"50 Years of Love and Adventure"

Our sons' title for their parents' anniversary celebration on August 4, 2007, aptly summarizes a half century's toils, tribulations, and triumphs. The weekend brought together several of the small group that witnessed our hastily assembled wedding in 1957, many members of our families, and a host of friends—people gathered from our various lives in Istanbul, Catania, Avella, Elba, Orange, and Amherst.

Throughout my adult life I've probably given more than the normal amount of attention to keeping friendships with people that David and I have met through our travels, our work, and during our residences in different countries. It has been well worth the effort; these encounters afford us exciting opportunities to discuss national and international issues, politics, books, plays, and music—comfortable as we are in our long acquaintance with one another. Friendships can so easily fade, given the constraints of family and career responsibilities and the high mobility level of Americans—time and distance ease the dissolution. In our seventh decade on this planet, at the celebration of our fiftieth year of marriage, the presence of so many friends from places far-flung and near was especially poignant.

Our sons, their wives and partners and children, provided a weekend full of entertainment, including such treats as a ride in a 1957 Chevy from our house to the party, and a series of skits acted out by the grandchildren titled, "The Courtship of David and Rosalie." A singular moment of unintended humor stands out in my mind, especially because it involves an assumption made about religion, a subject that was a source of tension in our marriage, one we never had much occasion to laugh about: At Sunday Mass at the Newman Center Chapel, we were called to the altar to receive a special blessing for our fiftieth anniversary. Since my husband never attends church services with me, and his name is David, Deacon Lucian Miller assumed my husband to be Jewish; he offered fulsome praise to our blessed union, this fine example of ecumenism in our community. The deacon was wrong—at least about David's Jewishness, although not about ecumenism in the broad sense of how it embraces differences—but we dared not make a correction, not when the whole congregation was standing and applauding! Family and friends quietly suppressed their laughter until we were outside, where our sons could not resist teasing their father. "Hey, Dad, why didn't you tell us you were Jewish, why'd you keep it a secret all these years?"

On Love and Marriage and Family

Several years ago I happened on a truly frightening view of love and marriage in *Bangkok 8*, a novel by John Burdett:

> I did try love once, I really did. It still gets so much hype, you feel you've got to give it a chance, right? I think in the States we're way past that stage, though. It's like in the first phase of industrialization, there's still marriage as in an underdeveloped agricultural economy, meaning it lasts for life. The next phase, people get married knowing they'll get divorced. One phase further on, and you find people marrying *in order* to get divorced. By the time you reach 21st century America, love is a blip on the career path, something that was capable of making you late for work for a week, before you got over it. The sad truth is it's incompatible with freedom, money and equality. Who the hell really wants to be stuck with their equal for life? Human beings are predators, we like to hunt and eat the weak so we can feel strong for a moment. How about you?[23]

I would hope this jaded view of contemporary life, so inimical to healthy adult relationships, is only a fictional exaggeration, but given the high level of marriage failure in Western societies, and the consequent devaluing of the traditional family, I really wonder. Monogamous marriages appear to be less popular with each generation following mine. Yet I still believe the rewards found in a long-term, monogamous marriage are unsurpassable— for the husband and wife, and for the children they raise.

And so it is that I am equally chilled by feminist Phyllis Rose who, as biographer-critic, describes marriage as "... parallel lives ... two imaginations to work constructing narratives about experience presumed to be the same for both. In using the word *parallel*, however, I hope to call attention to the gap between the narrative lines as well as to their similarity. ... I assume, then, as little objective truth as possible about these parallel lives, for every marriage seems to me a subjectivist fiction with two points of view often deeply in conflict, sometimes fortuitously congruent."[24] Ms. Rose, however, does concede that the family is the building block of society going back to the Romans, and confesses her abiding interest in the "... management of power between men and women in that macrocosmic relationship."

Over the years of a long marriage, two such ill-matched people as my husband and I have grown to *become* equals, tolerant of each other's faults, deeply appreciative of each others' strengths, of our individual successes in the public world, and of the immeasurable wealth of our family's love for us. We've come to realize a charmed life in the last dozen years within our immediate family—our sons grown up and established with mates and careers; our grandchildren amazing us with their intelligence, humor, and seeming delight in our company (and Grandma's cooking!). But the supreme satisfaction is in our daily enjoyment of each other's presence, our mutual delight *in just being together!* The rewards we have earned for our patience, loyalty, and faithfulness to one another are manifest—and achievable even in twenty-first-century America. My husband and I share this caution about aging with our contemporaries: that we balance our criticism of some new ideas and trends with tolerance for humanity; that we change with the times as our family evolves but not give up our basic values or the exercise of intelligent minds.

Fulfillment in Public Life

My personal good fortune has been in finding useful work for the past quarter century in an arena that grows more contentious every year with the variety and numbers of new arrivals to our country. I believe I have sufficiently chronicled the scope and trajectory of my career path, from being a classroom teacher, rising to administrative responsibilities and to research, and writing and advocating on a national and international level for our newest citizens. Much of my success rests on the timing of my entry in a developing field, and to the inestimable value of my husband's and sons' unfailing support. I do not discount my own passion for learning, and my ambition to succeed at evermore challenging occupations.

Helping immigrant children become successfully assimilated into American life is my contribution to this my adopted land, as well as raising three fine human beings who themselves are making a better world. One of our Roman ancestors, Cicero, made an observation that I find particularly appealing as a last word, "A life employed in the pursuit of useful knowledge, in honorable actions and the practice of virtues ... yields an unspeakable comfort to the soul."[25]

About The Author

Rosalie Pedalino Porter, Ed.D., advises school districts across the country, as well as the U. S. Congress, on the education of immigrant children. She is the author of *Forked Tongue: The Politics of Bilingual Education,* and *Language and Literacy for English Learners: Grades 7–12, Four Programs of Proven Success.*

Under the sponsorship of the U.S. State Department, Dr. Porter has delivered lectures on language and education policies for immigrant children in Bulgaria, China, Finland, Israel, Italy, Japan, and Turkey. She holds degrees (B.A., M.Ed., and Ed.D.) from the University of Massachusetts/Amherst, spent a year as a Visiting Scholar at the University of London, and was a research fellow at the Radcliffe Institute for Advanced Study at Harvard University.

Dr. Porter has served as an expert witness in court cases on behalf of non-English-speaking children in Arizona, California, Colorado, New Mexico, New York, and Texas. She was co-chairman of the English for the Children campaign, which won 68 percent of the popular vote in the 2002 election in Massachusetts.

She and her husband David Thomas Porter, Emeritus Professor of Literature, University of Massachusetts, live in Amherst, Massachusetts, and have three sons and four grandchildren all living nearby.

APPENDICES

Appendix A.

Selected Publications by the Author

Books

Forked Tongue: the Politics of Bilingual Education. New York: Basic Books, 1990. (2nd Ed. New Brunswick, NJ: Transactions Publishers, Rutgers University, 1996.)

Language and literacy for English learners: Grades 7–12, Four programs of proven success. Sopris West Educational Services, Longmont, CO: 2004.

Articles on Bilingual Education and English Immersion

"Bilingual ballot amendments damaging to schoolchildren." Worcester, MA: *Telegram & Gazette,* June 17, 2003, p. A-7.

"Question 2: How and why it won." Northampton, MA: *Daily Hampshire Gazette,* November 22, 2002, p. A-6.

"English immersion plan makes sense." Amherst, MA: *Amherst Bulletin,* October 18, 2002, p. 4.

"Let's replace a failed program." Boston, MA: *Boston Globe,* March 13, 2002, p. A-19.

"Debate on bilingual education should correct misconceptions." Worcester, MA: *Sunday Telegram,* September 2, 2001, Insight section, p. 2.

Statement of Testimony, Subcommittee on Education Reform, Committee on Education and the Workforce. U.S. House of Representatives, Washington, D.C., March 8, 2001.

"Educating English Language Learners in U.S. Schools: Agenda for a New Millennium." In James E. Atlas and Ai-Hui Tan (Eds.), *Georgetown University Round Table on Languages and Linguistics 1999: Language in our time.* Washington, D.C.: Georgetown University Press, December 2001.

"Accountability is overdue: Testing the academic achievement of limited-English-proficient students." *Applied Measurement in Education.* November 2000, 13 (2).

Abstract. *Bilingual students and the MCAS: Some bright spots among the gloom.*, Washington, D.C.: READ Institute, August 2000.

"Uniform tests crucial to public education." *Springfield Sunday Republican*, January 23, 2000.

"The Benefits of English Immersion." *Educational Leadership*, December 1999.

"The Future of Bilingual Education in Massachusetts: Lessons from California." *MATSOL Currents*, Winter 1998, 12–13.

"Why Voters Said No to Bi-lingual Ed." *New York Daily News*, June 8, 1998.

"The Case Against Bilingual Education." *The Atlantic Monthly*, May 1998.

"The Politics of Bilingual Education." *Society*, September-October 1997, Vol. 34/6, 31–39.

"Bilingual ed badly in need of reform." *Boston Herald*, June 7, 1997, 13.

"Bilingual education gets failing grade." *Springfield, Republican*, June 22, 1997, B3.

"On the State of Bilingual Education 1990–95: *Forked Tongue Continued.*" *READ Perspectives*, Spring 1996, Vol. 3/1, 5–58.

"The Politics of Bilingual Education Revisited." In Jorge Amselle (Ed.), *The Failure of Bilingual Education*. Washington, D.C.: Center for Equal Opportunity, 1996, 33–39.

"A Review of the U.S. GAO Study on Limited-English Students." *READ Perspectives*, Spring 1995, Vol. 2/1, 9–27.

"Goals 2000 And the Bilingual Student." *Education Week*, May 18, 1994, 36, 44.

"Language Choice for Latino Students." *The Public Interest*, Fall 1991, 48–60.

"The False Alarm Over Early English Acquisition." *Education Week*, June 5, 1991, 29, 36.

"The Disabling Power of Ideology: Challenging the Basic Assumptions of Bilingual Education." In Gary Imhoff (Ed.), *Learning in Two Languages: From Conflict to Consensus in the Reorganization of Schools*, pp. 19-37. New Brunswick, NJ: Transaction Publishers, 1990.

"The Case for English Immersion." *Teacher*, August 1990, 60.

"Reflections on the Politics of Bilingual Education." *The Journal of Law and Politics*, Spring 1990, 589–599.

"Language Trap: No English, No Future." *Washington Post*, April 23, 1990, B-3.

"The Newton Alternative to Bilingual Education." *The Annals— Journal of the American Academy of Political and Social Science*, March, 1990, (508) 147–160.

"Bilingual Education and Immigrants." In William Dudley (Ed.), *Immigration: Opposing Viewpoints*, pp. 207–214. San Diego, CA: Greenhaven Press, 1990.

Appendix B.

Court Cases and Consulting

Tucson, Arizona, *Flores v. Arizona*, expert witness for the State of Arizona, 2006-2007.

State of Arizona, English Language Learners Task Force, November 30, 2006.

Arizona Department of Education, May 2001, chief researcher, *English Acquisition Program Cost Study, Phases I and IV.*

San Francisco, California, *California State Board of Education vs. San Francisco Unified School District et al.*, 1998-2000, expert witness for the State of California.

Austin, Texas, *G.I. Forum et al. vs. Texas Education Agency et al.* 1998-1999, expert witness for the State of Texas Education Agency.

Sacramento, California, *Valeria G. et al. vs. State of California*, 1998-2000, expert witness for State of California, defending Proposition 227—"English for the Children."

Albuquerque, New Mexico, *Carbajal, L. et al. vs. Albuquerque Public School District*, 1998-99, expert witness for the plaintiffs.

Oakland, California, *Travell DeShawn Louie vs. Oakland Unified School District*, 1998, expert witness for the plaintiff.

San Francisco, California, *San Francisco Unified School District vs California Department of Education*, 1998-2000, expert witness on behalf of California Board of Education.

Sacramento, California, *Maria Quiroz et al. vs. California State Board of Education, Orange Unified School District*, et al., 1997-98, expert witness for Orange District.

New York, New York, *Bushwick Parents Organization vs. Richard P. Mills and New York State Department of Education*, 1996-97, expert witness for Bushwick Parents Organization.

Seattle, Washington, *Sang Van et al. vs. Seattle School District*, 1994-95, expert witness for Seattle.

San Francisco, California, *Theresa P. et al. vs. Berkeley Unified School District*, 1988-89, expert witness for Berkeley Unified School District.

Dearborn, Michigan; Denver, Colorado; Orlando, Florida; Westminster, Magnolia, and Orange, California, School Districts, consultant on developing English language programs, 1995-2000.

San Rafael, California, School District, designing an evaluation study, 1995.

Endnotes

1   David Brooks. "Open field? Open Question. An academic explains, then disparages, the American dream." *Wall Street Journal,* (February 12, 2003).

2   Jim Cullen, *The American Dream: A Short History of an Idea that Shaped a Nation.* 2003.

3   Nicholas D. Kristof. "Obama's Kenyan Roots," *New York Times' Week in Review,* (February 17, 2008): *13.*

4   Forrest McDonald. *Recovering the Past.* Lawrence: University of Kansas Press, 2004.

5   Maureen Freely. *Life of the Party.* London: Jonathan Cape Publishers, 1984.

6   "Possible Tragedy at Great Point Averted by Rescuers and Radio Dispatch." *Nantucket Inquirer and Mirror,* (August 1, 1968): 1.

7   National Commission for Excellence in Education. *A Nation at Risk: The Imperative for School Reform.* Washington, D.C.: U. S. Government Printing Office: 1983.

8   Arturo Tosi. *Immigration and Bilingual Education.* Oxford: Pergamon Press, Ltd. 1984.

9   James Atlas. "Emily Dickinson in the Ascendant." *New York Times,* (October 16, 1980).

10 Jonathan Kozol. *Death at an Early Age: The Destruction of the Hearts and Minds of Negro Children.* New York: Plume Books. 1985.

11 Author. "Cambodia Wasn't Invited." *International Herald Tribune*, (December 24, 1985).

12 Author. "It's Time to Restructure Bilingual Education." *Boston Globe*, (April 2, 1986).

13 Nathan Glazer. *Affirmative Discrimination*. New York: Basic Books. 1973.

14 Author. "Language Trap: No English, No Future." *Washington Post*, (April 22, 1990) B-3.

15 Robert St. John. *Tongue of the Prophets: The Life Story of Eliezer Ben-Yehuda*. Westport, CT: Greenwood Press, 1952.

16 Russell Gersten, John Woodward, and Susan Schneider. *Bilingual Immersion: A Longitudinal Evaluation of the El Paso Program*. Washington, D.C.: READ Institute, 1992.

17 Robert E. Rossier. "A Critique of California's Evaluation of Programs for Students of Limited-English Proficiency." *READ Perspectives*, II-1, (spring 1995): 27–51.

18 *Bushwick Parents Organization vs. Richard P. Mills, Commissioner of Education of the State of New York, and ASPIRA of New York Inc.* Index No. 5181-95.

19 Author. "Question 2: How and why it won." *Daily Hampshire Gazette*, (November 22, 2002): A6.

20 Bilingual Education Commission. *Striving for Success: The Education of Bilingual Pupils*. Boston: Commonwealth of Massachusetts, (1993): 2.

21 Walter Kirn. "Stone's Diaries." *New York Times Book Review*, (January 21, 2007): 1.

22 Paul Gervais. *A Garden in Lucca*. New York: Hyperion Press, 2000.

23 John Burdett. *Bangkok 8*. New York: Alfred A. Knopf, Inc., 2003, 157.

24 Phyllis Rose. *Parallel Lives*. New York: Alfred A. Knopf, Inc., 1983, 6-7.

25 Marcus Tullius Cicero. *De Finibus,* II 105.

For Product Safety Concerns and Information please contact our EU
representative GPSR@taylorandfrancis.com Taylor & Francis Verlag GmbH,
Kaufingerstraße 24, 80331 München, Germany

Batch number: 08153774

Printed by Printforce, the Netherlands